TO SERVE GOD AND WAL-MART

TO SERVE GOD

AND

WAL-MART

The Making of Christian Free Enterprise

BETHANY MORETON

HARVARD UNIVERSITY PRESS

Cambridge, Massachusetts   London, England 2009

Library of Congress Cataloging-in-Publication Data

Moreton, Bethany.
To serve God and Wal-Mart: the making of Christian free enterprise /
Bethany Moreton.
p.   cm.
Includes bibliographical references and index.
ISBN 978-0-674-03322-1 (alk. paper)
1. Wal-Mart (Firm)   2. Business—Religious aspects—Christianity.   3. Free
enterprise—Religious aspects—Christianity.   4. Discount houses (Retail
trade)—United States.   I. Title.
HF5429.215.U6M67 2009
381′.1490973—dc22   2008055621

For Pamela Voekel

Solidarity forever

Contents

Illustrations follow p. 144.

TO SERVE GOD AND WAL-MART

Wal-Mart Country: Bentonville, Arkansas, in the mountainous Ozarks region, is home to the international headquarters of Wal-Mart Stores, Inc. *Map by Wendy Giminski, University of Georgia Research Media, 2008.*

Prologue
From Populists to Wal-Mart Moms

In 1999, the Pew Research Center announced the appearance of a new force in American politics. The key to electoral success in the new millennium would lie with a voting bloc that Pew called "Populists." These voters were largely white Southern mothers, conservative Christians trying to care for families while wages stagnated and public services dried up. They staunchly opposed abortion and gay marriage, but overwhelmingly welcomed government guarantees of higher minimum wages and universal access to health coverage. Pollsters quickly assigned Pew's Populists a more contemporary moniker: The fate of the nation, they asserted, lay in the hands of the Wal-Mart Mom.[1]

One American woman in five shops at a Wal-Mart store every week. As early as 1995, the head of the powerful Christian Coalition understood the link between value shoppers and values voters. "If you want to reach the Christian population on Sunday, you do it from the church pulpit," explained the boyish politico Ralph Reed. "If you want to reach them on Saturday, you do it in Wal-Mart."[2] Just as frequent church-going has proved a reliable predictor of support for the Republican Party since the 1980s, frequent Wal-Mart shopping correlates closely with conservative voting. In 2004, George W. Bush won the votes of 85 percent of frequent Wal-Mart shoppers, providing a crucial margin to his victory. But two years later, enthusiasm for the administration had dropped significantly among this group. The lukewarm support of white women cost the Republicans the midterm elections and sealed the

1

choice of Sarah Palin as the 2008 vice-presidential candidate. "Republicans have to be able to compete for these women," explained a pollster for presidential candidate John McCain. "We can't win without them."[3]

The Wal-Mart Moms complicate the story of the conservative ascendancy since World War II. Thanks to a generation of historical scholarship, the broad contours of that narrative are by now widely familiar: Fueled first by the New Deal and then by the Cold War, federal spending shifted net tax revenue out of the industrial North and into the South and West.[4] During the economic expansion of the 1950s and 1960s that enlarged the American pie, the white workforce in places like Orange County, California, and Cobb County, Georgia, experienced their good fortune as virtue rewarded. But the revolution against white supremacy that played out internationally as decolonization and domestically as the civil rights movement strained the loyalty of the white working class to the Democratic Party. In the 1960s, African Americans at last won the ballot in fact as well as law, and demanded an end to what one historian aptly describes as affirmative action for whites—that is, the redistribution policies that deliberately favored white Americans for generations, from separate and grossly unequal schools to whites-only public housing to the exclusion of majority black or immigrant job categories like farm worker and domestic servant from Social Security.[5] Great Society programs finally sought to match entitlement spending on whites with comparable investments in citizens of color, just as international competition to American industry finally recovered from World War II. Coupled with the expense of propping up successive unpopular regimes in Southeast Asia, the return of Japanese and European industrial might eroded the surplus on which the security of the "greatest generation" had been built.

When wages stagnated and inflation and unemployment soared in the early 1970s, the conditions were thus ripe for a formal split between the constituencies who had been uneasily joined in the Democratic Party since the New Deal—black and white urban workers in the North, and rural white Southerners. In his prescient blueprint from 1969, Nixon campaign strategist Kevin Phillips predicted an emerging Republican majority, provided the GOP could grasp "who hates whom" and leverage that antagonism.[6] The shift, in fact, was already underway. From the ashes of Arizona senator Barry Goldwater's failed presidential bid in 1964 and the overtly racist third-party challenge from Alabama governor George Wallace in successive national elections, a new Republican coalition arose to push American politics rightward in the 1970s. Richard Nixon jettisoned the frank racism of Wallace's Deep Southern base. In the Sun Belt's booming white suburbs, the Silent Majority instead defended its privileges in color-blind terms. The self-styled New Christian Right mobilized grassroots voters at the precinct level. Armed with the lists of Goldwater's major campaign donors, Republican strategists used the new high-tech marketing tool of direct mail to energize voters around issues like abortion. Their efforts were complemented by a 1974 change in campaign finance law that inadvertently encouraged political action committees (PACs) as agents of influence outside the more staid party structures. Business donations through PACs quickly dwarfed those of traditional Democratic constituencies like organized labor, magnifying corporate power even as the hierarchy of influence within corporate circles shifted dramatically. The ethereal economic sector labeled "FIRE"—finance, insurance, and real estate—gained influence relative to older industrial players, and Sun Belt consumer industries became an organized political force. Many of these activist firms from the South and West shared a common profile: they were often family owned, labor intensive, and tied to their region's spiraling real-estate values. Working through PACs and think tanks, they found new audiences for their ideas.[7]

Innovative white Christians—many evangelicals, fundamentalists, Pentecostals, and Mormons, as well as some Catholics—animated the conservative counterrevolution of the 1970s and 1980s. Though the movement's public representatives were typically men, histories of the "kitchen-table activists" behind the rise of the New Christian Right show the centrality of white women to the new political dispensation.[8] The result was advance on multiple fronts. During the decade in which "it seemed like nothing happened," the probusiness wing could count among its victories deregulation of industries like trucking and airlines; antiunion legislation; and the Federal Reserve's conversion to the monetarist policies of economist Milton Friedman. The profamily constituency meanwhile could point to their influential new organizations like the Moral Majority, the Religious Round Table, and the Concerned Women for America; the defeat of the Equal Rights Amendment; and the success of Anita Bryant's antihomosexual campaign in Florida.[9]

Disappointed by the nation's first born-again president, Georgian

Jimmy Carter, the New Christian Right swung its support to another Sun Belt governor in 1980. The Moral Majority registered 2.5 million new evangelical voters, the new conservative political action committees raised 8 million dollars, and Ronald Reagan informed evangelical opinion-makers in Dallas, "I know you can't endorse me, but I endorse you."[10]

Reagan's overwhelming victory and the growth of his evangelical base forced a sea change in the political and cultural landscape, moving the right from marginal fringe to controlling center. The new Republican coalition comprised a pair of strange bedfellows: laissez-faire champions of the free market unevenly yoked to a broad base of evangelical activists. The ideology of the Reagan-Bush era was crafted in corporate-funded think tanks and conservative economics departments. But the foot soldiers of this long, patient political counterrevolution were Christian family women, galvanized to public action by issues like school prayer, gay liberation, and *Roe v. Wade*. Rather than absorbing a family-values agenda from their male pastors, conservative women themselves taught the Republican Party and the Moral Majority which issues would send them door to door in their precincts.[11]

Whether the profamily block voted for Californians, Texans, or Arkansans for the next thirty years, the politics they created underwrote promarket measures. Successive administrations deregulated financial markets; scaled back education, health care, and social services to for-profit industries; and ended welfare as we knew it. They pursued a foreign policy of free trade and austerity measures, backed by robust military budgets.[12] "What's the matter with Kansas?" demanded the left in frustration. Why did working Americans enable the very antigovernment, probusiness policies that undermined their own tenuous place in the middle class? Why did the citizens of Red America keep falling for the same trick, gleefully voting against their material interests every time someone hollered "abortion" or "gay marriage"? Couldn't they see that what really mattered was the economy?[13]

The Wal-Mart Moms offer another perspective, one that links them directly to America's original Populists. Like the rural insurgents of the old People's Party, they expect government to help citizens like themselves—white, hardworking, Christian family members. In the twentieth century, their home communities in the South and West flourished through deliberate federal redistribution of resources out of the Northern Rust Belt into the Sun Belt. Entering the waged work force under a service economy rather than an industrial one, they changed both work and family life, and crafted a new ideology to explain the relationship between the two. For the emerging Wal-Mart constituency, faith in God and faith in the market grew in tandem, aided by a generous government and an organized, corporate-funded grassroots movement for Christian free enterprise. Ultimately, they helped shape American-led globalization itself.

The postindustrial society grew from a specific regional history and the heritage of Populism. It was built in the aisles and break rooms of Southern discount stores, in small-group Bible study and vast Sunday-morning worship services. It spread through the marketing classes and mission trips of Christian colleges, through student business clubs and service projects. Although free-market economic theories captured the hearts and minds of elite policymakers in the later twentieth century, the animating spirit of Christian free enterprise shaped the outcome. The Wal-Mart Moms understood better than their critics: Family values are an indispensable element of the global service economy, not a distraction from it.

1

Our Fathers' America

Today, even the most casual reader of the national press has encountered some version of this formula: Wal-Mart is the biggest company on the planet. Its sales on a single day topped the gross domestic products of thirty-six sovereign nations. If it were the independent Republic of Wal-Mart, it would be China's sixth largest export market and its economy would rank thirtieth in the world, right behind Saudi Arabia's. And then the punch line: it's from a little town in the Ozark mountains where you can't even buy a beer![1] Bentonville, Arkansas, was typically treated in the business press as the unlikeliest of places to produce a world-class player. "The paradox," marveled one commentator in 2002, "is that Wal-Mart stands for both Main Street values and the efficiencies of the huge corporation, aw-shucks hokeyness and terabytes of minute-by-minute sales data, fried-chicken luncheons at the Waltons' Arkansas home and the demands of Wall Street."[2]

A more useful interpretation of the "Wal-Mart paradox" came from within its own management. In Wal-Mart circles, no single story of the company's early years was more treasured than that of the Chicken Report. Since the early 1970s, Wal-Mart had courted investors with laid-back annual meetings featuring fishing trips and barbecues, and by the mid-1980s the national analysts could not ignore the home office's overtures. The result was an irresistible target for the Arkansans: an audience of slightly bewildered city folk, struggling to comprehend the company's magic. With encouragement from Walton, Senior Vice President Ron Loveless elaborated on one of management's typical in-house gags and presented it to the attentive crowd. "People often ask us how we predict market demand for discount merchandise," Loveless began,

> and you've heard a lot of numbers today. But there is more to it than that. We raise a good many chickens in Northwest Arkansas, and we've come to depend on them for what we call the Loveless Economic Indicator Report. You see, when times are good, you find plenty of dead chickens by the side of the road, ones that have fallen off the trucks. But when times are getting lean, people stop and pick up the dead chickens and take 'em home for supper. So in addition to the traditional methods, we try to correlate our advance stock orders with the number of dead chickens by the side of the road.

With elaborate graphs, Loveless demonstrated the entirely fictitious relationship, gravely explaining the peaks and valleys of chicken mortality, describing one anomalous spike as a misleading head-on collision between two chicken trucks outside Koziusko, Mississippi, and projecting slides of a uniformed "Chicken Patrol" inspecting a bird's carcass on a two-lane country road. "And the audience sat there nodding and frowning and writing it all down!"[3]

Like the majority of the world's population, but unlike most other United States citizens, Wal-Mart's core constituency only left the agrarian economy in the third quarter of the twentieth century.[4] The frames of reference it carried into the age of terabytes therefore sounded anomalous to the representatives of industrial modernity. But as the Chicken Patrol suggested, anomaly was in the eye of the beholder. The high-tech redneck, the rustic with a Bible in one hand and a Blackberry in the other, was only paradoxical from the perspective of a stage theory of history. Innovation from the agricultural periphery only shocked those who assumed that the industrial North Atlantic led and everyone else would follow, at their own remedial pace, along the same path.

In fact, however, it was the reputed antimodernists who showed a consistent talent for innovation. The rural South embraced distance commerce back when it meant mail-order catalogues and global cotton markets. Fundamentalist preachers first seized the new technology of radio and then cable television to create a congregation of the air.

In the 1970s, the Moral Majority mastered computerized direct mail to remake national politics. And, indeed, one small-town retailer set the technological standard for a global economic empire.[5] Observers who thus mistook style for substance, as the Chicken Patrollers knew, revealed more about their own assumptions than about the objects of their interest. To reject Detroit as the universal telos, it turned out, was not to reject progress itself.

In order to raise up not only a large, successful service company but an entire economic model, Wal-Mart had to overcome formidable obstacles to its legitimacy. The megastore selected as its home the most inhospitable part of the country for big business: the very same rural, Southwestern counties that since the 1880s had fought against large corporations and for increased government safeguards in the nation's economy. Not only were these Populist strongholds hostile to the distant capitalists of Eastern industry and finance, they were also lousy customers. The early twentieth century's department stores and theme parks were creatures of the city, and their paying customers the beneficiaries of industrial profits and union wages. Placed next to this urban cornucopia, small towns and their rural trade areas looked distinctly unpromising as the raw material of retail dominance. The viability of the small farms depended on the low consumption levels of those who stayed put. Measured in access to electric power, farm machinery, running water, phone service, or automobiles, the Ozarks in 1930 ranked at the bottom of America's consumer hierarchy.[6] Several obstacles stood between the Ozarks and the culture of consumption before World War II, most fundamentally the absence of two nickels to rub together.

Yet the American periphery—Wal-Mart Country—won the economic commanding heights in the second half of the century precisely by creatively mobilizing its regional disadvantages, turning necessity to invention, hostility to triumph. The Populist critique of the industrial political economy provided the raw material for a new corporate populism, a distinctly Ozarks version of capitalism with broad appeal across the Sun Belt. At the same time, the region helped develop new circuits for the redistribution of national wealth out of the industrial North and into the pockets of the Populists' own grandchildren scattered across Arkansas, Texas, and Oklahoma.

In both cases—reversing the anticorporate revolt and tapping new income—the region's farms, small towns, and churches provided the cultural resources to enable a massive shift in the conditions of economic possibility. Wal-Mart Country strove for alternatives to industrial modernity, urbanism, and the "society of strangers" that terrified early observers. The specific terms of its critique shaped the postindustrial service economy, suburbanism, and the free-market global village that have marked the era since World War II. By the time the United States addressed the world as a lonely hegemon in the last decades of the twentieth century, it spoke in the accents of the South and West. In short, as the business press concluded, Wal-Mart was "a lot like America: a sole superpower with a down-home twang."[7] Wal-Mart's prehistory in the Ozarks reveals how globalization got its twang.

In Branson, Missouri, everything changed on or about December 9, 1991. That was the day when *60 Minutes* described the little Ozarks town as "the country music capital of the universe" to a national audience of millions. Nashville felt the slight—it remains the Vatican City of this popular music genre—but the phrase became a self-fulfilling prophecy. In three years, tax receipts rose 75 percent; now roughly 7 million people annually visit the town of 7,000. Branson, once the country industry's low-profile retreat from the tour circuit, now claims more theaters than Manhattan. Particularly during its boom in the 1980s and 1990s, the town attracted a distinct demographic: retirees who made it America's number one destination for bus tours, and families who preferred their children to meet the famous Veggie Tales Christian cartoon characters than the mincing Teletubby Tinky-Winky, whom Jerry Falwell castigated publicly for his effeminate man-purse.[8] Opting for what one satisfied customer labeled a "G-rated, country version of Las Vegas," these gentle visitors eschewed Sin City in favor of Silver Dollar City, the "old-timey" theme park that anchored an international chain of Christian tourist attractions.[9] The faux-vintage "saloon" served no alcohol. Instead, an actress portraying local temperance terrorist Carrie Nation staged a raid five times a day, smashing bottles and shutting down a kick line. Professionally produced stage shows blended country staples and gospel favorites like "I'll Fly Away" with patriotic anthems that brought the crowds to their feet.[10] Branson was a reservation for the stars television made, including the orange-juice promoter and antihomosexual crusader Anita Bryant and the singing Mormon family named Osmond. Sequins, lights, and glitz were welcome, as long as the entertainment remained free of both sex and sarcasm.[11] In the pages of the free *Branson Church Getaway Planner,* it offered tens of thousands of congregations a sanitized version of America's rural heritage, a family-fun-filled redoubt of Jeffersonian virtue in a republic gone wickedly metrosexual.[12]

But as much as decaying Detroit itself, Branson was wholly the heir of America's industrial moment, that high tide of liberal, industrial Keynesianism. The region drew visitors to a half-dozen recreational reservoirs built with taxpayer money by the Army Corps of Engineers.[13] Its graying pilgrims owed their retirement leisure to the New Deal and the Cold War, in the guises of Social Security, Medicare, and the long, liberal boom economy from the 1940s through the 1970s, primed with military spending. Like every community built on tourism, Branson employed a low-wage seasonal work force subsidized by federal and state funds. When the tourists went home, up to 20 percent of the town was out of work. "In the winter," one resident admitted candidly, "everyone sits around on unemployment."[14] Yet the little town boomed because in the summer it drew a curtain over this heritage of the liberal industrial state, struck up the band, and spun a different tale. In Branson's version of America, there was "no crime, no crack, no inner-city blight," reported a visitor in the early 1990s. "Almost everyone is white, speaks English, and shares the same values of God, family and country. Almost everyone who wants a job has one," and the state was just a bumbling, risible tax collector.[15] In this imagined homeland, rural white virtue offered a hiding place from the twentieth century's tempests of creative destruction.

Throughout most of the preceding century, the Ozarks periodically offered the same comfort to a nation deeply ambivalent about the modern incorporation of America. Urbanites dazed by sudden, unchecked industrialization in the early 1900s often located the new urban pathologies in the polyglot work force that staffed the factories and filled the tenements. The Ozarks presented a dramatic contrast. Northwest Arkansas and Southern Missouri have historically been among the whitest places in the country—over 95 percent white as late as 1996. The African-American proportion of the population in Wal-Mart's Benton County has stayed under 1 percent since the close of the Civil War.[16] Moreover, the oldest waves of American immigration predominated—eighteenth-century English and Scotch-Irish, pre–Civil War Germans.

Like much of the South's rural interior, the region remained virtually untouched by the Southern and Eastern European immigration waves of the late nineteenth and early twentieth century, the Catholics and Jews who made up the industrial work force in the North.

In the wake of that immigration, during the high tide of American eugenics, the Ozarks enjoyed a brief vogue as the source for a reserve supply of old-stock pioneers who needed only to be taken off ice to re-invigorate the nation with traditional republican virtues of thrift, hard work, and quaint Elizabethan speech patterns.[17] Then Progressive-era legislation reined in some of the most destructive effects of industry; the First World War made large-scale manufacturing patriotic; the Im-migration Act of 1924 virtually halted the flow of objectionable immi-grants; and for a while, America did not need the Ozarks.

The mountains next soothed the national imagination during the Great Depression, representing the simple independence of small farm-ing—an occupation in fact devastated by the collapse in agricultural prices in the 1920s—at a time when the perils of large-scale bureau-cratic enterprises were all too apparent. In a 1934 travel article, cele-brated muralist Thomas Hart Benton christened the area "America's Yesterday." This paean to a preindustrial, preurban, preimmigrant America located our collective past in a decreasingly representative white rural enclave while the country faced a grim present and an un-certain future. If the Ozarks sheltered "'the very last of our fathers' America,'" then our fathers must have been Scotch-Irish farmers—not slaves, not immigrants, and not factory hands.[18]

With the industrial boom of World War II, the national need for the Ozarks faded again for a time. But the hillbilly made a comeback as a cultural icon in the late 1950s, this time through television. Rural comedies like *The Real McCoys, The Andy Griffith Show,* and especially *The Beverly Hillbillies* regularly ranked among the top ten programs on the air and counterbalanced the theme of degenerate mountain pov-erty that ran simultaneously through the news programming. By the 1960s, many Americans felt that progress was not what it used to be, and the small screen's sturdy mountain folk offered a critique as well as an escape. Paul Henning, the *Beverly Hillbillies* writer and producer, was a native Missourian who had spent childhood summers hiking the Ozarks. Henning attributed the show's genesis to a 1960 report that people in a remote Ozarks county were fighting progress in the form of a proposed road through their mountain refuge. His sanitized, made-for-television Ozarkers regularly exposed the shallow materialism of their new California neighbors with their kindly common sense.[19]

Despite the excesses of this romantic tradition, the political economy of the Ozarks offered some plausible conditions for its independent reputation. Like the Appalachian counties further east, Wal-Mart's Ozark homeland avoided the pathologies of widespread tenancy and monocropping that characterized the South's old plantation zones. On the better lands, a diversified farm economy built around grain, fruit, and livestock did not require the extensive holdings and massive labor reserves that commodity row crops demanded. Family labor and modest capital could coax a stable living out of a 125-acre farm.[20]

But the penetration of railroads in the 1870s had begun a long process of transforming the mountains. The unlovely economic bases of lead mining and timber clear-cutting denuded hills and removed the forest game reserves that had permitted small-scale farming on thin soil. Pell-mell extraction produced a "'quick-rich, long-poor'" pattern of underdevelopment, and the remaining families on marginal farms became a reliable source of part-time labor in their struggle for solvency.[21] This one-foot-on-the-farm strategy had proved its utility in many previous settings where labor-intensive innovations sought a toehold. The earliest textile mills in the United States explicitly targeted the unmarried daughters of New England farmers. Twentieth-century boosters of the New South likewise assured restless Northern industries that low wages suited their citizens just fine, since the family collard patch could make up the difference.[22]

A hidden part of the equation was the constant out-migration of surplus adults from the farm throughout much of the twentieth century. Ozarkers played a major role in circulating these domestic migrants. Route 66, the storied highway that carried "Okies" and "Arkies" into the San Joaquin Valley, passes right through Wal-Mart Country. Willis Shaw, whose one-man trucking outfit grew into a national firm, carried his Ozark neighbors out to California for $15 a head.[23] "Oh, everybody went to California back then," remembered an Ozarker who lived in Fullerton during the 1960s. "Anaheim, Brea—that whole little circle there was just mostly people from Arkansas."[24] Another local family who spent time in California came back to their Benton County farm every year and sent money home from their gas station near Sacramento: "It takes good people working full time to make enough money to keep a farm going!"[25] Even Florence Thompson, the "Migrant Mother" of Dorothea Lange's iconic 1936 photograph, grew up outside Tahlequah, Oklahoma, home of Wal-Mart #10.[26]

Though Route 66 earned its reputation by flushing landlocked white folks downstream toward the Golden State, the Ozarks sometimes diverted the flow inward to its own counties. While ailing Iowans poured into 1920s Los Angeles, the Ozarks of the same era attracted hardier Midwestern white-collar clerks who had stagnated in their tedious indoor jobs. Romantic promotional brochures touting the restorative virtues of the self-sufficient rural idyll lured them to the Ozarks. Marshalling their life savings, many enervated desk-sitters bought marginal land sight unseen, then went bust trying to plant apple trees in chert.[27]

From the Civil War to the Great Depression, this devotion to a yeoman dream that only truly worked for a few exerted a powerful pull on individuals. It also periodically offered the nation a serious critique of the forces that threatened it. Chief among those were the large corporations and financial institutions that arose in America after the Civil War. In order for the world's largest transnational corporation to make its home in a mountain redoubt of independent farming, it would first have to overcome regional objections to the very existence of such an entity. In the process of making the Populist periphery safe for corporate capitalism, the Sun Belt service economy provided American business with a new economic vision: corporate populism.

The origins of Wal-Mart's successful model lie in the nineteenth-century Populist critique of the new industrial economy. Well into the 1800s, corporate charters remained a privilege rather than a right: the limited liability and diffusion of ownership they represented could claim legal protection only insofar as they could claim to serve the public interest. But as mass production encouraged increasingly vast organizations of capital and management in the 1880s and 1890s, the Supreme Court vested corporations with legal personhood under the Constitution and established a new category of protected property in the form of expected return on investment. The corporation entered the twentieth century as an immortal supercitizen.[28]

The growth of corporate power generated opposition from many quarters, for it threatened the traditional economic basis of national virtue as well as countless individual livelihoods. When most firms were small, often family affairs, Americans had enthusiastically embraced the market revolution and established business as a terrain on which men could prove their mettle. The rise of industries like the monopolistic railroads and the financial panics that struck half a dozen times between 1819 and 1893 maintained the constant threat of personal bankruptcies. The undeniable presence of a permanent, degraded stratum of hired labor thoroughly undermined one shared narrative of American identity. Even more fundamentally, it menaced the legendary source of virtuous independence: the small farm.[29] It was the rise of the corporation that put all but a few small farmers on the road to oblivion.

The small-farm myth lay at the core of national understanding, enshrined by Thomas Jefferson, the plantation owner who became the republic's third president. Rural Americans had never really dwelt in an Eden of subsistence farming, but small-scale commercial agriculture, in which both production and profits were based in the family, retained an aura of praiseworthy Jeffersonian independence. This tradition ennobled all it touched, allowing country merchants and small workshops to present themselves as just a variation on this pattern of American virtue. Its sanctifying function became all the more critical as the economic terrain moved farther off the farm: in the 1880s, manufacturing took over from agriculture as the country's leading source of value, and by the end of the decade, railroads and centralized distributors put the squeeze on the small players. Agricultural prices fell. The seemingly endless supply of "vacant" land abruptly ran out. The yeoman's latest sun was sinking fast.

Wal-Mart Country was key territory in the revolt against this corporate reconstruction of American society. At the end of the nineteenth century, large-scale enterprises scored abysmally low marks in the territory's estimation of social worth. Upland Arkansas, southwest Missouri, and the eastern sections of Oklahoma, Kansas, and Texas all hosted some of the nation's most vigorous popular protests against huge economic "combinations." The strikes and rebellions of 1886 that posed the nation's greatest collective challenge to industrial capitalism spread out of Sedalia, Missouri, future home of an early Wal-Mart.[30] The insurgent People's Party—capital "P" Populists—likewise grew out of the giant retailer's backyard. From towns like Searcy, Arkansas, and Cleburne, Texas —future sites of Wal-Mart's vast distribution centers—Populists demanded a variety of government mechanisms to prevent the growth of corporations and trusts. They sought legislative action to redress the unlevel playing field, including legal recognition of unions and cooperatives, punitive taxation on land speculation, and federally administered banking.[31] The People's Party national platform of 1896 vigorously charged the federal government with restoring the republic's "financial and industrial independence" usurped by "corporate monopolies."[32]

That election, in which the Republican Party first employed the modern tactics of public relations, sent the Populists down in ignominious defeat with their Democratic allies and wiped them out as an organized national political movement. Despite the electoral defeat of the rural crusaders, however, their broad economic and political legacy remained. Their ideas did not expire on the marginal back forties around Cleburne and Searcy. Though their victories in even local and state elections were short-lived, the Populists endowed much of subsequent Progressive-era policy with their agenda. In 1914, even the agrarians' antimonopolism became national law in the form of the Clayton Antitrust Act—ironically, just in time for the production demands of World War I to legitimate massive corporations in fact if not in principle.[33]

But it would be a mistake to read the various shades of agrarian populism of the late nineteenth century—the ideological heritage of Wal-Mart's home turf—as purely hostile either to business or to bigness. Economies of scale and efficiencies of centralized communications made good financial sense to many sworn foes of the Eastern corporate giants. The economic vision of some Populist leaders included large-scale buying cooperatives and producers' monopolies over the marketing of whole farm sectors. The federal intervention they sought in transportation, finance, and agriculture, which sounds so out of character for Wal-Mart Country today, was intended to help them join the monopolies rather than beat them.[34]

Most of their specific recommendations for popular economic reform never materialized. But within the first two decades of the twentieth century, the Populists' political mobilization reaped a bumper harvest of government aid and protective legislation. By the beginning of World War I, the U.S. Department of Agriculture boasted one of the largest staffs in the federal apparatus and expenditures near $30 million. Washington assumed the tasks of ensuring ground rules for agricultural markets, liberalizing credit to farmers, and promoting Populist-style cooperatives. The major antimonopoly laws of the 1910s specifically exempted cooperatives: big, centralized production was legitimate so long as it was composed of farmers themselves. By agitating for protective regulation, improved infrastructure, and practical education, the "farm block" remade American agriculture in the pattern of big manufacturing. Ideologically, Populism helped validate the expanded use of federal resources for a favored segment of the polity, the virtuous farmers. Their defeat lay in the form this federal help took. They had asked for statutory controls subject to their own votes. What they got were discretionary bureaucracies of distant Washington experts.[35]

Thus, in the fragmented legacy of Populism, the rural South and West nourished ideas that would become useful for the future megacorporations of the Sun Belt. Despite the dominant antipathy to corporations, the area that would become Wal-Mart Country was also familiar with arguments supporting modern, large-scale businesses, so long as they were operated by and for the farmers. The farm organizations that animated political debate in Arkansas, Oklahoma, and Missouri were friendly to new technologies of transportation and communication. Populist organizations justified demands upon the state to underwrite regional development and advocated keeping the money and power local. All of these intellectual legacies contributed to Wal-Mart's subsequent success. More significantly, they helped the world's largest company win hearts and minds to the cause of corporate capitalism in the old heartland of anticorporate agitation.

Before Wal-Mart could emerge, however, twentieth-century populism had one last battle to fight in what would become the company's backyard. This time the enemy was the chain store, a new and menacing face of corporate gigantism. By the time future Wal-Mart Country erupted against the chains in the 1920s, big business was an established part of the national landscape. The Republican victory in 1896, powered by previously unimaginable sums from banks, railroads, and industrialists, inaugurated a golden age for business interests.[36] A series of legal victories strengthened the claims of the corporation upon the state and the public.[37]

But while the industrial dynamo found its bards among both socialists and capitalists, real or imagined memories of country life retained an emotional claim upon the nation. One-third of city dwellers had been born on a farm, and many had left because the farm failed, not because they yearned for the bright lights of the big city. In economic folklore, the villains remained the same: distant Northeastern bankers, megacorporations with a stranglehold over the country's credit and distribution systems. The challengers saw their cause not as impinging on a competitive free market but in fact as preserving competition by denying the combinations their unfair advantages. In a society of self-identified producers, this logic commanded wide loyalty.

Country merchants walked a fine line in this cosmology. Although early Farmers' Alliances classed them among the producers, their relationship to monopoly distribution could tip them into the villain's role in agrarian morality tales. Moreover, rural merchants often doubled as informal banks in the cash-poor countryside, a position ripe for abuse given the South's many unlettered sharecroppers.[38] Since the advent of widespread railroad and telegraph access in the nineteenth century, the trend in distribution had moved steadily toward greater efficiency, standardization, and central control. Efficiency meant compressing various points in the distribution chain. First wholesalers and their representatives displaced innumerable small peddlers, then after the 1870s themselves felt the pressure of mass retailers large enough to deal directly with manufacturers. Depending on where you stood in this process, the charge of monopolism and unfair dealing sounded salient at different historical moments.

The urban department stores, the first mass retailers of any influence, faced cries of foul play from their small, single-line competitors in industrial cities of the Gilded Age. Reeling from the depression of 1893, Chicago's small merchants used their influence in the City Council to fight giants like Marshall Field's, but like their counterparts in urban New York and Massachusetts, they ultimately failed to carry their argument in state legislatures. Since the department stores were confined to larger cities, the rural United States played little part in this first debate over centralized distribution. But a decade later the mail-order companies challenged Southern and Midwestern country stores. Despite fierce, nationwide opposition from rural shopkeepers and wholesalers, the catalogues' future was assured with the Congressional approval in 1912 of extended parcel post service, by which taxpayers underwrote rural consumption. Farmers could not be dissuaded from patronizing the catalogue houses.[39]

The subsequent antichain movement of the late 1920s and early 1930s, however, dwarfed all previous attempts to arrest mass distribution. Chains, defined by the federal census of the time as four retail units or more operated by the same proprietor, had enjoyed gradual, steady growth in the early decades of the twentieth century, as the efficiencies of large-scale distribution allowed them to undersell smaller merchants. In the 1920s, many municipal governments experimented with licensing and taxation structures that penalized chains, but they often failed to meet court challenges and, given their local reach, could not address the chains at their own level of organization. State legislatures sought a formula that allowed them to single out chains for what some forthrightly described as punitive taxation. Georgia's 1929 chain tax, for example, was presented as a tool for curbing monopoly. It quickly failed a challenge in the Georgia Supreme Court, but Indiana's antichain law, passed the same year, was found constitutional by the U.S. Supreme Court. By 1936, over eight hundred such laws had been proposed and almost fifty had passed; eleven had survived challenges and were in effect.[40] "Isn't it about time for government regulation?" demanded Alabama's attorney general in 1930.[41]

Public outcry against chains, widespread and organized, brought this flood of antichain legislation even as the large stores offered lower prices in the midst of the rural and then national depressions. Over four hundred local organizations mobilized against the chain threat across the country. The issue became a staple of high school and college debate societies. Opponents of chains made their case in dozens of issue-specific newspapers and on radio programs. Traveling lecturers spread the antichain message in the pattern of the old Populist precursor, the Farmers Alliance—or, more ominously, on the subscription plan of the revived Ku Klux Klan.[42] A poll from 1936 found that almost 70 percent of the public had a negative impression of chains, with the highest proportion of antichain sentiment in the South and Midwest. The "'chain store menace,'" marveled *The Nation*, was "the question most talked of below the Ohio."[43]

Thus the South predominated in the antichain forces of the 1920s and 1930s, providing the congressional leadership, the most vigorous state-level regulation, and a broad-based popular movement.[44] This core of popular opposition to chain stores in turn fueled concern at the national level. In the antimonopolist tradition, Congress demonstrated its suspicions of unfair trade practices and collusion among chain owners in a series of investigations in the 1920s and 1930s. At the peak of public concern, national legislation sought to curb chains indirectly, through two fair-trade acts that set minimum pricing to offset the chains' economies of scale. Congressman Wright Patman of Texas and Senator Joe Robinson of Arkansas sponsored the first of these. The confused qualifications to the Robinson-Patman Act's major provision, however, rendered it difficult to enforce. The 1937 Miller-Tydings Act—sponsored by an Arkansan and a Marylander—sought to plug the holes in the prior bill, but enforcement continued to be a problem.[45]

These limitations and the resulting legal confusion led Congressman Patman in 1938 to introduce a "community preservation" bill that would have settled the question for good by deliberately taxing chains out of business. By that point, however, the chain corporations had launched a highly coordinated public relations campaign and won over significant constituencies. At hearings in 1940, the retail companies opposed to the tax produced supporting testimony from organized labor, commercial farmers, and consumers' groups, and the Patman tax died.[46]

In the worst years of the Depression, however, the antichain movement had generated serious public opposition for more than a decade, opposition that threatened to derail Wal-Mart's business model before the company was even a glimmer in Sam Walton's eye. More than an outbreak of retail protectionism or regional crankery, it offered broad, vigorous, and, for a time, effective resistance to a highly visible representative of the new corporate economic order. Chain stores increased their share of the retail market from 4 percent of sales in 1919 to 20 percent a decade later; total chain units in the country went from 300 in 1900 to more than 100,000 in 1930.[47] But the temporary success of the antichain forces suggested the potential for resistance to Wal-Mart in Wal-Mart Country itself as well as the cultural context that nourished it.

For in assessing the Southern attacks on chains, progressive opinionmakers of the 1930s impatiently attributed them to slack-jawed rural backwardness. *The Nation* magazine announced in 1930 that "a new battle on evolution is raging in the South" in which the small merchant represented the "fundamentalist position" against the chains, exemplars

19

of "modernism."[48] "In the age of greatest efficiency," it instructed, "there must be three classes of people, the consumer, the producer, and a minimum number of citizens involved in distribution."[49] Certainly there might be some problems along the way, *The Nation* conceded, but the market would handle those: Yes, chain wages for non-managerial employees were indeed inadequate, but they would soon improve without legislative intervention, for "the chains will realize that it is to their own advantage to pay their labor well."[50]

Wrenching as they were, the struggles that pitted independent proprietorship against the factory model of mass distribution were only one part of an organic political philosophy. To counter the enthusiastic support from industrial champions of both management and labor, the antichain forces deployed other cherished Populist tropes. One powerful axis of argument attacked "foreign"-owned big business generally, with "foreign" implying not just international but also distant and unfamiliar. Considered in the antichain fight, this charge shows how a robust skepticism about corporate capitalism became intertwined with assumptions about just who was a legitimate claimant to the national patrimony in the yeoman myth.

The geographic idiom implied that, in contrast to foreigners, locals were Christian, "old-stock" American whites. It could therefore easily slide into racist scapegoating. At the time, Klannishness proved uncomfortably compatible with the antichain movement.[51] Father Charles Coughlin, the radio demagogue who made defense of the local merchant a central theme in his Depression-era broadcasts, moved on to full-throated anti-Semitism after 1938.[52] A congressional committee even heard sensational—and unsubstantiated—charges that the National Anti-Chain Store League disseminated Nazi propaganda.[53] The wife of a small grocer wrote to the Louisiana antichain radio station KWKH that in her opinion, the future of independent industry was the most important question facing "the Christian people of America."[54]

In 1935, Congressman John Cochran of Missouri called for an investigation of the newly formed American Retail Federation. The resolution, which passed speedily, labeled the industry group a "super-lobby," a conspiracy by the country's wealthiest, most powerful retail magnates to undo the antitrust laws and "by propaganda and other methods inimical to the public welfare to attempt to control and influence the

Congress."[55] The investigation listed those accused, so that anyone following the story could read between the lines: surnames like Kirstein, Rosenwald, Lazarus, Straus, and Rothschild figured prominently alongside Sherrill and Burke.[56] As the committee's chairman, Wright Patman championed "a Nation of free people" against a corporate organization with "powerful interests in the world of finance."[57] The Retail Federation's most vocal defender on the House committee was New York representative Sol Bloom.[58]

For all its concern with secret meetings, holding companies, and interlocking directorates, the investigation against the American Retail Federation ultimately failed to return a smoking gun. At the same time, the distrust of these and other "foreign" corporations was often honestly come by, and could carry quite different valences. The sections of the country that opposed chains most vociferously had suffered at the hands of Northern railroads, Eastern banks, and industrial monopolies that demonstrably extracted wealth in a semicolonial relationship with the hinterlands.[59] During the nineteenth century's Populist moment, no crime of the Republican Northeast inflamed greater passions than the region's jealous monopoly on the money supply. Even after the Federal Reserve system and the Farm Loan Act liberalized credit somewhat in the 1910s and 1920s, the Northern hold on capital ensured that most Southern companies of any size would be only branches of Northern firms.[60]

This Northern "money trust" still smacked of conspiracy to the antichain movement a generation later. "I don't want to be bolshevistic," wrote one Texan in support of Depression-era antichain legislation, but "it certainly is no permanent relief or progress for the government to create temporary jobs and distribute money and in a few days it all winds up in Chicago or New York City in the hands of a few extremely wealthy men, owners of the chains and utilities."[61] Patman, the leading Congressional champion of the independent stores, pointed out that while 200 companies controlled more than half the country's corporate wealth, only eleven of these were based in the West and a mere nine in the South: "'How a true Texan can favor ownership and control of local business by Wall Streeters,' he concluded, 'I cannot understand.'"[62] Members of the Ku Klux Klan in Clarke County, Georgia, railed against the chain owners as a "'Little Group of Kings in Wall Street'" and warned that Jewish and Catholic immigrants were using the chain to pauperize native-born white Protestants.[63] Employing a metaphor familiar to rural Protestants, a 1937 novel cast chain stores as evidence of the approaching Apocalypse.[64] Even the fundamental myth of corporate personhood came up for debate: contrasting "artificial beings" like the American Retail Federation to tangible, "honest-to-God citizens," Patman attacked the premise that legal incorporation permitted companies to claim the constitutional protections of private citizens.[65]

The suspicion of "foreigners" was echoed in charges of shady business practices. Chains demonstrably received better prices from their suppliers than the smaller independent merchants, allowing individual chain stores to undersell their competitors. The manufacturers and the chains attributed this differential to efficiencies of scale: naturally a supplier would give a break to a big customer over a small one. Small proprietors and their champions were not convinced. Such savings, in their view, must come either from sly, thumb-on-the-scale tricks of the itinerant "gypsy" chain managers, or from the kind of illegal collusion that violated the antitrust legislation of the 1910s. Referring to the evidence that the A&P chain used its large market share to extract volume discounts from wholesale suppliers, a wholesaler from Georgia made the connection explicit: "ANY CONCERN LARGE AND POWERFUL ENOUGH TO EXACT CONCESSIONS THAT CANNOT BE EXTENDED TO EVERYONE HAS NO RIGHT TO EXISTENCE."[66]

Nationally, the chain retailers managed to turn the tide by mobilizing their own potential constituents. Growers' cooperatives—the farmers who had modeled themselves on the corporations a generation earlier—found that the chain buyers represented a stable market for their crops, though not always on the terms the growers would have chosen. This alliance of two large-scale, efficient operations—one of growers, the other of distributors—came into its own during a bitterly fought referendum campaign in California in 1936. Supported by organized labor, the chains outspent the competition using all the weapons in their arsenal: a professional ad campaign equating the chain tax with higher food prices; a letter-writing drive by chain managers and employees; a faux grassroots organization, the California Consumers Conference, to front for the chains in public statements; and, to win over the state's farmers, a well-publicized drive to help sell their surpluses.[67] The anti-chain movement in California was soundly defeated. True to the mod-

ernists' predictions, Southern California chain stores became a strong-
hold of retail unionism—until Wal-Mart entered the Los Angeles
market in 2003.[68]

In the decades after the antichain fight, the independents' critique did
not entirely disappear. Small merchants could periodically gain a hearing with appeals to "save downtown," "shop at home," or eventually
"Stop Wal-Mart." Acting in alliance with preservationists, labor advocates, and other citizens dismayed by a store's disruptive potential, they
sometimes succeeded in denying the giant company the zoning changes
or subsidies it sought in a specific location. On a larger scale, however,
they were dwarfed by Wal-Mart's successful expansion in particular and
the growth of mass distribution more generally. By the time the first
Wal-Mart opened, chains conducted more than a third of all retail
trade.[69]

Aside from its literal growth, Wal-Mart played a major role in winning hearts and minds to corporate actors. The Depression-era movement drew on a broad populist heritage, then still a living memory in
Wal-Mart Country. Antichain legislation was enabled in part by popular antipathy to the particular beneficiaries of mass distribution—the
cabals of "foreign" capitalists who ran chain retail and the financial institutions behind it. The South's long history as an agricultural periphery grounded the resentment toward these companies. Like their predecessors, the railroads, the paradigmatic corporations of the 1920s and
1930s, aroused rural ire by pulling profits back into Northern cities
while hoarding credit. Wal-Mart, in contrast, managed to turn the populist heritage into positive enthusiasm for a corporate giant.

2

The Birth of Wal-Mart

The world's largest corporation arose in the fiery heartland of anti-monopolism. From the massive railroad strikes of the Gilded Age through Populism and the chain store battles of the Great Depression, Wal-Mart Country had cast its lot with the ideal of yeoman independence. But its rejection of large-scale business was not absolute. Farmers also pioneered a sincere form of flattery: they could imitate the giant corporate "trusts" by banding together in cooperatives, leaving their political virtue as rural producers intact. The cooperatives exemplified the Populists' enthusiasm for modern communications and marketing, their embrace of technical and business education, and their successful efforts to win federal patronage for the business of farming.[1]

This example kept different options open for corporations themselves, particularly in the changed consumer markets of postwar America. The chain that would become Wal-Mart Stores, Inc., arose out of the populist tradition of farmers' cooperatives. When the company outgrew this format, the founders developed creative sources of financing for its expansion: first local partnerships with fellow Ozarkers, and then an Arkansas investment bank that linked the rural Southwest to circles of national power. Although this capital represented only a portion of the company's financing, it wove Wal-Mart and the Ozarks into the Sun Belt's rise to national influence.

Corporate legitimation came in two stages. First, in its early years as a chain of dime stores during the immediate postwar decades, the company was structured as a traditional family business and then an updated cooperative, uniting ownership and management. The founder,

Sam Walton, turned to manager-investors as a practical necessity, a way to attract talented managers and local resources when his in-laws' financing reached its limits. The investment capital he raised this way was not large; local and regional banks continued to play a much greater role in the chain's growth than did the neighborly partnerships behind individual stores. But Walton's aggressive promotion of his enterprise as an Ozarks affair showed how clearly he appreciated the symbolism involved: "foreign" capital, not capital itself, was potentially tainted. In the words of an antichain slogan from the 1920s, Walton would help "keep Ozarks dollars in the Ozarks."[2]

Then, when the growing chain outstripped the investment resources available locally as well as within the extended family, Walton found new streams of capital in the early 1970s. In order to take the company public, he turned first to the largest investment bank outside Wall Street, fortuitously located in Arkansas itself. This outpost of investment capital had drawn on new forms of federal redistribution into the South and West, federal policies that nourished a particular regional economic vision.

Tracing Wal-Mart's initial underwriting back to its sources offers a snapshot of the shifting economic geography that ultimately shaped American-led globalization. Wal-Mart Stores, Inc., of Bentonville, Arkansas, was the creation of Samuel Moore Walton and his wife Helen Robson Walton, both natives of Oklahoma. Sam Walton was a standout from childhood, a well-rounded and charismatic go-getter voted "most versatile" by his high-school class. The son of a rural loan appraiser, Walton enjoyed a relatively secure youth in the midst of the region's farm crisis. In college at the University of Missouri, he worked a series of jobs—waiter, lifeguard—and rose to the top of a bewildering array of organizations: the Reserve Officer Training Corps, student government, the honor society, adult Sunday school. He graduated in 1940 with a degree in economics and was elected permanent class president by his astute classmates. Clearly, this was a young man headed somewhere.[3]

The first place he went was rather unexpected: a J.C. Penney store in Des Moines, Iowa. At the time, college-educated men were rare among entry-level retail managers. From the frugal, well-run store, Walton absorbed the fundamentals of the business, and left only in 1942 when his military call-up looked imminent. During a brief stint in Oklahoma, he met and soon married Helen Robson, daughter of a wealthy

Oklahoma rancher and banker. The new Mrs. Walton had attended a Christian college in Missouri and held a degree in business from the University of Oklahoma. Walton spent his stateside Army career in the intelligence corps, supervising security at aircraft manufacturing plants and a prisoner of war camp. Immediately after the war, Walton and his wife took a $20,000 loan from her father to open a Ben Franklin variety store franchise in tiny Newport, Arkansas. This five-and-dime flourished under Walton's management, selling basic necessities like pots and pans, bed sheets, and tools.[4]

The Ben Franklin chain represented an alternate descendant of the populist revolt against corporate chain stores. From the earliest days of the chain-store menace, some independent merchants sought to imitate the large-scale rationalization of storekeeping by banding together. This solution echoed the earlier attempts to meet big business with self-organization. Nineteenth-century farmers organized rural cooperatives most successfully to market their own products. But they also experimented with cooperative stores in order to bypass the monopolies of small-town merchants. By the 1920s, the impulse had taken firmer hold among small proprietors themselves. Associations like the Independent Retail Grocers Association and the Rexall Drug network combined multiple small stores to bargain with wholesalers for the same volume discounts and advertising budgets that chains enjoyed. Even some explicitly socialist cooperatives gave up the nonprofit fight and affiliated with these "voluntary chains."[5]

Wal-Mart's own direct ancestor, Butler Brothers, followed a related path. Having grown from a Boston dry-goods store into one of Chicago's dominant wholesalers of general merchandise for the central and western states, Butler Brothers joined an increasing number of wholesalers who operated retail franchises to compete with variety chains. To the prospective franchisee, the firm offered management services that mirrored the chains' own central planning: a location bureau to scout out likely store sites; start-up loans to outfit the new store; and circuit-riding experts to advise the merchant on every detail of operation from window-dressing to bookkeeping. Butler Brothers' massive Chicago warehouse even housed a model store on its thirteenth floor, which its retailers could visit for an object lesson in modern, chain-style presentation.[6] These innovations built upon the "Success in Retailing" guides the firm published for its customers, making the element of control more concrete.[7] In return for this guidance and financing, the often inexperienced shopkeepers were required to buy 80 percent of their stock from Butler Brothers.

Whether the voluntary associations stretched up from existing retailers into the wholesaling function or down from established wholesalers into stores, the catch was the same. The price of survival was submission to chain managerial practices. The proprietor's independence gave way incrementally to distant, salaried experts who monitored every detail of the operation and even provided the capital that backed it. The distinctions between working *for* a chain and working *like* one became harder to discern, sometimes amounting to little more than the right to individualize a window display.[8] Walton chafed at the control.

When the Newport store's landlord refused to renew the lease on the profitable business, the Waltons relocated to Bentonville. In the northwest corner of the state, this county seat was only a short drive to the borders of Missouri, Oklahoma, and Kansas. The Waltons' new Ben Franklin franchise on the town's central square quickly replicated their earlier success. The restless Sam, again backed by his prosperous father-in-law, expanded and remodeled with gusto. He soon opened an additional variety store in nearby Fayetteville, home of the University of Arkansas. Keeping this store independent of the Ben Franklin chain, he began to experiment with postwar innovations in retail. The first of these was self-service, a labor-saving reorganization that removed sales clerks from behind merchandise counters and centralized the checkout stands at the front of the store. Once that gamble paid off, Walton looked for additional new formats while continuing to open more Ben Franklin stores around the region during the 1950s. For a time he considered developing a suburban shopping center, then turned to a larger format of variety stores that he christened Walton's Family Centers.[9]

Walton finally found the concept he had been searching for in the new niche of discount retailing, which originally took off in the Northeast in the 1950s. Discounters made up for their low markups by moving a large volume of goods and relied on urban population centers to pack the aisles. Walton, however, suspected that towns with populations as low as 5,000 could support a discounter, providing he went about it the right way. The merchant took his plan to Butler Brothers in the early 1960s and was sternly rebuffed. The Chicago company's resistance to discounting was hardly surprising, given its fundamental identity as a wholesaler: from Butler Brothers' perspective, allowing its retail chain to undercut its wholesale prices would vitiate the whole rationale behind the stores. The company refused to finance Walton's discount experiment. Instead, using his wife's family land and her trust fund as collateral, he borrowed enough money from a Texas bank to open his first Wal-Mart Discount City in 1962 in neighboring Rogers, Arkansas.[10] K-mart, Woolco, and Target all opened their doors in the same year as this first Wal-Mart, though in much larger towns and cities. Self-service, stripped-down physical plants, low profit margin, and unheard-of stock turnover characterized the discount genre, which catered largely to the newly flush working class of the postwar expansion.[11]

Walton's company grew steadily by avoiding the competitive environment of major cities and instead targeting small and medium-sized towns in Arkansas, Louisiana, Missouri, and Oklahoma, where it was invariably the largest merchant in town. The company saved on advertising and distribution by building out from headquarters in tiny Bentonville. The Waltons placed all the original stores within a day's drive of their own new warehouse. The stores' density in the small region insured that by the time a Wal-Mart opened in the next town over, word of mouth would have already created a customer base. The Waltons' horizons, it seemed, were only limited by the region's chronic problem, one that had inflamed the Populists themselves: the lack of investment capital, still jealously guarded by the Northeastern financial industries.

On the hunt for investors in the credit-starved Southwest, Walton offered his early managers the opportunity to become limited partners in return for investing in the individual stores they managed and subsequent ones yet to be built. Each store incorporated as a separate partnership—between Walton and his brother, his father, his in-laws, his managers. The resulting model blended the independent, small-scale family business with a cooperative-style voluntary chain. Unlike the Wall Street version of ownership, this one was modeled on familiar populist economic lore. Rather than selling shares in an operation to faceless speculators from who-knew-where, Walton's capitalization scheme drew on the cooperative model. By 1970, he had stretched these resources into thirty-two stores.[12]

Thus in the first phase of Wal-Mart's development, Sam Walton and his family and friends found new uses for the region's political heritage.

Populism had animated the rural fight against distant corporations for six decades. It had spurred a vigorous movement against multiunit retailers like Walton, resulting in legislation that cast corporate chains outside the pale of legitimate business. On a structural level, the farmers' cooperatives and, later, the voluntary chains offered corporate form with populist content. As a popular intellectual tradition, moreover, the critique of corporations and chains tied political economy directly to concerns about moral legitimacy and citizenship.

In Wal-Mart's evolution as a populist multinational, the second great leap forward came in 1970. Walton decided to solve his frustrating, jerry-built financing system by issuing stock for public sale. Even then, the company was still vigilant to link ownership to the work of the stores. In these years of rapid growth, the company's stock-purchase plan for employees broadened the local ownership to locals with no investment capital. By the mid-1980s, the Walton-owned Benton County *Daily Democrat* was regularly publishing the company's quarterly statements, and the editor reported that an accidental omission of the Wal-Mart stock quote produced a flood of irate phone calls at the paper's office.[13] An ad from the 1970s announcing the opening of a new Wal-Mart in the home area pointed out that the store would belong to "local Northwest Arkansas people," since the stockholders came largely from the two-county area.[14]

The Ozarks' procorporate populism succeeded because it addressed the underlying logic of the old anticorporate populism. What could have been a contradiction—federal money turned to private ends—was actually quite acceptable. The same 1896 People's Party platform that damned corporations also demanded federal redistribution of public land, free, to "bona-fide settlers." In virtually the same breath, they called for the redistribution of Indian reservations and railroad concessions.[15] The legacy of Populist economic radicalism meant that the white periphery could make its peace with joint-stock companies and banks as long as they were local stockholders, hometown financiers.

This tradition entered the Democratic Party along with many of the defeated Populists in the Great Depression. The Democrats had struggled to craft an alliance between urban labor and peripheral farmers for two generations, and now the two classes' joint desperation threw their common interests into sharp relief. Harnessed together in the Democratic Party with Northern black and immigrant workers, the Southern and Western white rural voters pushed for state intervention to stabilize the whipsaw economic cycles and put a floor under the conditions of their lives. But the racial logics of the white South—populist and patrician alike—also found expression in the systematic exclusion of African Americans from the new federal bounty. Social Security, minimum wages, health care, education—these were delivered largely to whites only by the Southern wing of the Democratic Party, home to most of the defeated Populists as well as to the plantation oligarchs.[16] The managerial state had first expanded to serve commercial farmers in the 1910s and then to provide similar help for commerce generally during the 1920s.[17] It now extended that largess to individual claimants, but mostly those with their bona fides in order.

Movements like the antichain crusade thus included this sense of racial entitlement in the argument to preserve small farms and businesses. As an ad for an antichain film exhorted in the early 1930s, "Mr. Independent Merchant, here is your opportunity to recapture your birthright."[18] The white periphery expected the federal government to play an active role in its economic viability, so long as it acted on behalf of that mythic original citizen, the yeoman. The state's legitimate job remained metaphorically what it had once been literally: It was to provide a stake in the country, to free up the land from its Indian claimants, to build roads, to restrain the "foreign" monopolies, and then to leave the decisions to the yeoman farmer, disdaining distant experts. To see this dimension of the Southwest's conversion from the sworn foe of corporate capitalism to its most fervent booster, we can follow Wal-Mart's own capitalization back to its origin in the New Deal state.

Seen in the *longue durée* of the Sun Belt's conversion, some of the capital that launched Wal-Mart on a world stage originated with an evangelical Texas millionaire named Jesse H. Jones. As a concession to more conservative elements in Franklin D. Roosevelt's Washington, Jones wound up controlling the country's first mass alternative to tight Northeastern credit. After making a fortune in timber and real-estate development— classic frontier wealth-producers—the Tennessee native used the New Deal apparatus to promote his progrowth, open-shop vision, then deserted the Democratic Party for good after the segregationist split in 1948.[19] As the overseer of the Reconstruction Finance Corporation

(RFC), the largest lending agency in the nation's history, Jones lies at one end of a chain of capital that terminates in twenty-first-century Wal-Mart. Jones's career put procorporate boosterism in the driver's seat, and suggests how the Sun Belt's signature combination of government subsidy and antigovernment politics made populist sense.

Christened the "man who runs Houston" by *Fortune* magazine in 1939, Jesse H. Jones reigned over that Gulf Coast city undisputed for more than four decades and once hoped aloud that his heavenly reward would resemble the swampy port.[20] As the first among equals within Houston's powerful business brotherhood, Jones enthusiastically expanded on a pattern of government-subsidized growth that dated to the years immediately following the Civil War. As federal land giveaways to the railroads stimulated Western commerce, these Texas businessmen wielded influence through their interlocking control of private associations and government agencies. By deliberately neglecting public services for Houston residents, the city's businessmen were able to capture resources for their pet project: development of the business corridors that linked the railroad stations to the downtown markets.[21]

From the get-go, Jones was an outspoken friend of public investment in private enterprise. Early in the century, he headed a party of local businessmen on a trip to Washington and succeeded in convincing the federal government to foot half the cost of dredging the city's harbor to promote shipping and trade. When Ford's Detroit reshaped the nation with private automobiles, Houston was well placed to profit as an oil center. Federal and local governments built up its national market for petroleum with $200 million in highway subsidies by 1919. World War I only heightened demand for Houston's signature product, and Washington followed up in the 1920s with tax deductions and tariffs to protect the oil industry.[22]

This was the vision of government that Jesse H. Jones brought to his federal service in the Great Depression. With the rest of the Houston elite, he believed the government's first priority was to underwrite private, profit-making expansion. Residential streetlights and sewers would take a distant second to massive infrastructure projects, and the decisions about public resources would be left up to alliances of businessmen.[23] Under Jones's autocratic leadership, the loan corporation shook loose credit both directly—through loans to businesses—and indirectly, by forcing banks to liberalize lending.[24] Jones and the New Deal

Reconstruction Finance Corporation thus answered the longstanding need of the South and West: access to credit outside the parochial interests of Northeastern financiers. The corporation did so, however, on a scale unimaginable to the nineteenth-century Populist advocates of currency and credit reform. *Fortune* magazine christened Jones's RFC the "fourth branch of government."[25] By 1940, Jones was the administrator of the Federal Loan Agency and the Secretary of Commerce as well, without relinquishing any of his previously amassed control over the RFC itself.[26]

Though President Roosevelt could not abide the sanctimonious parvenu and privately referred to him as "Jesus H. Jones," the Texan's conservatism made him an important link between the administration and business interests. The Houston developer proved an effective counterweight to the New Deal's liberal wing, defeating attempts to link federal loans and contracts to labor standards in the companies that benefited.[27] Building on his early experiences in Houston and reacting against the Eastern banking establishment's malignant neglect of Southern and Western financial demands, Jones envisioned an active, positive role for government in promoting private enterprise. "Be smart for once," he chided a truculent assembly of the American Bankers Association in the fall of 1933. "Take the government in partnership with you."[28] The economy was too large, too complex, and too many people depended on it for the era of laissez-faire to return. "But that doesn't mean," Jones elaborated in a 1939 interview, "that the government has license to dictate to business or"—in an echo of the Populist hero William Jennings Bryan—"crucify business men." Neither government nor business could survive without the other, he concluded, so why not accept a common future characterized by "cooperation and restraint"?[29]

This vision of federally subsidized free enterprise found a willing audience in Arkansas, which received more loans from the RFC than any other state.[30] It was in Arkansas, too, just minutes from Wal-Mart's future headquarters, that religious conservatism was decisively linked to Jesse H. Jones's economic hopes for the region. Jones's life became intertwined with Northwest Arkansas when a young evangelist, John E. Brown, staged a revival in Houston. At Brown's hands, Jones was born again. His conversion laid the cornerstone for a lifelong relationship to the young preacher. With encouragement from Jones, Brown founded a Christian college in Siloam Springs, Arkansas, on the western edge of

Wal-Mart's Benton County. As the little school struggled through near-constant financial peril in the 1920s and 1930s, Jesse Jones joined its board of trustees and coordinated donations from his circle of wealthy Houston oilmen. The Texan even used his influence to win accreditation for John Brown College. A grateful Siloam Springs declared "Jesse Jones Day" in May of 1938, by which point the Houston developer had become one of the most powerful men in the federal government. The evangelical school would go on to become a major training ground for Wal-Mart's Christian managers and a key player in the company's international promotion of free enterprise.[31]

Some of the federal largess from the RFC eventually found its way into Wal-Mart through the Little Rock investment bank Stephens, Inc. The founder, Wilton R. "Witt" Stephens, was the son of a Baptist deacon who had once counseled his boys not to go into the business of whiskey, women, or gambling "because it won't pay six percent."[32] Witt Stephens turned his first dollars in the 1920s at Fort Leavenworth, where he held an exclusive franchise to peddle military-style belt-buckles to unsuspecting country boys under the impression they were part of the required uniform.[33] This early lesson in the advantages of government contracting may have alerted Stephens to greater possibilities, but the Depression furnished his big break.

By 1933, the municipal bonds that had funded levees, roads, and schools in Arkansas during the 1910s and 1920s were in default and selling for pennies on the dollar. Certain that his honest neighbors would eventually make good on the bonds' value, Stephens borrowed from friends of his father—just elected to the state legislature—and began buying enormous quantities of the cheap Arkansas municipal bonds from the Eastern banks that held them. Racing back home, he would immediately sell them at a slim profit to Arkansans before the bill came due—usually a margin of only a week or two.[34] The profitable resale was possible in part because Jesse Jones's loan corporation had begun bailing out municipalities and agricultural districts, meaning that the depressed bond market slowly rose.[35] Stephens also happened upon a well-timed public windfall from the bonds of the Southeast Arkansas Levee District, selling in the Depression for ten cents on the dollar. In 1938, the RFC stepped in and refinanced them at more than seven times that amount. Three years later, with a war economy on the horizon, Stephens took the trip to Washington and won the RFC's permission to buy up

$1.3 million of the levee bonds on credit, refinanced them again at a lower rate, and cleared an almost instant profit in their resale.[36]

Witt Stephens, later joined by his younger brother Jack, went on to extraordinary wealth and power as a kingmaker within Arkansas. Eventually their influence was felt nationally and internationally, though their cultivated country mannerisms and their private ownership of the investment bank Stephens, Inc., helped them maintain a relatively low profile. Over six decades they continued to make astute use of New Deal agencies and state government, Medicare, and public schools, becoming the largest privately owned investment bank outside Wall Street. Jack Stephens joined the board of Wal-Mart, where he served with the governor's wife, Hillary Rodham Clinton.[37]

This prewar redistribution into Arkansas and the network of Christians and oilmen it empowered anchored the Ozarks' developing economic culture outside traditional Northeastern circuits. During the postwar decades, while borrowing from family and from regional banks, Wal-Mart founder Sam Walton energetically pursued loans from the usual big banks in New York. But he kept bumping up against the cultural gulf separating him from the closed social worlds of the Manhattan bankers, those sources of private capital that lunched at Delmonico's. The federally aided redistribution into a Southern bank like Stephens, Inc., helped not only Wal-Mart but other major Ozarks firms like Tyson Chicken and J.B. Hunt Transport. Through these alternative channels, the old economic backwaters hitched their wagon to the Sun Belt's rising star.[38]

For the Stephens brothers, and certainly for their client Wal-Mart, Jesse Jones's Reconstruction Finance Corporation itself ultimately faded, becoming a minor player against the backdrop of the Sun Belt. The canny marketing of Wal-Mart stock to institutional investors—a second stock offering in 1972 moved the company onto the New York Stock Exchange—and its formidable growth meant that by 2004, the Bentonville enterprise had brought more outside capital to the South than Coca-Cola and the Bank of America combined.[39] But the "cooperation and restraint" that Texan Jesse Jones had advocated for American business characterized the Sun Belt relationship to government for more than half a century. In Wal-Mart's home territory, this pattern of federal investment laid the basis for a broad new consumer market. At the top of Northwest Arkansas's wish list were the massive dams enabled by the Comprehensive Flood Control Act of 1938. In Harrison, Arkansas, later to be the home of the second Wal-Mart store, the city fathers organized in 1940 to urge Washington to add hydroelectric power capacity to the planned Norfork Dam. They couched their arguments in sober terms, but privately, most in the area would have leapt at any federal project that would stanch the economic hemorrhage from local farms. Their success with damming the Ozarks allowed many locals to leave their low-wage jobs for federal rates on the construction projects. Boom towns sprouted on the infusion of government dollars; suddenly the area was teeming with pool halls, garages, and retail shops.[40]

Thanks to the lakes that these dams created, by the 1960s the Ozarks had become one of the country's few four-season retirement destinations—Florida without the bikinis. Retirement communities fueled the area's staggering 80 percent population increase between 1960 and 1998, and its original resort town, Bella Vista, served as something of a national prototype for this new industry.[41] These migrations to Wal-Mart Country drew people who could plausibly imagine the Ozarks as their yesterday—indeed for some of them, the area was quite literally their own immediate past. "Arkies" who had, in the words of Woody Guthrie, followed the do-re-mi to California for generations sent their children to college back home, returned regularly to visit, and often finally retired near where they had been born.[42] The little old lady from Pasadena might well be on the road back to Bentonville. When she got there, Wal-Mart helped ensure she would feel right at home.

3

Wal-Mart Country

In 1989, the Ozarks added a new attraction. Many of the country music fans leaving Branson, Missouri, began to take a detour to Bentonville, Arkansas. It was not an easy route, following two-lane roads through the mountains in laborious switchbacks. But the beautiful drive only added to the appeal for fifty thousand people a year whose destination was the Wal-Mart Visitors' Center. Here they could see where it all began for the richest man in the world, through a museum-quality re-creation of Sam Walton's first local five-and-dime. The displays were dominated by the Wal-Mart founder's modest 1979 Chevy pick-up, a monument to his humility and rectitude. After Walton's death in 1992, many of the tourists became visibly emotional at the sight of the famous truck. A docent at the center reported five years later that the comment he heard most often was "'Oh, I wish I could have met Mr. Walton.'"[1] For those who had known him, like one long-time Wal-Mart employee from Pea Ridge, the truck was an apt symbol of his priorities. "He was a great man," she recounted in 2005 of the boss she had met dozens of times. "He was not, I don't believe, money-hungry at all."[2]

Turn the other way out of Branson, though, and you could wind up in another Ozarks town, one that many Wal-Mart insiders pointed to as the real birthplace of the company. By 1960, Sam Walton reminisced in his autobiography, the family business had already grown to the largest independent variety chain in the country—but that still meant only fifteen stores and only $1.4 million in trade. About that time, Walton wrote, "I began looking around hard for whatever new idea would break us over into something with a little better payoff."[3] The answer lay right up

Route 66. "I think Sam would agree," brother Bud Walton mused in 1987, "that St. Robert, Missouri, was the originator of the Wal-Mart stores."[4] Walton had chosen the site carefully, using the factors he considered in all location decisions. First, he would check the local bank deposits and the sales tax receipts in the whole county, aware that farmers in the surrounding areas were accustomed to coming into town on Saturday to shop and conduct their courthouse business. Then he checked the population—under a thousand, in St. Robert's case. In his plane, though, Walton flew over the town and spotted the military base, home to over 100,000 soldiers, "all shopping at the post exchange because there really isn't anywhere else! No wonder that store was always over the top in sales."[5]

The base in question was Fort Leonard Wood, begun late in 1940 as part of the Army Expansion Program. During World War II, more than 300,000 soldiers had passed through it for training, as well as captured European POWs. Deactivated in 1946, the fort sprang back into economic viability with the onset of the Korean conflict in 1950. Cold War priorities kept it funneling federal payroll into the tiny town. By 1962, when the Waltons opened their St. Robert store, it had become the Army's Engineer Training Center and a major conduit for soldiers on their way to Vietnam.

The St. Robert experiment taught the family that these larger variety stores could do "unheard-of amounts of business." The Waltons took that lesson to Wal-Mart, which they launched the same year.[6] The old Ben Franklins and Walton's Family Centers gradually converted to the new discount format. The business was careful to stress that much of its early growth was financed by local capital, not by creditors from the North. Early ads from the company's days as a privately held chain pointedly referred to local ownership. At the annual meeting in 1984, as the company began to draw national attention, the shareholders who came from Northwest Arkansas were asked to stand and be recognized. "I'm sure proud of these folks," enthused Sam Walton. "This is going to happen all over the country."[7]

Paralleling the company's innovations in finance and organization during the postwar decades, then, was a third trend: the conscious crafting of a populist corporate image from Ozarks culture and from Sam Walton himself. This development dovetailed with the rise of the Sun Belt, a blended South and West fundamentally reshaped by government subsidy. Whereas the postwar boom and progressive taxation helped create a new national consuming class, the Cold War also redistributed national wealth geographically, on the lines envisioned by Sun Belt boosters like Jesse H. Jones. As America became "Southernized" through the wartime migration and then the Sun Belt's growing consumer clout, the small-town Wal-Mart could spread across the South and West and even into suburbs.

The notion of Wal-Mart Country gradually underwent an official shift: from being a strictly geographic designation in the company's early days, it evolved into a more ephemeral community. The first fifty towns to host a Wal-Mart store had a median population of just under nine thousand people, and they were tightly concentrated in the Ozarks, home to no city larger than Springfield, Missouri.[8] But beginning in the mid-1970s, as the company's stock sales backed more exuberant expansion, the task of transferring its Ozark culture to non-Ozarkers forced a more self-conscious appraisal. The company laid claim to a growing "Wal-Mart Country," represented on the back covers of its newsletters as a circle radiating out from Bentonville and uniting a string of small towns in the Ozarks, the Dust Bowl, Texas, the upland South, the whiter parts of Mississippi, the less French parts of Louisiana, eventually even the Little Egypt triangle of southern Illinois. In 1980, again promoting the sense of organic cultural connection among the stores despite their growing geographic distance, the magazine began an occasional series of "community profiles" on the towns in which it operated stores. Now that the stores' trade areas were losing their territorial specificity, just what—and where—was Wal-Mart Country?

One common denominator that the descriptions often unintentionally illuminated was the heavy public supports that attracted Wal-Mart to town. Private colleges, public universities, military installations, federally funded artificial lakes, and state institutions like schools for the deaf, insane asylums, or public hospitals appeared over and over in the publicity provided by the towns of Wal-Mart Country.[9] Walton preferred county seats, since farmers were accustomed to traveling to them for shopping, but the additional payrolls of county government could not have hurt business either. And where the mark of government subsidy was less direct, it was often inscribed on the towns' histories by way of the great railroad land giveaways of the nineteenth century that established many of them as transportation hubs.[10]

In actively seeking government resources, Wal-Mart Country exemplified the success story of the rising Sun Belt. Thanks in part to the style of federal support begun under Jesse H. Jones, the high-tech, military, and service industries grew steadily across the South and West from World War II onward. In turn, the Sun Belt's growing influence in postwar America decisively shaped the country's political horizons. The one-party rule resulting from black disfranchisement in the South had produced a gerontocracy of powerful incumbents in the Congressional committee system. Making common cause with probusiness Republicans, these segregationist Democrats broke the back of the labor and civil rights Left in the years immediately following the war with a pair of crucial initiatives: The antiunion Taft-Hartley Act of 1947 essentially halted the spread of unions beyond their established territory in Northern industry by encouraging the states to pass "right-to-work" legislation. These laws made the benefits of collective bargaining flow equally to those who paid union dues and those who did not, thus giving workers no incentive to join the union. Southern champions of industrial development lost no time in promoting their region's antiunionism to lure facilities out of the Northeast. Arkansas, Wal-Mart's home state, passed one of the first "right-to-work" laws in 1947; by 1954, the entire South had enacted such legislation.[11]

When it came time to select sites for military bases and war contracts, the conservative congressional coalition made its power felt as well. Jesse H. Jones's lieutenant at the Reconstruction Finance Corporation—a zealous supporter of the free market from Houston—shaped the postwar sell-off of federal assets to private companies at bargain-basement prices.[12] This infrastructure anchored the Sun Belt's dominance of the high-tech "clean development" of the Cold War—NASA in Texas and Florida; Hughes Aircraft in Orange County, California; Lockheed-Martin in Cobb County, Georgia; the Air Force Academy in Colorado Springs. The Cold War defense industry and its single guaranteed client, the federal government, provided a reliable mechanism for redistributing national wealth to the South and West.[13] These high-tech industries in turn supported a secondary sector of service, entertainment, and recreation: McDonald's and Disney from California; the retirement industry in Florida, Arkansas, and Arizona; Blockbuster Video from Dallas; the country-music industry in Nashville and Branson; and, of course, Wal-Mart in Bentonville, discount commissary to the Sun Belt boom economy. Under the Reagan administration alone, military spending created over a million new service jobs—an increase of 65 percent between 1980 and 1985.[14]

Jesse H. Jones and his Reconstruction Finance Corporation had institutionalized a particular pattern of federal economic restructuring. The government would make public resources available to business decision-makers and allow them broad discretion to avoid social claims by other parts of the polity. The subsidies would flow even without guarantees that their benefits would be widely distributed. Frequently, faith-based organizations would take the place of those subject to democratic oversight. This pattern of regional development fueled industrial flight first to the American South and later to the global South.

This prototype nurtured a distinctive political culture in the areas dependent on high-tech defense spending and its related service economy. California's Orange County, for example, was ground zero of the "draft Goldwater" movement in 1964 and subsequently of the Reagan Revolution. Cobb County, Georgia, was the home district of Congressman Newt Gingrich, author of the 1994 Republican takeover of Congress. Since 1991, Colorado Springs has hosted Focus on the Family, the most powerful Christian family values lobbying organization in the country.[15] Wal-Mart's Northwest Arkansas, bolstered by the influx of retirees from traditionally Republican states, joined the national defection of white suburbanites and Southerners to the Republican Party.[16] Among the Ozarks' sons who ultimately traveled to Washington was the governor of Missouri, John Ashcroft, who became U.S. attorney general under the second President Bush.

Conservative electoral success after 1968 was only one effect of the Sun Belt's distinctive postwar political economy. As a dominant voice in Washington, it also shaped globalization itself. The New Deal liberals' hope had been to use federal procurement contracts in Latin America to insist on improved conditions for the workers, but Jesse H. Jones had put a definitive stop to this particular vision of U.S.-led globalization.[17] In effect, Left-labor influence was contained within the industrial islands of the North Atlantic, from which it might subsequently be rolled back.[18] Washington could place the orders and foot the bill, but managerial prerogative would be preserved, both at home and abroad.

In essence, Wal-Mart created a chain of little Bransons, theme parks of landlocked small-town life, reservations for an imagined homogeneous yesterday that only the technologies of tomorrow could render. The very culture it sold, the living diorama of America's Yesterday, was the product of the increased leisure time, consumption, and mobility that postwar growth generated. But it was also an explicit reaction against new claimants to that America. In the aggrieved tones of the conservative mobilization, a Wal-Mart stock man at a store in Paragould, Arkansas, greeted Christmas of 1972 with this frustrated poem:

> Have you ever just once tried to be
> Understanding, loyal, and true
> To all the men and women
> Who are fighting to see it through?
> They look to us with hope and faith
> That what they do is right
> But it seems that all we ever do
> Is have demonstrations, riots, and fights.[19]

Nixonian resentment was only one note in the political, economic, and religious culture that Wal-Mart nurtured. More often, the accent was on the positive contribution of the silent majority. Within the Wal-Marts of the 1970s, commentary from customers and employees regularly drew an implicit contrast between the courtesy, friendliness, and order within the stores and the chaotic world outside, full of malcontents and rioters. Wal-Mart was preserving a version of America that its constituents felt was endangered. "Thank God there are still some good, kind, unselfish people in the world whose joy is in serving those in need," was a representative comment from the early 1970s.[20] What made Wal-Mart different from other discount stores, asked *Time* magazine more than a decade later? Not the products—those had long been standardized across the country. The difference was the environment: "clean aisles, well-scrubbed shelves, and cheerful clerks." "'It's attitude,' explain[ed] Wal-Mart vice chairman Jack Shewmaker. 'Give me workers with the right attitude.'"[21] For their part, many store-level employees enjoyed pointing out elements of small-town life recreated under the blue roof. An employee in Covington posed for a photo alongside a pair of elderly women chatting away in the rocking chairs for sale one Saturday afternoon in 1975.[22] A group of retirees was such a regular feature

41

in the snack bar of a Florida store that the employees dubbed them the "Board of Directors."[23]

Ironically, the people who felt most comfortable in this replica of small-town life were in need of it precisely because they had become so mobile. Wal-Mart Country mapped an archipelago of familiar territory for a constituency that was increasingly on the move. The white Southern exodus that peaked around 1980 was an impermanent affair, with the prosperous migrants and their children cycling from the suburbs of Los Angeles or Cleveland back through the small towns of the border South.[24] "My companion and I traveled through Oklahoma, Arkansas and Texas with our light truck and travel trailer," recounted a grateful customer in 1989. Already familiar with Wal-Mart at home in Junction City, Kansas, the pair "looked for and found the same friendly and dependable service in every town where we traveled."[25] Taking an astute look at the 30 million recreational vehicle enthusiasts around the country and the potential for growth among retiring baby-boomers, the company later welcomed overnight RV parking at stores nationwide. Rand-McNally published a version of its driving atlas that located every Wal-Mart with addresses and map coordinates. In Anchorage, Alaska, a Wal-Mart dispatched employees to leave a welcoming note under the visitors' windshield wipers at night. Wal-Mart's RV guests developed their own subculture, swapping travel tips, guidebooks, and photos in the parking lots. "We don't like hotels. They're so impersonal," explained a retiree from Chandler, Oklahoma.[26] The Wal-Mart chain mapped a specific American culture within the larger one, and people knew when they were home.

Throughout the 1970s, the citizens of Wal-Mart Country self-consciously marked out the parameters of this community with elaborate pageantry that reinscribed their fathers' America onto the low-rise shopping centers and expanses of asphalt. In these spectacles, they asserted their connection to old-stock American folk heroes: farmers, cowboys, pioneers, hillbillies.[27] The store at the Ozark town of Harrison, Arkansas, annually tied its dress-up to the seasonal opening of the nearby Ozark theme park Dogpatch, USA, a commodification of hillbilly clichés based on the long-running comic strip.[28] The store in Leavenworth, Kansas, sponsored a children's costume contest for Buffalo Bill Cody Days in 1971, paying tribute to a man famous for pretending to be a cowboy.[29] The town of Claremore, Oklahoma, home of Wal-Mart

#12, boasted a memorial to the wholesome Rogers and Hammerstein musical *Oklahoma,* complete with the original surrey with the fringe on top.[30]

If one cultural idiom stood out above all as the lingua franca of Wal-Mart Country, it was country music itself. As a commodity for sale, as a comfortable backdrop for shopping, or as the living art form practiced by the stores' customers and employees, country music made Wal-Mart Country. The Lebanon, Missouri, Wal-Mart sold almost four thousand dollars' worth of records and tapes in 1971 during a three-day "Western" promotion, complete with an in-store band.[31] A country station in Salem, Missouri, broadcast its show from the local Wal-Mart every Saturday morning in the early 1970s.[32] Two fabric department associates and a stockman from Jefferson City played together in a country band, and the hardware manager in Broken Arrow, Oklahoma, sold a song he wrote to Loretta Lynn herself.[33]

Country stars were sure draws for in-store entertainment, especially since many of them had lived in the area at some point. George "Goober" Lindsey, star of TV's *Hee-Haw,* returned to his hometown of Jasper, Alabama, for a Wal-Mart promotion of Liberty Overalls, where he signed autographs for delighted customers.[34] When Barbara Mandrell visited the Wal-Mart in Belleville, Illinois, the store sold almost five hundred recordings, and Mandrell signed 1,500 autographs for the throng of fans. "In return," reported *Wal-Mart World,* "people brought special pieces of art like needlepoint and posters for her. The crowd was great and very polite."[35]

The Wal-Mart shoppers' and employees' identification with country music in the 1970s spread within the company to become a full-fledged identity politics, unifying a company that had outgrown its geographical base. When the musical genre dropped the "& Western" from its name in those years, it sought to free itself from a specific physical location and instead represent the nation. The country of country music was no longer defined by place. Its citizens were scattered from Orange County to Pentagon City, but everyone understood who belonged there.[36]

In later years, as Wal-Mart addressed a national audience remote from the Ozarks, this division came coded as urban versus rural. In this mental geography, "urban" implied a kind of person rather than a density of persons. Walton made the association clear in his autobiography.

In cities, he admitted, "We have more trouble coming up with educated people who want to work in our industry, or with people of the right moral character and integrity."[37] The geography of Wal-Mart shows a conscious urge toward the comfort, order, and unity of this homogenized, depoliticized space, one with a new appeal in the twenty-first century. "On September 12, 2001," explained an Ozarks developer, "our phones started ringing—lots of companies are seeing the wisdom of moving to the interior of the country, a small town area."[38]

Thus the original home of anticorporate populism came full circle, offering multinationals a haven in a risky world. In order to effect this shift, Wal-Mart Country needed the specific redistribution of income that followed the New Deal and a native son to redeem the managerial corporation. Wal-Mart's host cultures provided the specific identity that has come to represent the corporate vision of America. In its project of creative reconstruction, the Sun Belt's economic frontier found new uses for the old Populist possessive individualism, winning allegiance from Uncle Sam to Mr. Sam.

Sam Walton of Kingfisher, Oklahoma, was an ideal figure to fashion a procorporate populism. His family history exemplified the Southwest's growth pattern in which government largess was turned into individual virtue by the addition of sweat equity. Walton's grandfather served as postmaster, a form of federal patronage that provided a steady if hardly munificent wage amid the vagaries of farming. His uncle staked out a free land grant when the federal government drove Indian owners out of Oklahoma and made white settlers a gift of the territory. Homesteading, the federal subsidizing of the yeoman ideal, laid the basis for what was to prove a much longer-lived wealth engine in the future Sun Belt: not small-scale farming but land speculation. Two generations of Waltons profited from the loans and mortgages that underwrote land booms, taking time out to farm only when World War I guaranteed a government market for their crops at peak prices.[39] For their part, the Waltons worked hard with the capital their government furnished and became legendary for thrift: "He could squeeze a Lincoln until the president cried," exclaimed one long-time employee of Sam's father.[40] The family inspired more respect than affection, driving relentless deals, yet never crossing the line into dishonesty. And while their living was more comfortable than most, it was hardly extravagant. Walton was "no Donald Trump," an *Arkansas Gazette* reviewer pointed out approvingly in 1990, and *USA Today* christened him "a billionaire everyone can love."[41]

Walton blended his personal reputation for honesty with the company's strict codes of commercial behavior in a bid to address the persistent populist anxiety over unfair backroom deals. Wal-Mart publicly stressed a narrow form of procedural ethics, while simultaneously employing ruthless tactics against smaller merchants. Its buyers could not accept so much as a paperclip from a manufacturer's representative. In the waiting room at the Bentonville headquarters, visitors and employees alike could help themselves to a cup of diner coffee, but they were expected to insert fifteen cents in a box to pay for it. Rather than install a coin-operated dispenser, the company made its point by charging on the honor system. The secretive company's insistence on picayune transparency reinforced the sober, thrifty ideal of our fathers' America.

Walton's biography of finance, inherited security, and public inputs was hardly the stuff of a convincing Horatio Alger tale, but a host of mythologizers relentlessly forced Walton's personal history into the threadbare rags-to-riches plot line. A "family tradition of hard work and thrift" stood in for actual material hardship in most renditions.[42] The national economic disaster of the Depression and the regional one of the Dust Bowl were elided into Walton's personal biography. "While still a child, Walton moved with his family from one town to another in Missouri, where he observed Dust Bowl farms. He promised himself he would never be poor."[43] In fact, his father was repossessing those farms for the family mortgage company. Yet Walton's childhood seemingly converged with that of the busted farmer, not the moneylender.[44]

Communicating the legend of Mr. Sam required strategic silences and careful emphasis: Walton "got out of the military in 1945," ran one in-house version from 1976. "He and his wife, Helen, had managed to save a little money while they were in the service . . . he and Mrs. Walton decided to invest their savings in a small Ben Franklin store in Newport, Arkansas."[45] All the elements of meritorious bootstrapping were on display in this telling. The wartime military service—which, the article fails to mention, all took place in a stateside office—sanctified subsequent success. The considerable investment capital from family sources disappeared entirely; and the husband and wife together launched the modest store, named for an enterprising Founding Father.

After Mr. Walton's passing in 1992, when both presidential candidates paused to offer tribute, Wal-Mart made a conscious policy of reinforcing its identification of founder with company. "'After Dad was gone,' his son Rob reflected, 'we made a real strong commitment to keeping his name and his philosophy in the top of minds around the company, and, interestingly, it has gotten even stronger over the years.'"[46] Quotations from the Chairman hung on banners around the central meeting auditorium at Wal-Mart headquarters. His lean visage smiled gravely down from the walls, and taped clips of his firsthand advice were played for employees and stockholders alike. Even the retail union presented its case to Wal-Mart workers as an attempt to "Keep Sam Walton's Dream Alive." In an advertisement alleging false advertising on Wal-Mart's part, its competitor Target proclaimed, "This never would have happened if Sam Walton were alive."[47]

The Waltons were not alone in their rehabilitation of big business with a Southern twang. In the Sun Belt's boom years, Northwest Arkansas produced several outstanding examples of the boss as Everyman, the multibillionaire captain of his industry who wore his egalitarianism on his sleeve. Ostentatious displays of thrift, for example, marked the Ozark chicken king Don Tyson, who dressed in the khaki uniform of his employees.[48] The region's mighty trucking empires were founded by men in overalls with grade-school educations. "In Northwest Arkansas," explained the local trucking magnate J. B. Hunt, "the rich don't know they're rich and the poor don't know they're poor."[49] During the heyday of the industrial economy in the North, auto companies poured vast resources into the fledgling field of public relations in their efforts to personalize their gigantic corporations for the public. Similarly, advertisers strove unconvincingly to convert AT&T into a "friend and neighbor" or the GM headquarters into "the family home."[50] In contrast, the down-to-earth Mr. Sam and Mr. Don, truckers like Harvey Jones and J. B. Hunt, easily stood in for the companies that bore their names. As urban, coastal America came to look less and less like Northwest Arkansas, these entrepreneurial titans insisted ever more firmly on their Ozark identities.

The connection between the area's rural white virtue and its new corporate representatives was not confined to their uppermost ranks. Most store managers as well as hourly employees were raised in small towns or rural areas, "hard-working farm kids" in the words of another executive.[51] Since most upper management came out of related retail or distribution experiences—Walton was notorious for raiding other chains for talent—they were not necessarily local men themselves. But it helped to have some country in your background, as well as a family and a church membership.[52]

In fact, since Wal-Mart evolved out of the five-and-dime sector within mass retail, it was particularly well placed to harvest personnel from the farm. The first wave of limited-price variety stores from the late nineteenth century—chains like Woolworth's, Kress, and J.C. Penney, where the young Sam Walton briefly worked—had followed precisely the same pattern. Northern companies stated an explicit preference for "old-stock American Protestants from rural and small-town origins." They believed such employees would show personal thrift and abstemiousness, and expressed their unease with college-educated applicants or "Bolshevistic" urbanites. The S.S. Kresge Company, whose eponymous founder dabbled in genealogy and recruited through the Young Men's Christian Association, published in 1920 a management directory without a single surname from beyond Western or Northern Europe.[53]

But these sons of the soil had merely been employees in corporations that were controlled by the usual suspects: the New York financial establishment. As early as the 1910s, Woolworth's board of directors shared with the Sears board Henry Goldman of Goldman Sachs, Philip Lehman of Lehman Brothers, and the chairman of Chase National Bank. Merrill Lynch began in the same years to promote trade in chain store securities as well as mergers and acquisitions among regional retail chains.[54] Moreover, by the time of the postwar consumer boom, the old Northern five-and-dimes had lost their preferred talent pools. The Yankee farmers were becoming thin on the ground, the customer base more diverse, and the prejudices less intense.[55] Newer chains entered the field without any pretense to rural virtue, firms like E. J. Korvette's, which supplied the multiethnic Northern suburbs with cheap refrigerators and washing machines.

Only in America's Yesterday could the original pattern be successfully repeated, and then only with appropriate attention to the potential conflict between corporate structures and Southern rural priorities. The people who brought those priorities into the heart of the new Wal-Mart

Country were unlikely vehicles for an ideological revolution in corporate capitalism. Sam Walton had provided the face for the aw-shucks corporation, and federal redistribution created its conditions of possibility. Through the rising Sun Belt service sector, however, middle-aged Wal-Mart moms taught the country a new way to imagine the economy. The women that Walton hired gave Wal-Mart Country its soul.

4

The Family in the Store

In June, 2004, Judge Martin Jenkins of the U.S. District Court certified the largest private-sector civil rights class-action lawsuit in history, *Dukes v. Wal-Mart Stores, Inc.* The decision by the California judge allowed six named plaintiffs to represent the two-thirds of Wal-Mart's work force that were women, totaling over 1.5 million women who had worked at the company after December 26, 1998. Explicitly linking *Dukes* to *Brown v. Board of Education,* which turned fifty that year, the judge described the case as "historic . . . This anniversary serves as a reminder of the importance of the courts in addressing the denial of equal treatment under the law whenever and by whomever it occurs."[1] One of the plaintiffs' experts concluded in his report for the case that at the end of the twentieth century, Wal-Mart store management remained more overwhelmingly male than its competitors in 1975. "Such long-term persistence," wrote economist Marc Bendick, "is further evidence that the shortfall in female employment observed in 1999 reflects attitudes and practices deeply embedded in the organization's corporate culture."[2] A lawyer concurred, "Wal-Mart is living in the America of thirty years ago."[3]

Wal-Mart, these commentators implied, was still living on Arkansas time while the rest of the world had moved ahead. Who could forget how white Arkansans had interpreted *Brown*'s "all deliberate speed" two generations earlier, or the ultimate action their intransigence had required: federalized troops in Little Rock's Central High? Although this time around sex not race was at issue, the analogy suggested that the good ol' boys were just up to their old tricks. The federal power of the court might again prove necessary to frog-march them into the twenty-first century.

But thirty years ago, women did not emerge from inequality at work into full economic citizenship in "men's jobs"—the stable, well-paid factory or professional-managerial work that had been the backbone of postwar prosperity. Rather, under the stress of deindustrialization, men's jobs came to look more like women's work. Casualization, "flexibility," part-time or temp work, and the erosion of benefits, seniority, and tenure—the conditions that had once best described most women's work in an industrial economy became generalized to the work force as a whole. Unwaged household labor, personal relationships, and part-time jobs had supported the American breadwinner all along. This breadwinner was a husband whose wife packed his lunch box, a father whose children were trained by the state, an imaginary homesteader whose mortgage was subsidized with tax deductions, a craft worker—union carpenter or university professor—whose job was explicitly reserved for him by race and sex. Without the exclusions that had invisibly supported him, he disappeared from the economic landscape with frightening suddenness.

By adapting the management/labor dyad to a "natural" family hierarchy, Wal-Mart performed another of the Sun Belt's innovative sleights of hand. By drafting the labor of the yeoman's household into its work processes, it colonized a realm that industry had scorned. Like postwar evangelicalism, the country music industry, or the Republican Party's "Southern Strategy," the region's service sector spun traditional straw into radical new gold. Far from being thirty years behind the times, Wal-Mart pioneered an economic breakthrough of the sort that now undergirds globalization generally. Historically the workers in the nation's leading economic sector have constituted its natural "labor aristocracy," their contribution rewarded with stable work, high wages, and benefits. But the Arkansas discount store broke this connection.[4] Today the patriarchal organization of work ranks as a hallmark of the global economy, from maquiladoras of young Honduran women embroidering swooshes on shoes to the immigrant-owned family motels and convenience stores that dot the United States. Like the embrace of corporate populism, this social reorganization required a creative reinterpretation of cherished ideologies about work, sex, faith, and citizenship.

The South, relatively "backward" in terms of its industrialization, once again had the freedom to redefine the labor model following the post–World War II economic boom. It was this feminized, familial pattern of work that shaped the subsequent landscape for all of us.

In the middle decades of the twentieth century, while the snowbound capitalists and communists alike raised the assembly line to the status of cultural icon, the South was looking for the next new thing. Wal-Mart managers acquired an expanded role as the symbolic heads of household, the Jeffersonian "masters of small worlds."[5] Women—both employees and customers—structured a unique social relationship that had no precedent in the factory model of work. Middle-aged mothers in particular formed the stable backbone of the new workplace, training generations of male managers and providing a reserve of service skills. Workers and customers alike brought rural, Protestant family ideals into the workplace, changing the face of postindustrial America.

When Ozarks veterans of Wal-Mart's early years speak of their working lives, one phrase recurs with startling regularity: "I loved working at Wal-Mart," they say emphatically. "It was like a family." The term "family," like "populist," has been pressed into service in such a bewildering array of circumstances that it can be hard to recapture its particular meaning in a given time and place. For many Wal-Mart employees in the company's formative years, however, the white, Protestant farming region in which they worked and lived imbued "family" with a quite specific suite of associations that would fuel the rise of the service sector. Well after the companionate nuclear family had transformed households in the booming metropolitan suburbs, many Ozarkers maintained the sense of a family as a productive economic unit, not primarily the vehicle for individual self-actualization. This model helped Sam Walton's company meet another of the anticorporate critiques that had challenged his predecessors: the threat of the service economy to masculinity itself.[6]

The South had distinguished itself as a hotbed of agitation against chain stores before World War II. One of the activists' principal concerns about the demise of independent retail had been the reduction of independent workers to feminized men who would never know the possessive individualism of self-command. Like the intertwined critique of "foreign" capital, this polestar of antichain agitation likewise derived from the symbolic power of the independent yeoman and equally demonstrated his ambivalent legacy.

The original political virtue of the land-owning head-of-household lay in his literal self-possession: he could participate in the public sphere because he called no man master. But the implicit corollary to his independence was the legal *dependence* of the other members of his household: women, children, the infirm, and in various times and places, servants, tenants, or slaves. By the 1920s, with independent farming a distinctly minority occupation in the United States, the independence could inhere in other forms of proprietorship, providing the illusion of self-command.[7] The chains, owned by stockholders and managed "scientifically" according to the standardized principles of Taylorism, raised the specter of "a nation of clerks." The least industrialized sections of the country might see their sons fall prey to the same dehumanizing factory discipline as the immigrant masses of the North and East. These Americans weren't supposed to be working for the Man; they *were* the Man.

Thus a generation before the man in the gray flannel suit offered a bogey of the standardized postwar drone, middle-class Americans could gaze with horror on the permanent retail clerk. This man-boy would be relegated to the lifelong status of a "helper," classed by one outraged observer alongside such effeminate professionals as typists, stenographers, and secretaries. Chain-store employment could even strip him of political manhood in the form of the franchise, for constant mobility might prevent him from registering to vote.[8]

The economic logic of mass distribution demanded that many nineteen-year-old clerks would stay in that lowly condition throughout their productive years, never becoming the Pop of a mom-and-pop. "[Chain stores] stifle opportunity for local boys," charged an anonymous proponent of chain taxes in *Reader's Digest.* "[A chain] doesn't want bright boys—it wants plodders, dutiful machines."[9] Klansmen warned that chain monopolies, by shutting out the option of small-business ownership, were enslaving American children and turning young men into "'automatons.'"[10] As promotion opportunities at the chains contracted in the Depression, an Arkansan wrote his senator, "Do you really believe rugged individualism can be revived without legislation to destroy the 'Octopus' movement" of chain retailers?[11] A chain-store clerk's capacity for fatherhood could even fall victim to the chains' downward pressure on wages, for he could not earn enough to marry and have children, argued one opponent of chains.[12] Decked out in an apron, subjected to time-and-motion studies, trapped behind the produce counter of the A&P—the sturdy yeoman was indeed imperiled.

The franchise model of the Ben Franklin stores offered the illusion of independence but not the substance. Its champions shrilly asserted the independents' "virility" in the face of the retail revolution and denounced the parent firm's attempts at "forcing any additional authority or control on the owners."[13] But for all the concern over the fate of the male clerk, another model offered an end-run around his emasculation. During the Depression, the New Deal's economic administrators had referred to the small, independent shops as the "Mama, Papa, and Rosy stores."[14] The owner, in other words, managed the labor of his female dependents. This model in turn grew out of traditional agrarian economies, in which the household was the productive unit and its male head legally owned the labor of all its members. The uneven advance of women's legal rights to their own earnings left the home-based business in limbo. Generating income in a family enterprise was akin to domestic service, which the law still assumed a woman owed her husband.[15] In a mom-and-pop store, then, Pop united ownership and management, while Mom and Rosy were labor.

Sam Walton had made a virtue of necessity in his earlier stores when, in the absence of investment capital, he expanded the chain by bringing in family, friends, and neighbors as investor-managers. Then in 1970 he successfully wooed underwriting support from Little Rock's Stephens, Inc., and took the company public. The patchwork of manager-owners and family members all traded in their stakes for shares, and the stores moved to salaried management over waged clerks. In exchange for the infusion of capital, in other words, Wal-Mart no longer offered a connection between ownership and control, the distinction that had set this chain apart from the nation of clerks.[16] Loss of this literal possessive individualism was one potential pitfall for Wal-Mart in its home region, and it went hand in hand with the novelty of an entire workplace full of women. Despite chain managers' man-sized wages and their decision-making power, there were two, three, many Mamas for every Papa.

But the analogy held an answer to its own conundrum, for the farm family undertook its mission of economic survival as a diversified communal project under one head, not as a collection of competing equals. The man of the household—the master of his small world—did not lose prestige or authority by being a minority of one: to the contrary, it was his uniqueness that legally defined a household. A nation of clerks might indeed threaten the gender order, just as had the wartime entry of women into heavy industry. But as long as Rosy was ringing up sales rather than riveting, a nation of Mamas and Rosies simply reinscribed the family sexual hierarchy onto the workplace.[17]

In earlier American transitions from agriculture to waged labor, the destination had been the factory. Young women left their family farms to work in the Lowell textile mills in the antebellum North, then left the looms for marriage. After the Civil War, the mills moved closer to the cotton, building company towns across the Appalachian Piedmont and contracting for the labor of entire families. In both these moments, historically distinct concepts of family followed the women, men, and children into the factories—and often, back out again, for the first industrial generations rotated between mill work and farms.

In contrast, in the old core industries of metal, steel, and rubber, the family members were hidden from sight, even though the workers continued to depend on this unwaged domestic labor to fit themselves for industrial production. Likewise, the Victorian ideal of separate spheres supported the demand for a "family wage" that would maintain a wife and children outside the market. This vision of gender and work was enshrined as state policy through social provisions like Social Security and unemployment insurance that addressed men as workers and women as family members, regardless of the reality that both were usually both.[18] Though waged labor produced an official ideology of contracts between individuals, it was always a family affair; for all its reductionist talk of hired "hands," the industrial economy ran as well on hearts.

After World War II, there were few places in the country where a new industry could draw upon an agrarian population for its reserves of social capital, but the Ozarks was one of those few. The genius of Wal-Mart and its imitators was to mobilize the very resource that had been devalued by the earlier rise of industry. The ruling myth of labor enshrined a chain of association between masculinity, autonomy, and skill.

This suite of concerns was given institutional form in the New Deal social provisions, in most unions, and in firms themselves.

The burgeoning service economy then capitalized on this broad social agreement that women weren't really workers, their skills not really skills. The domestic economies of farm families provided a model and a vehicle for this appropriation, and companies in the Ozarks were working overtime to support the direct transition from farm to service corporation. The Second World War had put an end to the dream of small farm independence for all but those with outside income. Pricey new chemical, mechanical, and biological inputs—herbicides, automatic tomato-pickers, hybrid corn—took up the temporary slack in the labor market and made farming so capital-intensive that only increased acreage could support the great leap forward in mechanized production.[19]

For those who did not need to wrest a living out of their acreage, though, farming could still anchor a way of life distinct from national patterns. The small-farm allegiances that shaped local work culture were hinted at by the Tyson poultry processing plants scenting the air around Northwest Arkansas. This Ozarks *Fortune 500* company relied upon an agribusiness revolution: contract chicken-raising. Farmers received tens of thousands of day-old chicks, raised them in a computer-controlled climate according to a rigidly standardized schedule, and then returned the broilers and fryers to Tyson Foods for processing by a new work force of Spanish-speaking immigrants—a kind of factory farming for the outsourced era.[20] As one such grower put it, "'This isn't farming. It's going to a job in your back yard.'"[21]

In the Ozarks, the trappings of independent family subsistence remained a plausible goal for a generation of native-born whites in the mid-twentieth century. Much of the economic substance had been drained from the farm. But for the generations raised there, the form remained, with all its ideological power and all its resources of skill and social relations. Ozarks industry leaders in trucking and chicken capitalized on the area's historically late transition from farming by mobilizing the yeoman himself. Wal-Mart wanted the yeoman's wife as both a customer and an employee. To get her, it had to model itself on her family relationships.[22]

Undoubtedly, one signal effect of building corporate structures through a family farm model—as opposed to the military organization to which many older workplaces had aspired—was to lodge authority firmly in adult masculinity itself. The early Wal-Marts adjusted to their largely female work force by emphasizing the natural prerogatives of men *as men,* not as management. Nowhere was this conflation more obvious than in the occasional moments of ritualized inversion—the store turned upside down for "Ladies' Day." As celebrated in the Eldon, Missouri, Wal-Mart in 1975, Ladies' Day featured hourly female employees assuming the positions of store managers and assistant managers. Then,

> The first business of the day was coffee made by Jesse Mutz, in place of the ladies . . . The regular Friday morning meeting was conducted by Karen and her [elected] assistants . . . for one day the ladies were to be addressed as Mrs. or Ms. . . . Windows were washed by Jerry Pate, Assistant Manager, and the refrigerator was defrosted and destroyed by Ray Olive, another Assistant Manager . . . Approximately 25 red light specials were conducted by Mr. Olive and Mr. Mutz. They also, complete with smocks, ran the cash registers when business increased . . . Thanks to the co-operation and sportsmanship from the men at No. 44, Ladies' day was a huge success![23]

Not just sex, but the distinction of adulthood marked the appropriate manager, no matter how poorly the mantle fit. "Mr. Blankley will be eighteen years old next month . . . I'll bet he's the youngest Assistant Manager in the Wal-Mart chain!" wrote one store employee about the promotion of a recent high-school graduate in 1974—the honorific "Mister" transforming a teenager into a manager in two syllables.[24] Each company newsletter showcased an endlessly repeated vignette: store managers in their twenties presenting five- and ten-year service pins to women who could be their mothers or even their grandmothers.[25] Moving these young managers around—a common and long-standing practice in chain management—helped orient them toward the company as a whole rather than an individual store. The personal face of the company in the community could be maintained by the women whose rootedness meant they might spend two or three decades in one store. The requirement that a potential manager be "relocatable" at the drop of a hat has been cited by the company to justify the underrepresentation of women in management, and in the face of *Dukes v. Wal-Mart,* Wal-Mart announced it was dropping that official requirement.[26] But like the company's other claims in the class-action case, the policy looked rather different from within its original time and place than it did in the 2004 court documents applied to the national work force. Many Ozarkers had historically paid the price of seasonal mobility for the privilege of keeping a stake in the hills; the relief was finding a way for at least one family member to stay put.

Like much of the service sector that waxed as manufacturing waned, Wal-Mart and retail generally came to rely on additional categories of employees it could imagine as less than breadwinners: not just wives and mothers, but adolescents and retirees. An item from 1989 suggests the economic logic at work: when her Kansas high school sponsored a career day, Lawanda Faler chose to "shadow" her own grandmother in her work as a Wal-Mart greeter. Faler was so taken with the experience she announced her hope to work there herself. "Looks like Grandma's got competition!" joked a co-worker, in an apt epigram for the service economy's labor market.[27] Retirees carried the values of Sam Walton's own "greatest generation," along with the relatively stable pensions and federal benefits won under the New Deal order. At the age of 74, for example, Earl Phillip found working in the garden center of a Texas Wal-Mart a welcome distraction from monotonous retirement, but his wartime service with the Army Corps of Engineers and his thirty-year career on the Santa Fe railroad suggest his income and benefits were already assured.[28]

For the original Wal-Mart Country in the 1970s, what stands out is the overwhelming consensus on family roles—implicitly coded white by the yeoman model—as the common organizing principle. On special holidays, the conflation of adult masculinity and managerial legitimacy was reinforced with exaggerated symbols of patriarchal authority. Men found an extraordinary array of costumes that allowed them to arm themselves with dummy weapons, from cowboy pistols to automatic assault rifles. Usually these costumes formed part of a storewide or even communitywide celebration of frontier heritage. Harrison, Arkansas, for example—home of the second Wal-Mart—inaugurated each tourist season with "Dogpatch Days" in honor of the nearby Ozarks theme park. Dressed in "hillbilly" regalia, Harrison's store #2 topped off its Sadie Hawkins Day sale in 1972 with a shotgun wedding.[29] "Rodeo Week" in Hugo, Oklahoma, like "Western Week" in Idabel, provided an opportunity for the young assistant managers to fake a "stick-up" with bandanas and six-shooters. The Fulton, Missouri, version culminated in a faux shoot-out in the parking lot, with the lower-ranking bandits, fresh from terrorizing a female cashier, halted by the store manager.[30] For St. Patrick's Day, 1974, the young women on the night crew in a Missouri Wal-Mart dressed as leggy leprechauns; their male colleague outfitted himself as an IRA terrorist.[31] Even without the premise of costumed fêtes, men routinely posed with guns or prey. When an electrical storm disabled the store's alarm system in store #33, an assistant manager won kudos for guarding the premises with his shotgun.[32] Many stores annually gave away rifles as prizes to open the deer or quail season, posing the manager and winning male customer gripping the gun together. Once hunting season was underway, managers displayed their trophies, from turkeys to Canadian geese.[33] Sam and Bud Walton's enthusiasm for quail hunting entered the company lore as part of the logic behind the company's location: in the northwest corner of the state, Benton County allowed them to take advantage of Oklahoma's and Missouri's quail-hunting seasons as well as Arkansas's. The metaphor of male authority implied by weapons was not lost on the in-store audiences. In Manhattan, Kansas, a departing store manager transferred control to his successor by handing off a baseball bat in front of the largely female staff.[34]

In a structure that so unambiguously equated authority with adult masculinity, the metaphorical challenges to that authority took the form of ritualized gender humiliation. Throughout the 1970s, the late summer saw blanket sales across Wal-Mart stores. The promotion was organized as a team competition. Traditionally, each of two young male assistant managers played captain to an assortment of salesladies. In a "tremendously successful" version from Miami, Oklahoma, each sale over $3.00 won the saleswoman the right to cut an inch off the tie of the opposing team's manager.[35] By 1983, the bounty was up to $10 in Mansfield, Texas, and the clerk holding the most pieces of tie at the end of the contest won a day's paid vacation.[36] The stakes signaled the symbolic power of the managers' neckties, a badge of adult masculinity in a sea of girlish blue smocks.

If a manager's authority derived from his fatherly status within the store family, he could be unmanned by conversion into either a woman or a boy, and both forms of drag were rampant in early Wal-Mart stores.

The man-in-a-dress spectacle seems never to have aged: in addition to routine drag appearances for Halloween, men seized the opportunity to wear women's nightgowns at special "Moonlight Madness" sales or don poke bonnets and long dresses for "Old Timey Days."[37] In a 1975 version of "Crazy Days," an assistant manager in normal dress escorted his subordinate in drag, under the caption "Cute Couple."[38] In 1984, Walton himself wound up as headline news across the business press when he made good on a promise to dance a hula down Wall Street if the company posted profits over 8 percent: flanked by hula pros, the richest man in America donned a grass skirt and flowers and saluted his employees' hard work with public self-abasement, in the language of gender difference. The joke lay in the men's inability to disguise their maleness: beards, body hair, and muscled forearms appeared in high relief against floral prints and lace. This frat-house-style drag did not seek to pass off men as women. Rather, it underscored the irremediable differences between them.

Similarly, some Wal-Mart men lampooned their own adulthood in settings where a teenager might manage several women who could have given birth to him. "What better advertisement for blanket sales," inquired a store reporter rhetorically, "than Dennis Legg of store #54 in Springdale, Ark., with his bottle, bib, diaper, and of course his faithful blanket."[39] Christmas of 1973 found a store manager in Lebanon, Missouri, dressed in a Buster Brown outfit and sharing Santa's lap with his female employees.[40] A district manager punished the losing assistant manager in a 1978 blanket-selling competition by hauling him around the store in a little red wagon.[41] Humiliation, whether administered by the boss or cheerfully self-inflicted, comprised the symbolic loss of adult masculinity. The natural state of most hourly employees—young, female, or both—thus implied a permanent position at the bottom of the store hierarchy.

If this equation had held undisputed sway, however, the jokes would not have been particularly funny. The drag gag disciplined the managers by allowing their subordinates to invert the usual order, and also offered a legitimate avenue of critique among those who accepted its basic premise. Special events offered acceptable zones for blowing off steam toward the boss. In some stores a manager would traditionally submit to a birthday paddling or a force-feeding from a young woman employee.[42] Annual staff picnics and barbecues offered veritable theaters for ritual humiliation within accepted limits, beginning with the managers' gracious service as cooks. The 1975 picnic for associates in Wal-Mart #67 was typical. Management first raced one another on their hands and knees; then, "in keeping with #67's tradition, the store manager was chased around the park and thrown in the pond for his yearly bath."[43] Assistant managers routinely received the vaudevillian pie in the face, sometimes with an excess of enthusiasm on the part of the hourly employee.[44]

The little-boy trope could get a bit nasty: when Bentonville summoned the under-performing manager of store #42 to headquarters for a management training seminar, the employees outfitted him with schoolboy accessories:

> Off to school you go for a week
> A smile on your face and a blush on your cheek
> With your fat pencil, Big Chief [writing tablet] and lunch
> And good luck wishes from the Wal-Mart bunch.
> We can hear the echo as you go out the door,
> "Get the freight off the floor."[45]

And some of the off-stage commentary crossed a line from readily recognizable forms of "all in good fun" into the genuinely bizarre. An avid amateur baker in Aurora, Missouri, presented her four-man Wal-Mart management team with an arresting tribute in 1977: their own heads on a platter, in the form of meticulously decorated cakes.[46]

Two overriding messages, then, came through the zany company culture of spectacle. First, drag performances emphasized the fundamental contrast between adult men and their natural opposites. No one could mistake a hairy 200-pound manager in a dress for a woman or a little boy, so the differences must be real, unavailable to intervention. Second, the managers' willingness to invite laughter in the guises of their subordinates rendered their authority benign. Their ostentatious public humility emphasized the hierarchy's familial nature, for they declined to credit their personal talent for raising them to the top of the stores' command structure.

Conflating the family and the store was an obvious move for the labor-intensive service sector. Under the military-inspired corporate model of the industrial era, both management and unions had privileged skilled white male workers. This formula relied on a particular definition of skill that discounted nontechnical competence as both irrelevant and inherent: handling a metal press was a skill that merited pay, benefits, and respect; handling a customer was not. The identity politics of labor thus bolstered the class politics of business and offered service industries like retail an incentive to organize a new kind of workplace among new populations of waged workers. The dispersal of service industries into farm country allowed them to avoid the craft solidarity of unionism in favor of family partnership as the immediate context for work.

Blending the store with the family made sense in small-town settings where many employees knew one another's real families on sight. When Clarence Leis, long-time manager of the original Wal-Mart in Rogers, Arkansas, left for a higher post in the company, employee Betty Pike composed a tribute that included the line, "We have watched your children grow up and leave home/Just as you watched ours."[47] In-store fashion shows featured associates' children as models, and husbands could pitch in as Santa at Christmas or coach the store softball team.[48] The young daughter of one Missouri department head might have found the family togetherness more than enough: for a 1977 display of Polaroid battery packs in his camera department, Jim Gale decorated little Dolores' head with lights, ran them to a battery taped on her back, and instructed her to blink them on and off with a button control to attract customers. The sign she held read, "Wal-Mart prices really turn me on—ask me how!"[49]

In addition to this informal slippage between store and home, for some the family simile became quite literal through multiple Wal-Mart jobs in one household. A 105-year-old matriarch was the great-grandmother, grandmother, and grandmother-in-law of Wal-Mart associates in Clinton, Arkansas, where she had arrived in a covered wagon more than a century before.[50] At the Wal-Mart in Christiansburg, Virginia, twenty-nine employees had relatives in the company in 1992. Three generations—grandmother, mother, and a son with Down's syndrome—worked in the Slidell, Louisiana, store.[51] Sons and daughters often took Wal-Mart jobs in high school, and some stayed for a second generation's career with the company: one Springdale family clocked over eighty years of combined Wal-Mart service.[52]

The family career was not confined to hourly employees. In structuring management for a rapidly expanding company, the Waltons sought to bring to Wal-Mart the assets of two people for each one they hired. Attracting experienced managers to Bentonville could be a challenge, but Helen Walton teamed up with her husband to recruit the prospect and his wife as a couple. The Waltons asked prospective hires to stay in their home in Bentonville during the interview, where Mrs. Walton hosted and laid out the area's charms for the wives.[53] As Claude Harris remembers it, he was won over from Woolworth's when the Waltons invited the Harrises to their house for ice cream with another Wal-Mart manager, Bob Bogle, and his family. The Bogles' young son wandered out to the patio and unself-consciously climbed onto Sam Walton's lap. "[T]hat child's reaction made me really believe, this guy's for real."[54]

Hiring was just the beginning of incorporating management families into the early Wal-Mart. Gary Reinboth remembered that the Waltons knew his children's names "as well as they knew my name." His colleague Tom Jefferson, who defected from Sterling Stores to Wal-Mart in 1972 and brought half a dozen experienced managers along with him, found the transition smooth because "[t]he people in Wal-Mart are easy to make friends with. I'm talking about the wives and children—it's just a big happy family."[55] In Northwest Arkansas in the early 1970s, the growing group of Wal-Mart wives headquartered around Bentonville held a monthly bridge lunch.[56] Annual management meetings included a full slate of activities for the wives, with top executives addressing them as a group.[57] The 1979 meeting at the manmade Lake of the Ozarks included a question-and-answer session with a vice president, as well as classes in "microwave cooking, floral arranging, indoor plant care, cosmetic application, latch hook, disco dancing, furniture refinishing, and gourmet cooking"—courtesy of Wal-Mart vendors.[58] When the company instituted its first-ever training program for assistant managers in 1978, a representative of the personnel department reported an enthusiastic response from both the trainees and their wives: "'The wives want to read the manual so they can learn more about their husbands' jobs.'"[59] "When someone asks me what my husband does," reported the wife of a Louisiana manager, "I say *we* work for Wal-Mart. I don't say my husband works for Wal-Mart."[60]

That was the idea. Wal-Mart management traveled incessantly, whether from Bentonville across regions of responsibility, or as store managers from one posting to another. A wife's unwillingness to accommodate this pattern could pit the family against the career, and so Wal-Mart refused to render her labor invisible. Finding ways to include management wives had helped turn the company around in the early years, recalled vice chairman Jack Shewmaker. "It eliminates the negative influence of a spouse wondering about the long, unexplained hours of work."[61] As the pace of new store openings pushed management into overdrive, Walton early on made a point of thanking "our very fine group of assistant managers and their wives and families for the great job they've done" in allowing the company to open fourteen stores in a single year; soon enough, of course, that rate of expansion would look like a crawl.[62]

Given the relentless schedules demanded by its growth and its tight lid on labor costs, Wal-Mart sought to make the sacrifices worthwhile, and solicited input from management wives on how best to compensate them. Wives predictably agitated in the annual meetings for higher salaries and a less punishing schedule, with fewer moves and longer stints following each relocation. A 1977 survey of associates who had been transferred—in other words, assistant managers and store managers—revealed a significant form of wifely labor crucial to the company's expansion: wives managed the moves alone, since their husbands were transferred on short notice without time off. "The most frequent complaint voiced by survey participants was that they were not given enough time to pack or take care of business before transferring," reported a summary. "One thoughtful husband suggested that associates be allowed to take time off to help their spouse pack or unpack."[63]

While virtually all managers were men, not all men were managers, and the official attention to their family responsibilities underscored the overriding importance of gender in structuring an employee's experience at Wal-Mart. With the threat of the Teamsters for inspiration, Walton periodically addressed the grievances of truckers and warehouse men.[64] Among his more attractive options was stressing the family benefits of distribution work at Wal-Mart. Since the company's expansion depended on keeping all stores within a day's drive of a distribution center, drivers saw more of their families than did their long-haul colleagues. The company enjoyed a good reputation for accommodating specific family-related scheduling requests, and with special permission wives and children could even come along for the ride on occasion. As with the attention paid to managers' wives, this ride-along program consciously sought to enlist the families' support for the husband's demanding work.[65] "'Dear Mr. Michael,'" wrote the children of driver Paul Walter to a Wal-Mart safety instructor, "'We wish to thank you for making it possible for us to go on a trip with our dad. We surely did enjoy riding in a Wal-Mart truck and we can understand now why our dad is so tired on the weekends.'"[66]

One traditional masculine privilege honored by both management and labor in many workplaces was not automatically mitigated by the family model, however. Just as women entering "men's jobs" in factories and professional settings often met a sexualized hostility aimed at insulating the jobholders from new competition, some Wal-Mart settings made this aspect of masculine precedence explicit.[67] In the stores of the 1970s, the managers' birthday parties sometimes offered the occasion to acknowledge the potential subtext: Birthday cakes in the shape of a headless, buxom, bikini-clad torso required the manager to choose where to cut first with an outsized knife.[68]

The Equal Opportunity Employment Commission and state commissions later found that many women workers were subjected to sexual harassment at their Wal-Mart jobs and then punished for raising the issue. As in other service workplaces, like academe, the offending men were often simply relocated or even promoted.[69] Company policies against interemployee dating were often turned upon store employees while Bentonville executives left their wives for their file clerks with impunity.[70] The internal company videos that came to light in 2008 showed humiliating drag routines performed at management meetings in the 1990s, complete with pat on the ample, skirted rump of an executive from then-chief executive officer Lee Scott.[71] The depositions in *Dukes v. Wal-Mart* brought to light such sleazy managerial practices as taking routine trips to strip clubs, holding required meetings in a Hooters restaurant, and propositioning subordinates in the crudest terms. A mother of five working in a California Wal-Mart in the 1990s reported her supervisor's greeting: "Why don't you put your face in my lap and solve both our problems?"[72]

Overall, however, for many Ozarkers who made up both management and labor in the early company, Mama, Papa, and Rosy offered a familiar ideal of work and authority. The family metaphor unquestionably signaled the precedence of adult men and the theoretical dependence of everyone else. This segmentation showed up in the hard numbers of job discrimination and sometimes in aggressive sexual harassment. Within the new service workplaces, however, the numerically dominant women stressed other meanings of "family," ones that often delivered on their own priorities.

Wal-Mart's mobilization of Ozarks families into its labor process followed the age-old pattern of enclosing the commons, or removing a shared resource from its communal base and turning it to private use. Classically, enclosure imposes regimes of private property over the productive capacities of the earth: the right to hunt deer in the forest or run hogs on the range is replaced by absolute rights to property by a single owner. The landlord puts a fence around the deer park and the hog's owner becomes liable for his beast's forays into neighboring fields. This version of enclosure continues today to fuel the world economy, as Chinese peasants are squeezed off farms to make toasters for Wal-Mart.

But the raw materials of land, water, and life are only the most obvious, concrete objects to be fenced off. Economic relations require more ethereal enclosures. To make the factory system, artisans' skill was studied, codified, then built into machines and processes. To raise the service sector, a company like Wal-Mart likewise metabolized the knowledge and skill of its initial work force. This very late moment in the history of capitalism saw the enclosure of a rural, Protestant family ideology and a female work culture based on "people skills." The women in the stores—customers as well as waged employees—made their priorities known, and management responded accordingly. Not surprisingly, these priorities were distinct from those of men in industrial or professional workplaces as well as from those of women seeking access to such "men's jobs." The model the early Wal-Mart women created was therefore the product of a specific time and place.

For that reason, it cannot be repeated endlessly. The women who crafted this new economic zone in those decades are not even representative now of Wal-Mart employees, let alone of the army of workers who have made service the country's leading sector. But they do not need to be: their skills and knowledge, the creative pressure they exerted from the bottom of Wal-Mart's corporate structure, provided the original momentum. The company became a student of its skilled service providers, drawing their knowledge up the chain of command and building it into managerial systems.

The in-store experiences represent only one input among many. During the same decades that it was learning from its home base how to sell service on a mass scale, the growing chain also experimented with logistical efficiencies. Systematic innovations like bar codes, satellite transmissions, and containerization ultimately provided Wal-Mart with the leverage to command its suppliers and overwhelm challengers, and simultaneously imposed ever-greater pressure and rigidity onto the work processes within the store.[73] Organized in a historically unprecedented model of the labor- and communications-intensive firm, linked to new low-wage supply chains around the world, the Ozarks company could float free of its original base.[74] But a global economy is a relationship, not a thing. Human knowledge and beliefs are built into its mechanisms, though not necessarily as their original owners intended. The early women of Wal-Mart taught the company a new service ethos and watched it grow to an economic gospel.

5

Service Work and the Service Ethos

By drawing on rural families in its formative years, the world's largest company successfully mined an undervalued human resource of the industrial economy: white, native-born mothers. In the second half of the twentieth century, married white women with young children entered the waged work force in mass numbers for the first time.[1] Certainly African-American women had struggled for centuries to wrest their labor from market degradation or improve the return on it. Similarly, factories and offices had always found room for young, unmarried white "working girls" in jobs strictly segmented by sex. But Wal-Mart in contrast deployed a hidden store of skill and talent in one group of people no one was accustomed to paying.

"What a wonderful Christmas party we had at store no. 23 in Ruston, Louisiana," rejoiced one of Wal-Mart's female clerks in 1974. The managers' wives had prepared the food and organized the event, complete with children's games. "[T]hanks to Mr. Green [the store manager] for inviting the husbands, wives, children and dates of the younger ones. Anyone who didn't come missed a blessing, because the fellowship together was the greatest gift of all."[2]

It was a sentiment that would have rung true for Jolene Kinzel, who in 1972 moved from Salem, Missouri, to Benton, Illinois. Ms. Kinzel had worked in Wal-Mart #27 in Salem, a small but successful store that had opened only the previous year.[3] The Salem Wal-Mart was a lively work site. The local country station broadcast out of the store every Saturday morning, and for Easter employees had climbed onto the store roof and dropped 286 plastic eggs filled with gift certificates into the hands of waiting children.[4] The boss, Jack Brewer, maintained good relations with his staff: when he left for a new Wal-Mart posting that spring, thirty employees and their families hosted a farewell party for the Brewers in the basement of Salem's city hall. "We're very happy for Mr. Brewer," wrote employee Pat Plank about the manager's promotion, "but we also hate to lose such a fine boss."[5] No wonder, then, that Jolene Kinzel wrote back to her former Salem co-workers from Illinois that she was "homesick" for the store.[6]

Likewise Peggy Biggs, a former checkout supervisor at the Cleveland, Texas, Wal-Mart, echoed the sentiment at the end of the decade. Writing to Sam Walton after her move to the Wal-Mart-less Texas City, she confessed that back in the Cleveland store, "I took a lot for granted and I am sorry for it." Her new job at the Woolco, she noted, should serve as a cautionary tale for those currently at Wal-Mart to count their blessings, for the variety store couldn't hold a candle to her old work environment, and the management particularly suffered in comparison. Still, given the Arkansas company's expansion, the future looked brighter: "I hope when the Texas City Wal-Mart opens, I can get on."[7]

When early Wal-Mart associates expressed enthusiasm for their work, they did so in highly personal terms. Peggy Biggs opened her letter by listing all of her former Wal-Mart managers by name: the Cleveland Wal-Mart was a good place to work, she implied, because the men who ran it were themselves fine people, and she wanted the company's owner to recognize them individually. A quarter of a century after working at a Wal-Mart, many former employees around Springdale, Arkansas, could still reel off a list of their associates and job assignments from their earliest days at the store. Some even remembered where their favorite managers moved when the inevitable reshuffling happened.

Although few had friendships with their co-workers before coming to work at the store, work itself offered plenty of opportunities to gather off the clock. "We just had a lot of fun," a Springdale store #54 employee emphasized. "We would stand outside after we got off and just talk for hours."[8] For many, the weekly store meetings were more a social event than a work duty. Lunch-hour or after-closing parties in honor of weddings, birthdays, and retirements garnered the most enthusiastic participation, and the covered-dish lunch hour was a monthly feature at store #3 in the mid-1970s.[9] In addition to the usual company Christmas parties, some stores seem to have seized almost any occasion to gather together. Leap year, 1976, was celebrated with a covered-dish lunch at Wal-Mart #129 in Ardmore, Oklahoma. As one participant said, in the language of the church social, "A fellowship hour like this makes you realize that Wal-Mart is the only place to work. Thank you, Mr. Walton, for starting all of this for us."[10] The pull of a tight, supportive circle of colleagues was even enough to make Bea Scott think twice about accepting a management position. "As an hourly associate, you were buddy-buddy with everybody, you'd go to lunch, you'd go on coffee breaks. Then all of a sudden, they'd have to call you 'Mrs. Scott.' I had always been 'Bea.'"[11]

Mutual support counted doubly when the event was not a happy one. When a fire destroyed the Jonesboro, Arkansas, home of a checker at store #45 in 1974, the rest of the staff chipped in from their pockets.[12] After a Belleville, Illinois, employee's husband was seriously injured in an accident, her co-workers held a bake sale to help with the hospital bills.[13] Deaths in the family were met with a constant flow of calls, cards, and visits, and many stores were scarcely less solicitous of sick co-workers than of the bereaved. The store manager in Jefferson City, Missouri, placed a get-well ad in the local newspaper for the check-out supervisor as she recovered from an operation.[14] Associates at a Texas Wal-Mart went a step further when a department manager had major surgery: they donated blood right in the store.[15] And the kindness and generosity of the employees colored perceptions of the company itself: A woman who underwent surgery in 1979 reported that Wal-Mart co-workers visited her every day and sent a steady stream of calls, flowers, and gifts. "I wouldn't want to work anyplace else," she concluded gratefully.[16]

Personal ties among hourly workers and between workers and managers created in many stores a level of loyalty that other companies could only envy. With work so intensely social, where the bulk of the tasks involved human interaction, the fabric of the relationships loomed large in estimations of the work itself. A new hire in Springdale praised the "kindness, friendliness, and patience of the entire store staff and management towards a new employee . . . I hope to be worthy of being part of such a fine group."[17] By staying with Wal-Mart for decades, a lifelong Benton County employee emphasized, "you developed these relationships, and if that's not why we're on this earth, I don't know what is."[18] Some managers weren't up to standard, and one was a real problem, Alice Martin reports, but over her twenty-plus years at store #54, "I've been really lucky. And the [manager] I've got now—he's like my grandkid, and I just think the world of him."[19] It is a difficult sentiment to imagine coming from a General Motors assembly line.

Despite frequent paeans to *laissez-faire* competition in the company newsletter, *Wal-Mart World,* management exhortations sought to abstract and inculcate the rather precapitalist values that early employees brought into the corporation. One long-time manager remembered of the original company, "Most people came out of a small-town environment where teamwork was valued . . . Sure, people didn't want to fail, but it wasn't just because you wanted to keep your job—you also didn't want to let everyone else down."[20] An analyst pointed out in 1988 that although Wal-Mart's competitors eagerly wooed its management, they often found their talents did not transfer: Because Wal-Mart relied so intensely on cooperation and interdependence, no single employee lured away could reproduce the technique for a new employer.[21]

The classic rural goal of family subsistence—as opposed to individual advancement—meant that some early Wal-Mart employees in Northwest Arkansas evaluated their jobs in terms of their overall contribution to security, not strictly their wages or supervisory power. "During the years when I was not making what I felt like was a decent wage," Alice Martin explains, "every year when I got my profit-sharing, I'd sit down with my calculator and I'd say forty hours a week with fifty-two weeks and divide that into what that was. Some years I made an extra dollar an hour and some years it was fifty cents an hour, and that made it worthwhile."[22] "The eighties were the golden years," another remembered of the decade's frequent stock splits. "You could give yourself a raise" by buying Wal-Mart stock on the employee discount.[23]

Many interviewees remember to the penny the wages Wal-Mart offered when they started. While they do not hesitate to recognize the rate as low, they point out that no employer in the area was doing much better. "Back then, let's face it," says Bea Scott, "women didn't make much."[24] The way Pauline Crawford remembers it, when the Daisy air rifle company moved to Northwest Arkansas from Michigan, the town fathers talked its management out of offering the working women a higher wage, in order to protect the cheap labor pool for the existing businesses.[25] Nor were Wal-Mart workers entirely without recourse when it came to pay rates. After running the snack bar at store #54 for a while, Alice Martin asked to see the profit and loss statement for the area. "And so when I looked at it and saw the profits the snack bar was making, I went to him and told him I'd like to be considered for a merit raise. And I got one. It took me forever to get to five dollars, but I finally made that, too."[26] In most cases, the women's incomes were one of several contributions to a family's support. In-laws, sisters, and neighbors provided child care, or husbands looked after kids between hauls or took them on the road. Some former employees later babysat for their grandchildren while the mothers worked at Wal-Mart. Children or grandchildren might move home to help with sick relatives. At various points they have run small family businesses that employed multiple family members.

The ideal of an independent, self-sustaining, full-time wage, in other words, was not a prominent feature of their economic landscape. Rather, they emphasized Wal-Mart's contribution to overall family stability, the access it provided to insurance, Social Security, and even investment. Several of the longtime employees stressed their gratitude for the company's health and life insurance. Others mentioned that the old designation of "full-time" as twenty hours per week was an advantage, since it gave them access to benefits while allowing them to cover after-school child care. No one assumed these women were working for pin money, and no one thought their work ended when they left the store.

This was a calculus that paid off much better for these long-term employees during Wal-Mart's go-go years of expansion in the 1970s and 1980s than it did before or has since. Even during the company's growth years, the Ozarkers' experience was wildly atypical: in 1993, only one employee in seventy, at any level, had amassed at least $50,000 in Wal-Mart stock.[27] And as employees were to find across the economy of the 1990s from dot-coms to Enron, compensation based on stock appreciation was a short-term bet. One hundred shares of Wal-Mart stock purchased in 1980 and sold after fifteen years would have fetched over $300,000; the same one hundred shares bought by an employee in 1990 would have sold in 2005 for only $20,000.[28] Timing was everything.

Likewise, the Springdale employees' long tenure in the company's core territory meant their experience of benefits was quite different from most: Human Rights Watch calculated that in 2002, Wal-Mart spent only about three-quarters as much on *all* benefits per covered worker as other major retailers averaged for their covered workers' health care alone.[29] But for some, it was a bargain they found reasonable. In return for demanding work at underwhelming wages, they got to remain in the Ozarks, integrate work and family, and put a floor of security under their households' diversified earning strategies. "I had such a deep love for Wal-Mart," June Whitehead explained. "They were good to me, and I always tried to give them all I had."[30] "When I say 'we,'" Alice Martin summed it up, "I mean Wal-Mart."[31]

The family imagery that transferred from the rural heartland to Wal-Mart chain stores in the 1970s thus brought with it a variety of meanings: "natural" adult male authority, mutuality, sociability, subsistence over risk. Since Wal-Mart's early years, the same areas of the country that first welcomed Wal-Mart have also come to champion "family values" as the ruling metaphor of American public life. At the time, however, the family was not the only ideal available to a new workplace, nor even the most likely one. Married white women's mass entry into the waged labor force had sparked widespread concern over the mingling of men and women, the neglect of the domestic sphere, and the unsexing of women with independent incomes. In the case of Wal-Mart, however, the new work force's own meanings shaped the company's policies, both through emulation and through reaction. The result was a model that often boggled its principled critics: an economic colossus reliant on low-wage, part-time women's work, that nonetheless enjoyed an almost unshakeable reputation as a "family" company and that could command the loyalties of many with little in their pay packets to show for their devotion.

"What annoys me about the way some people talk about Wal-Mart today," asserted a former executive in 2004, "is that no one ever set out to create the biggest company in the world . . . it's an affront to so many people, especially a lot of women in those small towns, to say that their work didn't count for anything, that they were just being used. They gave their lives to this work."[32] A colleague concurred, "All of the policies and proceedings at the senior level—individual recognition, that kind of thing—were based on the importance of [women] department managers . . . Some of those department managers were with us their whole working lives . . . That's what makes a store click!"[33] Mrs. Scott remembered a district manager who mentioned that women between the ages of thirty-five and fifty-five were Wal-Mart's best store employees, an observation that squared with her own experience. By that age, their children were in school and "they know what it is to get a husband off to work, they know what it is to come to work on time, pick up kids on time, take them to school—they've learned the value of scheduling. I had some ladies that worked there, and if I'd had 12 like them, I wouldn't have needed anybody else."[34] Or as one Wal-Mart employee put it in 1980:

> It seems I've worked all my life
> In school, at jobs, as a mother and wife.
> Housework's important; the pay's not so well,
> But some of the jobs that I've had were pure_____, well,
> I've always put in my time for my pay
> Doing all of their work, *their* way.
> Why care if they rang up big sales
> If it all went to fill their lunch pails?
> They didn't care to share profits with me
> 'Cause I was only an employee.
> Associate was a term I never heard about,
> That I worked for *them,* there was no doubt.
> So you can see why I'm glad to find
> That Wal-Mart isn't *theirs*—it's mine!
> I won't ever be just an employee,
> If it's true that Wal-Mart loves me![35]

Since the regimented workplace was the zone where men lost the legal privileges of command and precedence that they took for granted at home, they unsurprisingly hailed militant independence as the worker's foremost virtue. But different concerns crosscut many women's experience of waged labor over two centuries: constant exposure to sexual humiliation, coercion, and even violence from their male supervisors; the excessive hours that ignored their second shift at home; the pressure to incorporate their children into the factory. Many unions structured around men's priorities wrote off women workers as insufficiently militant, even unorganizable. Yet in the 1990s, the only consistent bright spots in union organizing were in service industries and the public sector, where women and men of color, immigrants, and white women predominate.[36]

The work of service introduces a unique element that finds no parallel in production: the direct relationship of the front-line service provider with the customer, or, in white-collar service, with the client. Regarding service as merely manufacturing *manqué* obscures this key relationship and its considerable consequences.[37] Wal-Mart sources suggest the importance of this feature to the people who worked there in the early years. "On Saturdays," remembered Gail Hammond, "that was the place for everyone to go, to Wal-Mart! So we got to see all of the community." Although cashiers usually are at the bottom of the pay scale in retail, several Springdale women mentioned their preference for working checkout lines because of the increased customer contact. "I love talking to people," explained Mrs. Hammond, "so I liked being a cashier and moving on up to what we called the check-out supervisor."[38] Alice Martin was also glad to move to the cashier position, after finding her early work stocking housewares "kind of lonely."[39]

Shoppers met this interest with their own preferences for sustained interactions. Some regulars would deliberately head for a favorite cashier's checkout line every time they shopped.[40] In the ladies' wear department at the Fayetteville store, June Whitehead saw some of the same customers two or three times a week, and kept the product displays rotating briskly with them in mind.[41] Eleanor Cook, who started clerking in a Walton five-and-dime, still sees customers at store #54 "that I knew when I was working at Ben Franklin . . . they've been here all these years. It's so good to see them."[42]

If ringing up people's purchases and helping them choose clothes over many years suggested some degree of intimacy, then working at the Wal-Mart pharmacy moved the relationship to another level. Kathleen Hollins described her pharmacy job as "taking care of customers," using the vocabulary of health-care providers.[43] "I love my customers," said Alice Martin emphatically of her pharmacy work. She often saw her customers' funerals listed in the paper. "The young ones, that's the hardest. I went to the viewing the other night of a young man, and I went up to his folks, and I've got another one right now that's not good, and I'll go to his. He thinks he's taking a vitamin, but he's not."[44] With the prescriptions passing through their hands, the clerks ringing up the medications knew almost as much about their customers' conditions as the pharmacists, and sometimes more than the patients themselves.

Many service providers report similarly satisfying relationships with customers, and even the routinization of mass service work does not seem able to stifle entirely the pleasures of personal interaction.[45] In the small towns of Northwest Arkansas, moreover, the customer-clerk relationships weren't confined to the store. Springdale's store #54 often placed ads in the local paper that included photos of the hourly employees who headed up most merchandise departments. "Meet the Department Managers!" ran the headline, and thirty years later Gail Hammond could still name almost everyone in the photo: "There's Erma, Virginia, Rose, Dina, Wilma, and now I don't know him . . ."[46] The anonymous male department head may have moved on quickly to another store, but the core of local women became very familiar to area customers. "I'll be out somewhere else and people'll look at me and say, 'I know you from somewhere,'" says Mrs. Hollins. "A lot of them will recognize me."[47] When Alice Martin and her husband celebrated their fiftieth wedding anniversary, multiple customers clipped the article from the paper and brought it to her at Wal-Mart.[48]

Through this relationship between customers and clerks, the people in early Wal-Mart stores taught management how to function in the new economic niche it was creating. The manly ethos that had sanctified earlier forms of labor gave way in Wal-Mart to a corresponding ethos of service. Successful service work on a mass scale depended on "people skills." This development did not mean that bottom-tier service workers became the new aristocracy of labor, with the lion's share of job stability, compensation, or prestige. Nor did it mean they deliberately chose the "soft" rewards of human relationships over more tangible compensation. What it did imply, rather, was a new ideological basis for valuing work and for explaining the radical inequalities it produced.[49]

The corporate homage paid to the lowest-ranking workers was not a feature built into Wal-Mart from the first. In his 1992 autobiography, Walton made the by-then-familiar assertion that "the real secret to our unbelievable prosperity" at Wal-Mart had been "the relationship that we, the managers, have been able to enjoy with the associates." He continued with a confession: as much as he would like to claim that from the beginning management treated store employees as equals, the fact was that "none of it would be true."[50] As former vice chairman Jack Shewmaker candidly admitted, the early Wal-Mart chain treated its em-

ployees as "robots, or mere statistics." It had to learn a new style, to demonstrate that the company's purpose was "going to make life better for
others as well. That attitude does wonderful things."[51]

Here the top executives cannot be doubted. Neither the managerial
assertions of valuing store-level workers, nor the title "associates," nor
the much-touted profit-sharing and benefits packages appeared until
after employee unionization attempts at a pair of stores in southern
Missouri prompted Walton to call in an antilabor lawyer, John Tate, in
1970. Tate—and, evidently, Helen Walton herself—urged Wal-Mart to
"prove to them you care . . . Let them share in the profits. Let them know
you'll listen to what they have to say." With a certain lack of subtlety, this
became the official "We Care" program, a promise to employees that
raising concerns with management would not result in retribution.[52]
Only gradually did Wal-Mart learn from its employees and its customers to stress the emotional labor of service alongside the tight cost controls that had always taken the limelight.

Customers were explicit about what they valued in the service relationship. In 1979, a first-time Wal-Mart shopper wrote to praise a checker
for "show[ing] a true interest in every customer that came through her
aisle," and emphasized the evident sincerity of the woman's concern.[53] A
woman on a driving trip stopped at a Missouri store to buy an embroi-
dery pattern and thread, and then realized she had no way to transfer
the pattern to the material. The fabric-department staff borrowed an
iron and ironed the pattern onto pillowcases for her. "I don't know of
any nicer thing that could have cheered me, than the patience, consider-
ation, and genuine niceness of these four women," whom the magazine then went on to name. A woman from Mountain Home, Arkansas,
wrote the store manager of her local Wal-Mart to describe how she had
spotted a display in the fabric department featuring a kind of shawl she
had long been looking for. Upon asking to buy the pattern, she was told
that it came not from a pattern book but from a store employee, Donna
White. "I found Donna, who told me it was her grandmother's pattern,
and she would send me a copy, if I would like her to. Several days ago a
copy arrived. Donna took her leisure time and money to do a favor for a
total stranger. Personnel like Donna give customers like me a friendly
feeling toward the entire store."[54]

Customers praised employees as well for tracking down out-of-stock
items from other Wal-Mart stores, volunteering their own off-the-clock

time to deliver goods to a customer's home, or assembling a complicated piece of equipment with their own tools. Early Wal-Mart employees exercised considerable personal discretion in the lengths to which
they could go to help customers, a nonmilitant form of worker control
that nonetheless can enhance many jobs in service.[55] The home office
insisted that these were examples of employee loyalty to the company,
but the customers and store employees stressed the personal relationships involved and the high calling of service itself. "Sunday I witnessed
something I thought I would never see again, much less in a large and
very busy store," a customer from Kansas wrote with feeling. An elderly lady had come through the checkout counter to purchase a lone
bottle of perfume. In handing it to the checker, the customer dropped it.
The checker asked her supervisor what to do about the shattered item,
and he went back for a replacement vial. "He was so courteous, and so
nice—not even a frown over the mess on the floor," the letter writer
concluded. "It warmed the hearts of all who saw it."[56]

Although serving customers at the Waltons' stores in the postwar
decades had much in common with other forms of service work, certain aspects distinguished it as an unusually powerful model. As with
the nineteenth-century development of department stores, the spread
of mass consumption opened up a new category of "public" jobs for
white women in which low wages might well be secondary to a relatively
safe, agreeable workplace and service that did not automatically carry
the stamp of servitude.[57] But in contrast to earlier urban department
stores, Wal-Mart shoppers and Wal-Mart workers were not separated by
a gulf of class. Because of its small-farm heritage, Northwest Arkansas
was home to an unusually flat class structure, so that customers were
plausibly also "our friends, neighbors and loved ones."[58] Moreover, the
discount stores were not aiming for the luxury market; many women
applied for their Wal-Mart jobs while on their routine shopping trips.
The company's early avoidance of areas with large African-American
populations and its homogeneous labor pool of "old-stock" whites
meant that race and ethnicity rarely had a chance to differentiate the
served from the servers.[59] Unlike tipped jobs such as waitressing or
physical care like nursing and babysitting, store service did not have a
clear precedent in paid domestic service, nor were the women who performed it descended from servants or slaves, at least in recent history.
Instead, they were incorporated into Wal-Mart through the metaphor

of a family, and store-level managers especially were men of their own family backgrounds and education. For them, service did not come with the degrading associations that clung to it in other settings.[60]

Like their customers, and in contrast to official pronouncements from Bentonville, store employees themselves remarked upon acts of courtesy and respect as important managerial functions. When the break room at one store was improved in 1977, the workers thanked their all-male management for "the privilege and convenience of our microwave. We here at Store #55 have had many occasions to be grateful for Management's concern for our comfort and great working conditions."[61] A young clerk praised by a customer responded that the credit rightly belonged to her manager, who "work[ed] right along with his employees to help us build a better place for our customers to shop."[62] Their approval was especially marked in the case of Walton himself, whom they held up within the company as a model of service. After accepting a promotion to the home office, former store worker Ann Tuttle tutored newer employees with stories of the company's founder. "He came in one day," she related at her department's "culture meeting," "and he got down on one knee, and he said, 'If [the customers] ask you to kiss their behind, then you ask them which side they want you to start on.'"[63]

As a self-service store, Wal-Mart was organized on the pattern pioneered by the Southern grocery chain Piggly-Wiggly in the 1910s and 1920s. Rather than placing the goods behind counters with clerks to assist, in other words, mass retailers explicitly drafted the labor of their own customers and trimmed their payrolls by reducing the number of clerks required to turn the stock. By avoiding delivery service, they also shifted to households—to wives—the burden of transporting goods, significantly increasing the time and effort involved in family provisioning and, in the process, changing the sex of the task.[64] Thus the method of distribution in a Wal-Mart store combined the labor of mostly women servers and that of mostly women shoppers, who are themselves performing unwaged service to their families. The work formerly performed by clerks was divided between a proportionately reduced force of waged women and their customer counterparts—sometimes quite self-consciously. In 1974, a Springdale customer rated a photo in *Wal-Mart World* when she was discovered folding and straightening a T-shirt display.[65]

More commonly, customers also participated in the emotional work of service by their interactions with the regular store staff. Cashiers at a Texas store in 1992 would find their registers decorated with balloons, ribbons, and banners on their birthdays, ensuring a steady stream of congratulations from customers throughout their shifts.[66] When Ruby Holland, evidently an enthusiastic angler and one of the original employees at Wal-Mart #53, retired in 1977, her co-workers' tribute was structured to incorporate every customer in the store. Designating a "Ruby Holland Day," the managers pinned an orchid to her smock to encourage shoppers to congratulate her, and in honor of the avid fisherwoman, "all employees wore their fishing hats and jeans with a tag in the form of a fish, stating 'This Is Ruby Holland Day.'"[67]

Thus the result of this reorganization of work was a new social relationship—not a fully reciprocal one, to be sure, but one distinct from the boss-subordinate kind.[68] Early Wal-Mart publications bulge with reprinted letters from grateful customers who explained in precise terms what they found new and valuable about the emerging service ethos. "The clerks are always courteous, have smiles on their faces, making you feel like the most important customer to walk through the door," enthused one regular Wal-Mart shopper from Russellville, Arkansas.[69] "The girls that waited on me were two of the sweetest girls I have met working in public," wrote another lady. "They had a smile for everyone and treated everyone alike."[70] Among the items that women in Nashville, Arkansas, singled out as evidence of Wal-Mart's superiority was the longer hours, which "allow the working people to go shopping . . . [Also,] Mrs. Winnie Bell Young, who takes care of the clothing department, always has good taste . . . We are so thankful that she has seen to it that the stout women can be fitted as well as the smaller ladies."[71] Shoppers were not shy about explicitly contrasting Wal-Mart to the old central shopping districts. A letter printed in a Fort Scott newspaper by an irate customer of downtown stores complained about their rudeness, their credit-only returns policies, and their attempts to sell whatever was on the shelves when the items she wanted were out of stock. "No wonder the people of Fort Scott go out of town to shop and to the local Wal-Mart store . . . Why don't you downtown merchants shape up????"[72]

Though these extremes in customer service bubbled up from the stores, Wal-Mart headquarters was not blind to their cumulative effect. *Wal-Mart World* quoted a 1974 national survey, which demonstrated that two-thirds of the customers that a retailer lost took their business elsewhere in response to poor service. "This tells us how important it is for us to serve every customer as though he/she was the most important person in the world."[73] "Mr. Sam has always felt that the customer was number one," an early manager remembered in an interview. "He talked to us about how important it was to talk to the customers about their chickens, their pigs, their cows, their kids." More to the point, recalled another, he pounded the table and threatened to fire any manager who couldn't get with the program.[74]

Whether from the perspective of management or of labor, analyses of industrial work habitually divided workers by skill level, from the artisanal "aristocracy of labor" down through the "semi-skilled operative." But the measures of skill implicit in these rankings ignored the learned social skills that women brought *en masse* to the new factories of service. In its first generation of employees, Wal-Mart mined the resource of rural and small-town women's social training. After a high-ranking executive from a national chain visited half a dozen of the original Wal-Mart stores in 1973, Sam Walton reported, the rival told Wal-Mart's founder that what distinguished the stores in his mind was the employees' extreme friendliness and courtesy. "This is a quality that K-Mart, Sears, Penney's and many other regional discounters try hard to emulate," Walton wrote, "but, so far, haven't been able to get close to us. Whatever we have going for us, whether it's the fact that we're mostly small town folks or that people from Missouri, Arkansas, Kansas, Oklahoma, Louisiana and Tennessee are just naturally friendly, let's keep this great thing going for Wal-Mart."[75]

Adapting women's domestic labor to the retail store offered the new service workplace two distinct advantages. First, such labor was widely undervalued, and therefore cheap. Second, it incorporated customers themselves into service by way of their unpaid procurement of goods for families. Though the majority of American women had moved into waged labor by the late twentieth century, few American men today contribute any more to household labor than they did ninety years ago. Regardless of how many hours either spouse works for pay, wives perform roughly two-thirds of all housework, a category that includes all maintenance tasks from dish-washing to lawn-mowing. In child care, a separate category, a working father on average puts in three hours per week to his employed wife's eleven.[76] Since the standard full-time or salaried job was crafted to the specifications of a man with a wife, most women workers have been forced to evaluate a "good" job from the starting point of a savage time deficit. The jobs that look good in traditional labor terms—jobs as managers—do not always measure up from this vantage point.

The old factory model assumed that a position carrying more authority was more desirable, without considering how the role of front-line supervising itself changed under the service economy.[77] At Wal-Mart, the same standardization that hamstrung the old Ben Franklin franchisees tightly curtailed managerial discretion, substituting minutely detailed rules for individual power. From the music that played in the stores to the setting on the thermostats, decisions were made and even implemented from Bentonville. The fully automated stock-tracking system and the exhaustive analysis of consumer behavior eliminated important managerial functions altogether. Meanwhile, the 1947 Taft-Hartley Act provided employers with an incentive to expand the category of "manager" or "supervisor" to cover jobs with virtually no discretionary authority whatsoever: By declaring a given job supervisory, executive management could essentially exempt it from American labor law.[78] Whatever "management" meant at Ford in 1920, it meant something quite different at Wal-Mart in 1980.

In fact, Wal-Mart's managerial jobs were notoriously difficult. From the executive level on down, early burnout was endemic. The ferocious internal cost controls translated to grown men sleeping two or four to a budget motel room or even couch-surfing on business trips. This democratic frugality made for human-interest pieces in the business press but did little to enhance the job over time.[79] Determined to squeeze maximum profitability out of its salaried human resources, Wal-Mart pushed their exemption from overtime to the hilt. At the store level, managing meant brutal hours and constant relocation to new towns. Assistant managers from Arkansas and Tennessee reported in 1987 that they routinely worked sixty-five to seventy hours a week. "You could count on working a seven-day week at least once a month," one told a reporter.[80] At the next level up, a store manager made good money, but much of his compensation was pegged to the individual store's profitability. Bentonville demanded double-digit sales increases over the previous year. Especially as the merchandising and marketing decisions were centralized, this became a recipe for unrelenting pressure to squeeze additional cost savings out of hourly workers. Yet the labor-intensive company's reliance on its front-line workers meant that store managers were held equally accountable for employee morale, solicited directly via surveys. One manager described it as "living and working in a glass box."[81] In 1993, "over a hundred Sam's [Club] managers" anonymously forwarded to a union office an appeal they had circulated within the company, charging sharply worsening conditions for store managers and assistant managers: sex- and race-based discrimination, pay cuts, elimination of bonuses, lack of advancement paths to company-wide management. Given Bentonville's solicitous approach to hourly workers, they asserted, the Sam's Club store management was "being treated poorly, working longer hours, for less pay, while they moved Heaven and Earth to keep the Hourly Associates content." The unions were wasting their time on the workers, wrote "Sam's Management Team"; they ought to be trying to organize the managers instead.[82]

Regional managers routinely put 60,000 miles a year on their company Plymouths, traveling four or five days a week to visit the stores in their territory before returning for a bruising end-of-week meeting with Walton. Walton's visible hand of management was not a light one: the charming face he showed in the stores was not in evidence in the executive meetings, where vice presidents risked tongue-lashings and even on-the-spot firings for failure to produce. In Bentonville, the home office parking lot filled on weekdays at six or six-thirty in the morning, and a six-hour day on Saturdays was standard. "Of course," remembered Gina Dozier of the Sam Walton years at headquarters, "I didn't mind because I was hourly, not like when you go on salary and then you feel like you're not getting paid for it."[83]

Not surprisingly, then, when some early Wal-Mart employees talked about advancement within the company, they could be quite ambivalent about the costs and benefits of entering a salaried position. "Really and truthfully," emphasized Mrs. Martin, "there are no easy jobs at Wal-Mart."[84] Bentonville courted Bea Scott for months trying to get her to take a job as assistant manager, the training position that led to store management. She told them, "'I'm not tearing up my family. I'm not going to move.' Because it would have been kind of silly—they might have sent me to Podunk, Mississippi, somewhere!" The company relented and found a store for her in the immediate area. Similarly, in 1979 a Springdale man turned down a chance to move into salaried management because it would have required him to leave Northwest Arkansas.

Fifteen years later, the company relented and put him in charge of the Bentonville store. "I probably would be higher up in the company now if I had taken the position they first offered," he reflected, "but my wife and I are both from around here and once we had kids, we really wanted to stick around."[85]

Another local native who started as a part-timer in a Benton County Wal-Mart eventually accepted a promotion into the home office. But with her duties as a pastor's wife, she found the fourteen-hour days unsustainable over the long haul. "I couldn't take it anymore, working fifty, sixty hours a week," she remembered of her thirteen years in management. Returning from the long days on salary, she would then take up her pastoral duties with evening visits to congregants in the hospital or the funeral home. Finally she asked the home office to cut her job back. "They made an exception for me, and I'm very grateful to them for that."[86] A promotion likely meant losing precisely the personal contact with customers and other hourly workers that so many employees found satisfying. "I don't like that at all, the way they work them, and how they train them," summed up one longtime Springdale hourly employee in 2005.[87]

Authority, then, was not always the most appealing prize that work could hold out, even when sweetened by the concrete benefits it carried. Yet the company's reliance on women with more competence than ambition suggested a looming problem for male authority more generally: in strict economic terms, it was becoming an expensive luxury. Men ran the service workplaces on their borrowed prestige from more manly endeavors, but that justification could not hold up endlessly as they hired the majority of their workforce out of kitchens and nurseries. The identity politics dilemma of male workers was laid bare in the retail sector of the 1970s and 1980s. The baseball bats and guns that symbolized mastery in the early Wal-Marts implicitly argued that men earned their premium pay through some necessary blunt power. Their rivals at Sears, Roebuck similarly lauded the well-paid minority of men in their sales force by suggesting some crucial connection between muscular virtues and the work of selling washing machines on commission: The "Big Ticket Salesman," explained Sears, showed a "high level of activity" backed up by "considerable physical vigor. He has a liking for tools, likes work which requires physical energy, and carries much of this energy and drive over into his selling activities," which themselves were entirely sedentary and social. Identifying the Big Ticket Salesman at Sears required assigning applicants a "vigor score" with questions like, "Have you ever done any hunting?" and "Have you ever participated in boxing?" His "technical skills" and his "aggressiveness, drive, 'hunger'" all distinguished him for an elite calling. The much more numerous low-wage jobs, on the other hand, could be filled by any "sociable person with a pleasant, helpful personality and a reasonable ability to communicate."[88]

The specter that had haunted small-town America in the Depression—the nation of clerks—was back with a vengeance during the 1970s' economic stagnation. If masculine privileges in the workplace continued to justify themselves through deer slaying and boxing, men might well price themselves out of their jobs. The service economy could not have it both ways: a workforce segmented by sex and race reserved a pool of potential low-wage employees, but at the cost of men's illusions to self-sufficiency and natural mastery. What good was "aggressiveness" when more and more work called for "a pleasant, helpful personality"? How much was a service industry willing to pay for the luxury of irrelevant masculine virtues?

Wal-Mart's enclosure of the farm family brought with it considerable advantages: the absence of other significant employers and the farm traditions of long hours and low cash flow made the company's frugality and demanding working conditions acceptable. The industrial economy's scorn for women's work skills meant they could be had for a bargain price. The mixture of communal work and natural male authority in household economies offered a work force segmented by status but unified in effort. The persistence of the household as the economic actor and its diversified subsistence strategy ensured a steady supply of part-timers. But significant problems remained in the social organization of service work. Male authority in service could not endlessly define itself with reference to the gun-toting independence, especially as the managerial jobs themselves lost discretion and power. The sex-based hierarchy could undo the family metaphor with its abuse of sexualized power on the job. The reserves of social skills could be used up and not replaced when new generations came on line.

The militant factory worker and the profit-maximizing rational subject are equally unhelpful models for understanding this context. Neither can capture the creative response to these challenges that arose in the new world of mass service. For when Wal-Mart's hourly employees talked about their work, they did not automatically emphasize the elements that find ready parallels in manufacturing—elements like surveillance, automation, antiunionism, or supervisory authority. Rather, they stressed the one element of service work that distinguishes it from all others: the relationship between the service provider and the customer. They did not automatically claim the identity of "worker" or, indeed, of "woman." Their own preference was for a different cultural tradition, that of Christian service.

6

Revival in the Aisles

In the final days of 1977, a church bulletin from Dexter, Missouri, described a parking lot filling with cars and a stream of cheerful people pouring into a large building. "Friendly people were everywhere making sure that everyone was made to feel welcome. You have never seen such generosity among people. Everyone took out their wallets or purses and contributed freely. Some of the crowd spent several hours there but never complained about the time. Little children were everywhere . . . No one got offended if they didn't get special treatment."

No, explained the author regretfully, this was not a description of a holiday church service, though it ought to have been. Instead, she was among the throngs shopping for Christmas at the local Wal-Mart. Reversing the traditional relationship between Christianity and commerce, this shopper measured the church against the standard of the store, and found the former wanting in true religion.[1]

This reversal marks a victory in the task of sanctifying capitalism and consumption under Christianity. With stark prohibitions on profit, luxury, exploitation, sensual pleasure, even worldly work and ownership itself—"Leave all and follow me"—the way of the cross has been a difficult one for *Homo economicus* to travel. In the twentieth century, well-informed observers predicted the withering away of supernatural belief under the harsh glare of scientific modernity and the blandishments of the mass market. The possibility arose in many minds that a mature, complex society might give up the dream of a mansion in the sky. "Is God Dead?" demanded the cover of *Time* in 1966.[2]

In Max Weber's famous formulation, God did not die, but rather was incorporated into the very structure of secularism itself. Protestantism's unique theology of spiritual calling, Weber argued, reversed the traditional monastic withdrawal from the world that religion had encouraged. In place of this other-worldliness, the Reformation insisted that believers bring their duty to God into every activity of quotidian life. "Ascetic Protestantism" produced work values that promoted worldly success under capitalism. This worldliness in turn, Weber argued, undermined the original spiritual motivation, and gradually the habits of thrift, diligence, self-control, and industry took on a life of their own.[3]

According to this narrative, the Protestant ethic then ran up against mass consumption in the nineteenth and twentieth centuries. Prudence could not power an economic order built on the multiplication of desires. With the industrial degradation of labor and the growth of routine desk jobs, people increasingly sought meaning in leisure when they found none in work. This revaluation of desire even opened the horizons of sex and romance, making companionship, intimacy, and pleasure more important than the divine command to be fruitful and multiply. Faced with such challenges from consumer capitalism, it was argued, American Protestantism lost the battle. Salvation gave way to self-realization.[4]

The political impact of the New Christian Right in the 1980s forced a reappraisal of this narrative. Alongside liberal secularism in the postwar decades, it turned out, a powerful counterculture of conservative Christianity had been building strength. Beginning in 1943, the National Association of Evangelicals offered a new institutional network for a generation that had moved out from under the shadow of the Scopes monkey trial of 1925. Forward-looking, energetic young evangelists like Billy Graham filled stadiums over the next three decades. Outside the old sectarian boundaries, nondenominational organizations like Youth for Christ and the Christian Business Men's Committees galvanized Protestants for the great task of evangelizing America and the world. The secular tone of the mass-culture industries drove religious entrepreneurs to provide alternatives. Christian radio stations built on their earlier expansion in the 1920s and experimented with up-to-date formats to capture young audiences. New magazines like *Christianity Today* profited from the examples of *Life* or *Time*. The Christian Booksellers Association, founded in 1950, helped provide alternative outlets for evangelical and fundamentalist content. InterVarsity Christian Fellowship and the Campus Crusade for Christ nurtured a Christian student subculture. Rather than ending in secularism, self-realization placed salvation back into the center of American public life.[5]

Also in the decades after World War II, the faith-based industries followed the same pattern of federal subsidy as other Sun Belt growth sectors. Since the close of the war, finds historian Axel Schäfer, U.S. government support has totaled billions in such forms as tax exemptions, vouchers, and grants-in-aid to religious institutions. These taxpayer gifts to the sectarian faith sector included donating public land and former military installations; underwriting overseas missions; maintaining the military chaplaincy; and subcontracting services to religious aid organizations. Far from being a redoubt of private associational life, the faith arena developed a robust relationship with the state along the same lines as many for-profit industries: legal protection and public funding were welcomed, oversight rejected as government tyranny. As New Deal–style social provisions fell to the conservative ascendancy of the 1980s, the lightly regulated, tax-free informal economy of the faith industries steadily expanded for two decades. It grew with help from state lawmakers, government agencies, and court decisions that granted the religious organizations ever-wider access to government funds while proclaiming government itself to be the problem.[6]

The New Christian Right of the 1970s and 1980s combined religious efforts to regulate sex with an equally religious celebration of material comforts, self-expression, technological innovation, and secular success. These were supposed to be opposing currents, not mutually reinforcing ones. As the agent of mass consumption that emerged alongside this revival, Wal-Mart offers us a more specific form of this riddle: How did Wal-Mart make mass consumption safe for the white Protestant heartland, and mass service work an honorable zone of endeavor? Walton would not have made his fortune without convincing his notably underconsuming Ozark neighbors to buy in abundance. Ideologically, the challenge was to find a form of purchasing that did not suggest sensual self-indulgence. Unlike the lavish postwar suburban malls, the small-town discount store did not draw on the earlier department-store innovations in color, glass, and light that produced "a commercial aesthetic of desire and longing." To the contrary, the entire dime-store tradition marketed frugality, not opulence. Wal-Mart interiors were ostentatiously stripped-down, no-frills places entirely lacking in sensual ambience. The gridlike aisles and glaring fluorescent bulbs mapped order, abundance, and, ideally, cleanliness, but not mystery and exotic allure. The overall effect was suggestive of a warehouse.[7]

Rather than stoking individual desire, Wal-Mart imbued shopping with "family values." Drawing on the new relationships among managers, employees, and customers in its stores and on the regional evangelical revival, the company's emerging service ethos honored them all as Christian servants. Unlike the earlier department stores, Wal-Mart did not promote self-indulgent luxury. It did not encourage shoppers to imagine themselves as European aristocrats, recipients of fawning personal attention to their comfort.[8] The service workers therefore did not have to understand their attentions to customers in the humiliating metaphor of literal servants, promoting nothing more meaningful than individual comfort or acquisitiveness. The way was opened for a positive reinterpretation of shopping and service both, and evangelicalism offered the specific metaphors. The Wal-Mart mode of shopping removed several traditional stumbling blocks for Christian devotees of consumption. As long as mass buying could mean procuring humble products "for the family," as long as men could perform women's work without losing their authority, as long as front-line service workers could derive dignity and meaning from their labors, the service economy could survive its internal contradictions. Consumer capitalism could be born again.

In 2005, Don Soderquist, a former Wal-Mart executive, was asked at a prayer breakfast whether Wal-Mart was a Christian company. "No," he responded, "but the basis of our decisions was the values of Scripture."[9] This carefully qualified message, complicated by the overtly evangelical setting, accurately captures certain ambiguities. For most of its life, the company did not lay any claim to a Christian identity. Indeed, in 1993 Wal-Mart was forced to respond to a religious discrimination lawsuit right in the heart of the Ozarks when a Christian seminarian and Wal-Mart worker refused to work on Sunday. The managers dutifully congregated in Kansas City for an intensive training course on respecting the very religious belief they were widely perceived as exemplifying.[10] But mass merchandisers had been the vanguard in tearing down Sunday closing laws for the very good reason that many people shopped on Sunday, and the family-owned competitors could not match the longer hours.[11] Wal-Mart was no exception. Retail was a business, not a ministry, and any other suggestion would have been alien to its mainline Protestant founders.

To be sure, the founding generation of Waltons was active in a conventionally liberal Presbyterian congregation. The young Sam Walton held positions common to prominent local businessmen in small towns across the country—superintendent of the Sunday school, chairman of the finance committee, church elder. If the Bentonville First Presbyterian Church was not a cutting-edge congregation on the frontiers of social justice movements, neither was it part of the rising Christian right. The church opened the lay leadership position of elder to women in 1953, and only a few years later it began the process of integrating with black and American Indian Presbyterian churches into the same regional body.[12] Mrs. Walton, a public proponent of legal access to abortion and a donor to Planned Parenthood, went on to a distinguished volunteer career in the Presbyterian Church (U.S.A.), becoming the first woman on its national governing board. But some of Mrs. Walton's most notable financial contributions also tended toward distinctly secular, middle-class concerns, including performing arts centers around the Ozarks and a daycare facility for Bentonville. In short, neither Walton could be described as evangelical, born-again, Pentecostal, or fundamentalist, let alone as Christian activists outside their mainstream denomination. Their pastor neatly captured the place of religion in the founder's life by noting, "When it's not bird hunting season and he's in south Texas, every Sunday Sam Walton is in church."[13]

Yet for the nation at large, the company came to function as a sort of after-hours megachurch by the 1990s. "If you want to reach [the Christian population] on Saturday, you do it in Wal-Mart," declared Ralph Reed, then executive director of the Christian Coalition.[14] If the Waltons themselves are not responsible for this close identification, then, what has produced it? As with the evolving notion of the customer as the boss, the concept of family values through shopping seems to have moved up the company hierarchy from the women who predominated in the stores, both as customers and as employees. With conservative religion an increasingly commonplace feature of American life, Christian consumer demand drove Wal-Mart's conversion to some extent. In the early 1990s, the Christian publishing and media conglomerate Thomas Nelson, Inc., took a close look at the Wal-Mart base and began pushing the mass retailer to carry more than just the company's Bibles. It was "the whole family values thing," the publisher explained. Wal-Mart tested the potential market with Christian children's books and souvenir Bibles themed to weddings and births, and then added Christian pop music and novelty items. "They understand our business," a Wal-Mart executive explained of the Nashville-based publisher. "They've brought us a lot of winners." Sales were impressive, and in many stores customers asked for even more, leading to expanded Christian product lines in about three hundred stores by the mid-1990s.[15] Within ten years, Wal-Mart had become the country's largest merchandiser of Christian items, with over a billion dollars in annual sales.[16]

But as Christian books like *The Prayer of Jabez* and *The Purpose-Driven Life* topped national bestseller lists early in the twenty-first century, Wal-Mart's market dominance made the original Christian product distributors victims of their own success. Having made Christian culture a true mass culture, the network of small Christian stores watched their customers desert them for the discount version of the same merchandise. The share of Thomas Nelson's revenue coming from mass merchandisers like Wal-Mart and K-Mart jumped from 2 percent in the mid-1980s to about 15 percent in the mid-1990s.[17] At the same time, hundreds of independent Christian retail stores failed. From 2000 to 2002, the market in Christian merchandise grew by $200 million, but business at Christian stores contracted by $100 million. The Christian Booksellers Association responded with ads in Christian media outlets urging believers to shop in its member stores, and its members warned of the possible polluting effects of non-Christian products alongside appropriately orthodox ones. Said one Christian bookstore owner, "Our customers are looking for a safe place to shop."[18] That was precisely the problem. Wal-Mart was itself now thoroughly "safe," where the dangers to godliness were newly understood almost exclusively in sexual terms. It implicitly promised to desensualize shopping and the town square just as Disney had stripped the entertainment district of its sleazy elements. Wal-Mart stores reproduced the social spaces of disappearing small-town life in a setting much more morally sanitized than the actual streets and squares of those small towns.

In the original Wal-Mart stores, a mild degree of overt sexuality coexisted alongside active religion, though not without conflict. Some of the in-store fashion shows featured an impressive amount of skin, for example, and young women in bikinis or halter tops and shorts could be posed with products marketed to men, like sailboats and lawn mowers.[19] At the same time, the store in Helen Walton's hometown of Claremore, Oklahoma, hosted a bake sale by the Christian Women's Fellowship Group.[20] An Arkansas Wal-Mart helped out members of an out-of-state Baptist church when the congregation's bus broke down in the parking lot on its way to Texas: the store manager took the hot, cranky children and their parents home to his own house until their vehicle was roadworthy again.[21]

Early stores were to some degree contested terrain, and the religious themes that were present could be fairly quotidian. But beginning in the 1970s, the unremarkable small-town sociability of church and fellowship was swept by significant new currents. Only after this energetic resurgence of a particular conservative religion did Wal-Mart promote itself as explicitly Christian, through a series of widely reported product purges that spot-cleaned the shopping zone. In order to distribute its CD *In Utero* in Wal-Mart, the grunge band Nirvana substituted a new album image for the objectionable fetuses that appeared on the back cover. The retro model that graced White Zombie's tongue-in-cheek *Supersexy Swingin' Sounds* received an air-brushed bikini to hide her original coy nudity. Both Jesus and Satan disappeared from a John Cougar Mellencamp cover, and certain CDs by Tupac Shakur and Snoop Doggy Dogg were banished entirely, along with anything featuring Beavis and Butthead.[22] An evangelical mutual fund convinced Wal-Mart to shield its customers from the cover photos of *Cosmopolitan* magazine with opaque plastic protection.[23] The labels affixed to altered merchandise proclaimed it "sanitized for your protection." How did a stray glimpse of a fetus or a nipple become so polluting to shoppers, and why did Wal-Mart identify itself as their protector?

The elder Waltons and the early company did not embrace a Christian identity in the evangelical sense, but the people in their stores were in the midst of a religious realignment, and it was their values that Wal-Mart came to represent. In the 1970s, many employees and customers alike clearly cleaved to a different strand of Christianity than the owners. Their denominations included such literalist branches as the Church of Christ, the Assemblies of God, and Southern Baptists.[24] Unlike the company's owners, Wal-Mart employees readily combined their work and their spiritual lives. An employee of the Bentonville distribution center worked for seven years to earn a Doctor of Divinity degree, piecing together correspondence courses and night classes at institutions in southern Missouri.[25] In 1979, the supervisor of the Data Communications Department was lauded for publishing a Christian children's book.[26] A cashier at a Missouri Wal-Mart once accidentally led the blessing over her family's breakfast this way: "Dear Father, we thank you for shopping Wal-Mart."[27] A series of profiles of Wal-Mart women that appeared in 1989 revealed a consistent reliance on God to meet the challenges of their jobs.[28]

For many at the Wal-Marts in Northwest Arkansas, the connection seemed self-evident. Mrs. Eleanor Cook, daughter of an elder in the tiny First Christian Church in West Fork, relied on the Lord to help her raise six children on her Wal-Mart job in Springdale. She extended her faith to people she met at work. A young woman whom she mentored spiritually moved up in the company over many years to become a store manager and wrote back in thanks, "it has taken a lot of prayers and even more faith, both of which I learned through you, to be where I am today." In the absence of a Baptist church in her new town, she added, she conducted daily worship at home.[29] Mrs. Tuttle saw her twenty-seven years at Wal-Mart as a way to enable her real life's work: with her husband, an ordained minister, she has helped pastor a small Faith Baptist church for over thirty years. "My husband always put God first, and the church . . . So we could never have had much of anything if I didn't work and if Wal-Mart hadn't supported us."[30] The significant levels of Christian commitment that many Wal-Mart employees brought to their service-sector work formed a shared cultural terrain with the customers they served. One aspect of this trend never failed to win warm praise in the pages of *Wal-Mart World*: the increased respect for the eighth Commandment. "In the past I have taken some merchandise from your store," wrote an anonymous Fayetteville resident to Walton in 1973. Since then, the customer explained, she or he had become a Christian and was enclosing seven dollars to cover the stolen goods. "Praise the Lord!" the letter concluded.[31] An unfortunate Arkansan, sick and unemployed in 1975, sent in a dollar and thirty-five cents after shoplifting a bottle of hair dressing, "for if you can forgive me, so will God."[32] Most repayments arrived anonymously through the mail, but in one dramatic episode, a woman who had recently become "a converted Christian" walked into a store in 1975 and confessed to shoplifting there off and on for the previous five years. She gave the manager an envelope containing $100, her best estimate of her total take.[33]

Another artifact of this shared culture was the Christian music regularly performed in many Ozarks Wal-Marts, blending entertainment, worship, and work. After the Christian Cox duo made a big hit in 1971 at Wal-Mart Store #19, they returned to an even bigger crowd the following year, accompanied by the Christian Echoes. A local radio station broadcast the performance and mixed in advertisements for the store's daily specials.[34] The Cox family returned several more times, with backup from acts like the Sunshine Gospel Singers.[35] The Branson-area stores had regular access to more than the usual quotient of talent, like the Patriot Gospel Singing Group, which performed in Store #32 in 1973.[36] But they were hardly without competition. The Jackson Family Gospel Singers of Bentonville hit several early Wal-Mart stores *en route* to their performance on the Grand Ole Opry in Nashville.[37]

The blending of service, shopping, and religion was intertwined with developments in the spiritual geography of the Ozarks during the same years. Ozarks resort towns like Branson, Missouri, and Eureka Springs, Arkansas, aggressively developed themselves into thriving capitals of Christian tourism. Building on the rowdy nineteenth-century camp meetings, new commercial spectacles like the annual Passion Play in Eureka Springs and the theme park Silver Dollar City in Branson began to evangelize through entertainment.[38] New interdenominational "community churches" emphasized experiential dimensions of worship and downplayed theological differences among people who had been raised in a variety of fundamentalist, evangelical, and Pentecostal denominations.[39] Even some longstanding denominational churches remade themselves in the image of the new institutions. The First Baptist churches of both Springdale and Rogers, for example, transformed themselves during the 1970s and 1980s with bus service, high-tech programming, and expanded facilities, and grew from fairly staid, mainstream congregations into megachurches.[40]

Beginning in 1970, Springdale's First Baptist launched a remarkably successful "lifestyle evangelism" effort that more than tripled active membership. "Evangelism Explosion" teams targeted families with young children, presenting the plan of salvation in teams under neighborhood captains. In 1986, Pastor Ronnie Floyd took over the pulpit and implemented training programs that taught church members how to witness for their faith in their daily encounters outside church.[41] Over the next two decades, Floyd built First Baptist into a 16,000-member megachurch and opened a branch at the upscale office complex Pinnacle Hills with backing from Ozarks billionaire trucker J. B. Hunt. The pastor's most eye-catching innovation at First Baptist was the children's worship area, outfitted with video games, a light show, music videos, and a bubble machine. The centerpiece was a baptistery—a pool for full-immersion baptism—designed by a Disney artist in the shape of a fire truck. A child's baptism was accompanied by sirens and confetti fired out of cannons. "This is a visual generation," explained First Baptist's youth minister.[42] The host of a syndicated television show and author of *The Gay Agenda,* Rev. Floyd put Springdale on the map in 2004 when the national press picked up his Fourth of July sermon urging congregants to "vote God" with a huge picture of President George W. Bush projected behind him.[43] After coming in a distant second in the 2006 election for president of the Southern Baptist Convention, Floyd returned to regional fame. He currently hosts a weekly lunch seminar series for Northwest Arkansas's Christian business folk.[44]

Although First Baptist of Springdale was an unusually visible exemplar of the intensified experiential worship, it was certainly not alone. In a pattern repeated nationally, the most demanding, conservative denominations also showed impressive growth and influence at the expense of mainline Christianity.[45] Poplar Bluff, Missouri, became the expanded world headquarters for the stringently fundamentalist General Baptists.[46] The largest Pentecostal denomination in the world, the Assemblies of God, established its international headquarters and chief seminary in the Ozarks hub of Springfield, Missouri. J. Frank Norris, one of the most influential and controversial of the original fundamentalists, founded the Bible Baptist Fellowship in the same city in 1950 and opened a college from which Jerry Falwell graduated in 1956. Already home to several small Christian colleges, Springfield by the 1970s became "a factory for ministers."[47]

The growing emphasis the region placed on its religious life made itself felt in other ways as well. In reflecting on the declining fortunes of the Retail Clerks International Association—the main retail union at the time—Jack Gray, a longtime labor organizer from Springfield, attributed it to "quite simply, the churches." Yes, he explained, the union changed for the worse at the national level during the 1970s and 1980s, "but the people working in the stores changed, too. I'd go around these little old neighborhoods behind Evangel College, knocking on doors, and people making peanuts would tell me they tithe"—that is, donate 10 percent of their incomes to their churches. Meanwhile, the dwindling pool of RCIA members often paid union dues with rubber checks.[48] To the Christian tithers, Gray could only say, "'You're a better person than me.' But they are just one hundred percent about their churches, don't think the union means anything to them, and they won't say anything bad about the employers."[49] Nationally, organized labor in 2007 found that when asked, "Who do you turn to if you have a problem on the job?" working women named God far more often than they mentioned a union, government agency, or secular women's organization.[50]

If a single church could capture the religious transformation of the Ozarks during Wal-Mart's rise, a strong argument could be made for Fellowship Bible Church of Northwest Arkansas. The church home of many Wal-Mart executives, as well as management from Tyson Foods and other national powerhouses based in the retailer's backyard, Fellowship was at once an explicit companion to Wal-Mart, an inheritor of a specific regional religious history, and an active innovator of novel trends in postwar Christianity.[51]

To get to the Fellowship Bible Church of Northwest Arkansas, you first had to drive past the cows. Up to their knees in scummy pond water, the placid bovines watched streams of traffic pouring off Interstate-540 onto the two-lane Pleasant Grove Road. Neighboring their pasture was a small white frame church, its steeple poking up into a pleasant grove of old-growth trees. Perhaps two hundred worshipers could fill it. This was not Fellowship.

Rather, Fellowship lay another mile down the road, across an oceanic parking lot. Bolstered by a 10-million-dollar expansion, its campus in 2008 included offices, children's centers, and missionary housing. The worship center measured over 40,000 square feet and filled to capacity three times every Sunday. At the rear of the cavernous auditorium a team of volunteers managed the AV booth, projecting images and texts onto an enormous screen to accompany the sermon. In place of hymnals, the video screen provided the words to songs. An impressive choir was a regular feature, but worship included interpretive dance or a visiting Ukrainian orchestra. Between services, members milled about the mall-like foyer, drinking cappuccino from the coffee bar and looking over the new inspirational CDs for sale.

Fellowship began in 1984 with just seven families meeting in a rented Seventh-day Adventist facility in Bentonville. There was a vacuum in Northwest Arkansas, they felt, for the kind of ministry that could speak specifically to the family and the marketplace. Several Wal-Mart executives—or, more accurately, their wives—were active in the church's early incarnations, but the specific pattern of ministry was part of a national "church-planting" movement that grew out of a 1973 seminar at Dallas Theological Seminary. The style of worship would be participatory and interactive, incorporating drama, video testimony, and small groups. The professional, seminary-trained staff would be kept small, and instead the church would focus on cultivating talented lay people, a philosophy of "empower[ing] and releas[ing] leaders," many of whom would go form additional Fellowship Bible Churches elsewhere.[52] They drew insight from business advice on marketing experiences, engaging customers through entertainment, and monitored one another's faithfulness with close-knit, intense "accountability" groups.[53]

This new emphasis on the experience of worship, the high demands on lay people, the willingness to throw out received wisdom and downplay confessional doctrine were all characteristic of the broader religious restructuring that followed World War II in several waves.[54] The "Jesus Movement," a revival of the late 1960s and early 1970s that took root among the new mass population of college students, had an impact on Northwest Arkansas largely by way of organizations like Campus Crusade for Christ and the Fellowship of Christian Athletes at the flagship state university in Fayetteville. Under the energetic leadership of Pastor H. D. McCarty, a former realtor in his hometown of Dallas and a graduate of Southwest Baptist Seminary in nearby Fort Worth, the University Baptist Church on the edge of Arkansas's campus was a driving force in religious innovation. His background with some of the most energetic of the postwar Christian youth movements—Young Life, the Navigators, the InterVarsity Christian Fellowship—offered a pattern for working with Fayetteville's burgeoning student population, and over his nearly forty-year tenure at the University Baptist Church McCarty saw 300 student members enter full-time ministry. To reach the student population, McCarty drew material from the Campus Crusade for

Christ and formed small study groups, alternative Christian dormitories, and an additional Sunday worship service geared to younger tastes.[55]

In Rev. McCarty's analysis, the strict doctrine of biblical inerrancy that he imbibed in seminary actually paved the way for innovation, allowing him to jettison any Baptist traditions that did not seem to be meeting the needs of the new congregants. "We were one of the fastest-growing churches in America at that time," recalled McCarty proudly, and the area's economic quickening represented a new field for witness. "We begin from the premise that Jesus is at the center of everything, so there is no sacred versus profane—it's all sacred."[56] Similar patterns emerged at First Fellowship Bible Church in Dallas and Family Life Ministry and Fellowship Bible of Little Rock, forming a loose regional network of like-minded congregations. The enthusiasm and idealism of the young pastors fueled the booming megachurches of the Sun Belt.

Though linked to a broad national revival, Fellowship's phenomenal growth was marked by a self-conscious reaction to the newly sprawling landscape of Wal-Mart's home region. "During the summer of 2001, Morris and Millie Puryear were set to move into their new home in the new Pinewood Subdivision in Springdale," a church publication related. But "they desired something different from the typical 'come and go' lifestyle that most neighbors experience. They wanted to get to know their neighbors. They desired to experience community on a different level."[57] They wanted, that is, the kind of community that car-based sprawl had virtually destroyed. "Is it possible today," inquired a church publication, "in real life, to create a safe place where we can get to know our neighbors?"[58]

It was possible, those at Fellowship believed, through organized "cells" in the residential nodes across the region. Like megachurches across the country, the church niche-marketed specific programs to singles, to every age group of children, to women, to engaged couples, to retired men. The vast membership was subdivided by age, sex, language, and geography into regularly meeting units small enough to help replace the webs of association lost to sprawl. In tacit recognition of the expanding workday, one cell met in the nonresidential "neighborhood" of Fayetteville's downtown business district. Employed mothers had their own meeting time designed to avoid conflict with work schedules, and childcare was prominently positioned as one of the church's most compelling offerings. Fellowship Bible Church attracted a number of new managers at Wal-Mart's home office, just as churches nationally grew along with corporate organizations and their managements' high mobility.[59] Fellowship grew because it responded to a need. Wal-Mart executives looking for ways to integrate faith and the market recruited one another to the pews. Church members began a consulting firm specializing in integrating Christianity and work, whose newsletter *Life@Work* joined such advice books as *Spirituality@Work, The Living Workplace,* and *Jesus, C.E.O.*[60] In Wal-Mart Country as across the nation, the broad "faith at work" movement at the end of the century built on a 1972 liberalization of the Civil Rights Act of 1964: Where the earlier law had simply forbidden job discrimination based on religion, the subsequent revision required employers to accommodate religious practices and beliefs unless doing so imposed "undue hardship" on the business. Backed by the federal government, faith was increasingly welcome at work.[61]

This deliberate intermingling of the sacred and the purportedly profane is as old as Christianity itself, for religion seeks to connect the immanent to the transcendent. Even the most individualistic Protestantism promotes churches as venues for linking people together, bolstering the actual worship services with sociability and spectacle. The endless round of old church-based activities, remembered an aging Ozarker, were "a form of entertainment . . . That was what you went for." "The church was your outstanding social function, because there you met all your neighbors you hadn't seen for a week," another old-timer recalled of the area's farming days.[62] But the particular strain of "family values" Christianity that met mass consumption under Wal-Mart's roof was the product of historically new conditions. Among the most important of these was the eclipse of an agrarian economy not by modern industry but by postmodern service, and the revaluation of reproductive labor— the work of caring for others—that it demanded.

7

Servants unto Servants

In January of 1987, on a stage in Kansas City, Paul Faulkner found himself in a familiar role. Microphone in hand, the Wal-Mart director of marriage and family living was speaking on his specialty to an audience of Wal-Mart managers and their wives. The group of several hundred had gathered for a semiannual meeting that focused chiefly on marketing and operations. Sam Walton drove the meetings at a brutal pace, commencing activities each day at the crack of dawn and haranguing the road-weary managers into stunned exhaustion. But in this highly choreographed gathering, Faulkner's talk was not a sideline to the important business of running a retail giant. To the contrary, his disquisition on the changed relationship between husbands and wives was fundamental to Wal-Mart's business model.

Husbands, declared Faulkner passionately, were simply blind. They could enter the house at the end of their workday and walk right past the evidence of their wives' labors—the clean kids, the scrubbed floors, the hot meal. Men must realize that in dual-earner households especially, husbands had one job but wives had two. Still, Faulkner charged, somehow many men imagined that because they held a job, they were entitled to collapse into an easy chair at the end of the day and turn on the television, while their wives applied themselves to the second shift. But, he urged, "that's not the American way and that's not the fair way." Men should start expressing their appreciation to the overburdened women in their lives. After all, hadn't they been motivated this very weekend by Sam Walton's thanks for their own hard work at Wal-Mart?

Did they in turn show that appreciation to their wives? To the women working in the stores?[1]

During the late 1980s, at Wal-Mart management meetings, at store-wide weekend encounter groups, and through the company's personal advice hotline, Paul Faulkner promoted within Wal-Mart a widespread trend in evangelical culture generally. Urging the men in his audiences to "listen and learn" from their wives, the Abilene Christian University professor promoted a new style of Christian family life. He was well po-sitioned to do so. A 1952 graduate of the Church of Christ college, Faulkner had founded its Marriage and Family Institute. In the 1970s he developed a traveling twelve-hour seminar to "enrich, strengthen and vitalize the marriage relationship" for Christian couples; it was later filmed for distribution.[2]

As elaborated in such seminars and in churches, Christian advice books, parachurch organizations, radio shows, and evangelical families themselves, this new ordering of intimate relations ceded significant ground to women in exchange for maintaining masculine authority at home and at work. As evangelical men and women circulated through homes and workplaces, the revaluation of women's work provided the pattern for both. Men's precedence required respect for the second shift and for women's allegedly superior people skills, now indispensable for management and marketing.

For different reasons, many who met inside Wal-Mart stores and offices could see a significant victory in the company's gradual identifi-cation with its Christian constituency. In the stores, Christian women on both sides of the Wal-Mart checkout line successfully incorporated many of their priorities into the new workplace. More generally, many found appealing the growing religious identity of the discount store, which produced distinct experiences of mass consumption, low-wage work, and managerial ideology. This new identity did not cater to the citizen-consumer, that Northern shopper who defined her rights and responsibilities to the nation by way of the marketplace. Nor did it radi-calize the descendants of the Populists to pocketbook politics in the for-mal policy arena.[3] Rather, people within Wal-Mart learned to revalue shopping as selfless service to family, and service in turn as a sacred call-ing. In this context, the salient identity became not citizen-consumer nor worker of the world, but Christian servant.

The meekness of Jesus presented daunting challenges for modern masculinity. American Christianity had been a majority female faith since the early nineteenth century, and only the most strenuous efforts to privilege men within it kept it widely marketable to male congregants.[4] During the 1970s and 1980s, the eclipse of production by the service economy heightened Christian fears that the wellsprings of American virility were drying up: where would real men develop if work came to look too much like home? How could male authority survive the ascendance of service work and the mobilization of women as wage-earners? The experience of service labor itself offered the basis for a new ideology that met these challenges. Christened "servant leadership" by its formal adherents, this new ethic glorified the formerly humble, feminine reproductive labor against which the old manly producerism had defined itself. Taken up by Christian opinion-makers and embraced by many families in the pews, servant leadership offered something to everyone. Service workers found a measure of respect denied them by the heroic narratives of industry. Managers gained a new claim to authority just as their older ones came to look increasingly implausible. Christian husbands enhanced their status at home despite the loss of the breadwinner's mantle. And many evangelical women found wifely "submission" a small price to pay for men's reinvestment in the domestic sphere. Crafting this ethos was the cultural work of many people with a variety of perspectives and interests. Wal-Mart and its constituents, however, played a prominent role, drawing on the day-to-day experience of service labor and freely mingling their Christian priorities with the demands of the new economy.

In the early 1980s, when Wal-Mart's fame was still largely regional, an interviewer asked Sam Walton to summarize the single most important lesson he had learned through his Arkansas retail career. Walton did not hesitate: his business had taught him that "'all of us like to be recognized and appreciated and need to feel like the roles we play or what we do is important.'"[5] This sentiment found its formal codification in a sign hanging over one entrance to the home office: "Through these doors pass ordinary people on their way to accomplishing extraordinary things."[6] For all its obvious instrumentality, the phrase that Wal-Mart made famous was more than an off-the-rack slogan of spin. To many observers, it seemed self-evident that the way to value work was to reward it concretely with security, high wages, and benefits. To the extent that the average Wal-Mart job offered none of these, critics pointed out, the corporate cheerleading for its front-line workers was hypocritical. When low-wage employees expressed loyalty to Wal-Mart, the same critique was at a loss to explain it.

Such an appraisal assumed that service employees—the majority of whom were women—could be bought off with recognition, whereas more enlightened laborers at all levels would be less easily duped. "'A lot of people are pretty illiterate,'" a union organizer put it in 2002, "'and if Mr. Sam comes and shakes their hand, and listens to them, that's the greatest thing that ever happened. It don't matter that he did nothin'—just that he sat there and listened to you.'" Wal-Mart employees in this rendering failed on measures of appropriate worker militancy, debased by accepting celebrity paternalism over real rewards.[7]

But when some Wal-Mart employees related those encounters with Sam Walton, they emphasized his respect for them and their customers, not the other way around. By performing some of the humble tasks of running a store alongside the women who worked there, the chain's founder communicated his appreciation for their work. "He'd come in and sit down with me at the counter," recalled Eleanor Cook of the earliest Walton stores, "and make tickets with me, just talk to me. It was great—'How many of these do you need?' he'd ask."[8] When a woman in the Springdale store was operating a cash register one day, Walton came over and started sacking the customers' purchases while asking for perspectives on the new express lanes—were they going well? "He was sacking this woman's things," explained Ann Tuttle, "and she didn't have a clue who it was. And he said, 'Ma'am, would you like some help out to the car with that?'"[9] Efforts like these on the part of the richest man in America spoke forcefully to front-line workers of the value placed on their work. At least in the early Wal-Marts, service labor would not be rendered invisible.

Similarly, many Wal-Mart employees applied their value system to managerial priorities, selecting out which strains of corporate dogma resonated for these service-driven Christians. In communications to its work force, for example, Bentonville stridently emphasized individualism. Managerial exhortations to rugged individualism are textbook tactics of employer antiunionism. Wal-Mart's insistence on "respect for the individual" as one of the company's "core values" was part and parcel of its fear of collective action.[10] When employees at two distribution centers showed signs of affiliating with the Teamsters in 1979, Walton was moved to contrast their attitude with that of a model Wal-Mart store in Broken Bow, Oklahoma. This profitable store in a tiny town demonstrated the practical rewards of treating employees "on an individual basis." Walton lauded the store's manager as "attentive to each associate's individual needs."[11]

But where the executives put the stress on "individual" in these kinds of pronouncements, many employees heard "needs" and "respect" more loudly, and it was this interpretation that became company orthodoxy. A part-time Wal-Mart worker recently defined "respect for the individual" as incorporating "the ability to lead people while taking care of their needs."[12] Real individualism in the service workplace, of course, was about as impossible as it had been on a farm or an assembly line, since large-scale work processes are by definition interdependent relationships. Wal-Mart's own employees were not bowling alone but sharing casseroles in the break room. Rather than an individualism that asserted autonomy and independence, then, their version resonated with the language of self-esteem, the "craving for significance" in a mass society that vernacular Christian theologians popularized in these same years: not "Who am I?" but "*Whose* am I?"[13]

Employees read the company magazine, for example, in large part to join in applauding "the achievements of all these different people," according to Eleanor Cook.[14] Indeed, the pages of *Wal-Mart World* may have been among the few places many Wal-Mart employees saw themselves and their families in print. Their previous accomplishments had largely transpired within their homes, and no matter how worthwhile, they did not produce public praise. "It is not very often you get a curtain named after you—or anything else, for that matter!" one item mused in 1977. "But that's just what has happened to Peggy!" A textiles company had named a new style of window-dressing after Wal-Mart's Peggy Griffith, an assistant buyer for curtains and drapes, and was marketing it under that name in her honor.[15] The department head for cameras in Sallisaw, Oklahoma, proudly displayed her certificate upon completing a sales training seminar by the vendor Eastman Kodak in 1976. That same year, the warehouseman won praise for his freshly minted Doctor of Divinity degree, representing "a seven-year struggle, including campus classes, correspondence courses, and night classes at Southern State of Joplin and American Bible College of Kansas City."[16] Whole stores routinely printed their congratulations to the graduating high-school seniors on the staff, and proudly publicized their awards, club memberships, and college plans.

Articles and photos fed an appreciative audience for associate accomplishments within the company, as did the thrifty custom of using real employees in training slides and videos. Even more gratifying, Wal-Mart made its store associates the public face of the company.[17] In-store fashion shows, print ads, and local parades all featured the Wal-Mart corps in front of their neighbors. In 1983, an associate at the Belton, Missouri, store described performing in a Wal-Mart TV commercial: "It gives you a real sense of accomplishment and pride to see your co-workers and yourself on television. You know you can't help feeling a little proud and grinning from ear to ear when someone approaches you in the grocery store or at church and says 'Hey, I saw you on TV last night!' . . . Sure, we have to work hard for Wal-Mart, but just stop and look at the many opportunities the Company offers us for personal growth."[18]

For June Whitehead, Wal-Mart offered an attractive alternative to what she had known in nearby Elkins. When her children were small, she took in ironing, a dull job with no company but the television. But within three months of starting at the Fayetteville Wal-Mart in 1976, Mrs. Whitehead was a department manager in ladies' wear, with discretion over much of the product mix and marketing. Since many customers visited the store two or three times a week, the challenge was keeping new displays rotating through. "I used to get fashion magazines off the shelf and look at them in the break room, and I would get ideas about what people were wearing," she remembered. "I couldn't wait to get to work to try something out."[19]

"I am eternally grateful for what I have learned from Wal-Mart," said Alice Martin emphatically. "I graduated high school in Huntsville, Arkansas, in 1955, and there weren't but two typewriters at the whole school. Wal-Mart taught me the computer. When it started, I thought, 'There's no way I can learn a computer'—I was scared to death of it. They provided the equipment and the training to learn it, and I will always be thankful for that."[20] Bea Scott of Pea Ridge enjoyed the technical demands in the electronics department and the math skills required for stocking before the advent of barcode scanning. With her husband on the road hauling freight for the area's large trucking firms, Mrs. Scott had pieced together a series of jobs that could accommodate her four children—selling insurance and cosmetics with the kids in the back seat, taking in ironing, babysitting. She started at Wal-Mart during the Christmas rush in 1972, just to cover what was shaping up to be a lean holiday season, and wound up as the store's assistant manager. "Every day there was something different in Wal-Mart," Mrs. Scott remembered. "You didn't do an assembly-line type job at all."[21] Compared to the monotony of available options—household chores like laundry and child care, or their public equivalents like chicken processing and vegetable canning—the variety of early Wal-Mart work and the scope it allowed for personal development made it an attractive alternative for these Ozarkers. "People raised in this area didn't get to go to college, didn't have the opportunity," emphasized Mrs. Tuttle. "And that's why I've always appreciated Wal-Mart for the opportunity to grow and have a job that let you go as far in the company as you want to go."[22]

As company executives freely admitted at the time, it was the store employees who demonstrated just what would be needed to build a megacorporation on humble service work. Though the motherly Christian women in the original stores would not have seen themselves as making demands, they successfully held the workplace to their most important values. Management learned late the ennobling qualities of service. But as Bentonville gradually accepted the tutelage of its many wives and mothers, it was able to use the ideology. For just as the Christian workers and customers were shaping service work as paid employment, they were remaking the terms of service labor at home as well. Their activism on both fronts was ultimately codified by business and religious leaders in the twin canons of American mass readership, business advice and Christian self-help. From these platforms servant leadership achieved broad influence.

Certainly notions of both managerial power and business itself as service predated the era of Wal-Mart. Bruce Barton, innovative advertising executive and apostle of the abundant life, received hundreds of letters in response to his 1925 bestseller *The Man Nobody Knows*. Barton's treatise was the first popular treatment of Jesus as businessman, and while its entrepreneurial characterizations of the Christ may feel drearily familiar today, it is only because the genre has proved so enduring. Of Barton's fan mail, Jackson Lears writes, "Most are typed on business letterheads; but some are crudely handwritten, in pencil, on torn note paper, from secretaries, stock boys, and barely literate marginal men. Whatever their source, their main message was gratitude—for recognizing the spiritual nature of business enterprise, for making Jesus seem human and 'real,' for giving hope in times of despair."[23]

The executives, the secretaries, and the stock boys did not write to Barton as consumers. They wrote as producers of a new sort, service providers whose professional goal was not their own self-realization through consumption but that of their customers and clients. Barton and his fellows could not square the soft life of consumer society with the muscular Jesus they promoted. Consumption for oneself fell outside Protestantism's sacred circle. But helping others consume—especially helping them consume necessities "for their families"—*that* could be a sacred calling. It could even ennoble the men of the service sector if it could be shorn of its effeminate connotations. Servant leadership provided a way out of the conundrum of such labor for men.

By the early 1990s, the specific formula of "servant leader" became hard to escape. It attached itself with particular tenacity to the down-home, how-may-I-help-you image of Wal-Mart and its frugal founder.[24] Walton himself put it succinctly in 1992: "As servant-leaders, we must do all we can to exceed our associate-partners' expectations daily, one on one."[25] What disappeared in this formula, of course, was any notion of authority or ownership, to say nothing of the logistical advantages that fueled the retailer's growth. Rather, one's position of power within a system became de facto evidence of service, with no reference to the external structures that determined the distribution of power. The company's head of human resources held that "The higher up in the organization you go, the more of a servant you need to become."[26] In service ideology, there were no more bosses, only "leaders."

In the genre of business advice, the term "servant leader" actually dated to a 1968 essay by a former AT&T personnel trainer, Robert K. Greenleaf. Greenleaf, a sometime Quaker and restless devotee of human potential movements from phrenology to LSD, had taken early retirement from the communications company to pursue consulting, with the hope of spreading his humanistic values to other large bureaucracies. With a peculiarly blinkered approach to organizations in the abstract, he encouraged nonhierarchical management for clients as distinct as a Catholic sisterhood and the Business Roundtable, a lobbying consortium comprising the CEOs of the nation's 200 largest corporations that was responsible for many notable antilabor and deregulation victories of the conservative ascendancy.[27]

Greenleaf's work grew out of longstanding traditions in management theory. Since the initial military-inspired breakthroughs of Taylorization at the turn of the twentieth century, refinements on scientific management had proceeded from the analogy between a worker and a machine. The regime of mass production valued human effort in proportion to its efficiency and predictability. "Schmidt," Frederick Winslow Taylor's pseudonym for the "first-class laborer," embodied this breakthrough in the 1911 ur-text of scientific management: "He worked when he was told to work, and rested when he was told to rest," limned Taylor in the cadences of Genesis, "and at half-past five in the afternoon had his 47½ tons [of pig iron] loaded on the car."[28] Taylor understood his system as a branch of mechanical engineering, a logical extension of the machine itself.[29] As the ruling machines of the American workplace changed, so the analogy changed with them. The grinding cogs that broke Charlie Chaplin on the wheel in *Modern Times* were updated by postwar cybernetics revolutionaries into mechanical brains. As one leading architect of artificial intelligence put it, the "programmed computer and the human problem solver" were but "both species belonging to the genus IPS" or Information Processing System.[30] Yet whether manipulating Panzer divisions, pig iron, or punch cards, the human body at work always sinned and fell short of the glory of the machine.

Under the force of this reality, management theory repeatedly drew back from its initial infatuation with scientific rationalization to take into account human limitations. Even the earliest forays into Taylorism had incorporated personality and intelligence tests. In 1914, Henry Ford's "Sociological Department" began deploying inspectors to certify employees' housekeeping standards, sexual habits, and sobriety.[31] In the 1920s, a series of experiments in boosting employee efficiency suggested that merely taking an interest in a group of workers raised their output, perhaps by communicating managers' involvement or perhaps through the therapeutic effect of airing their concerns.[32] From these crude beginnings developed a self-styled "science" of human relations.[33]

But a funny thing happened on the way to the harmonious shop floor. Human relations, a field originally intended for improved supervision of industrial line labor, found a more enthusiastic audience among management itself in its ever-burgeoning office settings. The cold, dead hand of bureaucratization was forcing a new kind of worker into the updated machine metaphor, but the countervailing trend sought to ease the adjustment of the "organization man" to his new reality.[34] Emotions, sentiment, and social ties, argued HR's adherents, all had a place in the office.[35] And after World War II, offices gradually grew to replace factories as the paradigmatic American workplace. In 1956, the U.S. census reported more people employed in white-collar service industries than in blue-collar production for the first time.[36] Every year more managers, secretaries, and technicians found themselves governed for much of their waking lives by the ideologies of the company and the ethereality of nonmanual labor.

During these early years of Walton's expanding chain, the most widely influential model of this kinder, gentler management was Douglas McGregor's "Theory Y," developed at the Massachusetts Institute of Technology and published in 1960 as *The Human Side of Enterprise.*[37] According to McGregor's rather overdrawn distinction, "X" managers were rigid, authoritarian, and inclined to assume that employees will avoid work in the absence of strict disciplinary controls. "Y" managers, in predictable contrast, began from the insight that people seek meaning through work and will opt for greater responsibility when the structure of their jobs permits. Needless to say, McGregor promoted the latter style of workplace.[38] Down in Wal-Mart Country, a similar concept was percolating in the psychology department at the University of Texas during the mid-1960s. Professors Robert Blake and Jane Mouton's schema was called the "managerial grid." Though it came packaged in elaborate questionnaires, the managerial grid boiled down to the same distinction between managers with "a high concern for production . . . [and] a low concern for people," on the one hand, and those with the opposite priorities, on the other.[39] The ideal, of course, lay squarely in between. By 1973, between a third and a half of managers surveyed by the American Management Association were familiar with McGregor's Theory Y, Blake and Mouton's managerial grid, or one of the similar human relations theories.[40] At Wal-Mart, during a single month in 1977, headquarters held communications seminars for all warehouse supervisors in which they discussed the relative merits of "hard" and "soft" management, with the usual recommendation to strive for something in between, a "firm-but-fair" approach.[41]

Likewise, despite the scientific pretensions of its promoters, the managerial enthusiasm for small, nonauthoritarian groups both borrowed from and contributed to a parallel Christian tradition. With roots as old as Protestantism itself, evangelical small groups of the twentieth century included the Christian Business Men's Committee and the Oxford Group—forerunner to Alcoholics Anonymous—that bolstered conservative businessmen on their spiritual journeys and explicitly sought to connect faith and work. Church-based small groups of the 1960s and 1970s openly acknowledged their debt to the literature of human relations and bureaucratic group dynamics, and strove to replace theological instruction and rigid doctrine with expressiveness and intimacy. The result was a personal, practical faith and a God of fatherly love, not Old Testament wrath.[42]

The explicit inspiration for Greenleaf's servant leader was Hermann Hesse's *Journey to the East,* an indispensable text for a seeker in the 1960s. Yet the theological roots of Greenleaf's essay were obvious to the biblically literate. Dr. Martin Luther King's 1968 sermon "The Drum Major Instinct" suggested a trajectory for servanthood outside commerce, but other Christians found the concept more useful for sanctifying hierarchies than overturning them.[43] The Episcopal bishop of Atlanta encountered Greenleaf's writings soon after his appointment to the See in 1971. He was so inspired by the notion that he dedicated himself to "putting theology at the service of business" via an executive training institute at Emory University. "It's got to be the same God for General Motors as it is for the Episcopal Church," he explained.[44] The *Wall Street Journal* found the servant-leader message appropriate for the Christmas season of 1989. Citing Bruce Barton himself, a guest columnist introduced the readership to "the perfect executive." Jesus could have turned his awesome powers to accumulating worldly honors. Instead, he won glory though "his strongest leadership trait: the servant attitude." Putting aside your ego like Christ, the *Journal* assured its readers, did not mean renouncing your ambitious career goals, but rather furthering them through other people. Like Jesus washing the feet of the Disciples, management could earn subordinates' loyalty and business success through "the power of humble service to others."[45] Christian periodicals as well as management ones reviewed Greenleaf's work, and *Business Horizons* stated the obvious: "Christ was a servant leader."[46]

A key figure in the crossover of servant leadership from technically secular business advice to explicitly Christian capitalism was Kenneth

Blanchard, an early associate of Greenleaf's through an experimental program at Ohio University. Blanchard co-authored a widely used management textbook incorporating some of Greenleaf's insights and then went on to produce the 1982 success *The One-Minute Manager.* In the early 1990s, Blanchard experienced Christian conversion and founded the FaithWalk Leadership Institute to train managers in Christian servanthood. His popular manual, *Lead Like Jesus,* made the connection explicit.[47]

But at the same time Christian interest in service was working its way through other channels. It was precisely the advice flooding therapeutic Christian culture in the transformation of the male ideal at home: the expressive, communicative father who nonetheless assumed the weighty mantle of responsibility for those God had placed under him. "I am not recommending that your home become harsh and oppressive," wrote the Christian child psychologist James Dobson in his runaway 1970s bestseller *Dare to Discipline.* Rather, "when you are defiantly challenged, win decisively," then "take [your son] in your arms and surround him with affection."[48] Dobson, who anchored a Christian therapeutic empire with his Focus on the Family organization and eponymous radio show in 1977, became the foremost power broker of the politicized New Christian Right by the turn of the millennium.[49] But his organization's influence among American evangelicals over the decades was based upon its massive and sustained output of practical advice on childrearing and family life, with particular emphasis on changing the style of fathering from "X" to "Y." Authority, as Dobson and a host of imitators urged, should be "tender" as well as "tough."[50]

In many conservative Christian circles, too, the public challenges to male authority posed by women's legal and economic emancipation that began in the 1960s were met with renewed emphasis on male "headship" and female "submission" within marriage. The shift was more than a rhetorical flourish. In the mid-1970s, a rash of cultlike home-based churches popularized an extreme form of patriarchal authority, assigning an older male "shepherd" as the "servant leader" of younger men and women, who reported being unable to buy a car or travel out of town without the "shepherd's" permission.[51] The Assemblies of God announced a "paradigm shift" in its own internal concept of leadership with imagery that blended the corporate and the Christian: "Jesus reversed the 'power pyramid' by teaching us that 'the greatest is the servant of all.'"[52] The 1998 amendment on family life to the Southern Baptist Faith and Message—that is, the basic statement of the beliefs of the country's largest Protestant denomination—explicitly couched its controversial message about female submission in terms of husbands' "servanthood."[53]

Domestic interest in "servant leadership" signaled more than unilateral rearguard action by men whose legal precedence at home was in jeopardy. As organizations like the all-male Promise Keepers never shied from admitting, among the most fervent supporters of Christian men's familial authority were many Christian women. Here lay a clue to the persistent association between sexually conservative Christianity and postindustrial service workplaces like Wal-Mart. The feminization of men demanded by the post-1973 economy found in the new Christianity both an ally and an alibi. Elizabeth Brusco has supplied the useful term "reformation of machismo" to describe the effect of evangelical and Pentecostal Christianity on working families in Colombia. In contrast to liberal feminism, Brusco argues, the Protestantism she encountered "is not attempting to gain access for women to the male world; rather, it elevates domesticity, for both men and women, from the devalued position it occupies as the result of the process of proletarianization. It does serve to transform gender roles, primarily by reattaching males to the family."[54]

Elevating domesticity—publicly acknowledging its value and urging men to support it—offered many of the same benefits to conservative Christian women in the United States. A Texas woman interviewed in the mid-1990s explained that while she was growing up, her mother had been responsible for all the children's activities. In contrast, her husband James centered his own leisure time on family activities. "Where a [non-Christian] guy feels like it's his right to go out, James stays at home," she summed up. James even removed the computer from the house to avoid spending too much time in Christian chat rooms discussing homosexuality and abortion. "Now," he explained, "I'm freed up to take care of the baby, to clean, to cook." If he expected his wife to submit, he reasoned, it was only fair that he also submit to God's directives to respect and honor his wife by focusing his own energies on his family. Before their conversion, a Pennsylvania Christian couple recalled, the husband would "help out" from time to time, "but it was like, 'It's your job, you're the woman.'" Since being saved, though, they felt freed from dominant sex roles. In secular society, the husband explained, men worried that their peers would laugh at them for performing domestic chores. But as a born-again Christian, he was free to go against the grain.[55]

This novel interpretation of Christian manliness spread through evangelical, fundamentalist, and Pentecostal circles after 1970, bearing an unacknowledged debt to secular feminism but scoring a significant success of its own that still eludes the broader culture. Studies of Christian women who actively embraced this ideal suggest that the "submission" required of them was a minor concession for a divinely sanctioned domestication of their husbands. During its heyday in the early 1990s, the evangelical men's organization Promise Keepers struck a bargain that may well have been the best one on offer for many women. By submitting, they were rewarded with "husbands and fathers who forswear drinking, drugs, smoking, and gambling, who lovingly support their families by steady work, and who even choose to go shopping with them as a form of Christian service."[56]

This was a particularly attractive accord since "submission" in practice boiled down to little more than a rhetorical gesture at the husband's final say on major decisions. When asked how it played out in marriage, few conservative Christians seemed able to recall an example where husbands actually pulled rank in decision-making. Instead, the couples coded expressiveness—emotional labor—and family responsibilities—reproductive labor—as "leadership" to make them newly palatable to men. Bill McCartney, founder of Promise Keepers, explained on the TV show *Larry King Live* that "We're not talking about lording authority. We're talking about servanthood. There's a big difference there."[57] Speaking at a 2003 Promise Keepers rally, Bishop Wellington Boone, author of such bestselling Christian family advice manuals as *Your Wife Is Not Your Momma*, demanded of his multiracial all-male audience, "Who is the servant in your house? You should be, and you should learn how to praise and affirm your wife."[58]

Under the earlier industrial dispensation, in other words, labor and management disagreed over many things, but the unimportance of domestic labor and the women who performed it was an area of manly accord. Economic changes underway after World War II made such a position untenable in the long run, for paid work in general came to look more and more like humble service labor. At the same time, women were entering the jobs that had been structured for men supported by unpaid wifely services at home. Their husbands, however, overwhelmingly refused to make up the difference in domestic labor, and their employers likewise remained reluctant to admit the outdated particularity of their ideal worker. By elevating domesticity as an ideal for everyone regardless of sex, conservative Christianity gave women a powerful tool to redress some of the imbalance, while providing conservative Christian men with a new justification for their precedence.[59]

It would be easy to overstate the concrete advantages of this ideology to married mothers. The difference was fairly subtle in terms of a measurable addition to household labor. Though they evidently did spend more time in one-on-one activities with their children and undertake more of the emotional labor of parenting than more mainstream Protestant or unaffiliated men, churchgoing evangelical men were not shown to perform significantly more housework than their nonevangelical peers, which is to say about a half of what wives did regardless of paid employment.[60] What the model of Christian servant leadership did offer was two sets of significant if intangible benefits.

First, the sanctification of domestic work gave conservative Christian men an ideological stake in the institution of marriage itself. As fallible as this commitment may have been, it at least openly acknowledged women's greater economic vulnerability in reproduction. In the United States, rather than sharing some of the concrete costs of childrearing through social provisions, we assign the majority of these costs directly to individual mothers. Most of the persistent gender gap in wages—just over 21 cents on the dollar for full-time employment—is actually a gap between mothers and everyone else.[61] At work, mothers are held to stricter standards of punctuality and productivity, hired less often, and judged less promotable, less competent, less dependable, and less committed to their jobs—all demonstrated in experiments that control for actual differences in performance or qualifications. Fathers, on the other hand, find their earnings and approval enhanced by having the children that their wives are caring for eleven hours a week to the fathers' three.[62] The sacred emphasis on reproduction in the late twentieth century guaranteed a socially honored position, wrote Linda Kintz, "for women who have a deep and realistic fear that, without such a guarantee, they will inevitably be judged against men and found lacking. Then they and their children will be left at great risk in a society based on masculine competition, whether built by free-market theorists or liberal institutions."[63]

By "defending marriage," conservative Christianity straightforwardly acknowledged these quite unsentimental, concrete functions that Americans require of families. Thus Connie Marshner, one of the political and organizational founders of the "pro-family" Christian movement, asserted that the essence of family cohesiveness is not affective ties but rather the provision of vital services: "Families are strong when they have a function to perform," she explained in an interview. "And the more government, combined with the helping professions establishment, take away the functions families need to perform—to provide their health care, their child care, their housing—the less purpose there is for a family, *per se,* to exist."[64] Conservative churches could offer quite explicit support for mothers and potential mothers. In many settings around the world, a "family-values" church acted as a sort of screening agent for women seeking family-oriented husbands. Evangelical, Pentecostal, and Mormon congregations actively assumed the role of teaching men how to be expressive, affectionate husbands. Church-based daycare centers served both employed mothers and the congregations' bottom lines, as impressive untaxed revenue-generators.[65]

Through servant leadership, evangelical men made a measurable contribution to the "economy of gratitude." In this schema, the best predictor of domestic harmony was not an equal division of labor—that option has virtually never been on the table in American families—but rather husbands' consistent expression of gratitude for the gift of domestic labor women made to them.[66] Unlike their supposedly egalitarian male counterparts, conservative Christian men had at hand an ideology that allowed them to praise and acknowledge women's work at home without thereby running the risk of being required to share it equally. In contrast, nonreligious men who paid lip service to formal sex-neutral rights had no alibi for their demonstrated failure to split the labor at home, and may have found it safer to ignore the work altogether. Between the two, many wives preferred the former—especially since they seemed to have little hope of achieving actual parity.[67]

Conservative Christian fathers apparently offered significant displays of gratitude to their wives compared to other men. Women's approach to family life garnered consistent support in Christian self-help literature from the 1970s on. Focus on the Family's James Dobson opened a Christian marriage advice book with the expected rhetorical genuflection to absolute, divinely ordained differences between men and women. But he evoked them in order to urge husbands to adopt their wives' pattern of emotional investment in the relationship, and to emulate women's expressiveness.[68] Organizations like Promise Keepers even took up the task of training men in such traditionally feminized social skills as listening and consulting with others as equals.[69] In conjunction with the marital model of male leadership, then, many Christian men became more involved, emotionally expressive fathers and husbands, and many Christian women found their priorities elevated to a common goal.

The "stalled revolution" of American women's economic emancipation progressed only to the point of allowing some women access to formerly all-male labor pools.[70] It did not redistribute the significant penalties applied to women as the primary agents of reproduction and of reproductive labor. This was in large part, of course, because of political opposition from conservative Christians themselves. But it also signaled the failure of most men to make this second half of the bargain a policy priority. With the "problem" of motherhood not yet everyone's problem, many women found the solution best guaranteed by conservative Christianity, which elevated the domestic sphere for men and curbed the demands of the public sphere of paid work. This was a significant benefit for women, when so many avowedly liberal secular institutions continued to imagine a citizen or a worker as a person unhampered by domestic responsibilities. It also provided a valuable resource for the service industries like Wal-Mart, which found that gratitude for women's work and managerial homage to service likewise brought women workers meaningful benefits.

Conservative Christianity, then, adjusted to the feminization of work in surprising ways both at home and on the job. In a world where production was disappearing, reproduction would be the central ideological battleground. The rise of "family values" and the Wal-Mart voter were intimately connected to this transformation in labor. The principal figures in the battle were well aware of the change. One of the founders of the shepherding movement insisted in his oft-repeated sermon "Fatherpower" that "God's answer for the leadership crisis in our world today is the same as it was 3,500 years ago—fathers! The only way God's love and fatherhood is going to come into this world is through men who know how to rule and father."[71]

A 1979 article in *Eternity* magazine noted approvingly "all this talk about 'spiritual' parenthood and reproduction" and traced it to an emotionally charged, individual, male-on-male mentoring style pioneered by the Navigators.[72] This parachurch organization had started before the war in the naval port of San Pedro, California, as a ministry to sailors. Its distinctive approach combined small-group Bible study, rote memorization of Bible verses, and the homosocial discipling dyad that guaranteed moral "accountability" through constant personal monitoring. World War II gave it a stage on which to spread, and by the conflict's conclusion the Navigators could claim "cadres" in over 450 army camps and 350 navy vessels.[73] "Words such as fatherhood came forcibly upon us as leaders," recalled one influential founder of the 1970s discipling or "shepherding" movement, "causing us to recognize that the Church was not designed to be a frustrated General Motors, but a family built relationally, with spiritual fathers."[74]

Thanks to its founder Sam Walton, Wal-Mart was uniquely well positioned to benefit from Christianity's growing preoccupation with fatherhood and reproduction. Among the company's own management, the men of the service industry seemed to find in him a comforting exemplar of the soft patriarch. Those in Bentonville frequently described him as "like a father" or "like a daddy."[75] The retail industry unambiguously proclaimed him "Wal-Mart's Patriarch."[76] His fatherly significance marked the culture beyond his own business. In June of 1992, following Walton's cancer-related death that April, Doubleday released his memoirs through a million-dollar Father's Day promotional campaign featuring life-sized Sam Walton cutouts, patriotic window-dressings, and radio ads during Country Countdown.[77]

A retired Wal-Mart executive and influential evangelical made explicit the connection between the founder, the company, and the postindustrial Christian emphasis on reproduction. In his memoirs of life with Walton, Don Soderquist painted him as a man with a dream: "It wasn't to build the tallest building in the world or to build the longest bridge," the heroic masculine ambitions of industrial modernism. Nor did he seek to "make a million dollars before he was thirty years old," the sterile replication of wealth that folk Christianities have traditionally deplored.[78] Rather, wrote Soderquist with considerable authorial license, Walton simply wanted to "support his family" and "honor his Lord." Thus, appropriately, his humble store brought him unimaginable rewards.[79]

As long as the ideology could explain why a loss of formal masculine prerogatives and the indignities of postindustrial work actually *elevated* men's authority, then the danger to manliness might be contained. And there was no ambiguity about the nature of the threat. A management periodical recommended servant leadership for the new decade of the 1990s with the frank label "The Androgynous Manager."[80] Christian groups had another word for it: "Don't you know what kind of society we have today?" demanded McCartney of a 1991 Promise Keepers audience. "It's an effeminate society. It doesn't raise men."[81] Bishop Wellington Boone addressed the 2006 "Values Voter Summit" in Washington with the frank assertion that when he was growing up, if "we [saw] guys that don't stand strong on principle, we call[ed] them faggots."[82] "The demise of our community and culture is the fault of sissified men who have been overly influenced by women," wrote Tony Evans, an evangelist and former chaplain to the Dallas Cowboys who was in great demand at Promise Keepers events.[83] Indeed, McCartney had begun his public career as a board member of Colorado for Family Values, the sponsors of the state's Amendment 2, which specifically legalized discrimination against homosexuals.[84] In that capacity, McCartney denounced homosexuality as "an abomination against Almighty God," since homosexuals were "a group of people who don't reproduce."[85] Perhaps the most complete associational loop was produced when Bishop Eddie Long of Atlanta's 10,000-member New Birth Baptist Missionary Church called cloning and homosexuality "spiritual abortions."[86] Alert to the threats posed to reproduction by abortion and sterile sex, organizations like Promise Keepers and Focus on the Family strove to theorize a reproductive Christian masculinity for home and office, one with soft hands but not limp wrists. It was a fine line indeed. The vigorous promotion of "Adam and Eve, not Adam and Steve" became more urgent: reproductive sex had to carry the symbolic burden of an entire suite of lost male prerogatives.

Such opinions on these key issues of reproduction were widely held throughout the Christian men's movement. After interviewing a sample of active Promise Keepers on a wide rage of opinions, a social scientist found that "no other issues elicited such uniformity of belief" as did abortion and homosexuality. Every man interviewed stated unequivocally that homosexuality and abortion were sins, and that the pair of issues represented "perhaps the greatest threats to our society."[87] This intense focus on reproductive issues took shape in the early 1970s as public discourse about sex conformed less and less to conservative Christian standards. At first the targets were quite varied: the evangelical *Christianity Today,* for example, ramped up its coverage of sex-related issues in the early 1970s with concern over what it saw as increased promiscuity. But the focus soon narrowed sharply to the pair of sexual issues that insulated straight men themselves from criticism: Abortion and homosexuality—crimes against reproduction—eclipsed much more broad-based sexual issues like rising divorce rates or heterosexual infidelity.[88]

Anxiety over reproduction flared throughout the 1970s and 1980s. The Moral Majority, founded in 1979, cannily used direct mail to unite fundamentalists, evangelicals, conservative Catholics, and Mormons as a political force with attacks on abortion, homosexuality, pornography, and the Equal Rights Amendment. In 1977, Anita Bryant launched a campaign, "Save Our Children," to protect children from homosexual schoolteachers, who, unable to reproduce themselves, recruited unsuspecting young Floridians to their ranks. Her mobilization of conservatives succeeded in removing homosexuals from Dade County's antidiscrimination clause.[89]

The image of vulnerable human life tossed out as refuse likewise dramatically haunted conservative Christianity after the mid-1970s. Jerry Falwell's account of his awakening to an active pro-life position invokes a dumpster in Los Angeles overflowing with the dismembered remains of 1,700 fetal bodies and a trash incinerator in Wichita sending up hundreds more in smoke, like the victims of Auschwitz.[90] The postindustrial economy's accelerated drive to render people functionally obsolete was figured in the imagery of the political Left as the dispossessed, the economic refugees, the reserve army of the unemployed. But its mirror image on the Right was an equally visceral horror at the potential loss of meaning in human reproduction. The dispossessed in this cosmology were the children unconceived or unborn because of their economic superfluity. With children no longer welcomed as new laborers on a family farm or potential wage-earners in a nineteenth-century factory, refusal to reproduce could be figured as a selfish cost-benefit calculation, and bearing children could be understood as a stand against market values, a preference for people over profits, or at least over consumption. Hence the emphasis on abortion as the callous strategy of ambitious "career women" who could not be "inconvenienced" in their race to the boardroom, or on homosexuals as an affluent population that selfishly consumed without reproducing.[91]

"Most people in Carmi, Illinois, didn't think it could happen in any town, much less in theirs," a *Wal-Mart World* item began somberly in 1992. They were shocked to discover the remains of a stillborn premature baby in a garbage bin. After the burial, a young employee of Wal-Mart store #833 began visiting the grave site, calling the deceased "Joshua." She and her Wal-Mart co-workers began a fundraising drive to erect a suitable marker. Their energetic organizing eventually produced an engraved tombstone, which the clerk visited from time to time.[92]

The echoes of the broader debate were evident in the Illinois Wal-Mart. In contrast to earlier debates over abortion, the post-*Roe* movement focused on the personhood of the fetus rather than the power of doctors over medical decisions. The explosive shift in emphasis hinged on the visceral issue of the status of parenthood itself. For many women, the door that feminism opened onto the paid labor market led to precisely the undervalued, segmented sector of "women's work." If these service jobs were to be meaningful, the relationship of caregiver to client—of mother to child—had to be protected from purely instrumental logic. As sociologist Kristin Luker argued of the 1980s abortion debate, the issue aroused such novel passions because it served as a "referendum on the place and meaning of motherhood"—and, we could add, on the value of service providers more broadly.[93]

The new centrality of reproduction in the 1970s and 1980s reverberated at the institutional level of conservative American Christianity, redoubling its cultural impact. The Southern Baptists veered sharply from a mildly pro-choice position to absolute rejection of abortion except where it gravely threatened the mother's own life. The bellwether of conservative Christian priorities, the flagship Southern Baptist seminary in Louisville, Kentucky, shifted its bottom line of faculty orthodoxy from biblical inerrancy to gender exclusivity: of the four questions put to prospective teachers, three concerned abortion, homosexuality, and the ordination of women.[94] In evangelical publications, family issues eclipsed the second coming of Christ, and titles changed to include the word "family." Billy Graham and similar evangelists reminded their audiences now that God had created the family well before creating the church.[95] In 1977, Focus on the Family, founded by Dobson, the pediatrician son of an itinerant evangelist from Oklahoma and Texas, grew in two decades to generate more than a hundred million dollars annually through its 1,200-person media, research, and counseling activities.[96]

The same concerns underwrote the increasing currency of "family" as an adjective, one that could attach itself to the mundane task of purchasing paper napkins and ankle socks at the local Wal-Mart. In a 1992 article tracing the political rise of the "family values" trope, *Christianity Today* decoded its content as, first and foremost, opposition to abortion and to "pornography, the promotion of homosexuality, condom distribution in schools, sexual education that does not emphasize abstinence, violent and sexually exploitative entertainment media, and the National Endowment for the Arts," which at the time was under attack by a Christian Coalition direct-mailing campaign for supporting sexually themed art, especially by gay artists.[97] Pat Robertson's Christian Broadcasting Network became the Family Channel in 1988. The Promise Keepers began offering an internet service provider that filtered out unsuitable content under the self-explanatory name "pkFamily.com."[98] In short, "Christian" and "family" were increasingly represented as synonyms, and both referred above all to the regulation of sterile sex and the ideological elevation of reproduction for men as well as women. The gap between conservative Christian views of family life and mainline or nonreligious views widened over the last decades of the twentieth century.[99] Economic disruption has often expressed itself in the visceral language of vice. Anxiety over impersonal market relations focused attention on prostitution in the nineteenth century, and the metaphor of the body as a machine figured masturbation as a dangerous waste of vital energies. The desk-bound bureaucrats and experts of the federal government were "lavender lads" to the McCarthyites, internal subversives as dangerous as the communist conspiracy itself. And where sins against industrial production had galvanized some Christian activists in the days of the temperance campaigns, sins against reproduction evoked the most impassioned responses in the new economic dispensation.[100]

The evangelical revival associated with the Bible Belt became a significant national phenomenon in the later years of the twentieth century, and its growth paralleled that of Wal-Mart itself into deindustrialized areas of the country. Thus in 1992, Janet Rugg at store #1378 wrote to Wal-Mart's Bentonville headquarters explaining exactly what she valued about working for a Christian service company, beyond merely her paycheck.

> I come from a factory background, which meant work came first, before family, church, or anything else. Also you were treated as a person hired just to do a job. They did not care about you as a person at all. That is the reason I like Wal-Mart. I can keep God first in my life because Wal-Mart lets me work around church services. If there is a special function that my children are involved in I can work my schedule around that also . . . My days are filled with people with smiles . . . I treat them just how I like to be treated.[101]

Wal-Mart transformed itself into a national Christian icon from the bottom up. Pragmatic decisions at the home office in the early 1990s merely ratified a cultural change that took place at the store level and in the lives of key individual figures within the company. Far from building on or actively manipulating an unbroken Southern heritage of old-time religion, official Wal-Mart came rather late to appreciate its employees' and customers' spiritual priorities. Moreover, those religious values themselves were changing in patterns widely recognizable across nonindustrial peripheries that moved masses of people from farming to service work in a single generation.

The evolving Christian culture of Wal-Mart's host communities was clearly visible within its stores and regional churches after 1973. What the company provided was a quasi-public space in which mass consumption and waged service work could be represented as "family values," not simply "women's work." Removing the gender stereotype did more than simply bring men into the fold. Once service companies like Wal-Mart discovered that female labor produced higher profit margins, the mythical prestige of the male breadwinner began to erode. The hidden work of women in the part-time and unpaid economies that had supported the industrial "family wage" could not be ignored as real wages stagnated after 1973 and a steadily increasing proportion of families relied on two full-time wage earners.[102] For conservative theorists of male supremacy, this changed economic landscape presented substantial challenges. George Gilder, the bestselling economist who promoted Reaganomics' supply-side theories in regular opinion pieces for the *Wall Street Journal,* wrote that women needed to be excluded from the economic arena not because they were unfit for the work but because "males always require a special arena of glorified achievement from which women are excluded" in order to protect their manhood.[103]

Like more nuanced Christian authors that followed him, Gilder grounded his argument for male prerogative on a startlingly negative assessment of men. The future of civilization, he explained, depended on a sexual contract that would force young men—"barbarians . . . entirely unsuited for civilized life"—to give up their dangerous ways in return for regular sex and a guarantee of their paternity. Wives, in exchange for their domestic confinement, received their husbands' economic support and his reluctant fidelity.[104] What would become of this arrangement when women brought home their own wages?

Servant leadership showed the way out, for it transferred women's civilizing influence to the workplace itself, and recast male virtue in feminized terms. As revived Christianity increasingly identified sin with sterile sex virtually to the exclusion of other vices, a G-rated setting became Christian by default. Only with this process clearly underway did the world's largest private-sector employer fully apprehend the lessons of service labor and enunciate them as managerial ideology in the form of servant leadership. Thus the extremely rigid reproductive orthodoxy by which evangelical culture defined itself at the end of the twentieth century was a key technology of social control, but not a univocal one. Multiple meanings of "family values" made sense to people who shared the common experience of postwar urbanization and articulation into the global economy through service work. In a service economy, women's domestication of men was all the more crucial for the reproductive labor they now both performed and the functions of social reproduction that the state disdained. Moreover, elevating service affirmed managerial authority in an economic sector built upon the devaluation of women's work by industrial capital and labor alike. An economy that jettisoned heavy manufacturing had little use for brawn and speed, but desperately needed "people skills." Servant leadership, in other words, was how the service economy made patriarchy safe for postindustrial society.

8

Making Christian Businessmen

As a corporation and a workplace, Wal-Mart drew creatively on currents within its home culture during its early decades. The legacy of Populism, the social capital of a female labor force, and the Christian tradition of sacred service all contributed to a distinct corporate model, a specific work process, and a new definition of skill and power. At the same time, however, the company reached outward to connect with networks of people, institutions, and ideas across its original trade area. These new players brought distinct agendas to the emerging economic landscape of the Sun Belt. Although their priorities often fell far from the core concerns of a retail chain, all parties recognized the potential mutual benefits of collaboration. From these interactions, under the specific economic conditions of the 1970s, Wal-Mart Country synthesized its influential ideology of free enterprise as Christian service.

In the United States, the Keynesian response to the market failures of the Great Depression reduced inequality and coincided with the longest uninterrupted period of prosperity in the nation's history. When the industrial economies of Europe and Japan, decimated by World War II, roared back into full-scale competition with the United States in the 1970s, however, the trends of rising standards of living and decreasing inequality reversed themselves. Wages and household incomes stagnated even as productivity rose and women added another earner to most homes. Jobs proliferated at the lowest and the highest wage rates, but the middle was hollowed out: Two service jobs were required to replace one lost manufacturing position. Economic policies exacerbated the squeeze. In response to double-digit inflation, the Federal Reserve in

1979 began to ration credit through a tight money supply. Rising interest rates curbed inflation, but at the price of skyrocketing unemployment and household debt. The United States tilted from the status of net exporter to net importer.[1]

Yet this time the political response was to attack the safeguards Americans had put in place during the previous economic crisis in the 1930s. Under the New Deal, the country had penitently imposed adult supervision over the riot of laissez-faire and decriminalized collective efforts to assure basic physical security when markets failed to deliver it. In the 1970s and 1980s, in contrast, significant numbers of Americans transferred their loyalty to different solutions: privatization, deregulation, shrinking social provisions, proliferating financial speculation, job and tax cuts, and the general recasting of notions like the public sphere and the common good as fundamentally suspect.

Many sources contributed to the late-twentieth-century prestige of neoliberalism, or the belief that individual entrepreneurship, vigorous private property rights, and minimal barriers to trade best provide for personal freedom and well-being.[2] The economists who coined the term in the years around World War II blended the free-market enthusiasm of some nineteenth-century political economists with Adam Smith's classic image: the invisible hand of the market that mysteriously guided the most venal human concerns into the collective good. Thus neoliberalism envisions the economy as a sphere independent of other social institutions and relationships. It understands the market to operate by natural laws that will, if left to their own devices, optimize the conditions of human existence. In this logic, there is no such thing as society or community, only individuals; the commons are a crime against efficiency; and government action intrudes illegitimately on the sovereign territory of economics, to the detriment of all.

Since in practice neoliberal restructuring redistributed wealth upward, the rise of this "free-market fundamentalism" after the early 1970s left some observers demanding to know what was the matter with Kansas; why did those who lost out under the model's prescriptions continue to enable them politically? In much of the world, the free-market vision spent those decades as a contested ideology, subjected to debate and often found wanting. But for most Americans, it acquired over thirty-five years the status of common sense—a fact of nature as self-evident as gravity and considerably more certain than evolution. How did this exceptional state of affairs come about?

The prestige of the market in the last decades of the twentieth century grew from multiple sources. Among those were Wal-Mart and the Walton family, which supplied a highly productive laboratory of free-market faith during the 1970s and 1980s. First, through training within the company, Bentonville gradually blended national trends in management theory with the specific needs of its personnel and its core business. When Wal-Mart's rapid growth and increasing technological sophistication forced the retailer to recruit new managers on college campuses, it turned to the nearby Christian colleges. There, faith engaged with the market head-on, decisively shaping both.[3]

Wal-Mart first cultivated managers as they encountered them in the small towns of the Ozarks and the Dust Bowl, training men with limited formal education and little experience of corporate organization. Many of the original managers in the Waltons' stores had left school before graduating, not an uncommon experience for Americans who came of age before World War II. But in this precybernetic era of storekeeping, the stocking processes were both decentralized and heavy on math skills. The men in charge of the individual stores had to be up to the task, for it could not be controlled from Bentonville. The challenge for Wal-Mart's director of training was therefore to break the process down and communicate it to the managers in their own terms—not, he emphasized, "to talk down to them, but to make the re-ordering process clear for people from a variety of backgrounds, to write it from where they were coming from." The director's solution was to travel to the stores and observe a strong manager for a few weeks at a time, reverse-engineering a step-by-step description of his methods in classic Taylorist fashion. He would then run the codified steps past a new manager "in Kansas or Louisiana or Alabama. I would ask if a manager understood, and if he said yes, then I would ask him to explain it to me. If he could do that, then I knew he understood."[4]

Equally important to the new managerial class, however, were such intangible skills as good grooming, an appropriate speaking voice, "positive attitude," and enthusiasm.[5] As represented in *Wal-Mart World*, growing into the role of a manager was a fraught, anxious, neverending process of self-improvement and external evaluation. "Keep your work on the top of the desk where it will haunt you," the company advised.[6] "To get people to like you, to listen to you, it's important that you 'sell' your personality every day," *Wal-Mart World* reminded them. The process amounted to nothing less than "personal public relations," a task quite beyond the minimal requirements of earlier, less competitive small-town shopkeeping.[7] Instead, service management was now under constant scrutiny. "Every day of our lives, from early childhood to old age, our actions, our progress, and our performance are constantly being graded by someone," intoned the newsletter ominously. "The scores we get from our peers determine the number of friends we make . . . The same holds true in business."[8] Certainly Wal-Mart store managers were constantly graded. Given the inexperience of many, Walton instituted a weekly reporting system.[9] Their district managers averaged a visit to a given store once every two weeks, and these were not social calls.[10] Not only were others constantly evaluating them; anyone with ambitions to move up was expected to evaluate himself. "Self-analysis can be very painful to those who are unwilling to change," explained *Wal-Mart World*, "but it can be extremely rewarding to those who want to achieve maximum success." Usually, it elaborated, someone unhappy on the job could discover that the real root of the problem lay within, the product of a bad attitude.[11]

For such a large and rapidly expanding company, however, these rather scatter-shot sources of advice on going corporate could only be ancillary to a rationalized training program. The first in-house training seminar for store managers and assistant managers was held in Bentonville in the summer of 1973. The eight participants, summoned to headquarters for lessons in store operations, evidently improved enough to convince the home office of the program's potential. They repeated the exercise five times over the year, increasing the number of pupils.[12] As the operations seminar continued to grow, it also spawned other centralized training initiatives over the same time period: a department head seminar for the largely female hourly work force that ran each merchandise section; an in-store training program for new employees; and an assistant manager training program.[13] Video later allowed for mass in-store training, and eventually the entire effort solidified into a formal training center staffed by professional trainers. "In today's world of retailing," emphasized the head of personnel administration, advanced training was absolutely necessary, since "the company and its people must be thoroughly professional."[14]

Certainly some of this professionalism involved the increasingly complex nuts and bolts of running a store. But just as important to cultivating "professionalism" were questions of image, presentation, and communication, and many of the newly professionalized themselves sought out this instruction. At the request of many in the Bentonville office, the company introduced an eight-week voluntary seminar in communications in 1975. For two and a half hours every Monday morning, beginning at the rather agricultural hour of five A.M., this dedicated group of sixteen men and three women sought to improve their writing and speaking skills. They spent the first three weeks on "an in-depth analysis of the common barriers to communication," reported *Wal-Mart World*, followed by three weeks preparing and presenting speeches, which the class then critiqued.[15] "With trembling legs and shaky voices," reported participants, "we have made strides in gaining self-confidence to speak before groups to better ourselves" and to "communicate our thoughts and ideas to our fellow workers in the stores."[16]

The communications class was such a success that the next roster filled immediately, and the first crop of graduates requested a follow-up course in "human behavior."[17] This newly christened corporate training program "received an overwhelming response by the General Office personnel," the company summed up at year end, "illustrating once again the potential just waiting to be awakened and recognized" among "interested, ambitious personnel."[18] Jim von Gremp, a Wal-Mart training manager, added a public-speaking component to the training for district managers. The new responsibilities of speaking before Rotary and Elks clubs in the towns of their districts shook their self-confidence, and von Gremp searched for a creative way to inspire the new public face of Wal-Mart at the local level. "The way I found to help them was to encourage them to think of themselves as Sam Walton for half an hour. They were all familiar with Sam, they knew how he spoke and how he motivated people. 'Sam does this all the time,' I would tell them, 'but you can do it for half an hour.' And they would, they learned how to speak in public."[19]

Wal-Mart also helped make its internal constituency corporate by demystifying the technology for which the retailer was to become justly famous. Each major upgrade in computers, communication systems, or distribution automation was treated in detail in *Wal-Mart World* and grounded in the names and faces of the people who worked the new machines. A representative 1977 article inducted readers into a new realm:

> At the east exit of the General Offices lies a fairly unknown area ... Let's go inside the world of Word Processing for a few moments ... Just what happens to this spoken word once it is recorded on the small disc? Is it automatically transformed into the written document we see? ... What motivates [the women who work there]? ... PRIDE—pride in the ability to create a beautiful piece of work ... pride in being able to work together in a centralized atmosphere to achieve the results and realize the profits only an environment of this type can create.[20]

When the company introduced barcode scanning in the early 1980s, the vice president of data processing explained the switch in *Wal-Mart World*. It wasn't the scanners and computers themselves that sped up checkout lines and reduced stock loss, he explained. Rather, "We were able to put some new technologies in the hands of people and they achieved the results," not "the dumb computer."[21] During the company's explosive expansion, technology could plausibly appear to enhance rather than replace workers. Introducing the barcode scanner into Wal-Mart ultimately reduced the man-hours required for freight processing by 60 percent.[22] But since the corporation continued to open new stores and expand old ones, the change did not result in a plant closing or a mass layoff. The workers replaced by technology were largely hypothetical future employees never to be hired, not loyal associates long in the harness. In a move that owed more to the culture of new electronic frontiers than the erosion of manufacturing, Wal-Mart interpreted technology as a servant to service workers both at headquarters and in the stores. These two notes—Wal-Mart's increasing cultivation of managerial "people skills" and its careful presentation of technology behind the face of human interaction—put a particular cultural spin on postindustrial society, one related to national currents but lodged in the twin specificities of evangelicalism and service work.

At the same time that servant leadership was transforming male authority on the job and in the home, evangelical culture was busily disproving secular assumptions about religious hostility to technology. Keen appreciation for mass communication had fueled the popularity of such prewar figures as Pentecostal leader Aimee Semple McPherson, who founded one of the country's first Christian radio stations in Los Angeles in the 1920s. During the 1930s, religious broadcasting boomed with programs like the *Old Fashioned Revival Hour* and the *Radio Bible Class*. Then, frustrated by their lack of access to the staid Big Three television networks and mainstream publishing outlets, conservative Christians pioneered alternative communications techniques after World War II. Borrowing talent from Hollywood, evangelicals next broke new ground as an alternative film circuit in the 1970s.[23]

In the same years, Richard Viguerie, a former activist for the conservative Young Americans for Freedom and a co-founder of the Moral Majority, married humble direct-mail techniques to political mobilization via new computer technology. This innovation allowed the New Christian Right to mobilize millions of new conservative voters.[24] By the mid-1990s, the country boasted over 200 Christian television stations and nearly 1,500 Christian radio stations. Pat Robertson's *700 Club* reached one million viewers every day, and James Dobson's *Focus on the Family* radio advice program attracted an estimated 5 million listeners every week.[25] As long as the tools of technology could be put to use to spread the saving message, religious conservatives—evangelical, Pentecostal, and fundamentalist alike—found every reason to embrace them.

Wal-Mart's backyard was ground zero for much of the evangelical communications explosion. The faith healer Oral Roberts, for example, broadcast his weekly show from Tulsa on almost a hundred television stations as early as 1955.[26] Building on the success of the country and gospel station KWTO ("Keep Watching the Ozarks"), a pair of Springfield, Missouri, broadcasters sold programming like the Assemblies of God's "Sermons in Song" to over 200 radio stations nationwide during the postwar decades.[27] A fundraiser at one of the Walton-connected Christian colleges stressed in 1967 that thanks to its engineering department, "we have been able to supply the country's defense, military, and major industries engineers with a Christian testimony, and in addition we have engineers at Christian radio stations throughout the world."[28]

In this context, Wal-Mart's aggressive adoption of communications technologies seems less surprising. In 1977, after years of half-hearted flirting with IBM, a reluctant Sam Walton succumbed to the urgings of his lieutenants and permitted the installation of a computer network linking stores to Bentonville and to one another.[29] It was the beginning of the company's decisive technological advantage over the competition. In the 1980s, Bentonville launched the world's largest privately owned satellite network, putting it even more dramatically out front in data transmission. This time, the tech-minded executives overcame Walton's tight-fisted antipathy by pointing out the system's utility for the company's charismatic founder: wouldn't Walton like to be able to send out his own chatty broadcasts to the far-flung store personnel? This turned out to be the winning argument, and Wal-Mart took maximum advantage of the many talented communicators in its midst.[30]

Certainly not all of the technophiles in Bentonville were products of evangelical culture, but many of the key men were unquestionably well connected to the Christian embrace of technology. Wal-Mart executives and their families helped form Northwest Arkansas's innovative, high-tech churches like Fellowship Bible. Ruth Glass, the wife of the Wal-Mart chief executive officer David Glass, launched a personal ministry, offering her own Christian testimony to millions of viewers on Jim and Tammy Faye Baker's PTL network, on Pat Robertson's *700 Club*, and in presentations to Christian women's groups around the country.[31] Don Soderquist, chief operating officer of Wal-Mart and a graduate of the evangelical Wheaton College, joined the company in 1980. He combined a background in data processing with a winning personal style. After retiring from Wal-Mart, Soderquist became increasingly involved in Christian business circles through his friendship with the born-again management guru Ken Blanchard—key popularizer of servant leadership—and through a center for Christian business ethics named in his honor at one of the nearby Walton-connected Christian colleges.[32] Larry Holder, who reports that he joined Wal-Mart as a data processor in 1981 after a summer as a Baptist missionary, was gratified to find "many practicing Christians" in his tech-friendly workplace. President Jack Shewmaker, a major force in pushing the digital revolution in Bentonville, even attended the same church as Holder.[33]

These creative collusions between business, technology, and belief shed new light on the supposed "paradox" of Wal-Mart: how the high-tech rednecks mastered cybernetics and corporate culture without losing Christ or country music. Despite its gleam of pure scientific rationality, developing and deploying high technology has been in part a spiritual exercise from the beginning, no matter the political context. The countercultural devotees of Buckminster Fuller, Ken Kesey, and the *Whole Earth Catalog* brought their dreams of antiauthoritarian, transcendent elitism into the cyber revolution in California. Blending their privileged vision as "comprehensive designers" with the decentralized technologies they developed, this loose fraternity marked an entire wing of the postindustrial economy with their conviction that their new tools made them "as gods." From the Berkeley Free Speech Movement's rebellion against the university as "knowledge factory," the West Coast generation thumbed its nose at the men in the gray flannel suits—often their own fathers, whose bureaucratized work lives looked to them like a vision of hell on earth. The students found a short-term solution in their romantic dreams of country living, founding a wave of rural communes where virtually everyone was white, well-educated, and young, and where the chicks baked the bread. When that experiment foundered, they took their elite communalism to the electronic frontier. This historical trajectory ultimately produced the paradigmatic high-tech workplace, where entrepreneurial free agents rented out their expertise to near-virtual companies, played foosball, and counted their stock options.[34]

Thus one influential work culture of postindustrial society was definitively shaped by the networked Bay Area baby boomers. But their contemporaneous counterparts in the Ozarks had a similar influence on the other work culture of the service economy, the one comprising far more Americans than the free-wheeling, no-collar corporate campuses that dominate our imagination of postindustrial work.[35] Unlike the restless communards around Berkeley and Stanford, growing up absurd, the future managers of Wal-Mart were growing up rather strapped for cash. They were already intimately familiar with the rigors of the farm, and gray flannel suits could look more appealing next to a pair of overalls.

Becoming corporate, professional, and managerial was a task to which Wal-Mart's newly white-collar work force applied itself systematically and self-consciously. Personal transformation along these lines marked the creation of a new class in the rural, small-town social ecology of Wal-Mart Country. "Thank you for the delightful, informative tour of Wal-Mart's offices," wrote a local vocational-technical class after visiting Wal-Mart headquarters. "Our students were especially impressed by your poise and professional attitude. You were certainly an inspiration to them."[36]

Since his Ben Franklin days, Walton had sought managers wherever he sensed potential.[37] In the corporate offices, work experience carried somewhat more weight than it did in the stores, but a college education remained entirely optional. Walton asserted straightforwardly that "all our old variety store managers had a tremendous prejudice against us hiring college boys because they didn't think they would work hard enough." Though several of these first educated managers turned out very well for the company, he reported, "they had a heck of a time fitting in at first."[38]

But by the late 1970s, that picture was changing. With the company's phenomenal growth, more graduates began showing up at Bentonville. "Sometimes it was the actual content of the degree that helped," recalled Jim von Gremp, "but also it was the exposure to more of a big picture."[39] In the retail industry at large, palpable anxiety wafted from management on this score. "It is not unusual to find warehouse men with a college education," pointed out an industry organ in 1975, "taking the job because it pays better than the field for which they were educated. Coupled with their youth, these workers present a real challenge to any warehouse manager who may not be as well educated."[40]

To meet the challenge of the young, educated warehouseman, management itself would have to ramp up. At Wal-Mart, the subject of the college graduate was introduced rather tentatively, signaling the sensitivity of the issue. The home office figured college recruiting "a necessity for a growing company," rather than a self-evident good.[41] A 1978 *Wal-Mart World* article described for readers the new management trainee program aimed at college students, a year and a half after the program had started. Under the new recruitment plan, the company interviewed graduating seniors each fall and spring at universities in its ten-state trading area: "Qualities like aggressiveness, work experience and management potential are important factors in trainee selection," the magazine reassured readers. "Colleges visited are chosen for their business schools, good curriculums, and competitive environments"—places like Dallas's Southern Methodist University, Mississippi State, and the University of Arkansas, only minutes from Bentonville itself.[42] The twenty new trainees of each crop started out in the stores and passed through stages there that culminated in assistant managing after eight to ten months. Their degrees, in other words, did not replace the traditional male path of advancement so much as speed it up.[43]

As the rest of the industry was learning, however, it was not an easy sell. "[W]hether we care to admit it or not," wrote a Wal-Mart insider with long experience recruiting, "retailers—even Wal-Mart—do not attract the top students on campus."[44] Mass higher education in America was supposed to be about social mobility. "The thought of seeing your college-educated son or daughter trading in their graduation cap and gown for one of those blue smock-type vests," he concluded, was really "more than many parents can stand."[45] For Wal-Mart as for the retail industry generally, this shift to a formally credentialed work force thus represented an internal sea-change. It underlined the reality that once education was widely available and service industries the major employers, the result was an educated working class in service jobs, not a universal middle class. Someone still had to stock the shelves.

Over the long haul, Wal-Mart's college recruiting developed with the company's trademark sophistication. Ultimately, it provided substantial support not only to the retailing institute at the University of Arkansas, but to similar ones at Texas A&M, Brigham Young University, James Madison University, the University of South Carolina, Florida State, and Purdue. Bentonville brought student interns from those programs into the home office for summer jobs, with a twofold intent. Some were recruited to Wal-Mart after graduation, and since they had already experienced the punishing pace at headquarters, they proved less likely to wash out after a few years. But there was a second goal, too. Wal-Mart sought to send the student interns back in the fall as "ambassadors," "campus managers" outfitted with their own business cards and authorized to represent Wal-Mart by speaking at meetings and assisting the official recruiters.[46]

Wal-Mart's entry into the college campuses of its trade area took place in a unique moment in the history of American higher education. Until World War II, the proportion of college students had always remained under 10 percent of the total population between the ages of 18 and 24: attending college, let alone graduating, was a distinctly minority experience when Sam and Helen Walton earned their degrees. During the 1950s, however, college enrollment rose by almost 50 percent, meaning a quarter of young people were in college during any given year. The following decade, the increase was even more dramatic, a rise of 120 percent. One out of every three young people attended college, a ratio that was to hold essentially steady through the end of the century.[47]

The explosion of the college population that America subsidized after World War II had different effects in the Sun Belt than in the industrial North. In Detroit and Newark, the new crop of students came from the households of second-generation factory workers, the descendants of the late-nineteenth-century immigration wave. For some of them, the increasingly visible shift to a postindustrial economy produced a renaissance on the Left: If the industrial working class was to be replaced by scientific technocrats running automated industries, as theorists like Daniel Bell and Alain Touraine predicted, then students need not endlessly wait for their parents to charge the barricades from suburbia.[48]

In the South and parts of the West, however, the accounting and marketing students were fresh off the farm, encountering the punch card without prior experience of the assembly line. And often the vehicle for their orientation to this economy was the vocational business department of the small Christian college, where "the greatest good for the greatest number" remained an article of faith. Moreover, even as Daniel Bell was forecasting "the manufacturing sector as the prototype of industrial America," retail and wholesale companies outnumbered manufacturing more than two to one.[49] An economy in which factories became marginal could either call itself a service economy, with all the humble associations of reproductive labor; or style itself an information age, stressing the mastery of symbolic analysis, the power of knowledge. Thus many heard "postindustrial" and imagined a nation of computer programmers; Wal-Mart Country more realistically thought of clerks.

Once the necessity of hiring large numbers of college graduates was clear, Sam Walton realized the importance of establishing relations with their faculty mentors. For the annual stockholders' meeting, Sam Walton brought to Northwest Arkansas influential professors from the campuses where it recruited. As honored guests at the revival-like events, the professors found themselves the objects of personal attention from one of the most charismatic representatives of entrepreneurship they were likely to meet. Here was a role model to overshadow all the inarticulate, unprepossessing businessmen they might encounter. The discerning attention paid off; faculty recommendations sent a steady stream of graduates to the company. If their students couldn't all be entrepreneurs, at least they could work for a legendary one.[50]

Wal-Mart developed extremely close ties to several such campuses in Arkansas through sustained financial support, on-campus activities, and recruiting. This growing partnership took shape in the 1970s and 1980s when new financial pressures were being placed on small colleges; a regional market was emerging for trained, white-collar workers; and political imperatives were making the campus a key terrain for national corporate activism. In the eighteenth and nineteenth centuries, more and more young people raised on farms and in small villages left for factories, squeezed out of agrarian economies by the pressures of international farm commodity markets. By contrast, those shed from America's last agricultural periphery found their way to the postindustrial factories of service and knowledge work, places like retail chain stores and the high-tech offices that ran them. These new salarymen fitted themselves for work at the undergraduate business divisions of the colleges and universities that served them. The business program at the University of the Ozarks was one representative way-station between the old economy and the new, in which the children of farmers put on ties or pumps and peopled a high-tech white-collar workplace en masse.

The University of the Ozarks in the twenty-first century is an eager and self-conscious node in Wal-Mart's network, a major beneficiary of Walton largess and in return a stalwart ally of the company. But it began life in the nineteenth century as a project of the breakaway Cumberland Presbyterians, a dissenting frontier denomination that rejected predestination and seminary training and emphasized instead the sovereignty of the individual conscience. When the Cumberlands reunited with the larger Presbyterian Church (U.S.A.) in the early twentieth century, they brought these priorities with them. The college's bulletin from 1969 proclaimed its intellectual independence within Christianity: At Ozarks, "fearless delving into every aspect of knowledge is encouraged as a God-inspired search for truth."[51]

The tiny school—then titled the College of the Ozarks—struggled through its early decades until wealthy patrons back East took an interest in the "self-help work program" that allowed poor farm kids to work off some of the expenses of a college education. Then the Second World War brought a change of fortune when the landlocked institution became a training center for the U.S. Navy. Thousands of students cycled through technical programs on its campus. After the war, the GI Bill's educational provisions produced an enrollment boom at Ozarks as at campuses around the country. On this wave of federal prosperity, Ozarks expanded its infrastructure.[52] But the pool of students eventually slackened, and by the late 1970s the college was again concerned with finding friends. Then Reagan-era changes in the federal aid structures also hurt Ozarks and similar schools.[53] Drawing the bulk of its students from the immediate region, the tiny campus had only a limited base of support, and it struggled to stay solvent through a series of financial crises. Faculty dedicated to Presbyterian education accepted salaries far below market rates, sometimes teaching without pay when cash was especially short.[54]

A survey taken in the early 1970s suggests an insular, homogeneous community somewhat isolated from the currents roiling other campuses around the world: Compared to national student norms, Ozarks students were found to be "unconcerned about nearly every aspect of society that mirrors what other studies have shown to be basically American," and in contrast cared more about religion than their peers around the country.[55] Many at Ozarks were proud to be in this world but not of it, especially as "basically American" college students made headlines protesting the war against Vietnam or taking over administrative offices.

The Division of Business Education and Economics at the University of the Ozarks was born of the postwar demand for office personnel trained in the technologies that were automating management as they had production. In the academic year 1947–48, the college found increasing interest in a business major among its booming student body, and introduced a class in the "use and practice of business machines." In the same year, students formed the college's first business club. The first six business majors graduated in 1949, all with firm offers of employment, and the new discipline was off and running.[56]

Course listings through the postwar years proliferated, with new classes in salesmanship, business psychology, office routine, and filing. A practical two-year secretarial program, outfitted with war-surplus typewriters, augmented the four-year areas of business administration, accounting, or business education.[57] By the mid-1950s, business was one of the college's largest majors, and more than a quarter of all Ozarks students could be found in at least one business course.[58] The changing regional economy intruded into the curriculum. Offerings in agricultural economics and the economic geography of the Southwest disappeared, and the department requested maps of the five continents and one showing the United States and Mexico.[59]

Despite conscientious efforts to keep the new division true to the liberal-arts mission, the demand for vocational business instruction drove the department's development. The economics major was abandoned for lack of interest, but the advanced accounting offerings increased as those students were hired and promoted rapidly upon graduation.[60] Nighttime secretarial courses were added, catering to the young wives who worked for wages or cared for small children during the day, and the faculty begged the college each year for more up-to-date machines on which to train the new white-collar work force.[61]

The novelty of this encounter between a rural population and a post-industrial work site, with its new organization of work, time, and space, comes through most clearly in the field trips that the division's students regularly took to area businesses. The idea was to familiarize them with the environment of middle management, and their responses to professional-managerial workplaces are revealing. An office management class kept a scrapbook of reports from these visits during 1972 and recorded their responses in the sometimes stilted office idiom they were acquiring.

The students lavished a good deal of attention in their reports on technology, since for many it would have been their first exposure to computerized telecommunications. Stops in data-processing departments, communications departments, and punch-card operations at automated factories consumed much of the visits, for the students were as eager to see the new machines in action as the businesses were to show them off. At a bank, reported one business student, "If a man needed any information about a loan, he would punch the number of the loan in the computer and all of the information would be printed on a screen. If he needed a copy of this he would press another button and it would print out on paper."[62] Another student was captivated by the vast amounts of information the Arkansas Highway Department was able to capture on microfilm, which allowed the managers to "make a decision in seconds over the phone."[63] On a trip to the *Arkansas Gazette,* the teletype machines "seemed constantly busy although no one was in the room most of the time."[64] At Arkansas Best Corporation, one young Ozarker was struck by the elaborate communications office. "To hold a job in this department," she concluded, "was a note of prestige."[65]

The prestige factor did not escape more pointed comment from these new aspirants to middle-class job categories. Compared to more familiar workplaces, the expanding offices, after all, came with the trappings of professional status. The district office of the Western Arkansas Telephone Company excited admiration in one student, who noted that the "appropriate color schemes between the walls, carpet, and pictures were very impressing to the visitor." A bank executive's office, she reported, was decorated with a colonial theme.[66] The student assigned to reflect on the Arkansas Best Corporation recapped that visit in loving detail:

> There was nothing lacking for a perfect atmosphere throughout the whole building. The general office was very quiet and pleasant . . . The color scheme was pastel yellow with accents of pastel greens . . . There were a number of live plants [and] floor-length windows with a view of a fenced-in yard . . . I could not believe the building could get any more beautiful, but the executive offices were unreal . . . The board room was like a dining room you would find in a mansion.[67]

This was the world they were invited to join, and unlike the California techies' rejection of staid office culture, the Arkansans saw much to admire. Privacy, courtesy, tasteful decor, the power of high technology at your fingertips, a cubicle with a view—these were not dark satanic mills for which they were leaving the farm.

Meanwhile, the business club that had formed immediately after the war grew into an affiliate of a national business students' fraternity, Phi Beta Lambda (PBL).[68] The University of the Ozarks in Clarksville quickly became a powerhouse in the Arkansas PBL scene, routinely sweeping state-level competitions against bigger schools and winning state office for its members. Under the business department's early leadership, moreover, the student organization incorporated as PBL Enterprises, Inc., in 1972, and leased out the operations of the college's bookstore, snack bar, and post office as a source of income for the students.[69] This practical motivation could claim a proud lineage in Protestant higher education. For most of the twentieth century, small sectarian schools like Ozarks had searched valiantly for a way to fund their students with on-campus enterprises, from farms to laundries to the occasional ill-conceived pyramid sales scheme. In the absence of ample endowments, catastrophic debt stalked the struggling private institutions through mid-century. Increasingly, they turned to new patrons in the rising Sun Belt service sector.

At the University of the Ozarks, this move was symbolic of a larger change transforming the business department from a practical mission of training secretaries and accountants to more exalted realms of marketing and finance. Throughout the 1970s and early 1980s, this reorientation was evident both in the classes and in the extracurricular business clubs. Practical familiarity with mimeographs and teletypes could not suffice to win the Ozarkers a foothold in the cold new world of competition ushered in by the 1973 recession. Visiting speakers from the larger businesses urged their future white-collar labor pool to learn computer programming.[70] The students in turn evangelized for the automated office with great success. Annual "Office Machines Workshops" introduced the local public to the latest on-the-job technology, from calculators and electric typewriters to microcomputers. The response was "overwhelming." Visiting students from a high school were inspired to launch a fundraising campaign to buy their own photocopier. One student asked permission to return for a second day on "those newfangled machines." By 1985, the product expo had updated its name to "Technology Fair" and was pulling in more than 400 people.[71]

Along with their enthusiastic embrace of high tech, the young Ozarkers proved apt pupils of office life in their self-conscious adoption of white-collar discipline. Since "a businessman's appearance reflects his character and job performance," the students sponsored a "Dress Right Week" on campus to accustom themselves to office attire. They commented that while shedding their blue jeans was tough, the adults on campus "responded impressively to the appearance of members" in their business wear.[72] A clothier instructed them on "the correct business attire for interviews."[73] The PBL activities trained students through form as well as content, inculcating the corporate arts of meticulous documentation, enthusiastic presentation, and "accountability." Students spent tremendous amounts of time simply recording their projects in the most attractive light, and writing thank-you letters, press releases, flow charts, follow-up impact assessment reports, and solicitations.

An earlier curricular emphasis on the economics of farming and local resource exploitation gave way to the more ephemeral market currents penetrating Johnson County. Nationally, the inflationary spiral of the 1970s and the deregulation of Wall Street won over broad new middle-class constituencies to the stock market. With inflation running higher than the interest rates on traditional passbook savings accounts, money in the bank was losing value; investment became the new savings. Using marketing techniques they borrowed from consumer retail, innovative banks sold mutual funds and brokerage services just like Procter & Gamble sold "fifteen different brands of soap flakes," as one banker put it.[74] At Ozarks, this trend prompted an urgent new interest in finance. In 1974, PBL introduced a wall chart graphing stock prices from the *Wall Street Journal.* Student enthusiasm for the new project, the club reported, ran high, "fostering academic curiosity toward the market."[75] Speakers from banks, investment houses, and savings and loans addressed the students.[76]

Likewise, the lessons of consumption became increasingly visible in the classroom and out. Marketing was established as part of the department's "corporate orientation," a subfield designation.[77] The act of consuming appeared as an explicitly productive activity in itself, indeed sometimes as a duty of American democracy. In one PBL project, for example, students made presentations in the local schools "designed to give the children a basic definition of Free Enterprise and to stress the importance of preserving the system."[78] The pupils were instructed on the virtues of choice, the dangers of socialistic government control, and the importance of training from day one for their serious role as consumers, since "economic citizenship begins at birth."[79] As inflation undermined the traditional Protestant resistance to debt, students learned the importance of establishing good credit.[80]

The Dale Carnegie tradition was also well represented at Ozarks and similar schools by Zig Ziglar, the nationally known Southern Baptist motivational speaker.[81] Visiting the campus in 1980, Ziglar, a relentlessly cheerful former cookware salesman from Yazoo City, Mississippi, urged an attentive Ozarks audience to lose their negative "stinkin' thinkin'." In its place, they should accept both Jesus and Ziglar's own philosophy that "no matter what profession a man is, his positive thinking and believing can make him successful in all aspects of life."[82]

This emphasis on inspiration did not mean the business students neglected practical action. Area businesses enlisted them to conduct door-to-door advertising, hand out flyers, and create a slideshow employee orientation program.[83] The college itself put the students' marketing acumen to work raising funds in telethons and recruiting applicants with presentations at area high schools, even awarding each student a $200 tuition discount for every freshman they successfully attracted to campus. The director of admissions, the student paper reported, felt that "this is not so much a recruitment process as it is an experience in selling, and what better thing to sell than our own college?"[84]

Increasingly, then, the content of business education—of formal, organized socialization to white-collar work—encompassed training in attitude, self-presentation, communications, and salesmanship, plus the crucial ease with technology and finance. The lessons came from their own peers in state and national business clubs; from office-equipment salesmen and haberdashers, who presented the necessary accoutrements of middle-class work; and from area business owners, managers, and secretaries, as well as from the Presbyterian college's own growing business faculty. Students enthusiastically embraced both the tuition and the tutors, preparing themselves for the increasingly competitive and unpredictable service economy.

Meanwhile, despite its relatively diversified economic base, Clarksville itself was showing signs of the recession, and students took on their host town's retail health as a cause. Ozarks students from PBL joined merchants to promote the downtown area adjacent to campus. They helped raise money to hire a consultant specializing in revitalization and decorated all the vacant storefronts downtown with posters lauding Johnson County's assets. During the Christmas shopping season one year, they organized a patriotic promotion of the city center merchants, with discounts for shoppers wearing red, white, and blue, and coordinated a flag-waving corps of business students in the Christmas parade. Even Santa added blue gloves and boots to his costume.[85] Just as in the days of the antichain store movement, the small, independent merchant had a unique claim on economic citizenship. Like the bald eagle, his endangered status imperiled more than an individual livelihood: it threatened the nation's sense of itself.

All this intense activity on behalf of small, local retailers coincided with a gradually growing relationship with Wal-Mart through the 1970s. The Cumberland Presbyterian heritage of progressivism on women's preaching and education dovetailed with Helen Walton's mainstream, pro-choice Protestantism. As a young student at a Christian college in Oklahoma, Mrs. Walton had been impressed by the traveling musical ambassadors from the College of the Ozarks. So when Arkansas State University courted her, she declined, saying that the only college board position that would interest her was at Ozarks.[86]

It did not take long for the small college to come up with such an invitation. In 1975, Mrs. Walton joined the board of trustees, and ten years later she led a $15 million capital campaign.[87] In 1998, the Walton Family Charitable Foundation gave Ozarks almost $40 million, the largest donation to a private college in the state's history.[88] Mrs. Walton followed that gift with an additional $20 million in 2006. "'The College of the Ozarks,' Mrs. Walton affirmed, 'is an outstanding, caring Christian institution.'"[89] The students joked that it should just change its name to "Wal-Mart U."

The process underway at the University of the Ozarks was part of a larger national movement in which the demands on young members of the new postindustrial work force fed a coordinated campaign to win hearts and minds to corporate understandings of life, liberty, and the pursuit of happiness. This process took place at multiple levels of American public life under the specific conditions of the economic transformations of the 1970s. By wedding business policy agendas to the seemingly neutral notion of economic education and the philosophical trappings of youth culture, some of the nation's largest corporations naturalized a radical economic vision as mass common sense. In Wal-Mart Country especially, this vision was sanctified by the Christian colleges charged with producing white collars for the Sun Belt.

William Jennings Bryan, Populist standard-bearer and later a prominent fundamental-ist adversary of the teaching of evolution, speaks to a Northwest Arkansas crowd in Springdale during a tour of the state in 1899. The Ozarks region was fertile territory for the People's Party and similar populist movements, including the organized agitation against chain stores that observers labeled "a new battle on evolution" in the early years of the Great Depression. *Courtesy Shiloh Museum of Ozark History/Washington County Historical Society Collection (S-78-103-39).*

A farm in Wal-Mart's home county, photographed in 1979. In contrast to the large-scale plantations of the South's Black Belt, the upcountry Ozarks region was home to many small, diversified family farms. During the Depression, the area saw a marked increase in subsistence agriculture, supplemented by off-farm employment in timber or food processing. This pattern would continue after World War II as Ozarkers sought security by combining their new jobs in discount retail, long-haul trucking, and tourism with part-time farming. *Morris White, photographer,* Springdale News. *Courtesy Shiloh Museum of Ozark History/*Springdale News *Collection (S-2000-133-147).*

Beaver Dam and Beaver Lake, Eureka Springs, Arkansas. The transformation of the lower Ozarks into a center for tourism and consumer industries depended on the Army Corps of Engineers' construction of half a dozen dams and artificial lakes along the White River. Beaver Lake, which covers a resort village founded by Populist advocate William "Coin" Harvey, has supplied water to Wal-Mart's Benton County since the mid-1960s. *Courtesy of the Rogers Historical Museum, Rogers, Arkansas. Negative #10773.*

The combination of service and consumer industries and farming that characterized the development of the Ozarks after World War II is evident in this 1968 photograph showing beef cattle, a chicken house, a chain motel, and a feed mill virtually on top of one another. *Charles Bickford, photographer,* Springdale News. *Courtesy Shiloh Museum of Ozark History/*Springdale News *Collection (S-2000-133-48).*

A 1964 advertisement for a revival featuring James Allen, who toured the Ozarks throughout the postwar decades as part of the religious awakening that gradually gained strength in the region. Allen also taught for many years at the Wal-Mart-connected Harding University, a Church of Christ institution in Searcy, Arkansas, which has promoted Christian free enterprise and anticommunism since the 1940s through mass media, annual Freedom Forums and Youth Forums, student organizations, and teacher training. *Ray M. Watson, photographer. Courtesy Shiloh Museum of Ozark History/Ray M. Watson Collection (S-98-88-327).*

Opening day at the newly enlarged First Baptist Church of Springdale, Arkansas, 1988. Beginning in the 1970s, the area became home to many innovative megachurches, which combined contemporary worship styles and small cell groups with new services like daycare and sports facilities. Parachurch organizations like Campus Crusade for Christ and the Navigators nourished a generation of young evangelical leaders for the growing congregations. During this period of rapid expansion for Wal-Mart and other major Ozarks corporations, the "faith at work" movement developed among the new white-collar managerial class, and congregations as well as companies embraced servant leadership. *Charles Bickford, photographer,* Springdale News. *Courtesy Shiloh Museum of Ozark History/*Springdale News *Collection (SN 2-14-1988)*

Two of the exhibits at Enterprise Square, USA, a theme park at Harding University's sister campus, Oklahoma Christian University. During the 1980s, as entrepreneurial education and procapitalist student movements became common features of Sun Belt Christian campuses, this "Disneyland of economics" sought to popularize the free-market ideals of economists like Milton Friedman through imaginative interactive exhibits that stressed consumption and choice. Above, in an exhibit entitled "The Great American Marketplace," a visitor encounters the robotic speaking heads on outsized currency. These moving facsimiles of Franklin, Jefferson, Hamilton, and Washington chatted among themselves about the interdependent roles of consumers, owners, and workers, and briefly harmonized as a barbershop quartet. Below, in the Hall of Giants, visitors activate recorded messages from "giants of free enterprise" like retailer Sebastian Kresge and inventors Alexander Graham Bell, George Washington Carver, and Thomas Edison. In 1987, the institution presented Wal-Mart founder Sam Walton with the inaugural Libertas Award for achievements in free enterprise. *Courtesy Archives Division, Beam Library, Oklahoma Christian University.*

Wal-Mart founder Sam Walton, dressed as George Washington for the 1987 Wal-Mart shareholders' meeting, Barnhill Arena, Fayetteville, Arkansas. Skits, songs, and gags were a centerpiece of store activities and company events. While female drag was one common form of diversion for managers, the corporation's leaders were also well aware of the value of Walton's fatherly aura. *Jon Ver Hoeven, photographer,* Springdale News; *courtesy Shiloh Museum of Ozarks History/*Springdale News *Collection (S-93-94-517).*

In 1989, Sam Walton's original Bentonville variety store was restored and reopened as a small museum. Tens of thousands of visitors per year have since toured this replica of the old five-and-dime, the retail model that Wal-Mart effectively replaced as it grew through county seats and then suburbs. Today more than 90 percent of Americans live within twenty miles of a Wal-Mart store. *Photograph by Sherri Sheu, 2008.*

Linking value and values, the Bentonville Wal-Mart displays the amount of money the company's operating efficiencies have saved for "families" in 2008. Identifying its core customers and employees as women responsible for provisioning families—"Wal-Mart Moms," in the language of political pollsters—the company adopted many of their social and spiritual priorities into its managerial and marketing models. In the twenty-first century, political observers identified regular Wal-Mart shopping as an even more accurate predictor of conservative voting than regular church attendance. *Photograph by Sherri Sheu, 2008.*

This Bentonville development underscores the transformation of the Ozarks into a center of Christian free enterprise. Like several others in the area, the complex combines real estate offices, shopping, and worship. *Photograph by Sherri Sheu, 2008.*

9

Evangelizing for Free Enterprise

In 1971, Pepsico CEO and Nixon intimate Donald Kendall publicly lamented the country's "economic illiteracy," which he attributed to "the Generation Gap—the chronic alienation of youth and parents, youth and religion . . . youth and free enterprise." For evidence of this dangerous ignorance and anomie, his audience need look no further than the nation's campuses. So far, he cautioned, the hostile young had vented their spleen on draft boards and their own colleges. But could anyone doubt the day was fast approaching when the longhairs would come for American businessmen?[1]

Kendall's jeremiad joined a chorus from boardrooms across the country. Organized since World War II in vehicles like the Foundation for Economic Education and the American Enterprise Association, business elites in the postwar years had transformed themselves from "economic royalists" into the guarantors of individual liberty.[2] But their hard-won cultural prestige now was threatened by a student generation in open revolt against white-collar futures. "Business is in poor repute these days," counseled a retail industry magazine, "and for some obvious reasons: anti-establishment social upheavals spurred by Vietnam, Watergate and its attendant corporate scandals, oil price inflation, consumerism and the ecology movement."[3] "The young take for granted the affluence which is the rule," groused *Newsweek,* and California governor Ronald Reagan wanted to know what gave these arrogant children the right to sneer at the very men who had brought them the world's highest standard of living.[4]

Although business's crusade against economic illiteracy in the 1970s was not entirely new, the source of hostility to business ends and means came as a shock. In the postwar years, the main ideological opposition to big business had come from unions. Now it came from students, the future managerial class itself.[5] With impressive and well-funded resolve, the activist businesses of the 1970s chose to organize, not agonize. They reached out to the students on the young people's own terms. Indeed, for the youngest cohort, help was already on the way. Jack Williams, Arizona's Republican governor, took aggressive steps to combat the menace when in 1971 he enthusiastically signed into law a bill that created a new graduation requirement for the state's high-school students: economics. The class would provide the young student "some foundation to stand on when he comes up against professors that are collectivists or Socialists," its sponsor explained. Governor Williams, a former radio broadcaster who had decreed an annual "John Birch Day" for Arizona, heartily concurred.[6]

Likewise, Arizona's state superintendent of public instruction had long been a strong advocate of Christianity in the schools. He distributed materials from the Foundation for Economic Education that had been funded by sponsors like General Motors, Dupont, and Sun Oil, but he augmented them with his own, more theologically explicit views. "Collectivism as a way of life is a manifestation of the abyss into which men sink when not motivated by the pursuit of truth and justice," the materials explained to their student audiences. To place out of the course, students could demonstrate mastery on an exam by, for example, correctly matching the phrase "Government intervention in a free enterprise system" with its appropriate predicate, "is detrimental to the free market."[7] By the end of the decade, twenty more states had followed Arizona's lead, mandating economics instruction that amounted to little more than industry propaganda. In Texas, the legislature declined to appropriate public funds for the required class, opening the door to private sponsors like the Houston Natural Gas Corporation (HNG). In 1977, the gas concern provided teaching materials to twenty-three Texas school districts and trained fifty HNG employees as "business resource persons" for the schools. As the company's public relations manager put it, "Somebody had to take the initiative."[8]

Energy concerns became committed supporters of free-enterprise education. Standard Oil/Amoco of Indiana distributed 40,000 copies of its cartoon-based economics study guide to junior-high and high-school classrooms, while Phillips Petroleum underwrote a five-part miniseries entitled *American Enterprise* narrated by *Star Trek*'s William Shatner. *American Enterprise* was broadcast by ten state educational television networks, and by the end of 1978 the company's PR firm estimated it had been seen by 5 million students.[9] These materials stressed the risky economic climate faced by small, innovative start-ups, allowing the small businessman to stand in for corporations then in the midst of a wave of mergers. Heavy-handed PR tactics pioneered in the 1940s and 1950s by firms like General Electric increasingly gave way to more sophisticated, subtler messages as communications professionals took over from in-house spokesmen. By 1981, over 100 media consultants were renting their expertise to executives. Periodic "Communicator Workshops" taught businessmen to bond with audiences and leave their plaid suits in the closet.[10] In one innovative program from the early 1970s, nine groups of high-school "Union Carbide Scholars" traveled each year to Washington to observe sessions of Congress, meet Cabinet-level officials, and run their own mock Congress. Returning to their communities—all sites of a Union Carbide plant or office—these teenaged ambassadors then spoke to school and civic groups. "When a young man or woman comes back into your office after attending the seminar and tells you Union Carbide has changed his or her life," explained a manager, "now that makes your week."[11]

The communicators' efforts to personalize multinationals likewise included a renewed emphasis on direct contact with students, preferably by allowing smaller local businesses to stand for the whole. The U.S. Chamber of Commerce introduced its "Economics for Young Americans" kits into 12,000 schools in the mid-1970s on the condition that the local businesses who picked up the tab deploy one of their number as a "resource person" to accompany the materials into the classrooms.[12] The Knoxville Chamber of Commerce, impressed by the audiovisual materials' ability to "jazz things up" in the classroom, also instituted a program in which students and teachers would "run" a business for a day and then receive a business representative as a guest teacher in exchange. The manager of a Bay Area radio station used the Chamber's materials to tutor Boy Scouts on his own time.[13] Traveling around the country to local industry gatherings and fraternal lunches, a full-time speaker for Goodyear Tire urged greater one-on-one contact: "When's the last time you talked with local educators to see what is being taught in your schools?" he demanded of his audiences, and even warned them not to neglect the home front: how about those intimate chats with your grandchildren about the role of profit? The economic recession, he pointed out, was making young audiences noticeably more receptive to these messages.[14] A bank in Chattanooga that ran ads giving "basic facts about the private enterprise system" was equally gratified by the youthful response: "The thirsty acceptance of economic truth by young people was amazing," the bank chairman explained, pointing to a wave of appreciative phone calls and letters.[15]

Surveying the millions of dollars worth of "economic education" materials pouring out of corporate PR offices in the mid-1970s, though, the neoconservative intellectual Irving Kristol frankly proclaimed most of them propaganda, and ineffective propaganda at that. Even worse, he declared, honestly improving the quality of high-school economics courses would not guarantee the probusiness outcome the sponsors sought, for knowledge of economics did not necessarily mean favorable attitudes toward *laissez-faire*. Far more influential in shaping attitudes, Kristol contended, were experience and culture, including the culture of higher education. The repeated finding that college seniors were significantly more antibusiness than freshmen did not necessarily mean that they were failing to study economics in college. Rather, their animus had "more to do with their study of literature, or anthropology, or history, or political theory—the 'value-forming' humanities."[16]

The remediation Kristol had in mind did not include reducing students' academic exposure to the liberal arts. But through changes in higher education during the 1970s, this path became a de facto solution to the business demand for college-educated yet probusiness white-collar workers. Well before the 1980s "culture wars" over the academic canon, the undergraduate business major became America's default core curriculum.[17] Between 1969 and 1979, applications to undergraduate and graduate business programs both doubled nationally. The growth in business degrees conferred outstripped the growth in bachelor's and master's degrees in general. By the end of the decade, business was the single biggest major, approaching a 2:1 ratio over its closest competitor, education. A survey of college freshmen at the end of the decade showed one in four planning to major in business. Departments strained at the seams with the unexpected influx of what they conceded were usually the weakest undergraduate students. And at Berkeley, where only a decade earlier the Free Speech Movement had denounced the commercialized "knowledge industry," business classes were so choked with students that the university had to cap enrollment.[18]

As the cold wind of recession blew across the quad, the boom in university-based vocational training for business not surprisingly came at the expense of the liberal arts, or what *U.S. News* dismissed as "personal growth." An admissions officer at George Washington University explained mid-decade that entering freshmen were looking for majors that would be "more marketable than the liberal-arts programs have been in recent years." "The sitting-under-a-tree-and-wondering-who-you-are routine has diminished," agreed a Texas business professor. "Students are looking for layers of security." A longitudinal study by the College Placement Council stressed the low salaries and long job hunts facing liberal arts graduates, and recommended that the tree-sitters at least "take sufficient electives in business-related subjects to enhance their employability."[19]

The student demand for a career-oriented degree was indeed one half of the equation, but the changes in the structure of higher education that favored a default culture of business were much more profound. The stream of federal funding that had poured into research universities after Sputnik dried up under the demands of the country's land war in Asia. Under Nixon's prodding, the National Science Foundation (NSF) instead developed research partnerships between industry and universities. During his brief presidential receivership, Gerald Ford likewise called for a greater rapprochement between business and education, and Congress responded with 10 million dollars for career education. By 1978 the NSF required universities to find corporate sponsors for joint funding.[20]

But the lion's share of this tax-supported industrial R&D flowed to high-tech labs at the more prestigious research institutions. Less favored schools, unlikely to land a particle accelerator or a robotics program, turned instead to the self-styled science of management to attract new patrons. In 1971, a Texas business professor discovered a new market for this less capital-intensive expertise when he deployed his students to help the government's Small Business Administration (SBA) salvage local enterprises after a devastating tornado. Delighted with this new constituency, the SBA began paying other universities to award academic credit for free consulting by students, and christened the fledgling programs "Small Business Institutes" (SBIs). Squeezed for operating revenue, the colleges were happy to comply. By mid-decade, the number of SBIs was approaching 400, and the SBA was learning from its encounters with campuses. Its 1973 annual meeting focused on "changing concepts of education and integrating business management training into school curricula."[21]

Then in 1975, the dean of the University of Georgia's business school teamed up with California State Polytechnic to pitch the government agency an idea for an expanded program. As a result of their advisory efforts, the SBA launched a system of Small Business Development Centers (SBDCs) that would at last "make available to small business not only the services of the School of Business, but the full capabilities of the universities."[22] In other words, the very basis for judging academic legitimacy could potentially shift from the pointy-headed intellectuals to their snubbed colleagues in marketing and management. The SBDCs, as a congressional hearing established, were not to be "just an appendage, a stepsister" to the academic mission. To the contrary: the question was whether the American university could prove itself "a manager of resources," rather than "just another resource."[23]

To launch this ambitious dream, the SBA turned to a series of campuses that were already actively pursuing closer ties to business, including the University of Georgia and Cal-Poly. Clients for the free consulting services of students and professors were not hard to come by. The altered economic geography of postindustrial America was throwing many older, smaller concerns into a tailspin, while the downsized became the "newly self-employed." Congress signaled its approval by appropriating a whopping $20 million for SBDCs in 1981, with the requirement that colleges and universities find one-to-one matching funds from other sources.[24]

The political support behind this largess had little to do with the centers' effectiveness. Reports and hearings found a spotty record and a dramatic over-reliance on undergraduates. But many constituents understood that the utility of the centers could not necessarily be measured by their economic impact alone. The end of the Bretton Woods era stranded these bewildered small businessmen as window-dressing for the "vast casino" of international financial speculation.[25] Like a failed Missouri manufacturer, many could not understand "why, in a country as great as ours, a small business should have so much trouble surviving."[26] Like the personalized outreach programs, the college-based small business centers offered the businessman to impressionable campus audiences as a victim, not a bully. As Cal-Poly's Reed Powell put it, "Young students who know of American business only through stereotypes are changing their attitudes in favor of the private enterprise system."[27] The program benefited students, a Chicago instructor argued, by "providing an outlet for their social concern and youthful enthusiasm." It encouraged a consensus among the young in support of struggling small businessmen.[28]

Compared to the atmosphere of the previous decade, campuses by the late 1970s had become friendly places for business. A Harris poll of faculty at 150 colleges found over three-quarters of them favoring more contact between academe and the corporate world, and none at all urging less. "The welcome mat is out," the poll concluded with modest understatement.[29] As the stratification of the labor market accelerated and globalized over the ensuing decades, the American university loomed as gatekeeper to the land of the saved, empowered to distribute or withhold the credentials for economic survival. Unsurprisingly, rival claimants in this deadly serious contest struggled to ensure that the yardstick for success would be marked in the units they commanded. By 1981, graduating business majors already outnumbered their classmates in all languages and literatures, the arts, philosophy, religion, the social sciences, and history combined.[30] The Reagan cuts in higher education further helped transform the unmarketable liberal arts degree into a luxury, and programs that awarded academic credit for waged work inherited the ideal of democratic access to the life of the mind. As higher education assumed the vocational functions that high schools had developed at the turn of the century, they also elaborated an ennobling mission for future marketers and accountants. That this mission served the interests of the very corporations undermining small business did not lessen the appeal of its vision to the target audiences.

The intensified focus on business at the University of the Ozarks, then, took place within this national context of business colonization of education generally, both formally in high schools and colleges and informally through the media. It promised new resources for the wary employers of college graduates. In 1973, Oklahoma Christian College (now University) had commissioned a Gallup poll on the political orientation of college students. The results confirmed their worst fears.

Asked to rank professional fields by their ethical standards, students placed businessmen near the bottom. Consumer activist Ralph Nader won the honors in individual esteem, and the United Nations in the institutional category; the Republican Party and the CIA were last. Almost half favored nationalizing the oil industry. Moreover, while one-third of freshmen in the survey identified themselves as leftists, more than half of seniors did so. It was true: higher education in itself produced anticapitalist sentiment.[31]

But Oklahoma Christian College was quick to publicize the poll's silver lining: its own students were significantly more conservative than their rowdy counterparts at Princeton. This datum suggested a way out for corporate donors still wary of the restive campuses. In 1971, shortly before his elevation to the Supreme Court, Lewis Powell had penned a furious memo to the U.S. Chamber of Commerce: What was business thinking, he demanded, to tolerate college radicalism when the graduates would go on to vent their hostility as the next generation of lawmakers and regulators?[32] Two years later the chairman of Hewlett-Packard challenged the Committee for Corporate Support of American Universities to stop providing institutions of higher education with enough financial rope to hang the donors. In the future, he suggested, corporations should target support to those schools and departments that "contribute in some specific way to our individual companies or to the general welfare of our free enterprise system."[33]

Oklahoma Christian knew just the place. In addition to the poll, a 1976 study found that rural, male Protestants working more than thirty hours a week and studying business, math, or engineering were the most likely to be in favor of free enterprise. The most negative reactions, conversely, came from the nonreligious.[34] In Wal-Mart's backyard, for example, the Retail Clerks' union had begun noticing a disturbing trend among the students at Springfield's many Christian colleges. As union contracts came up for negotiation and renewal at groceries and variety stores, the employers would begin systematically packing the bargaining units with part-time students, diluting the more permanent, full-time workforce and with it, the commitment to pensions, vacations, and health provisions represented by the union. "I spent some time at the Bible College trying to talk with the students who are employed in the store," a union organizer reported in 1966, "but met with no success."[35] A few years later, with the students' antilabor attitude ramping up, the

Springfield-area local of the Retail Clerks passed a resolution to discourage labor organizations from recruiting at Baptist Bible College.[36] At the local's urging, the Springfield Labor Council decided to address the problem with the college's administration, but with no appreciable results.[37]

It was among these small-town Protestant students that Christian free enterprise took root with particular success. Expanding access to higher education had reached the children of unionized factory workers at places like Kent State, but at the same time small, Christian colleges drew students from rural and small-town settings. These colleges often had a long tradition of on-campus enterprises at which farmers' children could work their way through a degree in Bible studies or a teaching certificate. Students saw firsthand evidence in the Sun Belt that economic salvation, like its spiritual counterpart, was a matter best addressed at the level of the individual conscience—it wasn't Texas that was rusting, after all. The bureaucratic corporations that dominated industrial landscapes in the North were the entrepreneurial success stories of another century. The new ones building shopping centers and fast-food outlets in the South and West were the expressions of living individuals—small-town boys made good. The economic vision that defined insecurity as opportunity sounded more plausible with these object lessons in sight, and business clubs and departments served their Christian campuses by preparing country kids for Dallas's gleaming new high-rises. This tutelage eased their introduction to middle-class office culture even as secretaries and accountants actually became the new American working class.

The march of the business major, then, addressed antibusiness sentiment by incorporating much of the new student body into vocational training rather than the "values-forming" liberal arts curriculum. Merely by establishing themselves as the default perspective of educated America, business and marketing scored an enormous intellectual victory largely on the public tab. Thus Wal-Mart's task of making a managerial class with a corporate orientation dovetailed with significant developments at the national level. The creative agents of Bentonville first developed strategies for adapting much local talent to the conditions of the high-tech bureaucratic office, with particular emphasis on communications. Then, with their industry and the burgeoning Sun Belt service sector itself, Wal-Mart turned to the regional colleges and universities that now specialized in mass-producing white-collar employees to specification. On these second- and third-tier campuses, the employers' requirements for their new indoor workforce met the colleges' need for revenue and market share. The nonmarket values of Christian education in particular cultivated the crucial "moral sentiments," as Adam Smith would have it, the principles that the market itself could not produce but that it consumed in abundance.

Throughout the later 1970s and the 1980s, the growing relationship between their college and Wal-Mart gradually produced effects on the ground for the business students at the University of the Ozarks. For example, Wal-Mart's executives visited the campus to lecture on topics such as entrepreneurship and labor harmony.[38] The Ozarks Phi Beta Lambda (PBL) organization teamed up with the Bentonville headquarters to test market a toy the students had contracted to distribute.[39] Under a "co-operative education" model of vocational training, a PBL member earned academic credit for assistant-managing Clarksville's own Wal-Mart store.[40] "I don't think I can find words to tell you how much the Waltons' contributions have meant to the University of the Ozarks," said the school's vice president in 1992.[41] In 1983 Mrs. Walton herself, in her capacity as a trustee, helped kick off the opening venture of the business division's foray into entrepreneurial education, the first in an annual series titled Free Enterprise Symposia. "The main objective of this symposium," explained the student paper, "is to acquaint the students of our college community with the merits of the free enterprise system."[42]

The symposia were part of a more comprehensive re-orientation by the business department and the college at large. In 1977, when the national PBL launched a promotional campaign on behalf of free enterprise, the Ozarks chapter had thrown itself into the activities with its usual enthusiasm. They produced a billboard—"Supporting Our Heritage of Free Enterprise"—that found a home in thirty-five locations from Clarksville to Tulsa.[43] Flyers on the subject went out in the mail with local bank statements.[44]

One Thursday afternoon in the spring of 1985, the business faculty gathered at the home of the departmental chair at a nearby lake for a planning retreat.[45] They reported back to the college's president their recommendations for overhauling the department. In the cover letter to their report the chairman wrote that while the top concern was academic quality, a close second was "a program that the Administration and the business faculty can market to the business community in order to gain financial support and human resource involvement for the College."[46] Students appeared in the document as "target markets," and the report asserted that "the ideals of capitalism and personal freedom should be stressed."[47] Their objectives in the proposed changes, they asserted, should first and foremost adhere to the principles of Christian liberal arts education. They affirmed the freedom of the faculty to "transmit personal philosophies and business ethics" and "to personally guide the student," priorities which spoke to their sense of mission. In contrast to the efficiency of "state-supported institutions," Ozarks could offer "character development," "individualized attention," and "an appreciation for the arts." The plan of study they had in mind would involve an extraordinary commitment of time and care to the students, making their work as much a ministry as a job.[48]

Their biggest innovation that day on the lake was to lay the groundwork for a new concentration in entrepreneurship. Their holistic sense of the entrepreneurial function was evident in the academic requirements for the new major. It would include a course in the Old or New Testament; one in American national government; and one in ethics, as well as electives from the liberal arts. The core of the new program, however, would be the business division's own new offerings: an introduction to "innovative behavior, the successful entrepreneur's attitude, the resources needed for a small business, the risks and rewards of business" and "a comparative study of capitalism to other economic systems—particularly socialism/marxism. Emphasis on the advantages of free enterprise."[49]

This new focus connected tiny Ozarks to a regional movement with national and even international implications. From the early 1970s to the early 1980s, the number of colleges and universities offering courses in entrepreneurship and small business administration increased from eight to almost two hundred.[50] To shape their new major, Ozarks looked to Wichita State University, where a thriving entrepreneurship program had been centralizing information from similar initiatives all over the country.[51] One Saturday in 1977, Fran Jabara, a veteran business professor at Wichita State University, was enlivening his morning workout on a stationary bicycle by watching cartoons on TV. A stock character appeared in the midst of one animated sequence: out of a shiny limousine stepped a "high-powered, manipulating, uncaring businessman." The professor's interest was caught: no wonder people had such a negative impression of businessmen, if all they saw were cartoonish CEOs of megacorporations. In that moment, Jabara decided it was high time to change the public image of businesspeople. "'We spend all of our time talking to our students about becoming president of a major corporation,'" he explained, "'and we devote almost no time to thinking about the entrepreneurial process.'"[52]

Conceiving of entrepreneurship as a set of character traits rather than a function of an economic structure, the new field zeroed in on "the Entrepreneur as an Individual," in the words of a course at Georgia State.[53] The University of North Carolina treated "the psychology of the entrepreneur," while New Mexico Highlands University instructed students on "Entrepreneurs: care and feeding."[54] "The entrepreneur, through the process of innovation, becomes the principal actor in the drama of economic growth," explained the Chair of Private Enterprise at the Southern Baptists' Baylor University.[55] Southern Methodist University in Dallas elaborated: "The life of an entrepreneur is exciting, active, challenging and rewarding . . . The entrepreneur is the captain of the ship, guiding all facets of business while maintaining speed and direction."[56]

Here lay one answer to the postwar organization man, that other-directed drone who looked disturbingly like his Soviet counterpart. Texts assigned in the new classes extolled the entrepreneur as a rare and special type, not content with the ordinary round of bureaucracy in corporate life. In this guise, the entrepreneur inherited the mantle of Jeffersonian virtue from the independent farmers and the Populist rebellion—a hero for the age of the mass office, a foil to sissified bureaucrats and the distant Shylocks of Wall Street. At the same time, these young Turks embodied the countercultural values enshrined by the generation of '68: distrust of large-scale hierarchies, creative nonconformity, moral outrage on behalf of the underdog, even antimaterialism, since "their status needs are determined by achievements rather than clothes, office décor, or the automobiles they drive."[57]

But underneath these bold paeans ran the instructors' concern that their role models failed to live up to the virile image. Dull, uninspired visiting speakers often seemed ridiculously at odds with the entrepreneurial hero, and the risk-taking student was rarer still. The lack of "student aggressiveness," wrote a Tulane professor, had not yet been solved in his entrepreneurial classes. He had begun confident that students would demonstrate "boldness and breadth of vision," but was forced to conclude he had been too optimistic. At UCLA, even five years out from the graduate course, fewer than 10 percent of the alumni had actually started a business. Most, the professor noted, realized by the end of one semester that "being an entrepreneur IS NOT for them."[58] One professor found a pedagogical silver lining to the parade of incompetence represented by the visiting practitioners of capitalism: his students, he reported, often concluded that "'If that dumb bastard can make it, so can I.'"[59]

Most entrepreneurship students eagerly sought work in the secure, salaried jobs of large corporations, while others went into the same small family businesses they would have inherited anyway. In the face of this failure, many professors philosophically changed their objectives. They would try instead to teach their students to evaluate risky ventures cautiously, and train them to perform entrepreneurially within bureaucratic companies—"intrapreneurship," as Gifford Pinchot christened it in 1985.[60] Above all, they would strive to equip their students for the uncertainties that increasingly came along with the salaries. As one of their favorite textbooks had it, what was needed was an action plan for "the employed, the unemployed, and the self-employed"—after all, you never knew when or how you might change categories.[61]

If the professors and their students were having second thoughts about an entrepreneurial future, however, their institutions could not afford to acknowledge them, for these courses were proving tremendously valuable for the universities' public relations. In earlier decades, universities like Columbia and Harvard had enthusiastically released undergraduates from class to serve as strike-breakers for the Ivy League's corporate donors. The network of nonelite inland schools found less bloody routes to their funders' hearts.[62] At Wichita State, for example, Professor Jabara's success with his small-business courses convinced the university of the project's potential. An entrepreneurship major followed, and ultimately a concentration within the graduate degree. In 1986, the school's Center for Entrepreneurship acquired an historic monument to entrepreneurial innovation when it moved the original Pizza Hut restaurant to its campus and reconstructed it brick by brick.

The humble structure had housed the business in 1958, when a pair of Wichita State students turned $600 borrowed from their parents and a cook trained by the U.S. Air Force into the anchor of an international fast-food chain. Reconstructed, the landmark hut served as entrepreneurship headquarters on campus.[63]

Wichita State's center also ran the Association of College Entrepreneurs (ACE), a clearinghouse on extracurricular campus organizations devoted to the topic. Throughout the mid-1980s, ACE organized national conventions for such clubs and published a newsletter, making Jabara one of the more influential evangelists for the cause of entrepreneurial training within academe. Moreover, his own program modeled the potential payoffs to schools: "Wichita State (Fran Jabara) has been doing an outstanding job of raising private financing from a number of individual sources," one reporter concluded in a state-of-the-field survey in 1985.[64] This was not a minor concern. The demographic trough in the college-aged cohort, spiraling operating costs, and declining federal support for higher education led universities up and down the academic food chain to pursue alternative sources of funding.[65] Just as these factors pushed the University of the Ozarks into a closer embrace of Wal-Mart and drove Wichita State to laud Pizza Hut, the national academic hunger for patronage gave birth to an entire subfield of teaching and research, and convinced a new waged working class to identify with capital rather than labor.

Despite its ideological disdain for government, higher education's affiliation with business was a product of federal intervention. In the 1970s, the National Science Foundation channeled federal money to "innovation centers" intended to spur commercialization of technological and engineering inventions at three selected universities: the Massachusetts Institute of Technology (MIT), Carnegie Mellon, and the University of Oregon. This last was subsequently transferred to Baylor, the flagship Southern Baptist university in Waco, Texas. In 1977, the University of Utah joined them and then privatized its innovation center in 1980 as a for-profit venture when the grant ran out.[66] Karl Vesper, a University of Washington engineering and business professor, undertook in the late 1960s to track the development of the new academic field by sending out open-ended surveys to business and engineering faculty. From his own position straddling both departments, Vesper presumably expected to see entrepreneurship develop out of the marriage of business practices to technological innovation, as indeed the federal funders intended and as happened around elite schools like Stanford and MIT. But nationally it was overwhelmingly business departments rather than the schools of engineering that took up the challenge.

It was a two-way street. Corporate expenditures within these college business departments, especially among particular student populations, could potentially win friends and influence people. From the colleges' perspective, the new entrepreneurship programs offered a practical route to much-needed revenue. Costs for higher education began tacking up sharply in the late 1960s, and student fees and tuition showed increases of over 15 percent in just a few years. Moreover, revisions to the tax code in 1969 reduced the attractiveness of donations to foundations—a major blow when 85 percent of private donations came from individuals and philanthropic organizations, not corporations.[67] The burden naturally fell most heavily on those smaller schools without deep-pocketed alumni or the facilities for lucrative research. *Fortune* magazine even questioned their prospects for survival.[68] Oklahoma Christian College (later University) made national headlines when in the mid-1960s it introduced automated teaching to reduce faculty payroll. Rather than actual classes, Oklahoma Christian put teachers on tape and placed students in individual carrels with headphones. "The lectures were illustrated with voices of great speakers," explained a brochure, "and the progression of ideas was not interrupted by student digression or questions." The college boasted that the new system resulted in a 60 percent increase in instructor efficiency, and university representatives from Florida to California eagerly attended conference presentations on the technique.[69]

Cost-cutting alone could not save the smaller, less prestigious schools from their money woes. The entrepreneurial education programs and centers opened new doors. In Karl Vesper's 1987 survey that identified seventy such programs, more than half voluntarily reported that entrepreneurship education had generated funds for the institution or the faculty. Many of the most elaborate programs and centers were at smaller and middle-sized campuses, the survey reported. "These schools appear to view entrepreneurship as an underserved segment of the market for educational services and they pursue this area quite aggressively."[70] The marketplace of funders and paying customers shaped the new subfield more decisively than the marketplace of ideas.

Between the celebration of the pioneering entrepreneur and the realities of corporate backing, however, lay the danger that a contradiction might be laid bare. An entrepreneurial firm must grow or die. If it died, it could hardly serve as an inspiration for students, much less as a source of support. But if it grew, in short order it became a bureaucratic corporate organization in its own right and lost its entrepreneurial virtue. Neither outcome served the university well as a cultural symbol. Wichita State's Center for Entrepreneurship was intended to counteract the image of the bureaucratic captain of industry, yet the founders of Pizza Hut were precisely that by the mid-1980s. The contrast only remained plausible because with the Sun Belt's postwar boom, the arc of the entrepreneurial corporations' growth to oligopoly actually corresponded to the life cycles of the legends who founded them. The rebuilt restaurant at Wichita and Bentonville's downtown museum in the original Walton five-and-dime store provided a visible lesson in competitive dynamism. Like the picture of Dorian Gray, they stayed forever young and unblemished, even as the transnational corporations themselves burgeoned.

In these university programs that encouraged free enterprise, as in the wider movement against "economic illiteracy," an immense burden of cultural work was relegated to a mythical figure christened "the Entrepreneur." The Entrepreneur was the presumed lineal descendant of the independent small businessman—the hero of the antichain fight. His importance to Dow Chemical and Sun Oil needs little explanation. The University of the Ozarks and similar schools thus fit into a national context of entrepreneurial education that took off as the postwar economic landscape ruptured. Large, stable manufacturing concerns gave way to the shifting sands of service and finance. Contracts and clear career paths lost ground to casual, flexible, and contingent employment, as well as automation and off-shoring. Deregulation under both Carter and Reagan lowered entry barriers to some industries at the same time that it drove many of the established players into bankruptcy. In this period of flux, the ability to carve out a personal economic niche was both more possible and more urgent.

The in-class portions of the new entrepreneurship studies therefore ranged from earnest attempts at scientific legitimation to pragmatic tutelage for an uncertain future to unvarnished political advocacy in pursuit of patronage. The same could not be said of the various campus centers that mushroomed alongside them as straightforward PR tools in the colleges' struggle to win private backing. Although a 1987 survey found that fully thirty-six schools had established some type of center for entrepreneurship or small business development, only five of these centers conducted scholarly research of any kind.[71] Free enterprise centers, programs, and even endowed chairs made inroads primarily at smaller, less selective schools, where the explicit advocacy did not conspicuously offend academic values.[72]

Their adoption was self-consciously strategic, a marriage of convenience more than a love match. Small Protestant colleges and big business were not traditional allies. At least initially, their broader faculty constituency was rarely independently motivated by the cause so much as alive to the practical benefits, generally in favor of free-market economics—they taught business, after all—and alert to the interesting teaching and research options offered by the new subfield. Forging the alloy of Christian free enterprise required tremendous effort and resources, and the zeal of one or two ideologically committed proponents like Fran Jabara. Once the genie was out of the bottle, however, the equation shifted. The new centers and majors drew faculty as well as students with those interests, and the corporate sponsors' influence became ubiquitous.[73] The business major itself eclipsed the liberal arts that the colleges had once offered the faithful, and a powerful political alliance was born of unlikely lineage.

John Brown University (JBU; formerly John E. Brown College), an interdenominational evangelical school in Wal-Mart's home county, followed a similar path as the University of the Ozarks and many other small schools that ultimately staffed the Sun Belt white-collar workforce. Founded in a cornfield in 1919 by an itinerant evangelist, John Brown gradually transformed itself from a vocational institution for the children of poor farmers to a respected trainer of Christian businessmen and missionaries. John Brown University initially tried to offer students the means for funding their degrees right on campus, in carpentry or machine shops. But the books never balanced, and the blue-collar training became a net drain on resources.[74] The college found sources of income in subsequent decades with commercial enterprises like radio stations and private schools in California for the Dust Bowl's more prosperous descendants. Throughout the school's first three decades, too, John Brown could claim a powerful friend in his convert Jesse H. Jones, Franklin Delano Roosevelt's secretary of commerce and the formidable head of the Reconstruction Finance Corporation. Jones's influence kept the school in touch with potential donors.[75]

In the 1950s, as demand for white-collar labor boomed, John Brown University's president charged the school with expanding its vision of vocational training. Rather than milking the university's dairy cows or repairing automobiles, the students increasingly fulfilled the vocational requirements with "practicums" in churches, radio stations, and local businesses. The more sophisticated career orientation dovetailed with an explicit emphasis on "Christian Americanism" and a growing integration into the national evangelical movement. When rebellions erupted on high-profile campuses in the 1960s and early 1970s, JBU's clean-cut musical group Sound Generation toured wholesome Sun Belt venues like Disneyland and *Hee Haw* to proclaim that, through God's blessing, the United States was "still the greatest nation on the face of the earth." The evangelical college launched an annual week-long "Christian American Heritage Seminar" that showcased Sun Belt businessmen warning of the need to fight communism and protect free enterprise. Students needed little prodding: a 1968 poll showed their overwhelming backing for Nixon's presidential bid, and the student senate sent him a "vote of confidence" for expanding the war into Cambodia the following year. Editorials in the campus paper charged war protesters with treason and hippies with Satanism.[76]

With further support from Southwestern oilmen, JBU's finances had gradually stabilized by the 1980s, but it was the Wal-Mart connection that proved most mutually beneficial. Its proximity to Wal-Mart headquarters had suggested a potentially happy pairing. Executive Vice President Don Soderquist spoke at JBU's American Heritage Week in 1981, and the college made overtures by honoring Sam Walton at its 1983 Free Enterprise Week. The relationship flourished through the 1980s and 1990s. The Walton Lifetime Health Complex commemorates the $1 million John Brown University annually receives in student scholarships from the Walton Family Foundation.[77] Likewise, Soderquist expanded his relationship with the college, chairing the college's board of trustees in the 1980s and endowing a Soderquist Family Fund for Student Missions.[78]

In 1998 JBU dedicated the for-profit Soderquist Center for Business Leadership and Ethics, an institute for Christian management training that counts among its customers Wal-Mart, Tyson Chicken, and Little Debbie. In 2005, the Soderquist Center hosted a CEO Summit in partnership with the national evangelical men's organization Promise Keepers.[79] Soderquist, the center's patron and Executive in Residence, served at Wal-Mart for over twenty years, finishing as senior vice chairman. Known as a "keeper of the culture" after the death of Sam Walton in 1992, Soderquist published *The Wal-Mart Way* with a Christian publishing house in Nashville.[80]

Within Wal-Mart's network of academic ties, the process of wedding Christian vocational education to corporate concerns was most dramatically exemplified by Harding College (now Harding University) in Searcy, Arkansas. Sam Walton first made contact with Harding in the 1970s through Bill Cox, alumnus of the school's Bible department and an early pupil of Harding's unique American Studies program. Cox had gone on to an MBA at Southern Methodist University in Dallas, and after some years in the private sector returned to Harding as an administrator. He stumped Arkansas energetically for business support of the college and ran a series of promotional trips to cities like Dallas, Chicago, and his native New Orleans. As a concurrent sideline, Cox ran management seminars around the country, and at one of these he met Sam Walton.[81]

The encounter resulted in regular invitations for Cox to speak at Wal-Mart's Saturday morning management meetings, and reciprocal ones for Walton and other Wal-Mart executives to address the small Church of Christ college in the Ozark foothills of central Arkansas.[82] By 1992 Sam Walton and Jack Stephens—investment banker to Wal-Mart and to other major Ozarks firms—chaired the advisory board of Harding's American Studies program.[83] The president of Wal-Mart Realty also served on the board, alongside his fellow Ozark native and Stephens client, the president of Tyson Foods.[84] The relationship between Harding and Wal-Mart was solidified with the 1978 construction of an automated distribution center in Searcy on land sold to the company by the college.

For many decades following America's entry into World War II, Harding enjoyed an unusual level of fame for a college its size. Founded in 1924 out of the Bible school tradition, Harding College and its associated projects served during the Cold War as the "'largest producer of radical right propaganda in the country,'" according to the Anti-Defamation League of B'nai B'rith.[85] *Newsweek* concurred: "What M.I.T. is to engineering and Harvard is to law, Harding is to the far right . . . the academic capital of ultra-conservatism."[86] The *New York Times* called Harding in the early 1960s "perhaps the most prolific center of aggressive anti-communist propaganda in the United States."[87] Yet its roots were in a pacifist, antifundamentalist, world-rejecting apocalyptic tradition, and its transformation hardly a foregone conclusion.[88]

Harding's odyssey from struggling Bible college to national standard-bearer for conservative free enterprise began with the accession to the college presidency of George S. Benson in 1936. Though Benson was Sam Walton's senior by two decades, the two men's early years actually ran on parallel tracks. Like the Waltons, the Scotch-Irish Bensons acquired their initial capital stake in the free-enterprise system through the federal giveaway of Indian land in what is now the state of Oklahoma. Like his more famous friend, Benson grew up near Kingfisher and then moved to Helen Walton's hometown of Claremore to attend a federally funded boarding high school intended for the Indians who had lost out in the land transfer. Benson, like Walton, was among the small minority of American men with the resources for higher education prior to the G.I. Bill. This background, Benson later reminisced, demonstrated that "'anybody could get an education who wanted to work hard'" and, by extension, "'probably most any other goal could likewise be attained through perseverance and hard work.'"[89]

In 1925, while Sam Walton was still in knee-pants, George Benson and his new wife departed for China, the most storied mission field in Protestant evangelism. They interpreted the anticolonial sentiment they encountered there as the product of Communist indoctrination, and, unable to make inroads with ordinary working Chinese, concentrated on evangelizing elites. The government, Benson recalled in disgust, could not protect the missionaries, and even "Chinese businessmen lived in constant fear of being captured and held for ransom."[90] Benson returned to the United States with a new appreciation for his home country and undertook to train missionaries at Harding College.[91] When the institution's presidency was offered to him in the midst of the Depression, he put the fundraising experience he had learned in mission work at the disposal of the seriously indebted, struggling little campus.

Benson's new cause quickly came to the attention of Clinton Davidson, a co-religionist from Kentucky who made a fortune selling life insurance to wealthy New Yorkers. Inspired by his reading of the Bible as a financial manual, Davidson went on to plan the ultimate disposition of estates totaling over 3 billion dollars. Through his connections to Davidson's Estate Planning Corporation, Benson began "selling" Harding to men like Lammot du Pont and Alfred Sloan as a good buy for their potential donations.[92] As a way of cultivating business support, he started inviting executives to campus as speakers.

In 1941, lobbyist friends of Davidson's arranged for George Benson to testify before the House Ways and Means Committee, then weighing proposed tax increases as defense expenses loomed. Although the deficit was a clear object of concern, in three weeks of hearings members of Congress could find little support for cutting funding to the witnesses' own programs. Benson, in contrast, lit into the inflationary dangers of New Deal programs like the Civilian Conservation Corps, the National Youth Administration, and soil conservation. This unusual witness held up as exemplars thrifty Arkansas and his own plucky college, which had recently retired its crippling mortgage.

The reaction was electric. The *New York Times* reprinted the entire speech on the editorial page. The *Chicago Journal of Commerce* distributed 2 million reprints. Hundreds of speaking invitations flooded into Searcy, and Benson hit the roads and airwaves with his polished speech, "America at the Crossroads." Back in Washington to urge the dissolution of the National Youth Administration the following year—now with the war expenses a reality—Benson again made the front page when twenty Harding students wrote the White House that they would like to return their Youth Administration work-study allowances, but only if the funds would go to the military. The resulting flap kept the issue alive for months, and though Benson was denounced by some as a publicity hound, the offending New Deal programs were abolished in 1943.

There was no stopping the winning formula of corporate support, student involvement, and savvy marketing. Benson's syndicated column "Looking Ahead," begun in the wake of his testimony, was by the mid-1960s appearing in over 3,500 periodicals. Harding bought a radio station in Memphis as a revenue-generating concern, and Benson's own "Land of the Free" radio show was carried by stations in Little Rock and Memphis. By 1951 it was reaching a radio audience of 20 million people each week. The college produced and sold kits "designed to help individuals speak before groups to spread the gospel of Americanism."[93]

In the early 1950s, Benson tacked to the winds of corporate antilabor sentiment. He established annual Freedom Forums at Harding to bring prominent antilabor and then anticommunist speakers together for student audiences. The college housed the National Education Program (NEP), which produced and distributed anticommunist material to the U.S. armed forces, public schools, colleges and universities, local Chambers of Commerce, and American Legion chapters.[94] Hollywood's Metro-Goldwyn-Mayer voluntarily distributed the NEP's free-enterprise films in its 5,000 theaters around the country, claiming they were "the most popular short subjects ever distributed by MGM." U.S. Steel inserted 13,500 copies of reprinted Benson lectures into its employees' pay envelopes in a single year. A version of his syndicated column aimed at industrial union members ran in 1,500 newsletters and trade organs.[95] Industry was not shy with its gratitude. On average Benson's activities pulled in $1 million annually from donors like Gulf Oil; defense contractor Boeing Aircraft gave the program $1 billion.[96] In a 1961 report that censured a national campaign of "rabid, bigoted, one-sided" presentations illegally incorporating active-duty military officers to redbait the federal government, Secretary of Defense Robert McNamara singled out Benson for criticism along with professional anticommunists like Billy James Hargis, the fundamentalist radio preacher who memorably libeled the National Council of Churches as a communist front, and Fred Schwarz, founder of the Christian Anti-Communist Crusade and an early promoter of Ronald Reagan.[97] The *Journal of Higher Education* observed disapprovingly in 1967 that Harding served as "a kind of war college ... dedicated to the teaching of conservatism."[98] But in Searcy this was now a compliment.

The NEP spawned Harding's American Studies program, with over half a million dollars in operating funding for the first five years. This allowed the college at large to tap into the business network the NEP had already created for funding its physical plant. American Studies led weeklong citizenship training seminars for high-school students every summer, with speakers that included South Vietnamese refugees, missionaries, and former hostages. The Harding seminars grew to 350 students and were duplicated by the NEP in fifteen other locations around the country. In 1954, the campus also launched summer classes under the heading "American Studies for Teachers," featuring courses on topics such as "The Christian Constitution."[99]

At Harding, the free enterprise center established in the 1970s had grown out of decades of missionary anticommunism in a feedback loop with American business's PR needs. The American Studies department and the NEP—technically a separate entity, in the interests of Harding's accreditation—continued to devote themselves to promoting free-market economics as a sacred political cause. The NEP, for example, helped publicize a Young Americas Foundation study blaming the Reagan recession on pervasive Keynesianism in college economics textbooks.[100] American Studies regularly hosted supporters of the Austrian school of hard-right economics from the Mont Pelerin Society and its American offshoot, the Foundation for Economic Education. The college celebrated the nation's bicentennial with a program honoring the concurrent two hundredth anniversary of the publication of *The Wealth of Nations.*[101]

In 1979, Harding's business department took the additional step of establishing the Belden Center for Private Enterprise Education, named in honor of an independent Arkansas manufacturer. Its activities included the publication of an annual almanac of "mankind's onward march through the centuries to economic freedom and greater material blessings" and a quarterly pamphlet, *The Entrepreneur,* written entirely by the center's director and dedicated to articles on "capitalism, personified so well by Wal-Mart."[102] The Private Enterprise Center supported the student "Capitalism Corps" and the academic business club. In 1982 Harding also signed onto the federal subsidy available through the Small Business Institutes, creating a Center for Management Excellence to provide free consulting services to local businesses.[103]

George Benson's most ambitious vision for a free-enterprise center came to fruition at Harding's sister campus, Oklahoma Christian University. Beginning in 1957, Benson had served as the head of Oklahoma

Christian for ten years, most of that time simultaneously running Harding and commuting between the two campuses in a private plane. He immediately instituted the American Citizenship Training Center, which, like the National Education Program, conducted revenue-generating Freedom Forums and summer Youth Forums. At Oklahoma Christian, these programs ultimately gave birth to Enterprise Square USA, a theme park of free-market capitalism. At 60,000 square feet, the vast facility was, in the words of its own publicity, "the nation's only major visitor attraction designed to interpret the American Free Enterprise System." The product of forty years of experimentation in capitalist outreach, Enterprise Square aimed to "simplify economics and the free-market system and to provide a hands-on, fun experience for people of all ages as they learn about free enterprise and the role it has played in making the United States the greatest and most profitable of all nations."[104]

After publicizing the results of the Gallup poll that showed Christian students to be more reliably in favor of free enterprise than their secular peers, the college determined that previous efforts at economic education flopped because of their dull format and failure to connect to consumption, the aspect of economics most familiar to people's daily experience. The solution was arrived at in consultation with advertising executives, public relations professionals, television producers, and theme park designers: To "blend education and entertainment," updating the old Freedom Forums with "graphics, photography, animation, and computers."[105] "It has some traits of a museum, and some traits of an amusement park," explained its technical director.[106]

The challenge of executing this bold vision fell to Pepperdine graduate Bob Rowland, then in charge of Oklahoma Christian's American Citizenship Training Center. "I was a Dust Bowl Okie kid," Rowland characterized himself proudly, "when my family moved west to California. Steinbeck wrote about diehards like us." Rowland's idea was to take George Benson's Americanism seminars to a new scale. "Instead of reaching out to 5,000 people a year through structured programs," he explained, "why not have 250,000 people a year come to OCC voluntarily, sponsor themselves and get the same message in dramatic form?"[107] The fundraising committee for this mammoth undertaking was headed by William F. Martin, retired president of Phillips Petroleum

Company. It included the president of Halliburton, the chairman of Getty Oil, the CEO of Kerr-McGee, a Pew heir of Dallas's Sun Oil Company, and the Am-Way president, Rich DeVos.[108] Intellectual rigor was guaranteed by the chief economist from the American Enterprise Institute, a representative of the Hoover Institute, an Oklahoma State economist, and the chairman of Oklahoma Christian's business department, a real-estate dealer and former accountant.[109] Creative veterans of Disney, *Sesame Street, Mr. Rogers' Neighborhood,* and *The Muppet Show* provided the technical magic, with skills honed in producing in-house films and slide shows for companies like RCA, Union Carbide, and IBM.[110]

To a backdrop of fireworks and flags, the 1980 ground-breaking ceremony for Enterprise Square USA placed the theme park firmly in its Cold War context. Nearby Tinker Air Force Base provided full military honors and an air show of fighter jets. Dick Laird, Nixon's original secretary of defense, took the opportunity to remind the crowd of the need for a strong military. Senator David Boren declared the event a chance to help the United States win back its lost prestige as the "number one nation in the world."[111]

Fifteen million dollars and two years later, Enterprise Square threw open its doors to hundreds of eager visitors on November 20, 1982. The verdict was unanimous. "Absolutely the most sensational thing we have ever had in this part of the country," raved a local visitor. "I think they've got something here that could outdraw the Cowboy Hall of Fame," concluded another.[112] In its first six months, the indoor theme park attracted over forty thousand paying visitors, many of them schoolchildren on field trips.[113]

The initial experience of Enterprise Square was certainly impressive. After the visitors entered the flying-saucer-shaped structure,

> on silent cue, Bob Hope materializes on a nearby screen. Shortly into his quip-filled greeting, a news bulletin shatters the air. It's Ed McMahan at the news desk. A flying object, as yet unidentified, is skittering about the skies of Oklahoma City . . . Suddenly, lights flicker and dim. With a burst of laser-light and electronic sound, a metallic space craft plunges through the ceiling of the room, inches from visitors . . . A quizzical face pops from a module.

The face is that of one of three Muppet-like aliens, who serve as the visitors' guides for the rest of the three-hour tour. The trio's spacecraft, visitors discover, is out of fuel, and innocent of economics, the aliens must learn to navigate the marketplace to rectify the problem. Lucky for them, this is Oklahoma.[114]

From this dramatic introduction, visitors moved through a series of high-tech interactive stations, each with a catchy title. The first stage was a ride in a massive glass elevator through "Heartbeat Rotunda," where the three-story ascent passed "a flashing diorama of hundreds of giant transparencies—each depicting an economic transaction, each keyed to impart a fleeting but telling impression."[115] The next stop, "an entertaining panorama of giant whirring digital counters encased with soaring graphics," recorded real-time changes in the national debt and employment statistics alongside such humble figures as the number of cows milked, photographs taken, and phone calls placed. The two exhibits sought to link familiar consumer transactions to the wider concept of economic life, demystifying the dismal science with light, music, and graphics.

The ten-foot-high, grimly Orwellian "Great Talking Face of Government" covered one wall and housed nine separate video screens representing mouth, eyes, ears, and brain. "As the face expounds on the needs for 'more regulatory power to protect people,'" wrote an enthusiastic reviewer of an early sneak preview, "the tempo and action increase until the face short-circuits. 'It's overworked,'" explained the alien guide.[116] One passageway between exhibits mimicked a quiz show format, with questions and answers about living standards under capitalism and Soviet-style socialism. A video arcade offered games like Aliens, which, as an enthusiast explained, was "like *Star Wars,* but you are firing at the space invaders who would take away your right to own property, to seek a profit, or to compete"; Housebuilder, "a subcontracting venture of profit and loss"; and Oil Tycoon, a natural for Oklahoma. Those unable to visit could order the software from Enterprise Square.[117]

In the exhibit "Free to Choose," named for economist Milton Friedman's successful book and video series, blue-screen technology allowed visitors to select a profession—pilot, truck driver, president of the United States—and project themselves into the cockpit or the Oval Office. In the "Hall of Giants," heroes of capitalism like Henry Ford and Alexander Graham Bell towered over visitors, with slide shows and artifacts from their exemplary careers. Sonar devices implanted in the gargantuan heads activated the show when a visitor approached.[118]

With so much to choose from, it was hard even for the center's own technical director to pick a favorite exhibit. If pushed, though, the former Church of Christ minister had to admit he preferred the Great American Marketplace. "To me," he told a reporter, "it's the best show. The music, the talking heads, the big cash register—there's just a lot going on in there."[119] The talking heads belonged to gigantic one-, two-, ten-, and hundred-dollar bills: "Our Founding Fathers on giant currency talk, sing and teach," a promotional brochure explained.[120] A six-projector slide show helped them narrate the story of free enterprise. In 1990, a Soviet aviation crew visiting Oklahoma City for an aerospace show toured Enterprise Square. "The singing dollar bills," the newsletter reported, "stopped the group dead in its tracks."[121]

By the time Enterprise Square's original director retired in 1990, over half a million paying customers had visited the high-tech center on the Christian campus.[122] Its friendly space puppets had served as goodwill ambassadors at state fairs, trade shows, parades, and shopping malls.[123] Enterprise Square sold teaching materials, rented films, and hosted workshops, from in-service training for teachers to the old-style citizenship seminars from George Benson's day. Through the end of the Cold War, the "Disneyland of Economics" kept the faith.

An early recruiting brochure for the business division at Oklahoma Christian featured a photograph of diligent young women working various office machines that must have looked cutting-edge in the 1960s. The captions identified them by their small hometowns in Oklahoma and Arkansas, and the headline addressed their potential peers directly. "Why a college rather than a business school?" The chief reason, the brochure stated simply, was that "you will earn more money," perhaps in the office of one of the many employers in Oklahoma City aware of the college's good reputation. But there was another reason as well. "A recent survey indicates that 85 percent of the failures in business are caused by the inability of employees to get along with fellow workers. The character training given at a Christian college becomes an important asset in the business world."[124] The southwestern Christian college and the new mass white-collar workplace were just beginning a quietly historic partnership, and the terms of the bargain were clear enough.

Over the next thirty years, Stanford University's counterculture produced an antiauthoritarian corps of nerdy entrepreneurs for Silicon Valley, and institutions like the University of Chicago theorized a new economic orthodoxy for the policy elite. But just as important, the small regional schools simultaneously found their own calling among a different flock. The road from America's last agricultural periphery to the offices of the Sun Belt service economy ran increasingly through the vocational business departments that served as the primary destination of a booming new college population. The practical demands of this massive population shift of young adults into extended job preparation propelled their institutions into a new relationship with multinational corporate capital. The contradictions in this pairing in turn forced an ever more flamboyant ideological defense, visible in the fight against "economic illiteracy," in the burgeoning business major, in the entrepreneurial education movement, and in the free-enterprise centers on those same campuses. For Wal-Mart, the relationship reached its apogee in a market-oriented extracurricular organization it adopted, Students in Free Enterprise.

10

Students in Free Enterprise

It was the end of the Reagan era, and Hobbs was hurting. To be sure, the little New Mexico town was no stranger to tough times. It had begun life eighty years earlier as an arid cow pasture, distributed to white settlers under newly liberalized homestead law.[1] Then an oil strike in the late 1920s turned the remote village into a regional hub. Humble Oil, based in Texas, developed the local resources. The usual trappings of pell-mell development quickly followed, with chain stores, bars, and revivals jockeying for attention under the shadows of the pluming crude wells. Fluctuation became the norm. The entire Permian Basin of New Mexico and Texas was continually whipsawed through the boom-and-bust cycles of extractive industry over the course of the twentieth century. The oil economy peaked in the 1970s, and by 1989 it was in the midst of a devastating slump, the most protracted oil bust in American history. Businesses on Hobbs's placid main drag were shuttering at a frightening clip.[2]

But in that difficult time, young people at the local Christian college knew it was all a matter of attitude. Into Hobbs's main intersection, the indomitable students of the College of the Southwest dragged an "armed tank" to do battle with capitalism's only true enemy: fear itself. The tank came not from an armory but from a defunct oil field, and its ammunition was the painted words "FREE ENTERPRISE WORKS, ALL IT TAKES IS GUTS."[3]

This project, along with more than eighty like it, helped win the 250-student college first place at the annual national competition held by a nonprofit from the Ozarks called Students in Free Enterprise

(SIFE), whose biggest corporate sponsor was Wal-Mart. By 2003, the company hired 35 percent of its management trainees out of SIFE.[4] "Wal-Mart always finds the most economical way to do everything, and we're an economical way to get talent," pointed out SIFE's chief executive officer.[5] An explicitly ideological organization that trained young activists, SIFE offered an outstanding laboratory for the elaboration and dissemination of Christian free enterprise. Just as the Young Americans for Freedom was the poster-child organization of the electoral Reagan Revolution, SIFE was its economic counterpart. Today SIFE is active in over forty countries, teaching principles of "market economics, success skills, entrepreneurship, financial literacy, and business ethics" from Albania to Zimbabwe.[6] It even claims a high-school counterpart, Students for the Advancement of Global Entrepreneurship, with chapters in over 100 American high schools and ten countries.[7]

Already in 1989, the organization's successful pattern was well established. Working under the guidance of a faculty sponsor and a local business advisory board, the students of Hobbs's College of the Southwest and over a hundred peer institutions worked feverishly throughout that school year to bring the good news of free enterprise to their host communities. The SIFE team at Arkansas's Harding University mobilized in the fall around the national elections, handing out promissory ballots for citizens to pledge their votes to candidates supporting business. Participants at Mount Vernon Nazarene College in Ohio started off the school year dramatically by halting each car delivering a freshman to campus and distributing leaflets on the federal deficit to its occupants. In a reference to the Boston Tea Party, Lubbock Christian University mobilized their host town to mail tea bags to Washington to protest a congressional pay raise. In April, the students took their tales of the year's activities to nine regional competitions in cities like Fort Worth and Cleveland. The representative teams of four delivered painstakingly rehearsed presentations to corporate judges.[8]

From this round, the finalists then faced off at the annual expo in Kansas City, Missouri, competing for close to $100,000 in prizes at a downtown hotel. Special awards went to projects designed to draw public support for reducing the federal deficit and capping tort awards. Students in neckties or lace collars made their pitches to panels of executives from AT&T, Hallmark Cards, General Foods—and above all, Wal-Mart. Many graduating seniors took a turn through the job fair, meeting formally with the corporate representatives they had encountered all weekend over lunch and in the halls. "We have extended several offers to the students we visited with during the fair," confirmed a Wal-Mart recruiter. "One in particular I believe will be a Regional Vice President for us some day. Thank you for giving us exposure to such talent."[9]

Students like these were the shock troops of the postindustrial economy: the first mass college-educated generation in history, their childhoods largely underwritten by farms or oil wells, but their futures dependent on corporate offices. With their spirited defense of capitalism at the very moment of capitalism's unqualified international triumph, the SIFE champions of 1989 passionately promoted a new economic folklore. They were not alone: in the early 1980s a network of procapitalist clubs at colleges and universities formed an association and organized national conventions of club representatives. Though examples could be found in all sections of the country, the South and West predominated.[10]

These young probusiness enthusiasts from the College of the Southwest saw Hobbs's misfortunes as evidence that capitalism itself was under attack—or, perhaps even more ominously, that it was so fragile, such a creature of collective faith, that any wavering in the face of recession might lead to a wholesale desertion and collapse into socialism. From their organizational franchise at a small, private, Christian school, the students demonstrated their conviction that economics, like salvation, was a matter best addressed at the level of the individual conscience.

Moreover, their activism allowed these new entrants into a white-collar hierarchy to share a recently acquired expertise. They came to college as shy rural kids encountering business administration with trepidation. SIFE helped them transform themselves into the charismatic leaders and speakers required by their new economic niche. Their faith struck a sharp contrast to the sour mood of blue-collar America in the 1970s and 1980s. The form reigned supreme: small groups with internal accountability mechanisms; public presentations; team competition; networking opportunities with executives from consumer industries. The content was only vaguely apprehended, a secondhand smattering of Adam Smith and "this guy named von Hayek," as one student put it.

Beyond the sheer audacity of SIFE's accomplishment is its contingency. The program, whose roots reached back into the 1960s, did not begin with an emphasis on free-market economics, but rather on law enforcement. It originally drew in business sponsorship as a rather conventional corporate public relations vehicle, offering a forum for teenagers on the model of a Boys' and Girls' Club. Even when corporate anxiety over business's bad image suggested a more specific mission for SIFE as a nonprofit corporate communications outlet, the organization could have easily been orphaned by a recession, shed by its erstwhile benefactors when hard times came in the mid-1970s.

Even SIFE's subsequent safe haven in the world of Ozarks evangelicalism was as much a matter of institutional expediency as of natural affinity. Free-enterprise programs allowed cash-poor Christian colleges to catch the eyes of potential benefactors when public sources of revenue dried up under Reagan, a move that foreshadowed the entrepreneurial shilling of even well-endowed Ivies and venerable public universities in the 1990s. SIFE truly hit its stride, however, when it caught the eye of a farsighted Wal-Mart executive and morphed into a training and recruitment tool for the world's largest company and many of its suppliers. In the process, it transformed itself from a Cold War vehicle of "100% Americanism" to an exemplar of Wal-Mart's own corporate globalism.[11] The arc of SIFE's biography captures the creative elaboration of a new, postindustrial economic folklore, one that both responded to the new Sun Belt dispensation and shaped it decisively.

The earliest version of SIFE was born of adult anxiety over the "juvenile delinquent," a new character on the mid-century scene. Initially public concern grew from World War II's disruptive effects on the home front. The specter of returning war veterans, potentially unemployed and psychologically damaged, likewise heightened public fears for young men in 1945. The Federal Bureau of Investigation proclaimed a national epidemic of delinquency. In 1955 alone, Congress considered roughly two hundred different bills relating to youth crime. Mass-circulation magazines addressed themselves to the problem in a stream of stories, and Hollywood created a subgenre of causeless rebels and their B-grade imitators. Civic, church, and fraternal organizations in municipalities joined the crusade. Under the catch-all category of juvenile delinquency, a Texas study analyzed offenses from shooting spitballs in public to murder.[12]

Students in Free Enterprise was born out of this history in Austin, Texas, in the ominous year of 1963. In August, just a few short months before the assassination in Dallas transformed Texas into a national pariah, the state's attorney general, Waggoner Carr, lent the prestige of his office to a new antidelinquency effort. Under Carr's leadership, the legislature recodified the state's juvenile laws and launched an annual youth conference on delinquency. Sponsorship of the conference then passed to the Texas Law Enforcement and Youth Development Foundation, an advocacy group that had already logged several years in its mission to "arouse greater respect for the law" among Texas's young people. The Law Enforcement Foundation worked the oil industry, the insurance companies, and individual donors for private sponsorship of its antidelinquency programs.[13]

These programs' striking ability to channel teenaged enthusiasm in support of conservative goals owed a great deal to Assistant Attorney General Robert T. "Sonny" Davis, who went on to found SIFE. His early antidelinquency activities laid down the contours that the free-market organization would follow.[14] In the mid-1960s, Sonny Davis turned the law-and-order Texas Youth Conference into a forum for teenagers themselves to propose solutions to the juvenile threat.[15] The idea was to win teenagers' allegiance by ceding some traditional adult control. Texas's "teen juries," for example, heard misdemeanor cases involving their high-school peers. Rather than letting their friends off lightly, the juries reportedly handed down stiff, if unusual, punishments.[16] Though the fresh-scrubbed student council presidents who gathered in Austin were hardly the population most at risk for mayhem, Davis's approach nonetheless stood out in the national wave of antidelinquency efforts for this emphasis on student input.[17] Here was an idea that might have legs.

Sonny Davis tackled juvenile delinquency with the same fresh ideas that proved so compatible with servant leadership: the human relations school of management, which encouraged intimate teamwork and non-authoritarian control. Davis had encountered human relations management theories as a student at the University of Texas, where a team of its professorial avatars performed HR fieldwork at the legendary Texas company Humble Oil. These University of Texas management researchers introduced the term "synergogy" in 1962 to describe classrooms that "shift the responsibility for learning from the teacher to the student," thereby leaving "no authority figure for students to rebel against."[18] Meanwhile, Humble Oil was looking to burnish its image with a philanthropy focused on young people. Some of the oil executives had children who participated in Davis's antidelinquency Texas Youth Conference, and so the oil company's philanthropic arm backed the conference organizer with a $100,000 grant. Davis's mission was to create a marketable, traveling form of leadership training based on the "synergogy" concept.[19]

Throughout the later 1960s, Davis honed training tasks that allowed students to arrive at appropriate conclusions through their own small-group interaction. An exercise might involve setting each group the task of listing the U.S. presidents in order. Invariably, the group demonstrated that it collectively knew more decontextualized facts than did any individual member. The point was to dispense with both the individual striver and the authority figure of the teacher, and thus demonstrate the superior outcome of cooperation. "So how does one become an effective leader?" inquired the project's manual rhetorically. "Simply by helping the uninvolved grow and experience a sense of belonging and contribution to the organization . . . [P]eople support what they help create."[20] Davis seized on the program's potential to integrate the private sector into the colleges and nonprofit organizations that contracted with his organization for full-day workshops on leadership. Humble Oil grasped the potential early, but an even bigger opportunity for Davis's leadership program was brewing in a paradigmatic Sun Belt boom town.

It was in Dallas that the future SIFE consciously combined corporate concerns over the public image of business with the private evangelical convictions of a rising generation of Sun Belt businessmen. Even before Lee Harvey Oswald made Dallas the national capital of political violence, the railroad town had been periodically campaigning for the title of "the city of hate." During the Depression, the local Ford Motor Company operations had assembled a paramilitary force that vigorously discouraged labor organization, with the collusion of police and the business establishment. The National Labor Relations Board eventually found the corporate vigilantes guilty of "indiscriminate ruthlessness and organized gangsterism," but the point had already been made to a generation of potential progressives. With dozens of activists brutally maimed and the survivors cowed or run out of town, Dallas entered the postwar years as a hotbed of quiescence.[21]

The professionals and managers that migrated to the city after World War II tilted the city more sharply to the right. Bruce Alger, a Dallas congressman and realtor, distinguished himself on the national stage in the 1950s and 1960s as a staunch opponent of such transparent communist plots as free lunch for schoolchildren. The city's public library purged a Picasso from an art exhibit on the grounds that the Spanish master was too pink for Dallas.[22] When United Nations Ambassador Adlai Stevenson visited the city in October 1963, for United Nations Day, a "National Indignation Convention" met him with ferocious heckling, and cameras captured a Dallas woman smacking the ambassador over the head with an anti-U.N. sign. President Kennedy's visit the following month was heralded by flyers bearing his likeness and the slogan, "Wanted for Treason."[23]

Students in Free Enterprise's first official corporate sponsor, the Dallas insurance firm Southwestern Life, represented the Sun Belt financial services corporations that were gaining the upper hand on the "Silicon Prairie." After half a century as a staid Texas concern, Southwestern Life had expanded into the southern tier of states beginning in the mid-1950s. Within a decade, it stretched from the District of Columbia to California, diversifying its financial instruments as it went. A handy stock deal with data-processing *wunderkind* Ross Perot allowed the company to shift to state-of-the-art computing in the early 1960s for virtually nothing.[24]

Sonny Davis's student leadership program fit well with the growing insurance company's optimism. Eager to demonstrate "that business does care about young people and their future," Bill Seay, Southwestern's chairman and chief executive officer, invited Davis's organization to host a training weekend at the company's headquarters in 1970, the first in what was to prove a highly successful run. Seay epitomized the Sun Belt Christian entrepreneurs who were to make up the backbone of SIFE support and shape a distinctive corporate culture. The Seays were deeply involved in the city's evolving evangelicalism, with Mrs. Seay drawing praise for her skills in teaching the Old Testament and Mr. Seay eventually serving as a director of the Dallas Theological Seminary and the Billy Graham Evangelistic Association.[25] He went on to join the board of Wal-Mart Stores, Inc., and to chair George H. W. Bush's 1980 presidential bid in Texas.[26]

The 1970 student leadership institute at Southwestern Life Insurance reflected a growing concern in business circles nationally. "Along with hundreds of other businessmen," a former Southwestern executive recalled, Bill Seay had been disturbed by the "gathering clouds of anti-business attitudes in college and university classrooms." The intensive weekend institute was to impress emerging campus players while they were still reachable and provide them with human relations skills for influencing peers. Almost a quarter of the 100 attendees were presidents or vice presidents of their student bodies.[27]

The plan for the on-site leadership institute included a formal banquet in Southwestern's futuristic corporate headquarters, which would bring together company executives and their wives with the young people attending on the company's scholarships. Southwestern's managers had been nervous about burdening the cafeteria staff in its home office with the task of feeding over a hundred collegians—on a weekend, no less. But in a gesture to be echoed endlessly by SIFE itself, the banquet culminated in a standing ovation for the assembled food service workers. For their part, the students took home precisely the intended lesson: "It really makes me feel great to know that a company like Southwestern Life is here in America," wrote one young trainee. "It builds up my confidence in the U.S.A. to know that someone really cares about the future leaders of America." Davis and Southwestern had united the elements for a fantastically successful endeavor: a nonprofit organization backed by corporate PR departments that raised the status of business among potentially rebellious students through the efforts of their own peers; that saluted the contributions of the humblest service workers; and that employed an antiauthoritarian, cooperative human relations model taken from law enforcement and management theory. *Public Relations News* crowned the event one of the ten most outstanding PR projects of 1970. A star was born.[28]

Over fifteen years the organization had gradually evolved from combating juvenile delinquency via public funds to promoting youthful faith in business through corporate donations. Sonny Davis's program boiled down to a collection of familiar human relations techniques. His own charisma and his ingenuity in packaging and marketing them certainly set his leadership training institutes apart, but fundamentally he taught organizations how to achieve whatever collective goals they had already adopted. As merely techniques of group dynamics, in fact, "leadership" was an empty category: "leaders" could theoretically coordinate a war protest or a strike as well as a demonstration against deficit spending. It was not until the mid-1970s that Sonny Davis's organization took the leap that at last transformed it into Students for Free Enterprise, an explicit advocacy group franchised to college campuses and deploying the energies of students and faculty for corporate ends. Like the Dallas efforts in 1970, this move came at the instigation of Bill Seay. This time, though, the stakes were distinctly heightened.[29]

As Southwestern's historian remembered it, the first SIFE gathering convened 100 students from ten different Sun Belt campuses near the theme park Six Flags Over Texas in January 1975. The students gathered there in order to "discuss what they might do to counteract the stultifying criticism of American business which was flowing from the campus, the press, and elsewhere, seeking to tear down the very system which gave the critics their jobs and their warm, comfortable homes . . . The kids loved it."[30]

The sponsors and students came up with a new mechanism for counteracting this corrosive antibusiness sentiment. The idealistic young free-enterprisers were to return to their campuses and develop their own projects for promoting American capitalism locally, then present these public education plans in a competition to be judged by a panel of Dallas businessmen. The winning student collective would take home a $2,500 grant to its university.[31] Corporate backers stepped up briskly, for they had watched recent campus developments with growing concern.

In 1978, Wal-Mart executives attended a three-day conference on the image of the retail industry. After listening to assortments of young people, the media, and consumer advocates both governmental and private, they concluded that "the retail industry, as a whole, does not enjoy a good image at all . . . Consumer agencies and individual consumers alike felt that some retailers could not be trusted and therefore, had to be monitored by governmental regulating agencies."[32] From 1967 to 1973, Congress considered hundreds of consumer-protection measures and from them enacted twenty-five major laws. Increased scrutiny and new regulatory agencies—the Environmental Protection Agency, the

Occupational Safety and Health Administration, the Consumer Product Safety Commission—meant that in the span of a few short years, the nation now specified standards for every stage of the life cycle of consumer goods, from the effluents released in their production to their packaging to the highways they moved over and the credit available for purchasing them.[33] Ralph Nader troubled the sleep of many executives with proposals like the 1976 manifesto *Taming the Giant Corporation,* which advocated an employee bill of rights and community involvement in corporate decision-making. Though Nader's initiatives lacked the activist muscle to present a real threat, they kept the legislative alternatives to *laissez-faire* in sight.[34] The free-market economist Milton Friedman visited Harding College in the winter of 1973 to ask urgently "Can we halt Leviathan?"[35]

Consumers were not the only critics, nor Wal-Mart's sector the only one criticized. Business at large faced serious PR challenges during the 1970s. Watergate, after all, had required two to tango: the Nixon administration put up the manpower for the tawdry string of illegal operations, but corporate America had provided the sea of unreported donations that floated the felonious Committee to Re-elect the President, the bribes for foreign government contracts, the multimillion dollar secret slush fund that funneled money to Republican candidates in the 1970 midterm elections. Some major companies also won an unwelcome high profile for their obvious financial stake in the Vietnam War, most notoriously the chemical manufacturers like Dow Chemical and Dupont, producers of the incendiary petroleum jelly napalm and the carcinogenic herbicide Agent Orange.[36] A 1974 Senate subcommittee raised the restless ghost of past war-profiteering when it heard testimony on the Nazi collaborations of DuPont's General Motors division, which had won a decoration for its chief executive for overseas operations from Adolf Hitler himself.[37]

The executives, then, were not paranoid: they really did have enemies. Public confidence in CEOs of major corporations plummeted from over 50 percent in the mid-1960s to 20 percent by the mid-1970s. Even the executive branch of the federal government fared better in public esteem over the same period, and this with both a president and a vice president resigning in disgrace.[38] In a 1973 poll, respondents asked to rank the professions by prestige put businessmen last, below even lawyers.[39]

This startling reversal of fortune owed much to the new economic dispensation, the end of the postwar boom. In 1971, America saw its first year of a trade deficit in the twentieth century, and inflation edged out the war in Vietnam as citizens' number-one concern. They were right to be worried: the increase in imports signaled the end of America's long postwar economic dominance, built on the destruction of the European and Japanese industrial capacity in World War II. Beginning in 1973, real wages in the United States reversed their long upward trend and actually began decreasing for the first time in more than a generation. Median family incomes stagnated even as more women added wage-earning work to their unpaid domestic labor. Corporate profitability dropped from a mid-1960s high of almost 10 percent to under 6 percent after 1975. The recession of 1974–75 finally registered the impact of the new international division of labor on America's high-wage, high-consumption accord. The party was over.[40]

Through these dark days, SIFE developed as a bridge between the tarnished business sector and the newly prominent campuses. SIFE made its initial campus contacts through the deans of college business schools. Each fall, these administrators selected a faculty member to head the team, who then put together a squad of four students. All five from each school received "extensive motivational leadership training" and "information about current problems of the free enterprise system." Alert to the potential charge of indoctrination, SIFE hastened to assure its audience that the orientation was based on "intellectually creditable materials" from such mass-circulation magazines as *Fortune* and *Business Week*. SIFE acquainted the participants with promotional materials that were already in existence and available for the students to take to local audiences, turning the participants into an effective grassroots distribution mechanism for corporate films. Local Rotary clubs provided "dialogue resource persons" for the trainees, teaching students how to present their cause professionally and garner support for their activities.[41]

Once the teams had concluded their training, the competition was opened for the year. SIFE groups had most of the school year to develop "innovative, creative, imaginative, and effective programs for projecting the positive side of our free enterprise system on the campus and in the community." Back on campus, the four students and their faculty sponsor first set to work cultivating a Business Advisory Council to support each team during the year, five to ten local businessmen who could be counted on for advice and often in-kind contributions. The cell of four also recruited as many as 100 additional students to log time on the projects themselves. The intercampus competition could spur each team to a frenzy of activity. For their efforts, most of the students received academic credit, as well as valuable exposure to the unfamiliar world of corporate America.[42]

Through the Ford and Carter years, SIFE was still a regional sideshow in the struggle to redefine corporate capital's prerogatives under the new conditions, as yet dimly understood. But there were signs abroad that might have given hope to a careful observer. In spite of its justifiable anxiety in the 1970s, business was rallying to self-defense with unprecedented creativity. While older corporate advocacy groups like the U.S. Chamber of Commerce and the National Association of Manufactures slowly regrouped, a new configuration grew out of the united corporate opposition to bills proposing stiffer consumer and environmental protection and advocacy of deregulation.[43]

The Business Roundtable, soon to become one of SIFE's most significant benefactors, was born in this period. It sprang from a merger between the Labor Law Study Group—representing venerable industrial giants like General Electric, General Motors, and U.S. Steel—and the awkwardly named Construction Users Anti-Inflation Roundtable, which focused on controling the costs of union labor for rapidly expanding physical plants. The March Group added world trade to the Business Roundtable's agenda when it joined in 1971. The Business Roundtable now comprised about two hundred CEOs of major American corporations; membership was by invitation only. This was no Elks Club.[44]

With the Business Roundtable as its standard-bearer, business scored a string of impressive policy victories, even under the anti-Watergate backlash. Deregulation of trucking, telecommunications, and airlines, for instance, all occurred before Ronald Reagan's election. After inflexible positions cost the older business lobbies early legislative losses on occupational safety and employee pensions, the Roundtable's approach produced wins on unemployment insurance and labor law.

By 1977, the mechanisms were in place for a coordinated counterattack on labor's drive to reform the National Labor Relations Board. Presenting a united front, the largest employers' associations financed a campaign against the reform that made skillful use of new technologies like direct mail. Sensitive as ever to the PR value of independent business, the coordinated lobbyists of the National Action Committee organized small businessmen under thirty-one state chairmen in targeted states. An easy win for the reform proposal in the House raised the stakes for the Senate debate going into early 1978. The longer the process took, the employer lobbyists felt, the better their own chances, for the state-level lobbying apparatus needed time to generate constituent mail, place editorials, and run media campaigns.[45]

The fight against labor reform galvanized Wal-Mart to national lobbying action. For the first time since the early 1960s, by his own account, Sam Walton traveled to Washington to lobby in person in early 1978. What he found there evidently alarmed him, for he immediately addressed an article to Wal-Mart's employees. Sam Walton castigated himself for neglecting the political arena too long, until this threat was upon the company, and he warned employees that from now on both he and they would be called upon to address specific legislative issues. For the moment, he was deeply concerned about "this so-called Labor 'Reform' Act." Far from reforming anything, he instructed readers, the proposals would amount to forcing employees into unions against their will. "We need everyone's help to put down this labor law that is now being debated by the Senate," Walton wrote. "In my opinion, such a legislation could wreck our Company and largely negate the future for us all . . . It may be too late, but I'd like to enroll all of us in all our stores, our general offices and the distribution centers in the fight to preserve our free enterprise system."[46]

Business campaigns like the one Sam Walton proposed slowed the progress of labor reform in the Senate. Stalwart senatorial allies of the employers' association like Orrin Hatch and Jesse Helms filibustered the bill through the spring of 1978, and *Wal-Mart World* offered an article on "How to Write a Letter to your Congressman."[47] If the magazines' readers took the lesson, they were in good company: 8 million pieces of mail poured into Congress as the fight dragged on. Finally, in September, the legislation crawled back into committee, never to reemerge. The employer lobbyists' victory had demonstrated once again the effectiveness of the new organizing tactics.

In retrospect the election of Ronald Reagan in 1980 marked a turning point for the public fortunes of corporate capital. But the reality on the ground at the time was far from clear. Reagan's inheritance of the Goldwater movement was not necessarily a plus in corporate circles, where many had actively opposed the Arizona senator. Small business considered Nixon one of their own, but large multinationals had seen little to applaud in Nixon's wage and price controls or his proposed guaranteed national income plan, and in the 1980 race the bulk of big business only rallied to Reagan after the defeat of his Republican rivals John Connally and George H. W. Bush.[48] For their part, SIFE's sponsors were not about to let down their guard just because the executive branch had passed to a Republican.[49]

Among the campuses playing host to a SIFE chapter in these uncertain times was Southwest Baptist University (SBU), in the pleasant Missouri Ozarks town of Bolivar. Southwest Baptist's mission today is to prepare "servant leaders in a global society," but it began life in 1878 in a former Baptist church and sometime feed store, with a student body numbering fewer than seventy. In a familiar pattern of struggle, the tiny school moved from site to site, burned, closed, and reorganized before gaining four-year accreditation in 1965. Many of SBU's professors were also preachers, and continued their lives in the pulpit on the side. This dual career had a practical dimension: Like many small, underendowed denominational schools in the region, SBU struggled constantly to meet payroll and keep its doors open. Experiments in solvency included a college-owned broom factory and a farm that supplied the dining halls. Dependent on tuition for much of its operating costs, the college was frequently left casting about for revenue.[50]

The conversion of SBU into a center for free-enterprise education and ultimately the national home campus of SIFE followed the pattern at schools like Ozarks and John Brown University. After making the leap to four-year status, the college in the 1970s was focused on judiciously expanding its curriculum under the sharp-eyed intelligence of President James Sells. Sells, a native of Illinois and holder of an Ed.D. from Columbia, preferred the liberal arts program, but "it became clear that it was an era when that was just not feasible," he recounted many years later. So the college shrewdly selected areas of professional preparation that could stand up to economic downturns, focusing on solid curricula in accounting and health care.[51]

As the new areas drew in more faculty, many fired with enthusiasm about free enterprise, the business school became a more vocal segment of the institution. A small grant from the Kansas-Missouri Telephone

Company sponsored a "free enterprise forum" in 1978, dedicated to the "uniting of business and professional interests into a consistent voice for free enterprise." The event attracted the attention of Missouri congressman Gene Taylor, the owner of a car dealership in Sarcoxie. His interest piqued, the congressman returned to campus the following year to help cap Free Enterprise Week with a formal introduction of SBU's new Education for Business and Community Leadership Program. "The essence of the program," Taylor affirmed, "is to implement a solid ongoing effort to educate the people of Southwest Missouri and our nation to the need for a return to the 'three R's' of Americanism—respect, reverence, and responsibility." By 1980, the new program was holding a series of talks billed as an Economic Education Seminar for Opinion Leaders.[52]

With a healthy stream of future Christian ministers among the entering students, moreover, Sells saw a potential use for the business offerings that would put them in service to the Baptist mission. "In my opinion, these students are often terribly naive about finance—all aspects of finance, personal and institutional. They would have a general pull toward Christian work but little sense of how it is organized and funded." In 1982, Sells instituted a mandatory business course for all students, and the institution began developing an identity as a center for Christian business education.[53]

The earliest efforts in the late 1970s had involved little more than additional courses, workshops, and seminars on free enterprise, but the overall expansion of the university put President Sells in constant conversation with potential donors. The college, after all, could look to its alumni for little material support, for most had graduated when the school was a junior college and gave instead to their later four-year institutions. Few were making fortunes in missions or ministry, anyway. With more students now cycling through the business department, the college focused on a new building to house it—and, though less remarked upon in the promotional efforts, to provide space for the liberal arts faculty, too. Where would the new infrastructure come from?

Nearby Springfield, Missouri, was home to a chain of supermarkets called Consumer's Market, with about thirty-five stores in the area. Sells had been cultivating their owner for a while with little success. But then, as he drove around Springfield on various errands, Sells began to register that the designs of each individual Consumer's Market actually varied; despite being part of the same chain, they showed signs of experimentation from one to the next. Sells realized that the chain's owner was deeply involved in designing the stores himself. The college president went back to the chain's founder and tried a different approach. "Here's what you can do," Sells told him. "You can build us a Consumer's Market on campus, and we'll turn it into a Science Center." The grocer was so overcome, Sells recalled later, that tears stood in his eyes. "He used to get down on the floor of his own house and try out different tile patterns for a new store, trying to see what would look best, what would lead people down an aisle. And it meant a lot to him that what we wanted was one of his buildings that he had put so much of himself into," President Sells explained. Southwest Baptist got its science center.[54]

This experience was fresh on the president's mind not long after when he drove past the Wal-Mart in Harrison, Arkansas. He stopped in for a bag of chocolate peanuts, and as a token gesture toward walking the calories off, parked at the far edge of the store's parking lot. Back outside with the peanuts in hand, President Sells walked across the wide asphalt to his parked car. "And then I turned and looked at that Wal-Mart, and I thought to myself, 'There it is. That Wal-Mart, that's our new library.' I knew Sam Walton slightly, and I said to him, 'Sam, you build a Wal-Mart on our campus, and we'll use it as a library.'"[55]

Thus Southwest Baptist learned to approach its potential friends where they already stood. The little college would not put on airs, not consider itself too good for the humble service industries that produced the donations. Instead, it would memorialize retail stores right into the buildings for the colleges, rather as if Carnegie-Mellon University had put a library in a steel mill.

While these relationships were developing, Sells also figured out how to get the free-enterprise center up and running. Rather than antagonize the college's board—composed entirely of Southern Baptist ministers—the president increased its size and filled the new chairs with businessmen. The Gene Taylor National Free Enterprise Center was dedicated to the service of Christ by Vice President George H. W. Bush in 1982. "As Christians," the audience recited *en masse*, "we dedicate ourselves to practice free enterprise in our own lives by being productive and hardworking, by being good stewards of God's bounty, and by upholding our Christian responsibility to our communities and to those who are in need."[56]

This was the environment that greeted Alvin Rohrs, the son of a minister who ran a local boys' ranch, when he became one of SIFE's earliest recruits at Southwest Baptist. By his own report, Rohrs made a poor spokesman for free enterprise during his undergraduate years. But at the University of Missouri law school, Rohrs specialized in tax law and business regulation.[57] Degree in hand, he found himself underwhelmed by the prospect of a future at the bar. Rohrs instead accepted Southwest Baptist's invitation to return to campus and take up advising the SIFE chapter, as well as heading the college's new National Free Enterprise Center.[58]

It was not a propitious moment for SIFE. The sharp economic contraction of the early 1980s decimated the organization's backing. From a hundred corporate sponsors in 1981, it plummeted to eighteen two years later. Perhaps not coincidentally, Sonny Davis had begun to tire of the project, and went looking for a buyer. At a meeting in St. Louis, he suggested to Rohrs that the national organization needed a permanent home on a college campus. Southwest Baptist's enterprising chancellor sealed the deal in a trip to Dallas.[59] The SIFE board hired Rohrs as national director to rebuild support, and he took on the task with gusto.

In his new position, Alvin Rohrs threw himself into expanding SIFE's corporate backing by shaking the bushes for influential board members.[60] His early efforts paid off in the form of support from local Southwest Baptist benefactors like Springfield's Consumer Markets, as well as traditional SIFE regional supporters like Texas energy interests Sun Oil and Conoco. Dart & Kraft, the conglomerate that helped launch Reagan's supply-side guru Arthur Laffer, came on board.[61] Collectively, corporations contributed over half of the annual $200,000 budget in the early 1980s. In general, the formula for the organization did not change much in the early years of Rohrs's leadership. Sonny Davis still led the fall leadership training, and students still directed the bulk of their energies to such tried-and-true outreach vehicles as voter registration drives, lectures, and general lessons in free enterprise for public schools. They financed these activities and the travel costs to their competitions by peddling Easter baskets and pizzas on their campuses.[62]

During these lean years, the young champions of beleaguered free enterprise took their infectious optimism where it was sorely needed, to the front lines of the service economy. In July 1984, SIFE held its year-end competition at the financially troubled New Orleans World's Fair, which declared a "Free Enterprise Day" in their honor. President Reagan himself penned a hearty endorsement of this effort, advising SIFE's gathered competitors that free enterprise "needs new advocates to hold aloft its ideals of freedom and justice and to demonstrate to others why, with its admitted imperfection, it has achieved the highest standard of living that mankind has known."[63] The fair closed in bankruptcy a few months later, dragging the city's hotel industry into depression after the expected bonanza in tourism failed to materialize.[64]

While in New Orleans, students heard from an executive at Pan American Airways that "the free enterprise system should welcome, not fear, the effects of governmental deregulation" begun six years earlier.[65] These were brave words: as he spoke, the airline industry was already littered with failing carriers, and Pan Am itself was shortly to join the nearly two-thirds of major airlines that eventually wound up in bankruptcy.[66] Under such conditions, free-market capitalism looked like a cause in need of resourceful, dedicated champions. In the midst of these trials, one new area of development for SIFE in the early 1980s showed particular promise. Director Alvin Rohrs's aggressive rebuilding effort was leading the organization to experiment with new advertising techniques. The report from 1984 celebrated new expertise in "making SIFE ideas visible and getting the public to recognize the virtues of capitalism." Through trial and error, SIFE chapters discovered untapped audiences for their message. They constructed information booths in malls, produced public service announcements for radio, silk-screened tee-shirts and imprinted their message on bumper stickers, milk cartons, Frisbees, billboards, and mud flaps.[67] The headquarters began to lend a videotape with interviews of participating students, professors, and corporate representatives. It hired a former advertising representative for Bell South and a marketing intern, and the two launched a direct-marketing recruitment drive for 1985 with over a thousand calls to colleges around the country. Their publicity, aimed at corporate sponsors, highlighted the 30 million Americans reached with the SIFE message. This optimistic number included "all north-bound traffic on the Golden Gate Bridge" that passed by a billboard proclaiming "Free

Enterprise Works!" as well as the cable audiences absorbing thrice-daily public-service messages from SIFE teams.[68]

One innovation loomed larger than any other in SIFE's renaissance of the mid-1980s: the fortuitous adoption of the small, nonprofit Ozarks institution by the growing for-profit one, Wal-Mart Stores, Inc., and the Wal-Mart Foundation. Working out of Southwest Baptist, with a staff of only a half dozen, Alvin Rohrs put his early education in local networking to use and created a support club. The Leaders of the Ozarks, as it was known, formally organized some of the area powerhouses for "mutual fellowship and social interaction." Each member paid $1,000 annually to the organization, which went to the support of SIFE. Members ranged from small local proprietors like the owner of Bolivar Insulation to high rollers like the founder of Wendy's fast-food chain, Dave Thomas, and the governor of Missouri, John Ashcroft. Some of the Leaders were already linked through their contributions to Southwest Baptist. Sam Walton, of course, had contributed to the college's library through the company foundation, and the Wal-Mart founder appeared on the Leaders' first roster in 1985 along with Wal-Mart's vice chairman and chief financial officer, Jack Shewmaker.[69]

Though Walton's was the blue-chip name, it was Shewmaker who provided the crucial bridge between SIFE and its new corporate protector. Shewmaker was an Ozark native, son of a car salesman in the small Missouri town of Buffalo. He had studied to be an architect at Georgia Tech in Atlanta, but his fiancée's close call in a car accident reordered his priorities before graduation. He left college for marriage, and took a job in Springfield.[70]

Shewmaker moved fast, cycling onward and upward through a series of sales jobs around the Midwest, but he wanted a way to stay in the Ozarks. In an episode that would be recounted to audiences at SIFE and Wal-Mart over the years, Wal-Mart invited him to Bentonville in 1970 for an interview that the company founder left to his lieutenant Ferold Arend. Arend made the almost insulting offer of an assistant manager post in a store, which Shewmaker refused. Sam Walton himself then invited him back to speak one-on-one, with the implied expectation of a job more in keeping with Shewmaker's experience. Annoyed by the added trouble and expense of a second summons to Bentonville, Shewmaker turned him down. Walton then made him the counteroffer that was to be enshrined as an expression of his fundamental fairness: If Shewmaker could get himself to the Howard Johnson's in Joplin, Walton would "meet him halfway." Shewmaker then joined the company as author of its first training manual, a new necessity for the growing network of stores. He rose quickly, a "demanding but fair" executive. By 1978 he was Wal-Mart's president and Walton's heir apparent.[71]

And for SIFE, Shewmaker was the man on horseback. In 1985 he accepted the organization's chairmanship and brought with him a $50,000 donation from the Wal-Mart Foundation.[72] He augmented the $1,000-per-member Leaders of the Ozarks by launching the Chairman's Club for donors of $20,000 or more. The goal was to bring in up to fifteen private contributors who wanted to support a major marketing drive with backing for new videos, word processing, toll-free phone lines, recruiting staff, and PR materials.[73]

Through Shewmaker's stewardship, Wal-Mart Stores, Inc., and the Wal-Mart Foundation in 1985 created twenty-five fellowships for the faculty advisers to SIFE on college campuses within the retailer's trade territory. Two years later, they doubled the number of fellowships, reminding interested parties that "[t]he degree of free enterprise education on a college campus has always been a criterion of our selection of schools from which to recruit our employees and provide financial support."[74] By 1986, Wal-Mart in one form or another—via company donations, personal donations by Walton and Shewmaker, or company foundation grants—accounted for a third of those honored by Chairman's Club awards for major donors.[75] By 1991, the retailer was providing over 10 percent of the total budget and much of the entrée that enticed other backers on board.[76]

Within its first six years, then, the relationship led to the proud announcement that "Wal-Mart is #1 with SIFE—#1 in support . . . #1 in establishing teams . . . #1 in judges . . . #1 recruiter."[77] Student outreach projects found new homes in local Wal-Marts and Sam's Clubs.[78] SIFE alumni peopled the management tiers in Bentonville and at many of Wal-Mart's most closely associated suppliers, and its chosen colleges astutely made the club a star feature of their offerings. Looking back on the organization's progress from the turn of the millennium, Rohrs commented with his usual modesty, "Almost through sheer accident we have developed a leadership program that fits what business needs these days."[79]

11

"Students Changing the World"

If you were to tour the Ozark foothills today, you might meet middle-aged Arkansans who could recount the day the six-foot-tall pencil visited their sixth-grade classroom. In the public schools around Searcy, in the late 1980s, the bigger-than-life pencil was one of the projects with which the Harding University Students in Free Enterprise sought to impart faith in free-market economics to schoolchildren.[1] Invigorated by powerful new patrons—RadioShack, Dow Chemical, the Business Roundtable, but above all, Wal-Mart—SIFE in the late Cold War offered an extraordinary proving ground for the themes and techniques of the New Right, a training laboratory that turned a white-collar cadre into enthusiastic marketers of economic restructuring at home and abroad. By the end of the decade, 40,000 SIFE students on over 150 campuses claimed to have reached over 100 million people with their message, or that of their corporate backers.[2] The giant pencil was part of that extraordinary effort.

Though the Searcy sixth-graders would not have known it, the big pencil claimed an international intellectual genealogy. The concept it illustrated was fairly straightforward—namely, that even an item as simple, cheap, and familiar as a pencil was the product of complex processes played out on multiple continents and involving literally millions of people, none of whom individually knew how to make a pencil. The pencil arose from miners in Ceylon who dug up the graphite, and the people who made the string that tied the sacks in which the graphite was shipped, and those who loaded the sacks onto boats, and so forth, at exhaustive length. The miracle in this process was said to lie in the absence of any central mastermind, or even any intent to make a pencil on the part of most of those implicated in the process. So what brought it all together? SIFE's answer was clear: The invisible hand of the market.

The Harding students who toured with their giant pencil referred to themselves as followers of Milton Friedman, the passionate *laissez-faire* economist and 1976 Nobel Prize winner. Soon after retiring from his teaching duties at the University of Chicago in the late 1970s, Friedman and his wife, fellow economist Rose Friedman, were approached by the renegade CEO of a Public Broadcasting Service (PBS) affiliate in Erie, Pennsylvania. Bob Chitester was that rare breed among public broadcasters, "a libertarian rather than a socialist," as the Friedmans recalled later, and he carried around a tattered copy of the pair's 1962 treatise *Capitalism and Freedom* as his personal bible.[3]

The public broadcaster proposed capitalizing on Friedman's sudden celebrity with a privately funded PBS project: a television documentary that could later be sold as audio and video cassettes and packaged with educational resource materials for a complete course at high schools and colleges. The ten-part series, *Free to Choose*, aired early in 1980. Later that year it appeared in book form, preserving the simple, colloquial style of the spoken lectures, and became the year's bestselling nonfiction book in America. The series enjoyed some secondary circulation in the form of 16-millimeter prints, and then in 1987 it became widely available on video cassette.

The pencil illustration appeared in the very first episode, along with a stirring testimonial from body-builder Arnold Schwarzenegger, entrepreneurial refugee from Austria's tyrannical bureaucracy. But as Friedman freely acknowledged, the pencil illustration did not originate with him but with Leonard Read. Read had started his adult career in the 1920s as a produce vendor in Michigan, only to see his independent business decimated by the coming of the chain stores. Like many disappointed Midwesterners, he moved to Southern California and wound up as manager of the Los Angeles Chamber of Commerce. His energetic advocacy work caught the eye of the National Industrial Conference Board, an employers' organization in New York. Hired there in the waning months of World War II, Read was charged with coordinating a national PR effort "for the restoration of individual freedom and the market order."[4]

Frustration with the organization's balanced debate format, however, drove Read to leave in less than a year, and corporate backers from General Motors and B.F. Goodrich staked him in a new, more aggressive organization. One of the very first of the conservative think-tanks that were to remake public policy, the Foundation for Economic Education focused on popularizing strict free-market theories—"neoliberal" economics, in the terminology that confounds Americans' political binary—by organizing potential opinion-makers. Led by Read from its 1946 founding until his death in 1983, the Foundation for Economic Education drew its initial intellectual resources from economists like Ludwig von Mises, Fred Fairchild, and Leo Wolman.[5] In 1947, Read was present at the creation of Frederick Hayek's Mont Pelerin Society, the international gathering in Switzerland that launched the hard-right Austrian school of economics as a force in the United States and Britain.[6]

Over the next decades, the staff of the Foundation for Economic Education spread their alternative economic vision around North America. To influence the climate of opinion on college campuses, the Foundation in 1948 began hosting short-term seminars, exchanges, and conferences on its Hudson Valley estate. Individual academicians were sponsored by corporations like Bristol-Meyers, Caterpillar, Dupont, and Westinghouse.[7]

Read wrote "I, Pencil: My Family Tree as Told to Leonard E. Read," in 1958, laying out the theory of the invisible hand of the market in the first-person voice of a humble pencil.

> The lesson I have to teach is this: *Leave all creative energies uninhibited.* Merely organize society to act in harmony with this lesson. Let society's legal apparatus remove all obstacles the best it can. Permit these creative know-hows freely to flow. Have faith that free men and women will respond to the Invisible Hand. This faith will be confirmed. I, Pencil, seemingly simple though I am, offer the miracle of my creation as testimony that this is a practical faith, as practical as the sun, the rain, a cedar tree, the good earth. [8]

Friedman's example on the nationally broadcast *Free to Choose* thus adapted the former public relations man's homily aimed at schoolchildren. SIFE teams then repackaged it for personal visits to elementary classrooms. Harding University's team added the marketing pizzazz of the giant pencil, and other colleges dramatized the lesson in other ways. Malone College took "I, Pencil" to elementary schools to illustrate "the power of the market, *not government control,* to produce private goods." Malone's team tested the youngsters before and after the presentation. They were gratified to note that while before the lesson, almost half the children answered the question "Who is responsible for the output of goods?" with "government," the post-test revealed that "SIFE instruction reduced that percentage to three percent."[9]

In its new incarnation as a Wal-Mart project, the nonprofit SIFE made friends in high places and learned to shape its message to their demands. SIFE specialized in popularizing simplified free-market principles, using the cutting-edge communications techniques developed by PR professionals and the New Christian Right. It aimed equally at rousing local opinion in favor of corporate capitalism and at grooming the student activists themselves for management positions with Wal-Mart and the other major sponsors. They filled a market niche created by the entrepreneurial education movement: elementary and secondary-school teachers knew little of economics, and while by the mid-1980s almost half the states mandated some form of instruction in the subject, teachers reported little interest in equipping themselves through course work. SIFE offered free public instruction in the dismal science.[10] During the 1980s and early 1990s, in other words, SIFE developed a successful mechanism for creating a grassroots free-market constituency—"sort of a trickle-down approach to business education," in the assessment of *Entrepreneur* magazine.[11] The corporate and political backing that the organization attracted after 1984 definitively shaped its every facet, from the location of its headquarters to the petitions it circulated and sent to Washington to the students' subsequent career paths.

It would, however, be a mistake to reduce SIFE to its material components and interest groups. The various players recognized their stakes in the project, but it worked because it convinced its participants that each was serving a higher good. "SIFE is not just an enterprise that gives a member experience for the future, but an organization for those who want to make a difference in the economic situation!" wrote a student in 1986.[12] The thrill lay in the struggle, for SIFE was reborn under conditions of wild economic flux and uncertainty. With America's postwar economic dominance at an end and capitalism in a struggle with its Soviet foe, nothing less than the fate of the free world rode on their efforts.

"Economic freedom," the students asserted, "is the foundation of all freedoms," and they were its guardians. The free market was about faith, about community, about cooperation, and about devotion to principle. Though students recognized the resumé-building potential of SIFE, they passionately donated their energies to what they perceived as an idealistic cause, not a mere system for the production and distribution of goods and services. In exchange for a token annual grant and the honor of a title, faculty advisers dedicated their time and energy to their students. Even the corporate sponsors, though they responded to the public relations and recruiting potential of SIFE, donated their personal time, not just their money. And they were saluted in the terms that businessmen had struggled to popularize for two generations. "There is a noble calling in going into business and creating jobs," Ross Perot told a SIFE audience.[13] SIFE paid all its participants in a currency not easily reducible to the substantial flow of funds in play: recognition, appreciation, the chance to give advice, the opportunity to make a voluntary, personal contribution to a recognizably momentous era. "I envy you," the CEO of H&R Block told a gathering of procapitalist students during the dizzying collapse of the communist world. "You're here at a great time in the history of this country."[14]

In 1985, Wal-Mart's vice president Jack Shewmaker hitched SIFE to the company's shooting star, marking a clear turning point for the student organization. The new vigor and resources had an immediate impact. New students could come into the club by direct recruitment from the current team members or by faculty selection, but the core group remained a small, carefully chosen cadre.[15] Each team was headed by a faculty adviser, and the instructors and students together gathered in a dozen regional centers for essentially the same training session Sonny Davis and his team had honed. SIFE's method minimized lecturing in favor of small-group teamwork. With this training element, headquarters emphasized, SIFE was "the most motivated and effective college free enterprise program in the country." Key techniques included "getting commitment from a group," "keeping presentations moving and stimulating," and "recruitment of volunteers."[16] Said one of the 800 participants who trained in 1985, "I feel like I'm ready now to go out and evangelize the country for free enterprise."[17]

The following year, the fall workshops in thirteen cities were revamped with the materials endowed by the Business Roundtable and a more top-down design for about a thousand attendees. In this "completely new experience in strategic planning," the staff walked the small groups through the process of setting up "outreach projects," so that every college team left with at least three such projects organized under the supervision of the SIFE trainers. Additional material for the workshops came from TV news magazine segments, like the *60 Minutes* story subtitled "Strip Mining in Appalachia." The clip demonstrated how coal companies used the federal two-acre exemption to avoid environmental standards for surface mines. SIFE creatively used the story to demonstrate "the negative effects of an excessive government regulation." Perhaps not surprisingly, it "resulted in stimulating discussions" from Orlando to Dallas.[18]

Keeping each campus's core SIFE team to a small cadre of hand-picked students remained an important element of the package. One SIFE adviser, formerly of Standard Oil, noted with satisfaction "the dedication of a relatively small group of students, who believe they have been given tremendous responsibility and who respond with vigor."[19] Another stressed tight control over the team's make-up by guaranteeing membership only on a year-to-year basis, removing unproductive members promptly, and allowing graduating seniors to choose their own replacements.[20] Three-quarters of the colleges offered the students academic credit for their work.[21] But equally important were the enthusiastic "support and recognition" lavished on the team members by their small communities, both on campus and off.[22]

Elementary school groups were a favorite audience for SIFE's message because, as one faculty adviser put it, "their attitudes are not yet set."[23] The corporate campaign against "economic illiteracy" made many schools anxious for precisely the kind of instruction SIFE could offer, and businesses were looking for less heavy-handed ways to get their message into classrooms. But the SIFE teams and their corporate sponsors experimented with other venues as well. "SIFE team members have even been invited to individual workplaces," a promotional video pointed out. "There they successfully motivate employees to higher productivity." And the growing proportion of Americans who passed through colleges and universities were always an available audience. Instead of lecturing about the virtues of business to student audiences, SIFE made the students the bearers of the message to their own peers, since "students reach students much more effectively."[24] It was a familiar policy in SIFE's circles. The administrations of Harding University and its sister campus Oklahoma Christian University, for example, had decided by the 1960s that their "Americanism" programs ought to concentrate on "training student leaders whose influence will be felt after they return to their home communities and multiplied through years of future leadership."[25]

The key to attracting financial support, SIFE's leaders understood, was lavishing honors and attention on businessmen who had felt themselves unfairly maligned in the 1970s. In this they built on the techniques developed by schools like Harding and John Brown University. Awards multiplied at a brisk clip, and were seldom confined to a single recipient. Regional competitions and even individual rounds of judging within them bore the names of friendly corporations. These honors complemented the major gateway to sponsorship, the invitation to potential sponsors to serve as "distinguished judges." The attention frequently paid off handsomely: The conservative Adolph Coors family— foundational backers of the Heritage Foundation, the Committee for the Survival of a Free Congress, and other key institutions of the conservative ascendancy—came on board as sponsors of the magazine *SIFE Lines* after careful courtship.[26] In a pattern repeated by Wal-Mart, Coors gave generously to SIFE both through the company itself and through the family's philanthropic foundation.[27]

Alongside its growing ties to national conservative networks, SIFE clear-headedly maintained its regional connections and watched its circle of friends expand concentrically. Tyson Foods, Northwest Arkansas's other stunning corporate success story, lent a hand. Legendary Dallas realtor Ebby Halliday and her husband galvanized new support from the Big D with personal letters to several hundred business associates, urging their contributions to SIFE.[28] Congressman Eldon Rudd of Arizona gave $200,000 in 1987, crediting SIFE with "one of the greatest impacts on American citizens' current attitudes towards the free enterprise system."[29] Likewise, the energy industry continued to support SIFE. Standard Oil of Ohio contributed $5,000 to the 1985 fall training session and created cash prizes for the best projects on the theme "The Role of Energy in Free Enterprise."[30] The founder of the Empire Gas Corporation, in the Ozarks town of Lebanon, Missouri, led the club in creative funding ideas and hosted the recreational get-togethers that "built a strong sense of community among the SIFE Board." All told, the organization estimated that Empire Gas's founder personally helped raise hundreds of thousands of dollars and recruited many fellow board members over the years.[31]

SIFE was not shy about making explicit the connection between its presence on campus and business support for the participating schools. When asked in 1986 what benefits Lubbock Christian College had received by having a SIFE chapter, a faculty adviser noted that in addition to publicity, "it has accounted for $70,000 to $80,000 in contributions in six years."[32] The group's director, Alvin Rohrs, summed it up: colleges used SIFE "to recruit students to their campuses and to build lucrative bridges between the local and national business communities."[33] Thus its presence paid off twice, first in tuition from an increased pool of students and second in direct corporate support.

In 1988, after traveling to various cities in the central time zone, the Students in Free Enterprise International Expo landed in Kansas City, Missouri, at the invitation of Hallmark Cards, Inc., headquartered there. The greeting-card company's gift of $25,000 led a wave of financial support from the city's businessmen when the card company's executives introduced SIFE around town. The metropolis closest to SIFE's Ozark home, Kansas City also served as the site for Wal-Mart's annual year-end meeting.[34]

The sponsoring corporations were the first to see the potential for SIFE as a recruitment tool. The gathering in one mid-American city of a self-selected pool of collegians, proven free-market enthusiasts who had already contributed substantial unpaid time and effort to supporting profit-making ventures, must have struck the employers as an unparalleled opportunity. Wal-Mart and Memphis-based Holiday Inn were the first to the plate, though SIFE took care to introduce the 1986 initiative in terms of "the benefits to the individual students" rather than to the companies.[35] And indeed, this message required no exaggeration: Leslie Gutierrez, a SIFE student on her way to graduating that spring, wrote that the "hard work, dedication, and responsibility" she had learned as president of her local chapter had led to her new management job at Wal-Mart.[36]

The fruits of these efforts began showing up regularly in SIFE materials, which highlighted alumni's jobs at sponsor corporations.[37] Where else, asked the organization rhetorically, could students find such an unparalleled opportunity "to market themselves to America's greatest entrepreneurs and top corporate executives . . . It is no wonder that executives that served as judges are now hiring SIFE graduates."[38] Thus when the Findlay College SIFE team won the national competition in 1986, one of the judges was so impressed that he offered to back the students in launching a business. Jennifer Payne took him up on the proposal and opened "Gifts in Time," a service that provided appropriate gifts for companies to distribute in appreciation of their employees.[39] When Missourian Joe McGennis turned to State Fair Community College to earn an associate's degree in business, he quickly found a home in SIFE. His role models became the team's adviser and Wal-Mart's Jack Shewmaker. "By making contact with members of Wal-Mart through SIFE," he later wrote in gratitude, "I recently was interviewed and hired by Wal-Mart Stores, Inc., as an associate manager. I owe my future employment to SIFE and the fact I was introduced to Mr. Shewmaker and the Wal-Mart family."[40]

The reborn SIFE understood its mission to be as much about form as content, as much about its consumers—the corporations willing to pay for its services—as about the collegians or their community audiences. The distinguished judges' concern with communications, presentation, and style; their insistence on attitude, enthusiasm, and the power of positive thinking; their obsession with documentation, quantification, and growth—these signaled their interest as potential employers of a new generation in a postindustrial workplace. The promiscuous devotion the organization lavished on its sponsors—awards, honor rolls, the seemingly infinite supply of places or events that could be named for someone—hinted at its history in Sonny Davis's consulting business. And though Wal-Mart and its fellow service providers quickly realized SIFE's potential for recruiting, screening, and training new employees, the organization first entered corporate funding streams through PR departments concerned with specific image issues. Accordingly, SIFE addressed not Karl Marx or Rosa Luxemburg but Rachel Carson and Ralph Nader, and it did so in the idiom of Christian free enterprise.

With Shewmaker chairing the SIFE board and the energetic Rohrs at the helm, the organization kept SIFE's potential in front of its friends. Missouri governor John Ashcroft, a member of Leaders of the Ozarks, proclaimed a statewide "Free Enterprise Week," as did his Arkansas counterpart, Bill Clinton.[41] In 1985, the Leaders hosted an "Ozarks

Against Government Waste" fundraiser for SIFE featuring chemical magnate J. Peter Grace. Grace's eponymous commission of over 150 executives had been charged by President Reagan in 1982 with working "like tireless bloodhounds to root out government inefficiency and waste of tax dollars," a two-year mission underwritten by the heads of many of the country's largest corporations. Peter Grace's personal motives in trying to "get government off our backs" were not utterly disinterested. As a subsequent guilty plea revealed, at the same time he was serving as the chair of the antiwaste commission, Grace lied to the Environmental Protection Agency about the quantities of hazardous materials used at its plant in Woburn, Massachusetts. Ultimately, the EPA also found the company guilty of illegally dumping carcinogenic chemicals that poisoned Woburn's water source, resulting in the deaths of six town residents and $8 million in settlements.[42]

These revelations, however, lay in the future. Grace had used his high-profile experience chairing the Grace Commission to found Citizens Against Government Waste, and SIFE took up the message with a new initiative in 1985. More than fifty SIFE chapters took part in an intensive, ten-week effort to "educate Americans on the need to reduce the federal deficit caused by government waste," explained the new SIFE newsletter. The clubs distributed pamphlets, books, and articles on the topic, and reached out with classroom seminars, media events, and petition booths in shopping centers and on street corners. Competing in a special category for $10,000 in prize money, the student activists claimed to have exposed millions of Americans to their message about "the threat posed to our free enterprise system by the federal deficit."[43]

The Business Roundtable, the lobbying organization comprising two hundred CEOs from some of America's largest companies, shared Peter Grace's anxiety about the deficit. For the annual fall orientation meeting of SIFE teams in 1985, the Business Roundtable provided each SIFE team with materials for getting across an urgent message: "Halt the Deficit!" Led to SIFE by its sponsor and Roundtable member Dow Chemical, the employers' organization outfitted the collegians with a how-to handbook; posters and bumper stickers bearing a stop-sign logo; postcards addressed to Congress; printed petitions; and "a professionally produced slide presentation, pre-written speeches, articles, letters and research booklets," all designed to awaken communities to the threat and stir them to "demand that Congress stop waste and inefficiency."

The 170 campuses reached through SIFE turned the nonprofit into "the foremost voice on American campuses for the deficit message."[44] For the high-quality campaign materials, SIFE graciously thanked Business Roundtable executive director James Keogh, formerly President Nixon's chief speechwriter.[45] "Halt the Deficit," in other words, represented the state of the art in the new media-ready mobilization campaigns that were increasingly taking the place of party machinations.

The content of the campaign, however, is a reminder that the conservative coalition behind Reagan hardly spoke with one voice. Certainly the argument that the burgeoning federal deficit—a record $110 million in the president's first year—resulted primarily from spendthrift politicians and inefficient bureaucrats was intended to draw responsibility away from the promised tax cuts and increased military spending that Reagan was delivering in his early months. But the deficit critique nevertheless insisted on holding the new president to the third element of his tripartite program, that of a balanced budget. The tough sell for Reaganomics lay in the evident incommensurability between the first two desiderata and the third. Cutting taxes on business, after all, did not ensure that the funds thus freed up would go to build another factory— or at least, not another factory in the United States. Business appreciated the supply-side generosity of Reagan's 1981 tax cuts—a 25 percent reduction over three years—but the predicted recovery did not follow. By early 1982, with unemployment and bankruptcies at alarming levels and the deficit at a peacetime high, businessmen broke ranks. The Business Roundtable informed the White House there would be "no more blind following" of the administration's economic policy. The president should cut back on his exuberant military appropriations, raise excise taxes, and delay the scheduled 10 percent reduction in the income tax, they counseled him in a private meeting.[46]

It was in the context of their failure to rein in Reagan and the uncertain fate of a balanced budget amendment in Congress that the Business Roundtable launched an appeal directly to the public. The "Halt the Deficit" campaign made a dramatic debut in a four-page advertising spread in *Reader's Digest* in 1985. Almost a million readers tore out and mailed in the accompanying postage-paid postcard. The magazine helpfully kept a tally by state and reported daily to Congress and the president. The overwhelming response caught all players by surprise. When the initial count reached 30,000, the *Digest* stated flatly, "We have never seen anything like this for anything we have done, and know of no other response like this in any magazine at any time." Not one to rest on its laurels, the Business Roundtable also distributed kits to each of its member companies, equipping them with postcards for employees and shareholders.[47]

This effective advertising tool became an enduring theme for SIFE, even as the landscape of business lobbying continued to shift.[48] In 1986, the Business Roundtable gave the organization $10,000 in prize money for a "Halt the Deficit" competition and another $5,000 to develop a teacher's guide to complement the deficit handbook that SIFE students were getting into junior-high and high-school classrooms around the country. A SIFE-produced video incorporating the Roundtable's message could be bought or borrowed from headquarters. Some Business Roundtable CEOs—heads of the largest companies in the country—served as SIFE judges at the regional and national levels of the competition.[49] Ross Perot spoke out against the deficit at a SIFE gathering in his trademark Texas twang, an early taste of what would become a key theme of his 1992 presidential bid.[50]

Students threw themselves into what they considered a fairly transparent issue: Keynesian deficit spending, after all, did not work on the individual level, so it must be equally pernicious for a nation. Lubbock Christian College, for instance, gave more than twenty presentations on the subject to area civic clubs in their 1985–86 academic year.[51] In the same year Findlay College in Ohio got out the word on the Grace Commission via radio and provided a hundred area clergy members with materials on the deficit to transmit to their congregations.[52] Some of the most successful antideficit projects hinged on dramatic strategies for concretizing an issue that could seem rather remote from most citizens' daily concerns. The key was to dissolve any distinction between individuals and institutions. Students at the University of Steubenville sent out invoices for individual portions of the federal deficit to the members of their campus.[53] At Mount Vernon Nazarene, in the cachement area of the Appalachian exodus to industrial Ohio, SIFE members teamed up with a local tombstone carver for their project. At a busy intersection, the monument business set up a headstone inscribed "Bury the Deficit." With this backdrop, a SIFE student made the local news, carrying the message of federal waste to "all of West Virginia, Eastern Kentucky, and Southern Ohio."[54]

Malone College collected almost 20,000 signatures on a petition "demanding that the federal government stop wasting money."[55] Like many schools, the Tuskegee Institute produced public service announcements about "the dangers associated with the runaway deficit" and had them aired on TV and radio stations near the historic university.[56] In awarding cash prizes, the judges considered such criteria as: "How successful were the students in bringing about attitudinal change?" But in their communications, the training manual stressed, the competitors should make it clear that "the opinions are exclusively those of the presenting students."[57]

SIFE's top corporate supporter, Wal-Mart, adapted some of these methods and materials for its own subsequent in-house campaign against the deficit. A two-page spread in a 1992 *Wal-Mart World* instructed employees that they should be working to elect congressional members who would curb government spending. The article warned that when the time came to pay off the federal deficit, "it might be through confiscation of wealth; re-valuation of currency; or *government seizure of retirement plans to support spending habits.*" Echoing the primary sources for "Halt the Deficit," Wal-Mart recommended to its employees J. Peter Grace's 1984 polemic on congressional waste and *The Coming Financial Earthquake,* by the Christian financial counselor Larry Burkett.[58]

The federal budget deficit remained a major focus for SIFE until the late 1990s, though the political issue fizzled and the Roundtable eventually dropped its support. As it turned out, a balanced federal budget was achieved under President Clinton, after the income-tax increases of the George H. W. Bush administration and of the first Clinton administration bore fruit.[59] But through its sponsors the organization also shone a spotlight on other potential political interventions in economic issues. Beginning in the 1987–1988 competition cycle, Dow Chemical Company provided prize money for a special division on the "liability crisis."

This issue was certainly timely. In April of 1987, a federal appeals court had upheld a $200 million settlement against seven chemical companies, including Dow, on behalf of 20,000 "utterly disabled" veterans exposed to Agent Orange during the war in Vietnam. The corporations specifically denied responsibility in the settlement, but as the appellate judge noted at the time, it was a landmark decision nonetheless.[60]

The case, moreover, took place against the backdrop of the devastating Union Carbide disaster in Bhopal, India, which resulted in legislation toughening requirements for disclosure of dangers to employees and communities. Suddenly everyone knew what was coming out of the smokestacks at the edge of town. Meanwhile, with industry regulation and enforcement drastically cut back under Reagan, lawsuits had become the only effective tool for those concerned with potential hazards.[61] In response, virtually all the industry's insurers began to drop pollution liability coverage.[62] There was, indeed, a liability crisis.

The Dow Chemical liability representative to SIFE was Debbie C. Nute, the company's manager of government affairs resources and a member of the Chemical Manufacturers Association's Grassroots Task Force, a subgroup of its own government relations committee. This latter organization had been formed in 1983 under the direction of Dow executives with the ultimate goal of producing "a positive impact on the Association's top legislative priority: Superfund/public compensation legislation." According to the committee report in 1985, "extremely important results were achieved" and the lessons learned would prove useful for other industry priorities like "toxic air pollutants [and] contaminated groundwater."[63] But as the industry association noted, "a new but rapidly growing issue at the state and federal level is liability insurance and the related issue of tort reform." As liability insurance premiums grew by as much as 500 percent, liability reformers could look for federal support from the Reagan administration's Tort Policy Working Group and from their number-one congressional champion, Senator John Danforth, a Missouri Republican. But much of the fight would take place in the states.[64]

Concerned, the chemical companies joined a coalition under the auspices of the American Legislative Exchange Council and set out to generate a citizen outcry against tort abuse.[65] It was an uphill battle, but as the SIFE competition demonstrated, Dow and the industry group Chemical Manufacturers Association had a valuable asset in Mrs. Nute, wife of Dow lobbyist Leslie F. "Lee" Nute. At an association meeting, Mrs. Nute described Dow's grassroots campaign. "Everyone was very impressed with the quality and comprehensiveness of this program," the minutes recorded, "and it was recommended that every company strongly consider such a program. Debbie said that all of their materials are readily available to anyone."[66] Liability law reform advocates reported "dramatic gains" for state-level tort reform in mid-1987 and pre-dicted even more adjustments in the months ahead.[67]

At Southeastern Louisiana University, bordering the state's "chemical corridor," SIFE students took up the liability challenge with gusto. Twenty separate projects got the message out to various audiences in a commu-nity lacking its own newspaper and TV station. The students estimated they reached over 100,000 residents with "[r]adio interviews, letters to the editor, oral presentations, handbills, and personal interviews."[68] At Findlay College, not far from Dow's Ohio state headquarters, the team took the fight "to college and high school classrooms, holding discus-sions on what product liability does to the economy."[69]

In west Texas, just up the road from Midland, Lubbock Christian University's SIFE chapter distributed Dow's own PR package entitled "Lawsuit," including the chemical company's issue briefs, a video, and frequently asked questions, with Dow's suggestion for solving the prob-lem. Repackaged by the students, the same information made it into over 12,000 "teacher aid packets" distributed around the southwest by Lubbock Christian under a $10,000 grant from Southwestern Bell's foundation. Through the local Chamber of Commerce and the Lubbock public schools, the team distributed sample letters and postcards to congressmen "with a plea to act quickly to halt this crisis and restore common decency by limiting liability awards and legal fees." Their zeal sparked a letter-writing campaign by the local Kiwanis club, and at a retreat for high-school students, SIFE members were able to "produce marked attitude changes from their previous biases . . . These students were amazed at the misunderstandings they had held."[70]

The crusade did not shy from addressing electoral politics explicitly, although it avoided applying party names to its white and black hats. Before the Super Tuesday primaries in 1988, SIFE members at Lubbock Christian University organized a straw vote for their campus that was covered by local media. At a campuswide meeting, over 600 audience members received instruction on the candidates' degrees of free-market devotion. SIFE's efforts were justified by the tally, which revealed that "over 80% understood the need to maintain a strong free enterprise system."[71] One of the stated objectives of Southern Illinois University students was to create "interest in citizens' responsibility to preserve the free enterprise system through the elective process." Students estimated that they reached 88,000 households in one year with a middle-school essay contest on the theme "How voting preserves our free enterprise system."[72]

Not every SIFE supporter came from a *Fortune* 500 company's public relations department, of course. The smaller employers in Wal-Mart's original trade territory displayed a range of concerns for the area they also called home, and while their economic values fit easily under SIFE's roof with those of the major players, their tactics sometimes contrasted sharply with the professional marketing initiatives of a Sun Oil or a Dow. In 1986, for example, a Missouri community college SIFE team hosted a panel that matched a labor representative with SIFE supporter Glenn Stahl, president of the antiunion Missourians for the Right to Work.[73] SIFE's message resonated with Stahl, who was equally concerned with students' attitudes and their vocational skills. "Often kids come out of school with no practical knowledge," he explained. "We can't afford to have people around here who look down their noses at people who produce things."[74] While certainly the open-shop crusade was a high priority for many industry lobbies, Stahl's worldview was more Bentonville than Business Roundtable. SIFE stayed in the Ozarks for good reason.

For Stahl, as for Wal-Mart's Shewmaker and others at the organization's top ranks, there was evidently no inherent contradiction between doing well and doing good through SIFE. They were sincerely glad to know that the kids were alright, even while deploying them for straightforwardly self-interested ends. Certainly many of the decision-makers were clear in their own minds about the difference between economics as a field of academic study, on the one hand, and the procorporate agenda they were promoting, on the other. They simply preferred the latter. Wal-Mart's chief operating officer, Don Soderquist, explained that the retailer supported SIFE because the organization taught young people "not what capitalism is, because I cringe a little bit with the word 'capitalism,' but what free enterprise is and how it fits in with the democracy we enjoy in these United States." In promoting SIFE to potential corporate sponsors, its material emphasized that it was "an action program, not a study or discussion group." Teams were judged on their effectiveness at shaping public opinion to the industries' chosen legislative priorities rather than opening up debate or providing context. "Remember," wrote an influential SIFE adviser from Harding University, "a university's goal is to search for truth. The SIFE goal is to promote the things we believe in."[75]

Although this distinction was thus explicit within SIFE's upper ranks, the content entered publicly funded channels as "economic education." Students at a Baptist college in Muskogee managed to get their workshop certified for staff development points for public-school teachers, meaning that a SIFE training session on free markets counted toward the teachers' state licensing requirements. Missouri Southern University's team established its two-week mini-course as a permanent element of the curriculum in area junior high and high schools, reaching 1,600 students a year. The complete package they distributed to teachers included lesson plans, tests, a list of objectives, and films, readings and "academic assistance" for the teachers who "admittedly do not have an economic background."[76] The teams routinely provided advertisements for their economic causes as public service announcements to local radio stations, aired for free under federal regulations.[77]

Much of the program's success depended on the committed faculty leaders, who saw their work as a form of ministry. Many of the Sam M. Walton Free Enterprise Fellows, as the advisers were known after Walton's death in 1992, showed extraordinary devotion to their students. The fellowships amounted to only a token sum, but the honor was deeply appreciated. As in other sectors of the service economy, the faculty members were front-line service providers, motivated by the higher calling of self-sacrifice and the pleasure of caring for their "customers." As one adviser put it, when a small group of students was willing to put so much into the projects, with no reward but "the satisfaction of having accomplished something this important, the least I can do is give them my total support."[78]

Becoming faculty adviser to the SIFE team at Malone College was the fulfillment of a lifelong dream for E. William Dykes. The Canton, Ohio, architect dated his passion for capitalism to 1948, when he heard a lecture by Leonard E. Read. Dykes eventually became a trustee and chairman of the board at Read's organization, the Foundation for Economic Education. As he put it, the organization played "a very important part in my life as they articulated the close connection between freedom of the individual and freedom in the marketplace." In 1981, Dykes was considering a partial retirement from his architecture business when his local college approached him about a new opportunity. The Greater Canton Chamber of Commerce had offered Malone College a chair in free enterprise, and Dykes was their choice to take the post. Modeling its program on the University of Akron's, Malone College tied SIFE into the curriculum from the outset and concentrated on "correction of the economic fallacies which are the result of poor economic education at all levels." Malone sent college students into area schools to promote free enterprise for course credit, with such presentations totaling close to 200 when Dykes retired in 1986. His next project, he mused, might be the writing of a textbook on the subject for schools, but he was conflicted: How could he justify teaching about free markets in public schools when the economic model depended on "belief in the Creator of all good things. This latter view is not consistent with what can be advocated in public schools and therefore such a text could have only limited acceptance."[79]

Similar views held sway at Kent State University in Ohio, where in 1970 the National Guard had fired on a student protest against the secret invasion of Laos, killing four students. At this campus, formerly a national symbol of the antiwar movement, a free-enterprise instructor was gratified to imagine himself in 1978 as a "business missionary." His mission: "to break down the walls of Jericho and correct the many negative misconceptions about business."[80] His example inspired student activists at Kent State's SIFE chapter. In 1979, the energetic club organized a "Battle of the Bands" at a bar a few blocks from Kent State's campus, awarding donated prizes to the best probusiness rock song.[81]

As its architects intended, the core of SIFE was not economics as a discipline but economic education as a practical trade. Children were the default audience and business literacy the bottom line. Some faculty advisers qualified themselves with a prior career in small business, left behind for the security and prestige of college teaching or tacked onto the end of a corporate career.[82] Others came from backgrounds in business training, at a further remove from economics even than economic education or practical business experience. Dr. Gary F. Young, a SIFE adviser, earned his doctorate with a cost-benefit analysis of the "self-paced" trend in vocational training. By the time he connected with SIFE, Young held an endowed chair in free enterprise at the University of Tennessee–Martin, where his activities included directing a "Kinder-Nomics" course for preschoolers and a Business and Economics Leadership Camp for high-school students.[83] Some brought explicit interests in Christianity to their scholarly work, like the adviser at Western Kentucky University who analyzed "the areas of money management dealt with in the Holy Bible."[84]

SIFE's focus on public outreach and especially on schoolchildren meant that the economic concepts in play remained extremely basic: profits are beneficial; government is wasteful; unions are illegitimate; corporations are natural persons; free markets abhor environmental regulation but not cartels, monopsony contracts, or military-supported access to foreign raw materials. Even at schools that taught economics as a theoretical discipline, SIFE invariably entered through the business departments. A small number of committed ideologues provided some of the fire in SIFE's belly, but only at a remove from the core theories they represented. SIFE students read "I, Pencil," not *The Wealth of Nations* nor even *The Road to Serfdom*.

Sometimes, however, the students veered toward contradictions between their ideological models and conflicting economic values. In the midst of the intense focus on entrepreneurial heroism and government profligacy, Malone College's 1987 project stood out for its explicit reference to the basis of the postindustrial economy. The program they presented that year in more than thirty elementary, junior high, and high schools was boldly titled "Consumer Sovereignty." It "explored the importance of the three main areas of the private sector economy: households, producers and markets."[85] Harding University, confident that "business is moral [because] it practices the Golden Rule voluntarily," was nonetheless moved to establish a business ethics retreat after national reports of insider trading, tax evasion, falsified records, safety violations, check kiting, the use of public office for personal gain and various other scams.[86] Southern Illinois University's team started off its rookie year in the fall of 1987 with a stock-market simulation competition that featured teams drawn from high schools and senior citizens' programs. The participants may have learned some unintended lessons, for the final awards banquet in January included a comparison of the crashes of 1929 and 1987 and asked the winners to reflect on whether they would really choose to play the market.[87]

A more fundamental contradiction, however, was the same one that plagued the field of entrepreneurship education. The students in SIFE, like their peers in free-enterprise centers across the Sun Belt, did not seem very interested in striking out on their own. Indeed, with the recruitment function that SIFE was playing for its biggest sponsor and the colleges' interest in postgraduation "placement rates" for students with employers, a wholesale exodus to the entrepreneurial frontier would not have been in SIFE's long-term interests. Still, the entrepreneur wore the mantle of capitalist virtue on this public stage.

In service to this ideal, SIFE received targeted support from the National Federation of Independent Business (NFIB), the small-business lobbying organization whose moral authority and grassroots support were so crucial to many of the Business Roundtable's efforts. Starting in 1986, the federation awarded two $1,000 prizes to the teams that had "developed the most creative and effective lesson plans" for instructing students on "the role of the entrepreneur in the free enterprise system."[88] Every SIFE team continued to cultivate a local Business Advisory Board to guide them and serve as inspiration for budding businessmen. In the superheated financial climate of the mid-1980s, however, the local Chevrolet dealer might not be the object of desire. In a 1989 segment for the TV show *Nation's Business Today,* an interviewer asked the SIFE director Alvin Rohrs the obvious question: Who were the business heroes of these young people? Were they dazzled by the "glamorous comings and going of a Donald Trump?" Just who were their role models?[89]

Rohrs responded diplomatically that there was a range of figures that the young people looked up to, starting with "the entrepreneur," who could be anyone from a local restauranteur to Sam Walton himself. When the interviewer pressed him to choose the big corporation or the independent business as their ultimate destination, the SIFE director concluded with the same theme of countless professors of entrepreneurship: As best he could tell, "a lot of them would like to own their own business, but a lot of them have the entrepreneurial spirit that they want to bring to corporations."[90] Again, the unique power of the Sun Belt's entrepreneurial corporations squared the circle: with Sam Walton as the exemplar, entrepreneurship could be a character trait, not an economic function.

By the winter of 1987, SIFE had outgrown its home at Southwestern Baptist, both practically and symbolically. The association with a regional, denominational school limited its national appeal, and with its growth to 180 campuses and a $540,000 annual budget, the organiza-

tion was seeking new quarters. Meanwhile, Joe Straughan, a businessman from neighboring Springfield, Missouri, had a proposition.
Straughan had judged at two national SIFE competitions and joined the
executive committee of the student group's supporters, the Leaders of
the Ozarks. He had a 4,000-square foot office standing empty in Springfield, and even better, it was already outfitted with a late-model telecommunications infrastructure, for Straughan was president of an advertising agency.[91] This move anchored SIFE in Springfield, the de facto
capital of the tri-state Ozarks region. It also cemented the organization's
connection to public relations, advertising, and increasingly sophisticated communications technology.

Wal-Mart, of course, had finished the 1970s with a new understanding of the possibilities for political involvement, or conversely for the
price of forgoing it. The vehicle for refocusing its attention had been the
proposed labor reform law that consolidated the power of a new business lobby. Meanwhile, many of Wal-Mart's fellow Sun Belt industries—
especially the chemical and petroleum concerns—were aggressively organizing to regain the advantage in the public sphere. SIFE's market
opportunities expanded in proportion to this increasing respect for activism coming from businesses of all sizes.

Business's extraordinary recovery of political influence under adverse
circumstances was not just a triumph of the will. The president of the
National Association of Manufacturers credited "the decline in the role
of the party" first and foremost. A wave of reforms in the congressional
committee system devolved power from the small clutch of super-senior
members to the lush undergrowth of the proliferating subcommittees.
Even the hoary Senate allowed a thousand flowers to bloom in its first
serious organizational reform since 1946. The revolt against the seniority system and the influx of new members to the House in the mid-
1970s unintentionally weakened the influence of both party apparatuses
back home. Shaping policy became less a question of elite access to a
handful of powerful committee chairmen and more about maintaining
a web of relations with multiple players. Even more disruptively, a corporation's aims could not be achieved without finding new ways to generate massive public support for single issues. It was in this context of
an influence vacuum that the ability to mobilize voters outside party
structures became a pressing concern.[92]

Three distinct avenues of mobilization ranked particularly high for beleaguered business under these altered circumstances. The white-collar class that filled the multiplying layers of middle management represented a powerful new resource. A union could always recommend political action to its members, but the explicit function of a company's top management was to give orders. Suggestions to its salaried strivers about political action, in the context of a command hierarchy, could hardly sound like an exchange of views among equals. An executive of the California Savings and Loan League, for example, suggested to his constituent corporations in 1978 that the firms hand out to employees "specific assignments to work in politics" and further urged that a subordinate's raises "might well be tied directly to his involvement in the political assignment you have given him." There was nothing hidden in this form of persuasion.[93]

The second innovation with which business met the changed congressional environment was the explosion of sophisticated, systematic attention to federal policy-makers through both professionalized lobbying and elite, business-funded think tanks. Existing trade organizations moved their headquarters to Washington or expanded their staffs there, and hundreds of new ones sprang up. Changes in election finance laws encouraged the efflorescence of political action committees, which could funnel money to issues rather than candidates. Trade- and business-oriented PACs quickly overtook those the unions had fielded, raising $50 million more in 1982 than their labor rivals.[94] Think tanks like the Heritage Foundation, the American Enterprise Institute, and the Hoover Institute turned the fortunes of Coors and Dow Chemical to the painstaking task of disseminating ideas. An admiring observer rejoiced in the early Reagan years that neoconservatives had successfully sustained their message for years "through journal articles, press briefings, seminars, essays for newspaper op-ed pages, television and radio panel discussions and workshops for congressional staffers and corporate executives. The very weight of this intellectual output," he concluded, "is tilting the scale of opinion to the right."[95]

This emphasis on ideas over political mechanisms opened up the third avenue for re-establishing business influence in the new dispensation. Access to Washington was priceless, but with party loyalties weakened, Washington itself now depended more decisively on the approval of mass numbers of voters, issue by issue. The prize would increasingly go to the side with the most effective grassroots mobilization tactics.

It was under these conditions that effective communications suddenly commanded the most respectful attention of SIFE's corporate constituency. The changed playing field elevated business esteem for the emerging New Christian Right, whose constituents had been training in effective communications for two generations. Frustrated by their lack of access to the Big Three television networks and mainstream publishing outlets, conservative Christians had pioneered alternative communications channels since World War II. Like the Moral Majority and similar direct-mail mobilizers, SIFE benefited from the New Right's superior grasp of communications.

In his role as vice president, Jack Shewmaker brought an appreciation for forward-looking communication techniques to Wal-Mart and to SIFE. Smart and self-confident yet unpretentious, Shewmaker displayed the classic accoutrements of a Wal-Mart executive: the pickup truck, the hunting trips, the durable marriage. He once told a reporter that his favorite material possession was his father's shotgun.[96] Though supremely competent in multiple aspects of retail, Shewmaker's passion was communications. He had been a driving force behind Wal-Mart's early adoption of ever more sophisticated technologies to link up stores to Bentonville.[97] From this context of relentless innovation in commercial communications, Shewmaker simultaneously threw himself into rebuilding SIFE, stumping for the organization around the country.[98]

The emphasis became a permanent feature of SIFE. Shewmaker's successor as SIFE board chair was Stanley N. Gaines, CEO of an automotive battery manufacturer that counted Wal-Mart as a major distributor.[99] Though Gaines kept a fairly low profile beyond the business world, his wife Gay Hart Gaines served as chair of the board for William F. Buckley's National Review Institute, and held positions at conservative think tanks like the Hudson Institute, the Heritage Foundation, and the American Enterprise Institute. Mrs. Gaines was a charter member of Newt Gingrich's political action committee GOPAC, organized in 1985. Elevated to serve as its chair in 1993, Mrs. Gaines became known as the capital's premiere conservative hostess.[100] She traveled the country raising money for the Republican takeover of Congress in 1994.[101] A few months before the upset victories that brought the "Contract with America," Mrs. Gaines confidently asserted that "Republican candidates are just beginning to reap the benefits of years of educational outreach and training, which will become apparent in the November elections."[102]

Like SIFE, GOPAC focused on early investment in a "farm team"—in this case, not of potential corporate talent but of state-level candidates who might ultimately make successful congressional bids. Instead of directing the majority of its contributions to individual campaigns, Mrs. Gaines explained in the wake of the Republican insurgency, the organization aimed at a broader cultural program. "GOPAC's primary mission is political training and education of candidates, party activists and the voting public."[103] "We have trained thousands of people—activists and candidates—to become more enlightened and effective citizens and elected leaders," she explained, making them able to bring "conservative ideals of lower taxes, smaller, more efficient government and citizenship responsibility" to the public agenda.[104] During Mrs. Gaines's years at GOPAC, moreover, the political action committee focused on the skillful use of language as a "key mechanism of control," sharpening the self-presentation skills of candidates and answering the "plaintive plea" of local spokespeople, "'I wish I could speak like Newt.'"[105] Through her husband's leadership of SIFE, then, the Springfield headquarters was positioned to learn from one of the New Right's most talented architects of communication.

Other SIFE supporters through the 1980s brought to the organization an increasingly sophisticated conservative expertise in public relations. SIFE board member Charles W. Hucker of Hallmark Cards also served on the board of the Public Affairs Council, an organization dedicated to increasing the influence of corporations in government policy.[106] Personal donations to SIFE came from the Dallas oilman Bill Clements, Jr., the first Republican governor of Texas since Reconstruction and an early client of Karl Rove.[107]

Some of the organizations' communicators learned their skills in the alternative media outlets that flourished in the shade of the mainstream media during the 1970s and 1980s. Kenneth Meyer, an Ozarks native, joined the board of SIFE in 1991 with a degree in business education and a background in broadcasting. Meyer and his wife had launched radio station KTXR in Springfield in the early 1960s, carving out a loyal base with easy-listening music, a popular Ozarks nostalgia feature called "Remember When," and the hometown sports events too small for the larger networks. In the days before cable, Meyers was among the pioneers of UHF TV, the local, low-budget alternative to the major networks. Meyer Communications grew to include several radio stations across southwestern Missouri and into Texas, with some stations ultimately affiliating with conservative news leader Fox.[108]

The emphasis on communication—on both technology and presentation style—was evident at the campus levels as well, where the small-town Sun Belt Christians enthusiastically embraced the glamorous new means to get the word out. Lubbock Christian University's SIFE, for example, took computer games that simulated starting a business and trading on the stock market to high schools.[109] Buying an electronic message board at the local Sam's Club, Harding University's energetic crusaders installed it in the campus business building and "displayed in a dynamic fashion over 100 short, simplified expressions of back-to-the-basics free enterprise economics."[110] Harding's SIFE adviser urged the students to take classes in speech, communication, and writing skills early on and to "get to know your college public relations staff and educational media staff."[111] "SIFE is more than just another student group," the 1989 annual report stated, "SIFE is . . . a media network."[112] As the techniques grew more sophisticated, some of the exuberant drama ebbed; giant pencils and puppet shows were less common. But in 1996, judges at a regional SIFE competition in Memphis's historic Peabody Hotel could still encounter acts like "SIFEMan," a "business superhero" in tights and a cape emblazoned with a large dollar sign. "Everybody needs a hero," explained the senior chemistry major from Union University.[113]

Long after their student days were behind them, SIFE alumni remembered their early lessons in persuasion. One alumna hosted a regular show on the cable shopping channel QVC in the 1980s before moving up to serve in its corporate offices.[114] Another, employed in the software business, credited her team's hard work in promoting "Free Enterprise Day" with teaching her the promotional skills she used in her $1.5 million company.[115] Jeff Shipley went from SIFE to Wal-Mart's recruiting office, and judged that "SIFE graduates who are Wal-Mart hires have better presentation and teaching skills than other hires."[116] In the postindustrial workplace, the ability to get the message across mattered as much as the message itself.

Even during its time of troubles in the early 1980s, SIFE had understood the international implications of its probusiness agenda. Its students back then drew heart from Reagan's 1982 speech to the British parliament, challenging the Anglo-Saxon democracies to take off the gloves and meet Red subversion with similar tactics: "Since 1917 the Soviet Union has given covert political training and assistance to Marxist-Leninists in many countries," the telegenic president declared, but two could play at that game. "It is time that we committed ourselves as a nation—in both the public and private sectors—to assisting democratic development."[117] SIFE took up that challenge with relish.

Within the strictures of the East-West conflict that shaped most of the students' worldviews in the 1980s, some glimmers of a post–Cold War developmentalism were visible. SIFE participants at Mount Vernon Nazarene College traveled to Belize to promote free enterprise with high-school visits, though the former British colony was hardly a citadel of Marxism. The eager young Christian visitors laid the groundwork for several micro-enterprises, such as a handicrafts exporting link, a small canning factory, and a cut flower business.[118] In the booming suburbs north of Atlanta, SIFE students at Kennesaw College developed a Spanish-language puppet show on entrepreneurship aimed at the area's growing immigrant population in the late 1980s. The management association of the aerospace defense contractor Lockheed-Martin used the company's facilities to produce a videotape of the show with plans to distribute it internationally and to Hispanic audiences in the United States.[119] Pan American University in Edinburg, Texas, focused the attention of that border town with a project it forthrightly entitled "Export the Trade Deficit."[120] And while the titanic struggle with the USSR overshadowed almost all other potential international contexts, an alert observer might have seen which way the wind was blowing in the patterns of SIFE's institutional growth. In 1984 the Ozarks organization established its first international connection, to Monterrey, Mexico. The private Centro de Estudios de Economía y Educacíon, founded in 1981, was dedicated to promoting the theories of the radically *laissez-faire*

Austrian economists, then slowly growing to prominence in Britain and the United States.[121]

Monterrey, in the northern Mexican state of Nuevo Leon, was an appropriate choice for SIFE's first foray abroad. Since the extension of railroads to the city in the nineteenth century, Monterrey had always looked to the bordering regions of the United States for its economic future. While Mexico as a whole supported the Union in the U.S. Civil War, Monterrey built a thriving business smuggling to the Confederacy, and used the profits to mount an industrial challenge to the Mexican heartland further south.[122] The northern city's export-oriented businessmen bitterly opposed the leftist economic policies of President Lázaro Cárdenas in the 1930s and 1940s. Cárdenas's conflict with Monterrey's most powerful industrial family, the Garza-Sadas, prompted his famous observation that if Mexican capitalists were "'tired of the social struggle,'" they could "'turn their industries over to the workers or the government.'"[123] In explicit reaction to the Mexican President's scolding, the renegade Monterrey industrialists in 1943 established the Instituto Tecnológico y de Estudios Superiores de Monterrey, a university patterned on the American models of MIT and CalTech. El Tec, as it was universally known, became a center for training the region's future CEOs, many already related to one another by blood.[124]

In this context, it was hardly surprising that some of the same families behind El Tec backed SIFE's man in Monterrey, J. Rolando Espinosa Ramírez, in his new project of promoting the Austrian economists, or that SIFE found its first foreign berth at El Tec under Espinosa's tutelage. Espinosa wrote feelingly of his nation's need to accept modern economic ideas of foreign origin, rather than endlessly returning to its own dual heritage of indigenous peasantry and an "absolutist, mercantilist Imperial state"—a message with which the optimistic, forward-looking businessmen of Monterrey heartily concurred.[125] By 1986 the team reported having reached 3.5 million people in Mexico and South Texas with its TV and radio messages on free enterprise. Seminars were conducted to reach target groups with programs such as "Women and Free Enterprise."[126]

These early ventures foreshadowed the importance that parts of Latin America would ultimately have for SIFE and its corporate patron, Wal-Mart. Likewise, the growing role of East Asia was hinted at by SIFE's early efforts in South Korea. There SIFE found a friend in the chair of the venerable missionary operation Far East Broadcasting Company, one of the early evangelical inheritances from the Pacific theater in World War II.[127]

For years, though, the foreign affiliates were something of a sideshow. The exigencies of the Cold War struggle meant patriotism came first, internationalism a very distant and symbolic second. The collapse of the Soviet bloc changed this equation. Louis Lataif, a vice president of marketing at the Ford Motor Company, celebrated the incredible transition before a SIFE student audience in 1991. As they launched their postcollegiate careers—"many, God willing, in free enterprise"—Lataif assured the young SIFE members they could do so as the proud heirs of Adam Smith. With the communist experiment exposed in all its ignominy, they had proved themselves on the winning team. "But nowhere in sacred Scripture does it say that America will continue to be a dominant industrial force in the world," he cautioned. "It will depend on how it is led and how it is managed, and that is where you come in."[128]

In 1991, the reorientation became official: "SIFE Goes Global," proclaimed a headline in the year-end review. The organization explicitly linked this move to the fall of the Berlin Wall, and though it mentioned the Mexican and Asian contacts in passing, the focus was on the recent converts from communism. Rogers State College, the article reported, inaugurated the new era by contacting East German colleges to offer their help in the economic transition. The result was a two-week sojourn in Oklahoma by three students of the Technische Hochschule-Zwickau, who "quickly became believers in our free market system." A permanent exchange between the institutions followed. Teams translated their entrepreneurial materials into Polish and Russian and shipped them to their erstwhile foes by the thousands. Other teams seized the opportunity to do the traveling themselves: SIFE members from East Texas Baptist University went to East Germany and distributed a booklet called "Texas Road Map to Starting a Business." And in the *coup de grace*, the University of Findlay SIFE spent spring break in the Evil Empire itself, where they found their Russian hosts "very open and receptive."[129]

The war had been won, but the struggle continued. The sudden dissolution of the Soviet bloc ratified years of patient spadework for free enterprise and offered capitalism's proselytizers the most poignant object lesson they had ever been able to deploy. The end of the Cold War did not mean that the organization could rest on its laurels. SIFE, its chairman reminded students, must "press on and hold even higher Free Enterprise as an example to the emerging economies of the world."[130] Like Wal-Mart itself, the students had a new calling in the era of free trade.

12

On a Mission: The Walton International Scholarship Program

In 1992, the champion economics student in Arkansas bore the demographically unlikely surname "Díaz." Competing in his second language, Mr. Díaz placed first in a statewide contest for collegians and went on to a fourth-place showing at the national finals in Anaheim, California. His accomplishment was publicized in a nationally syndicated column by the Tulsa-born Christian radio personality Paul Harvey, who proclaimed him a "Sam Walton success," since his education at an evangelical college had been funded by the Wal-Mart family's philanthropic foundation. The young Nicaraguan made it to the Ozarks by an unusual route, through a scholarship program based on the Wal-Mart retail fortune. He had passed his teenaged years in the Sandinista army, fighting the U.S.-backed *Contras* and translating CNN broadcasts for the intelligence service. Upon graduation he was offered a job in the Ministry of Economics in the new, U.S.-backed Chamorro government that replaced the leftist Sandinistas in the 1990 elections. A dozen years after graduation, he still dreamed of a public career. In the meantime, he worked as a marketing manager for Esso Standard Oil in Guatemala, the regional arm of Texas-based ExxonMobil.

Raised as a Catholic, Díaz was born again while in the Nicaraguan army, his religious commitment forced into high relief by the constant danger of death. But he attributed his real spiritual growth to his experiences in Arkansas, where his professors modeled a Christian life for the students and gave of themselves unstintingly. "Praying at the beginning of every class," he said, was "unforgettable." Asked about the lasting impact of his years in Arkansas, Díaz recalled, "I met Sam Walton twice in person and quickly came to learn that financial success and Christianity were perfectly compatible: being successful and humble, being loving and demanding, being competitive and caring for others—all of these were compatible."[1]

Díaz's Christian testimony—his inspirational biography of salvation, success, and humility—is the quiet back story of free trade in the Americas. The official story focuses on the hemisphere's "Washington Consensus," the term applied by a corporate think tank in 1989 to a suite of economic reforms that would encourage "the magic of the market" as the basis for hemispheric relations. Backed by the lending muscle of the World Bank and promoted by conservative economists like Milton Friedman, these recommendations included privatizing state enterprises, flattening tax rates, liberalizing trade, and relaxing government regulation.[2] Though their consequences were uniquely devastating in much of Latin America, these policies were part of the overall economic transformation evident in the rise of the Sun Belt. The global economic slowdown of the early 1970s had hit the growing economies of Latin America hard, pushing them into private loans from the increasingly mobile investment capital of the deregulated First World banks. Latin America's total debt grew eightfold from 1970 to 1980. The pain was compounded by rising fuel prices and the U.S. Federal Reserve's new high interest rates, themselves inspired by Friedman's economic theories. In the United States as well as for its southern neighbors, the result was a new era of federal austerity in every realm but defense. Social programs were slashed, from education to infrastructure to public health, while military spending increased by almost 50 percent over the Reagan years. States like California and Texas with significant defense industries received billions in contracts.[3]

The Washington Consensus, in other words, functioned as the hardware of economic restructuring in the Western hemisphere. At the same time, conservative Christians took up the cause of anticommunism in Central America with new fervor in the 1970s and 1980s. As the Reagan administration funded right-wing counterinsurgencies in El Salvador and Guatemala and sought to overturn the Sandinista victory in Nicaragua, it had no better stateside allies than religious conservatives. Hundreds of tons of material aid went directly to the *Contra* rebels from mainstream evangelical organizations like the Full Gospel Business Men's Fellowship, Gospel Crusade, World Vision, and the National Association of Evangelicals. The Christian Broadcasting Network raised money for Guatemala's right-wing dictator, Efraín Ríos Montt, even as he presided over the slaughter of tens of thousands of civilians. Christian student organizations like Campus Crusade for Christ energetically countered the growing opposition to Reagan's Central America policies. The White House Office of Public Diplomacy, staffed by psychological warfare experts from the Army and the Central Intelligence Agency, coordinated a multimillion dollar PR campaign to "defin[e] the terms of public discussion on Central America policy."[4]

Against this backdrop, the intersecting lives of a Nicaraguan student, an Oklahoma journalist, and an Arkansas merchant sketch a web of relationships between people and institutions that shadowed the Washington Consensus—a private-sector "Bentonville Consensus," a software of globalization. Through a Walton Family Foundation program, this human network bridged the transition from the last Cold War proxy battles to the new frontier of hemispheric free trade in the 1990s. It was not part of the coordinated Christian and neoconservative campaign of direct aid to anticommunists, but rather a parallel incubator of promarket Christians. When the devastation of the 1980s ground down—taking with it 300,000 civilian lives at the hands of U.S.-backed regimes in Central America—the Bentonville Consensus helped fill the vacuum.[5] For the grateful students involved, the scholarships offered a rare chance at economic security and broadened options for their entire families. For Wal-Mart and its suppliers, the program yielded a network of bilingual, bicultural potential managers throughout Mexico and Central America, just as the free-trade agreements the companies had long sought were encouraging new outposts for American corporations after the Cold War. Many graduates of the program became enthusiastic agents of economic restructuring. The cross-border cosmology of Christian free enterprise provided common ground between Wal-Mart Country and its new frontier.

In 1985, President Reagan's National Bipartisan Commission on Central America—better known as the Kissinger Commission—issued a report calling for private donors to fund closer educational ties to the region; too many young Central Americans, it warned, were imbibing communism while studying in Cuba or the Soviet Union. The first respondent to this challenge was the founding family of Wal-Mart Stores, Inc. Sam and Helen Walton established four-year scholarships to educate young Central Americans in free enterprise at a trio of Christian colleges in Wal-Mart's home state of Arkansas, offering the following explanation:

> The purpose of the program is to expose students from Central America to the benefits of a society and an economy that flourish under a free, open, elected government. "Reports show that several thousand Central Americans are studying on scholarships in Communist Bloc countries," [Sam] Walton commented. "If we want future leaders of Central America to know the benefits of a free society, we need to get large numbers of the student generation up here to the United States."[6]

The timing was fortuitous: the Ozark merchant had already been mulling over such a move on his own, ever since a Panamanian business associate had urged him to consider the potential influence of young communists taking jobs in "sensitive" areas like government.[7] The Cold War's East-West binary provided the original context for the Waltons as well as for the Reagan administration.

The Kissinger Commission, like its eponymous chair, certainly saw Central America as a battle turf for Washington and Moscow. To some extent the commissioners' view was a foregone conclusion. As Reagan's aggressive stance toward the region prompted increasing public unease in the United States, the administration had conceived of a bipartisan commission to review the situation and make recommendations for U.S. policy. The commission comprised hand-picked hawks from both parties, notably innocent of prior experience with Central America and exposed overwhelmingly to testimony that supported the administration's view of the problem.

Unsurprisingly, they urged precisely the positions that Washington had already adopted: military and material aid for antileftist governments despite the mounting evidence of their appalling abuses. The commissioners urged increased support, for example, to the Guatemalan government's counterinsurgency efforts, even while admitting to "the brutal behavior of the [government] security forces. In the cities they have murdered those even suspected of dissent. In the countryside, they have at times killed indiscriminately to repress any sign of support for the guerrillas."[8] The commission's report likewise admitted "short-comings" on the part of the Salvadoran government—including "mass reprisals and selective killing and torture"—but concluded that the 1982 elections carried out under these conditions, with millions of dollars of partisan political spending by the United States, proved the country democratic.[9] Maintaining an analytical division between politics and economics, the report then addressed the latter. "What is now required is a firm commitment by the Central American countries to economic policies, including reforms in tax systems, to encourage private enter-prise and individual initiative, to create favorable investment climates, to curb corruption where it exists, and to spur balanced trade."[10] In fact, the region had been pursuing this sort of export-led development for a generation, watching indicators like child malnutrition reverse their previous twentieth-century improvement as subsistence farming gave way to coffee and bananas for foreign markets.[11]

The Kissinger Commission heard from powerful Central Americans concerned about the ideological content of higher education for the re-gion's students. Rather than chiding American allies for torturing and killing student activists, the report instead raised the alarm that com-munists were providing thousands of university scholarships to Central Americans, whereas the United States offered only a few hundred. More-over, the United States was known as the place where the elite Central Americans sent their children, while the other countries provided op-portunities for poor students. "Thus," the report concluded boldly, "we recommend a program of 10,000 government-sponsored scholarships to bring Central American students to the United States." In an effort to recruit and retain nonelites, these scholarships would include intensive English language instruction. To make sure the program did not just turn into a migration route, they needed "[m]echanisms to encourage graduates to return to their home countries." The commission knew this sounded extravagant, but they did not expect the U.S. government to shoulder the whole burden; instead, they encouraged the private sec-tor to get on board. After all, the report shrewdly pointed out, university enrollments were declining all over the country, and those schools would jump at the prospect of a new source of paying students.[12] Thus the Kissinger Commission's recommendations—understood less as an educational outlay than as a contribution to national defense—stepped into a market niche.

In support of their new project, the Waltons donated $3.6 million from the sale of Wal-Mart stock, matched by funds from the U.S. Agency for International Development (USAID).[13] But as one early staffer put it, "You team up with the government and you have to do it their way!" Within two years, the Waltons had decided it was worth the price tag to run the program privately, and severed their ties with USAID. Besides their objections to government interference, the Waltons could legitimately claim the entire idea as their own. During a 1984 trip to Panama, the Waltons had been hosted by a millionaire brewer and director-general of the Panama Canal named Gabriel Lewis Galindo, the "Sam Walton of Panama" from an Ozark perspective.[14] Although part of Panama's hereditary wealthy class, Lewis Galindo was something of a maverick. When General Omar Torrijos gained the presidency in a 1968 coup, the businessman was one of the new regime's few elite backers and helped it maintain good relations with the country's thriving private sector even as it aggressively pursued economic policies favorable to the poor. As his country's ambassador to the United States during the Carter administration, Lewis Galindo had won congressional support for the return of the canal to Panamanian sovereignty, with the help of his effusive bonhomie. He experienced a rather sudden reversal of fortune, however, when Torrijos died in a mysterious plane crash in 1981. The presidency cycled quickly through a couple of military figures before landing firmly in the hands of General Manuel Noriega in 1983. Though both Lewis Galindo and Noriega had been allies of Torrijos, there was no love lost between the two men. In 1987, the former fled to Washington and organized a businessmen's opposition-in-exile called the Civic Crusade.[15]

But in 1984, such an open break with CIA client Noriega lay in front of the unconventional entrepreneur; he and Walton talked business. The Waltons responded well to the charismatic Panamanian, and when he raised for them the issue of communist investment in Third World education, they responded eagerly. The concerns of a variety of actors thus converged in the days following the release of the Kissinger Report. The soft-power priorities of Lewis Galindo and the Waltons merged into the stark ones of the Reagan administration, and for a time they coexisted in the project of Central American scholarship.

The University of Arkansas lay right down the road from Wal-Mart headquarters, but the Waltons had other ideas. Public education, they felt, was not the responsibility of private funders.[16] Moreover, the sort of holistic experience the Waltons had in mind called for more personal attention than a large university could provide. Fortunately, both the Waltons and Lewis Galindo already had ties to an appropriate school: the College (later University) of the Ozarks. Mrs. Walton sat on the board of directors and a major donor was Mary Anne Stephens, wife of the Little Rock investment banker shared by Walton, Lewis Galindo, and Arkansas megafirms like Tyson.[17] The Waltons invited Ozarks to put together a proposal for a Central American program stressing free enterprise and entrepreneurship.[18]

The University of the Ozarks was an easy choice for the Waltons, given their decade-long attachment and Lewis Galindo's shared connection. But to accommodate the number of students they had in mind and to distribute the resources to other strategic clients, the foundation needed additional appropriate colleges in Wal-Mart's home territory. A second receiving school prospered by proximity to Wal-Mart headquarters. Located in the company's home county, the evangelical John Brown University had long nurtured a connection to the retailer. It also had the advantage of a tradition of cosmopolitanism, as a popular college choice for the children of overseas missionaries and a major training ground for foreign missions. Finally, Harding University, the Church of Christ institution that won a national reputation as a Cold War probusiness warrior, built on ties to the company going back to the 1970s.

Into these three distinct traditions of American Protestantism—frontier Presbyterianism, nondenominational evangelicalism, and hard-right fundamentalism—the Waltons brought young people from what Reagan's ambassador Jeane Kirkpatrick had recently proclaimed "the most important place in the world."[19] In the small towns of the Arkansas Ozarks, the Wal-Mart family began to offer these students undergraduate degrees in business, marketing, and communications, the better to combat communism and build free-market democracies. As Sam Walton put it, the Arkansas schools recommended themselves because "we thought we could stay close to them . . . we know what they teach and how they think."[20]

Sixty new students a year at each Christian campus, majoring primarily in business-related subjects, found themselves defining a new category of the globalized: a transient white-collar class conversant with Protestant evangelicalism and service-sector office culture, employed by U.S.-based multinational corporations. Moreover, their presence in the Ozarks presaged that region's own growing awareness of its hemispheric context. Drawn by jobs in construction and chicken processing, pushed by the calamitous effect of repression and economic restructuring in their home countries, a steady stream of Mexican and Central American newcomers poured into Northwest Arkansas in the 1990s. Two peripheries met along paths worn by war, work, and worship.

In 1985, the three colleges scrambled to get the program off the ground with little warning and no experience in the region. Language posed the biggest initial problem. With so little lead time, finding candidates with enough English to stay afloat academically was a daunting task, especially since their mandate included recruiting outside the countries' tight oligarchies. One solution lay in the pockets of English-speakers on the margins of the isthmus: tiny Belize—formerly British Honduras— and the U.S.-influenced Panama.[21] Once recruitment began in Nicaragua—the Waltons avoided it the first year because of its "strained relations" with Washington—the English-speaking Caribbean coast offered another source of native speakers.[22] When approaching an unfamiliar region, the Christian colleges naturally turned to their closest counterparts. "We started by working through the churches," explained one of the program's early administrators, "Presbyterian, Catholic, and, around Bluefields [Nicaragua], the Moravian church. The question for us wasn't which church they belonged to, but how they conducted themselves there."[23] In 1987, two representatives of John Brown University (JBU) took a weeklong recruiting trip though the region. Working through contacts at Christian aid agencies like World Relief and Christ for the Cities, as well as a Baptist minister in Nicaragua and a Bentonville woman on staff at the U.S. Embassy in Managua, the pair secured eighteen new students and reported that they hadn't noticed any weapons.[24] The Reverend Harold Caballeros, the politically outspoken pastor of Guatemala City's megachurch El Shaddai, visited JBU in 1991 to discuss recruitment and arrange a meeting between JBU representatives and President Jorge Elías Serrano of Guatemala, an evangelical businessman.[25] At Ozarks, the Central Presbyterian Church in Guatemala City was a logical connection; in 1988, its senior minister gave a seminar at the Clarksville campus on "The Situation in Central America" and counseled individual students.[26]

Officially, the recruiters were tasked with selecting students "from the low to lower middle income families," with a cutoff of $6,000 annual family income.[27] Certainly the program wanted to help promising poor kids, but too many of them strained the school's cohesion and isolated the foreigners. On the other hand, accepting the most academically prepared students sometimes yielded an even more troublesome crowd, the Central American elite. Instead, "I tried for a mix," a recruiter remembered. "We had to have some mid-level kids for the social training they provided the others." In addition to modeling good behavior, the ideal student had to show ambition and tenacity: "I was looking for candidates who had energy, you could just tell by the look in their eyes."[28] A Walton alumnus applied that same standard to students he selected: "It has to come from the heart," he explained. "I look for the spark in their eyes."[29] One alumnus in Guatemala described a split among the alumni in that country between the more well-to-do, better-educated students from the earlier years and the younger ones from *"familias muy humildes."*[30] Back when he was recruited, a successful 1994 graduate explained, the JBU representative had emphasized educational preparation over background—quite appropriately, in his view.[31]

Regardless of the recipients' class background, though, the scholarships marked a distinct watershed in their lives. Federico López Bolaños, who heard about the program from a friend in the late 1980s, was so certain of failure that he kept his application a secret in order not to disappoint his family and friends. "I was very discouraged," he said about that time of his life, a few years after leaving high school in Guatemala City. He would run into friends and hear what they were doing— one studying at the national university, another working with computers—and "I'd just try to change the subject." Never a stellar student, he had failed his final year of high school, and now his family's limited resources meant he was trying to hold down a job and take classes at the same time. Invariably he would drop out after the first month or six weeks, overwhelmed. To his surprise, López Bolaños made it to the interview stage for the Walton scholarships, but at the posh downtown hotel where the interviews were held, he saw the other applicants lined up and knew he was entirely outclassed; he almost walked away before his turn. "When I got home after the interview," he related,

> my mother met me at the door. She was crying, and all she could say was 'They called . . .' I thought someone had died, that they had called from a hospital. 'Who is it, mother? Is it my sister? Who's dead?' And then when she told me 'They called from the scholarship!' I couldn't believe it. I went up to my room and just cried, for ages, and all that discouragement, all my sense of failure and self-doubt came flooding out, and I never felt that way again. And right there I thanked God for the opportunity to start over. I am very, very grateful to the Walton family for what this has meant in my life."

López Bolaños went to the University of the Ozarks, where he majored in business.[32]

The campus political climates that the Walton scholars encountered ranged from apathetic to actively conservative. To begin with, many students remained unconvinced that a Christian had any place in political debate whatsoever. In an article criticizing antiapartheid activists as unknowing dupes of international communism, a Rhodesian member of the Harding community flatly stated, "Christians have little place in politics" and asked "How can we as Christians, talk about rights? . . . When we start shouting about justice and rights, we get caught in a vortex with everybody's cries of 'I want my rights!' irresistibly pulling us down into a cesspool of greed, lust and ambitious desire." Conceding that black South Africans had a legitimate complaint, however, the author was forced to conclude that "there are no good workable solutions while man is in control."[33]

By contrast, a JBU student editorial urged graduating seniors to consider just where they would invest the money they were about to start making: "For Christians, investing decisions can be very difficult," wrote Randy Doyle. The South African regime raised the question of ethical investing for Doyle, but his concrete examples all involved classic Protestant sins of personal vice, not structural injustices like apartheid. A Christian investor, he concluded, should think carefully before turning his capital over to a publishing stock if the company had a line of pornography, or, in an example close to home, "Do you invest in a chemical company that makes fertilizer for Arkansas rice fields, knowing that a great percentage of that rice is used to make alcohol?"[34]

Perhaps most dramatically, the nuclear threat that hung over the late Cold War struck some as beyond the scope of human concern. A Harding professor of political science was convinced in 1983 that nuclear annihilation was "inevitable," but felt that Christians should not waste time worrying about the coming war. "If one is prepared to meet the Lord we shouldn't be overly concerned about leaving the world," he reasoned, while a physics professor pointed out that human beings could "adapt" to low-level radiation.[35]

Although spiritual matters tended to trump geopolitics regularly at all three schools, and the argument for Christian aloofness could command a respectful hearing, the events of the 1980s could intrude in terms readily legible to Christian audiences. The organized movement opposing Reagan's Central America policies, after all, had firm bases in a variety of Christian institutions and organizations, including not only Catholic communities inspired by liberation theology but also the pacifist evangelical Left.[36] A case in point was Dennis Godby, a native Californian and Catholic who had worked on hunger issues in Central America and who raised the area's concerns for the College of the Ozarks in 1985.

Godby had become convinced that the administration's policies in the isthmus were unjustly costing thousands of lives and conceived of an "Emergency Run for Central America" to draw attention to the crisis. Godby was particularly outraged by the Immigration and Naturalization Service's policy of deporting refugees from U.S. client regimes, even while it publicly welcomed refugees from Eastern bloc countries. The 3,000 miles he would run corresponded to the distance the Central American refugees were covering to enter the United States, where the administration found the refugees' stories of torture and murder conflicted too openly with official accounts of increasing respect for human rights by the governments it funded.[37] Granting them asylum would mean tacitly accepting their indictment of U.S. allies. Instead, the Immigration and Naturalization Service shipped them back, often to their immediate imprisonment and even death.

After running an average of thirty miles a day for two and a half months, with stops for speaking engagements, Godby arrived in Clarksville, Arkansas, to address a small group of students at the College of the Ozarks. Like most of the activists opposing Reagan policies, Godby was at home in front of Christian audiences. The courage of the many nuns and priests who regularly risked their lives in allying themselves with the region's poor made him "proud to be a Catholic."[38] The resistance movement was overwhelmingly based in churches and spearheaded by clergy and lay leaders, and Godby's itinerary had taken him to congregations across the country.

But the College of the Ozarks was different. As the student newspaper reported, Godby found the Ozarks students his toughest audience by far. The students challenged his interpretation, casting the issue in strict East-West terms. "Asked if he denied Soviet involvement in the overthrow of the Somoza regime in 1979, Godby in effect said yes, he believed they were not involved . . . [A]nother student expressed the fear of Nicaragua creating a domino effect." The visitor suggested a more nuanced understanding of Third World insurgency, invoking an unaligned peasant soldier who would buy arms from whoever would sell them, if that allowed him to fight back against a viciously repressive regime. The Californian urged the students to imagine Central America as "our neighbors," people with a stake in their own destinies, not as "our backyard." "What emerged," the student report summed up, "was a clash of two distinct belief systems. Godby maintained the guerrillas and the governments in Central America must fight things out on their own without U.S. involvement. Many students viewed the region as too close not to be addressed with more severity, and would not accept the view that the Soviets were not behind many of the problems."[39]

The Walton International Scholarship Program moved Central American concerns to the fore during Reagan's second term, but the genesis of the program in Cold War ideology restricted the campus discussion. John Brown III, president of the university founded by his grandfather, sounded a thoughtful note in his musings at the program's outset. He noted the region's "historically valid distrust" of the United States. Brown referred to a recent article in *Christianity Today* on America's thirty military interventions in the region since 1850, including eleven in support of the brutal Somoza regime in Nicaragua before the Sandinista Revolution. He saw the Walton scholarships as part of a "positive, nonpartisan effort to change the harsh pattern of our relationships in Central America," and looked forward optimistically to the transformative power of free-market economic integration.[40] President Ganus of Harding likewise called Walton's initiative essentially economic rather than political, citing the benefactor's wish that graduates "go home and build their country" on free-market principles.[41]

This outlook, which defined the economy as inherently nonpolitical, was bolstered in the classroom.[42] The Walton Scholars overwhelmingly majored in business or related subjects. Some reported considerable pressure in this direction, but for many the program's preferences merely coincided with their own best chance at later employment. They enriched their marketing and accounting classes with vigorous participation in business-related extracurriculars. In the program's first semester, a Panamanian freshman at JBU served as her class vice president and participated in the business club and Campus Crusade for Christ, in addition to an eighteen-hour course load.[43] By 1987, a business club at Ozarks had a Panamanian president, a double major in marketing and management who went on to earn an MBA.[44]

The other half of their education, though, did not respond to market logic at all. Walton Scholars performed ten hours a week of community service, a requirement that Helen Walton had insisted be incorporated into the terms of the scholarship. English tutoring for the growing public-school population of Spanish speakers in Northwest Arkansas quickly became an obvious venue. At JBU, Héctor Martínez of Chihuahua started the tutoring ministry in the early 1990s. "We saw how much need there was for English, and how eager people were for this," explained the program's 1995 student director, Guatemalan Sussy Bracamonte.[45] Tyson chicken-processing plants in Northwest Arkansas and the Wal-Mart grocery warehouse in Clarksville attracted immigrant workers, and the Central Americans taught them enough English to fill out a job application.[46] True to its organizational credo, Harding's SIFE incorporated the new students as both pupils and teachers. After exposing the Central Americans to the U.S. Chamber of Commerce's program "*Como trabaja la empresa libre* [How Free Enterprise Works]," the club recruited two of them to narrate an audio portion for a traveling slide show based on the material.[47]

Community service dovetailed with the larger Christian mission of each school. "It was a new experience to be a Christian at JBU because I was so used to always being in the minority here, and suddenly everyone around me was a Christian," rejoiced one alumna.[48] As a Catholic

Guatemalan put it, the program selected for students prepared to handle a "Christian *ambiente*."[49] The colleges all required regular attendance at worship services, from several times a week at Ozarks to daily chapel at Harding. In 1985, a weekly Spanish-language Bible study group at Harding led the newcomers in studying the Book of John. A Honduran communications major there stressed in 1985 that he particularly enjoyed the daily chapel services and singing in the a capella chorus.[50]

"Most students have been selected through churches and other Christian institutions," noted an early account, and as the earliest classes coalesced into formal alumni recruiting networks, these initial associations reproduced themselves.[51] "I'm not much in contact with the Walton alumni," explained one Guatemalan, "since I'm Catholic. With them it's religion first, and then everything else."[52] Graduates filled charismatic evangelical churches like Guatemala City's El Verbo—spiritual home of the former military dictator Efraín Ríos Montt—Lluvias de Gracia, and El Shaddai, or studied for the ministry at the Church of Christ's Baxter Institute in Tegucigalpa. Alumni included the pastor of a Moravian Church in Nicaragua, a broadcaster on a Christian TV station, and the assistant director of a Presbyterian school in Guatemala.

Carlos Estrada Román, a 1994 Walton graduate of John Brown University, worked for a variety of Christian aid organizations around Latin America upon returning to the region. He was struck at work not by the disparities of wealth between the North American donors and the local staff and clients, but rather by the brotherhood between them regardless of class. "The beautiful part of my work is to see very different people crying together, laughing together," he explained. "I've seen a millionaire crying alongside a poor campesino—I get to work from the heart."[53]

The similar intimacy of the three colleges stood in marked contrast to the large state universities that predominated in the students' home countries. Although all three colleges soon changed their names to "universities"—"*colegio*" in Latin America denotes a high school—there was no confusing the intimate, personal commitment of their professors for the anonymity of an urban, nonresidential national university. "Teachers seem to care about their students," marveled Honduran Lina Arzu. "I try not to bother them too much, but they are willing to give me extra help when I need it."[54]

The colleges also learned to incorporate their unusual resource into the U.S. students' education. In the first year of the Walton scholarships, JBU implemented a Latin American Studies Program that included Spanish language study, service projects in Central America, and home-stay visits with Central American families, whom the college assured students were "dedicated Christians with stable home lives."[55] The Walton program gave JBU "an academic focus on Latin America, on international business to Spanish-speaking countries."[56] Ozarks introduced two new Spanish classes, along with a Spanish table and a Spanish club, for the 1985–1986 school year; the instructor pointed out that both business and religion majors stood to benefit from the new emphasis.[57]

The newcomers occasionally took on the task of educating their hosts on regional concerns. In settings where the return of the Panama Canal to Panamanian sovereignty had been taken as at best a strategic error, and at worst as evidence of Democratic treachery on par with the Yalta Conference, a Panamanian student patiently explained the view from the canal zone: "Americans were obtaining all the benefits—the money, work, and control. Panamanians became upset because, although the zone was in their country, they felt that they have no voice in its management."[58] Likewise, students at JBU were treated to a Panamanian account of the relationship between the United States and its client Manuel Noriega following the American invasion of Panama City in 1990.[59]

The Walton Scholars stimulated considerable interest not just at the colleges but in the small towns that hosted them. The arrival of the first class to the University of the Ozarks was the lead story for the county-wide paper, and the First United Methodist Church honored them with "a tour of the city and a welcoming fellowship dinner."[60] The colleges made a point of publicizing their economic contribution to the host communities, especially after a mid-1990s report by the Institute of International Education calculated that each foreign student contributed almost $9,000 annually to area economies.[61] A student writer in 1988 proclaimed an El Salvadoran Walton scholar "a bona fide JBU student" because she shopped at the local Wal-Mart.[62] Central America had arrived in the Ozarks.

Though it ultimately outgrew a strictly Christian context, the Bentonville Consensus developed directly out of the missionary encounter with decolonization. Whereas earlier European and North American missionaries had arrived in their fields in the context of their own countries' expansion and conquest, those who came after World War II faced quite different geopolitical conditions that made their task more challenging in many ways. Across Asia and Africa especially, former colonies shook off the direct control of the imperial powers, and First World missionaries discovered that they were not always as welcome as they had supposed. Many individuals withdrew entirely. Institutionally, though, evangelical missionaries grappled creatively with the new postcolonial terrain.[63] Doug Ross, a retired recruiter for the Walton International Scholarship Program, would date this confrontation from 1956. That year, five American missionaries lost radio contact with their home base after a daring flight into the Ecuadoran rain forest to evangelize the Auca people, one of the exotic "unreached tribes" that so inflamed the missionary imagination. With intervention by the U.S. military command in Panama, the bodies were recovered. They had been speared to death and thrown in the Curaray River. A *Life* magazine reporter was helicoptered in for the mass burial, and his photos made the Auca massacre "the missionary story of the century" for the general public. Subsequent biographies of Nate Saint, one of the slain men, enshrined them all as martyrs within evangelical circles. An entire generation of young evangelicals was deeply affected by the incident.[64]

The massacre touched Ross personally. The martyred Nate Saint had been among his classmates at Wheaton, and the dramatic episode had fueled his resolve to bring the gospel to Latin America. After studying Spanish in Costa Rica, Ross and his wife moved to radio station HCJB ("Heralding Christ Jesus' Blessings") in Quito, Ecuador, where the five lost men had begun their journey in 1956. Rachel Saint, Nate's sister, invited Ross to take over the administration of the mission's interior hospital. "I wound up baptizing some of the same Auca men who had speared the martyrs," he recounted.[65]

From Ecuador, the Rosses moved to the Rio Grande Bible Institute, a training post on the U.S.-Mexico border that taught Spanish and practical skills for success in the Latin American mission fields. He administered an intercultural studies program at a southwestern Bible college in the 1980s, as an increasingly sophisticated field of academic "missiology" grew and took on some of the trappings of anthropology. Then in the late 1980s, Ross heard from a church friend about John Brown University's struggle to absorb its new international population. For a student body of about eight hundred and a town of only 8,000, integrating sixty Central Americans presented "a challenge," he recalled, and one his missionary background had prepared him to address. As the new director of international studies, Ross took on not only *"los Waltones,"* as they came to be called, but also the school's traditionally sizable pool of "MK's"—missionary kids, students who had been raised in the mission field and felt like foreigners themselves. "The missionary kids and military brats just gravitated toward the Walton kids immediately," and by 1996 a quarter of the school's population had grown up outside the United States.[66]

The experiences of the Rosses and of JBU were part of the most successful transnational movement of the later twentieth century: world Christian evangelism. The same creative pragmatism that was making the New Christian Right a force in domestic politics after 1968 likewise reinvigorated Christian missions abroad. The roots of the new movement lay in the mass mobilization of World War II. Hundreds of thousands of small-town Americans found themselves deployed across the globe in the armed services, often operating advanced communication technologies. For Christians concerned with the Great Commission— Christ's charge to evangelize the nations—the world seemed suddenly, tantalizingly reachable. Many returning veterans founded new overseas mission organizations or brought fresh inspiration into existing ones.

The fertile cross-pollination between the Cold War American military and evangelical power centers followed lines of mutual affinity. On a technical level, evangelical enterprises showed a consistent romance with air power, in the forms of both broadcasting and flight. The "gospel of the air" was a recurring image, and with the relatively low capital demands of independent radio and a veteran generation trained in radio technology, innumerable Christian enterprises put the Word out on the airwaves. In 1948, the Pentecostal Assemblies of God—Attorney General John Ashcroft's denomination—bought a pair of decommissioned war planes to ferry their newly cosmopolitan staffs to the mission field. Their Ozarks hometown of Springfield, Missouri, acquired an international airport to support the flights. Publications and mission campaigns carried titles like "Gospel Rocket" and "Global Conquest."[67]

The 1966 Berlin World Conference on Evangelism explicitly addressed the shifting center of gravity in Christianity, as its base of support shrank in most wealthy countries and swelled in the global south.

In a key theological shift, attention was drawn to a one-line text from John 20:21. In place of the imperial command of Jesus recorded in Matthew 28:19—"Go therefore and make disciples of all the nations"—the Berlin gathering emphasized John's rather different rendering of Jesus's commission to evangelism: "As the Father has sent me, I am sending you."[68]

Here was a radically different image, with authority deriving not from the Christ's kingship of all nations, but from the patriarchal family relation within the Trinity. A familial version of the Great Commission was better suited for the new era, for it recognized the changed context of power and made a virtue of necessity. The imperative to reject white supremacy on the mission field and simultaneously buttress male "headship" built a new world vision in tandem with the rise of Christian "family values."

The support for this altered emphasis grew after Berlin, and its further elaboration at the 1974 International Conference on World Evangelization in Lausanne, Switzerland, gave its advocates the name of the "Lausanne Movement."[69] Writing in 1973 in a handbook used at John Brown University, Herbert Kane owned up to the former relationship between missionaries and colonial domination, although he found redeeming characteristics to their interdependence. Regardless, though, decolonization had forever changed the conditions under which missions operated: "The countries of Africa and Asia are masters in their own house . . . Now that these countries are independent, their governments insist on ordering their foreign policy as well as their domestic affairs."[70] No longer children available for tutelage, the colonials had grown to a man's estate, to be approached with respect.

This new mastery challenged American missionaries to put their own house in order. The key to galvanizing missions lay in raising the status of the missionary, and a crucial component to this was masculinizing the work force. Echoing generations of concern over female preponderance in missions, many evangelicals pointed to the Peace Corps as the missions' main competition for adventurous personnel. The stringent living conditions demanded of "corpsmen" no doubt contributed to their favorable male-female sex ratio—three men to every two women, the reverse of the missionaries' own ratio.[71]

But the surplus of women was only a symptom of the real problem. Simply put, the desirable recruits—white-collar men—had too many options to find mission work attractive. The massive redistribution of wealth into education had done its job all too well. The children of the Protestant heartland had college degrees and high hopes now, and even second- and third-generation evangelical men were staying away from church work in droves. "How can the Christian church compete with Hollywood, Madison Avenue, and the Dallas Cowboys?"[72]

How indeed? Faced with these new challenges, the service ethos could save the church as well as the office and the store. Whereas missionaries in the nineteenth-century mold had been "the astronauts of their day," this moment had passed. "At home he was a hero; on the field he was a leader. Now he is neither hero nor leader—just a plain servant."[73] Outfitted with anthropology, linguistics, and the toughness to endure physical rigors in the field, this servant would win followers by humbling himself, on the Cold War pattern of the Ugly American. In another man's house—Mauritius, Guatemala—he would lead men by declining to command them. The Lausanne movement, like the racial reconciliation initiatives in the Christian men's movement, signaled a new racial dispensation within white evangelicalism.[74]

Thus the shift to a service ethos profoundly altered American Christianity's encounters abroad, as it had at home. Faced with new "masters," the missionary enterprise began to shed its nineteenth-century association with white supremacy. Without the pith helmets and penicillin that had signaled racial superiority, the compensatory hierarchy of sex enshrined by St. Paul became ever more important. Forced into the role of servant, the old masters of small worlds discovered that in fact servanthood was the best basis for leadership.

For its sponsors and administrators, although they took pleasure in the students' accomplishments on campus, the real test of the Walton program lay in their careers back home. "It's exciting to look down the road 10 to 15 years and see the places of influence these people will be working in," JBU president John Brown III declared in 1992.[75] Sam Walton himself seemed pleased with the early results. "We've now graduated two or three classes," he told an interviewer in 1990, "and when they get back they are going into journalism, government, IBM, teaching, et cetera. They are becoming influential citizens in their countries, and it will help Central America. And anything that helps Central America eventually will help the United States."[76]

For some, the combination of a U.S. education, international experience, and family connections at home could propel them into positions of unusual influence. Two weeks after Marcia Hernandez graduated from JBU in 1987, her father, a physician, mentioned her new American degree in journalism to a patient whose husband worked at the Costa Rican newspaper *La Nación*. Within a week of her return, Hernandez had an interview with the editor, wrote a sample article, and was assigned a beat that included the country's president, major political parties, senate, and ministry of foreign relations. From the JBU student paper, Hernandez moved straight to covering national political affairs for an influential daily. "I'm certain that this is where the Lord wants me right now," she told a JBU representative, "and I plan to stay around for a while."[77] The program "impacts our country more than [Sam Walton] could have known," emphasized an engineering student from the tiny nation of Belize. "All the people from Belize who were Walton students are leaders and policy makers. They are making an impact that is tremendous."[78]

Some Walton Scholars pursued their business studies further upon returning to the region, linking the Christian colleges in Arkansas to a network of conservative economists. Several undertook master's degrees in business at Guatemala City's Universidad Francisco Marroquín (UFM). Founded in 1970 by a future president of the Mont Pelerin Society, the university was fiercely loyal to the Austrian school of free-market economics and the U.S.-based Foundation for Economic Education, home of "I, Pencil." They explicitly intended UFM as an alternative to the public Universidad San Carlos, where the ideal of institutional autonomy offered the Guatemalan Left what little freedom of speech it enjoyed in the 1970s before the systematic official murder of students and professors.[79] The Guatemalan economists and businessmen who promoted the new free-market university found San Carlos "too political." UFM would concentrate on economics, understood as neutral and nonpolitical. Meanwhile, founder Manuel Ayau gave 2 million dollars to Ronald Reagan's presidential campaign, and entrepreneurs forged ties to the homicidal Guatemalan Army.[80]

Whether in higher education, business, or Christian service, then, the Walton Scholars established a collective track record of accomplishment. From its inception, though, the Walton Scholarship Program reflected U.S. fears about immigration from Latin America: could anyone really go home again, once they'd spent time in the United States? In 1985, John Brown III had quoted "a Panamanian businessman"—likely Gabriel Lewis Galindo—to the effect that if the United States could offer Central America "no jobs, no peace, no opportunity, then you had better contract with the East Germans for expertise on border security—they will all try to come to the United States."[81] However, if such opportunity were to come in part from American educations, what exactly was to keep the program's own beneficiaries from staying? A scholarship application in 1992 posited two potential situations that might face a graduating Walton Scholar, and asked for an essay explaining how the applicant would respond. "What would you do if a company in America offered you $40,000 to work for them?" read the first; "What if you fall in love and want to get married?" inquired the second.[82] Neither love nor money could be allowed to prevent repatriation.

But in practice, money fared better. Especially after the Cold War nightmare of leftist revolutions subsided, the program and its sponsor seemed increasingly to tolerate employment outside the home country. Asked to describe some of the scholarship's biggest success stories, a former recruiter spoke warmly of an exemplary Salvadoran graduate. Upon finishing his BA in business in 1994, he married a Guatemalan Walton alumna and went to work in Guatemala City for one of Wal-Mart's biggest vendors, Procter & Gamble. His wife worked for another, Kellogg's. Subsequently, though, he moved up rapidly through the corporation's human resources department and by 2003 was living in the Ozarks, managing Procter & Gamble's relationship with Wal-Mart, a position in which he could hardly be effective if the Walton Family Foundation felt he had undermined their goals. "Walton graduates are all over the world now—I mean, they've been sent there for their jobs," the recruiter wound up proudly.[83]

Similar success stories dotted the Sun Belt—a Kodak manager in Miami, a Christian aid specialist in Colorado Springs, a center for evangelical organizations like Focus on the Family. But though migration circuits tended to follow lines of military and economic penetration, not all of them ran directly north and south. A returning Walton Scholar found that his job as brand manager for Shell in Guatemala led to similar work for the same company in Puerto Rico, Jamaica, Haiti, and the Dominican Republic. One Walton alumnus who began his career scouting Guatemalan maquilas for a Korean firm found himself a few years later setting up laundromats in Indonesia for a German company.[84]

With capital freed to travel the globe in the 1980s and 1990s, keeping people in their place proved harder than Sam Walton imagined. More to the point, it turned out to have some distinct advantages for Wal-Mart and its supplier network. The Walton Scholars' geographical and cultural flexibility proved particularly adapted to the post–Cold War terrain. "Certainly my experience in Arkansas helps me here at Kellogg's [in Guatemala]," affirmed Roberto Guzman Ayala, a business graduate from JBU. "They're looking for people who understand American culture, how things are done in the U.S."[85] An alumna elaborated, "When you come out with a U.S. degree—it could be in anything—the assumption is you're more used to technology. You understand professional presentation, e-mail, and of course you have the language skills."[86]

One of the program's most successful graduates put it in concrete terms of hiring decisions. "Look, multinationals operating here are very concerned with U.S. culture, they want someone who knows how things work in the U.S.," he explained. In hiring for Coca-Cola's Guatemalan headquarters, for example, he himself would automatically pick a candidate with a bachelor's degree from a college in the United States over one with a master's in business from the leading regional business school, the Instituto Centroamericano de Administración de Empresas. The graduate of an American college would win out, explained the Coca-Cola executive, because "he would really have learned things that are culturally so important in multinationals. You can't get it in class alone."[87]

The roster of alumni employers reads like the *Fortune* 500: Coca-Cola, Compaq, Continental, Cargil, Colgate-Palmolive; Purina, Procter & Gamble, Pepsi. Alumni left Arkansas to run textile *maquilas,* handle sales for multinational telecom services, and supply plastic products to Wal-Mart. The returning Walton Scholars brought with them the specific business culture of the Christian service sector. The service ethos that animated the Christian business world at Ozarks, JBU, and Harding bolstered the less well-connected students who often struggled to find appropriate work upon their return. A low-level post was a starting point, they had learned, and every position could be an influential one if you approached it in the right spirit. One alumnus found work in

Guatemala responding to letters of complaint from disgruntled airline customers. His very first letter came from an extremely irate client, and rather than responding with the company's trademark indifference, he asked permission to take a "service-oriented approach." His boss allowed him to respond to the complaint with a "very polite, a very conciliatory letter . . . And even though we turned down the customer's request for restitution, she was very impressed by the letter and told us she appreciated that kind of treatment. It's small, but that's the kind of thing we can do."[88]

This sense of the fundamental dignity of service work resonated in many evangelical settings. The president of the Guatemalan Christian Businessmen's Association addressed a group of Walton alumni from the University of the Ozarks and described their shared vision in terms that would resonate in Clarksville and Bentonville: "There's no shame in starting small: cut people's hair, change the oil in people's cars, make hamburgers, whatever—just make the best hamburgers, offer the best service, and you will succeed."[89] As in the United States, Sam Walton erroneously appeared in Central American accounts as a rags-to-riches model of this pattern. "I think it was sophomore year," remembered a Harding graduate, "that we went on a trip to Wal-Mart headquarters in Bentonville. It was great to see that little museum, you know, with the signs on the wall like 'The Customer is #1!' and all that—because you know here was Sam Walton, a good man who started with nothing."[90]

The earliest classes of Walton Scholars met Walton himself, and were impressed by his humility and wise avoidance of the "riotous living" he could so clearly afford. Rather than indulge himself in luxury, Walton "has instead chosen to invest his fortune" in the Latin American students.[91] "Integrity," Walton emphasized to the visiting Central Americans, "that's the most valuable asset on our balance sheet."[92] The example of Walton and Wal-Mart made a lasting impression on many graduates. The daughter of a Guatemalan seamstress, for example, dreamed of designing mass-market clothing "that lots of people could afford. Really, that's something else I learned while I was there at JBU, that whole value of equality."[93]

The program has no legal mechanism to force students to leave the United States after graduation, yet the vast majority of Walton graduates have at least returned home for the minimum four years.[94] In the absence of strict controls, the Christian program achieved its purpose through moral suasion, requiring the students to sign a legally null contract that was all the more sacred for being unenforceable. Walton Scholars stress their sincere gratitude to the Walton family for placing so few requirements on them in return for the chance of a lifetime. If the program demanded that they repay their scholarships by working a set number of years at a particular company, one alumnus explained, the Central Americans might feel they had closed their account at the end of that term. But since nothing specific is asked, "I think we feel the need to keep giving back, especially collectively" in organized groups of alumni.[95]

Example spoke louder than ideology. Isabel Rueda Navas initially found Harding University's worship style a little bewildering. Every morning at nine, the entire campus shut down for a thirty-five-minute chapel service. Everyone from the college president to the cleaning staff was invited to worship for a slice of every workday. For the students, attendance was mandatory. "At first I didn't understand," says Rueda Navas, "I mean, going to church every day? But I really enjoyed it, I enjoyed the singing. Thanks to this experience I really grew as a Christian. I got baptized at Harding." To Rueda Navas, the salient feature was not the rule of daily chapel attendance, but the communal pleasure of group worship. Likewise, she felt gratified when trusted to uphold Harding's strict standards of purity when she was given permission to start the college's first Spanish-language radio program: None of the administrators spoke enough Spanish to monitor the show's contents, but they had faith that she would avoid "songs with bad words."[96] In her account, their trust is the take-home point.

Honor codes against cheating were often a new experience for many students, accustomed to a culture of academic mutuality in which the better students often wrote papers for their peers or shared their test answers. The colleges made their concern about plagiarism clear and put it in the context of respect for intellectual property rights as well as Christian ethics. "Now I try to teach that respect for intellectual property to people around me," Federico López Bolaños related, by turning down his co-workers requests that he author their reports at work. "This is hard, because they don't always understand my objection, but look now at all the problems with international property rights, knock-off CDs, and so on—it's important, and this is how I try to teach respect for those rights."[97]

The Walton program's elevation of individual responsibility over individual prestige or even individual accomplishment echoed the formula developed by Students in Free Enterprise: Construct a closed context, encourage team cooperation, set the terms of debate, but leave the decisions up to the students. Students coming from Central America's highly stratified societies found not selfish individualism but egalitarian mutuality the dominant note in Northwest Arkansas. The sense of teamwork at John Brown University struck Walton Scholar Olga Nuñez as a dramatic contrast with her experience in Guatemala City. During her first years back from Arkansas, she had taken a job that required menial work, below her qualifications. Asked to clean up the establishment where she worked, Nuñez turned to a co-worker for help. But the other young woman refused: if she started performing these low-level tasks, she explained to Nuñez, they would become part of her job description. Instead of earning respect for her willingness to pitch in, she would be punished with de facto demotion.[98] The contrast to the service ethos could not have been more stark.

Many Walton alumni have used their improved circumstances and connections to send siblings on to higher education, as was the explicit hope of the program's American administrators. "The program gave hope to our whole families," agreed two alumni. "It demonstrated that someone could actually make it."[99] Getting ahead in this cosmology was not about leaving others behind, but about offering a visible counterexample to the region's pell-mell immiseration. The biggest problem in Guatemala, opined an American faculty member from one of the Arkansas colleges, was the lack of a concrete alternative to mass collapse. "Guatemalans are so pessimistic, so discouraged. They can't see a Wal-Mart."[100] The returning Central Americans understand their role as exemplars. "I have five people working under me now," explained a manager at a communications company. "I can raise their expectations, make them aware of what they can do."[101] They perceived their own careers and free-market policies generally as a form of public service, on the pattern of the Christian business departments they attended. For its part, Wal-Mart and its suppliers reaped tangible rewards from this network of skilled graduates. In 2005, the Bentonville company entered the Central American market, drawing together existing chains in Costa Rica and Guatemala that had employed Walton graduates. The technological integration into a global corporation was a challenge, acknowledged the president of Wal-Mart Centroamérica, but the cultural front was going quite well: labor relations, for example, were being rethought along more Wal-Mart lines. "We are incorporating aspects of Wal-Mart culture that are consistent with our values and that bring us advantages in making the personnel feel an identification with the company."[102]

In the post–Cold War era of economic integration, the Walton Scholars helped create the new common sense of globalization. The positive inputs many brought home included technical skills, a pro-market orientation, an activist Christian faith, and personal relationships in Arkansas and the larger evangelical world. The impact of these contributions was magnified by the extreme situation to which they returned. In Guatemala and El Salvador especially, a generation of the educated Left had been decimated, hundreds of thousands of civilians wiped out, tens of thousands more tortured into submission by U.S.-backed regimes.[103] This extermination of the country's educated class, recounted a Guatemalan Walton Scholar grimly, was "worse even than just killing people, because it hurts the whole country to lose all these intelligent, educated people, professors, writers, artists . . . the students who were in the student association, the leaders."[104] The Walton Scholars offered new student leaders to take the place of that generation. Their Christian business educations in Arkansas linked them to a specific vision of globalization with direct roots in Wal-Mart's own stores and offices. Their hearts and minds were won to the free-trade gospel while singing in chapel, surrounded by people who trusted and cared for them. When the Cold War ended, the Bentonville Consensus made a virtue of the Washington Consensus's necessities.

Selling Free Trade

The annual Wal-Mart shareholders' meeting in 1991 was like those that had gone before, only more so. The most visible guests were the more than one hundred Gulf War veterans who were also Wal-Mart employees, sitting together in a dedicated section. Enormous American flags provided the backdrop. Baseball great Joe DiMaggio put in an appearance, and the radio commentator Paul Harvey celebrated Wal-Mart's invention of something "better than communism, socialism, and capitalism. We have created enlightened consumerism." A band of Wal-Mart truck drivers sang "Jesus, Hold My Hand," a group of musical computer specialists from the Bentonville office got a standing ovation for their performance of "America the Beautiful," and the country music star Lee Greenwood dedicated his aggressive hit "God Bless the U.S.A." to the troops. Sam Walton was appointed an honorary brigadier general in the Arkansas National Guard by order of Governor Bill Clinton, husband of Wal-Mart's first woman director. The name of George H. W. Bush was also invoked, in a ritualistic jeering at the ungrateful federal government and the parasitical Internal Revenue Service.[1] Wal-Mart Country was riding high.

Five years later, a regular attendee might have wondered whether he had strayed into the annual gathering of a different company altogether. In place of the straightforward nationalism, that year's meeting featured a video informing the assembly about the company's new International Division. It was followed by a parade of flags held aloft by employees from the new countries where Wal-Mart was operating stores. Against this radically changed backdrop, CEO Don Soderquist instructed the audience "We have pride in our country, and they have the same pride in theirs. What's transferable is the culture of Wal-Mart—making people feel good, treating them right." The shareholders rose to sing "The Star-Spangled Banner," now designated "the national anthem of the host country."[2] Was Wal-Mart America? Or was it just in America?

In the 1990s, with the sudden disappearance of the Cold War enemy, companies like Wal-Mart helped the nation work out its new international position. In important ways, the end of the superpower standoff brought back onto center stage some key themes of American foreign policy for over a hundred years. Chief among these was the search for new markets. From the "open door" forced upon Japan and China to the acquisition of Caribbean and Pacific islands and the "dollar diplomacy" practiced on Latin America, employing military force in support of free trade was a long-standing option in United States foreign policy. As President William Howard Taft explained, it was an "axiomatic principle" that the United States government would "extend all proper support to every legitimate and beneficial American enterprise abroad."[3] In the first two decades of the twentieth century alone, American troops intervened in Cuba, the Dominican Republic, Haiti, Mexico, Nicaragua, and Panama, all in service to American corporate or financial interests and all with unabashed reference to white supremacy. During the Cold War, the defensive imperative of containing communism was matched by a positive drive to integrate the free world into an interdependent, American-led economic bloc.[4] Certainly covert intervention was not off the list of American options—in 1954, for example, the Central Intelligence Agency engineered the overthrow of Guatemala's democratically elected Leftist president, to the great relief of the United Fruit Company's operations there.[5] But sending in the Marines was no longer the simple solution to enforcing its economic vision, for the United States was locked in a competition for international prestige with the Soviet Union. Open military intrusions could not win hearts and minds in the dozens of former colonies that declared their independence after World War II. Even if they had little truck with Moscow, the new nations might choose the path of economic self-sufficiency or join together in an independent bloc, as nonaligned conferences in Indonesia and Egypt seemed to portend in the mid-1950s.[6] The same pressures that animated the Lausanne Movement among missionaries shaped American foreign policy at the highest levels.

If free trade was often a hard sell outside the United States, it was not a foregone conclusion at home, either. In the decades after World War II, successive administrations faced an uphill battle in selling the American public on integrationist foreign policy. Beginning with the United States Information Agency's "People-to-People" initiatives in the 1950s, Washington enlisted broad coalitions of cultural agents to help individual Americans feel they had a personal stake in the Cold War. American religious communities were essential to this effort, having harbored some of the country's most vigorous traditions of internationalism. For his speech introducing the programs, which educated private citizens in diplomacy through vehicles like Sister Cities and the Christian Children's Fund, President Eisenhower chose the Southern Baptist Baylor University in Texas.[7]

To this dynamic tradition of missionary globalism, Christian economic thought in the 1980s added an expansionist bent that was invigorated by its triumph in the Cold War. The New Christian Right's many Pentecostals often embraced "health-and-wealth" optimism, certain that God rewarded his faithful with ever-increasing abundance. This prosperity gospel was an international movement, linking Christians from Colorado Springs to Kinshasa to Seoul.[8] Many evangelicals, meanwhile, saw entrepreneurs as public benefactors who brought the blessing of goods and services to an ever-wider public. "The man who makes the highest profit," explained the Texas-based Institute for Christian Economics in 1981, "is the man who is best serving the public."[9] Evangelical opinion-makers enthusiastically adopted the economic visions of George Gilder and Michael Novak, putting a Christian spin on globalization.[10] Georgia congressman Newt Gingrich, a family values standard-bearer, championed a high-tech, high-growth, expansionist entrepreneurship that condemned trade barriers alongside other big-government intrusions. In this context, transnational corporations opened up new opportunities for evangelizing around the world. At Regent University's School of Business in Virginia, the Christian Broadcasting Network's Pat Robertson promoted "Entrepreneurial Tentmaking." This program prepared Christian men and women to start businesses abroad in order to "revolutionize nations economically and provide platforms for spiritual revival."[11] The end of the Cold War—the defeat of godless communism—gave both markets and missions a new chance to win souls around the world.

The Bentonville Consensus won hearts and minds in the United States—not least in the U.S. Congress—as the implications of post–Cold War free trade became the subject of national debate. Like the Walton International Scholarship Program and the international expansion of Students in Free Enterprise, Wal-Mart's development of international operations drove the company to experiment with private foreign policy. Figuring free trade as service to humble Third World consumers, it dovetailed with missionary optimism and servant leadership. In the brief historical interlude between the Cold War and the War on Terror, Christian corporate globalism imagined that economic restructuring could come not at gunpoint but at the point of sale.

Initially in the mid-1970s, Wal-Mart was concerned with overseas procurement, not expanding its retail outlets beyond the United States. Cheap goods from Asia had grown in importance to the entire discount industry since the beginning of the decade, gradually providing them with more leverage vis-à-vis suppliers. But while its stores' proportions of imported goods were estimated at over 40 percent by the mid-1980s, Wal-Mart was not a notable pioneer in the drive for Asian procurement. Where the industry led, it followed, and quietly.[12] In 1976 the Waltons traveled to "the Far East" without much fanfare to lay the groundwork for a direct importing program.[13] In 1980 the company first opened its own buying offices in Hong Kong and Taiwan that grew over that decade to almost 100 employees, but the company strove to contain its offshore operations in the existing paradigm of Wal-Mart Country. "These associates are no different than their American counterparts," the company magazine stressed rather laboriously.[14] Wal-Mart used a "global sourcing agent" from 1989 until 2002, when it took over the entire function and established a buying office in the Chinese free-trade boom town of Shenzhen. At that point, 80 percent of its suppliers were in China.[15] But for American retailers in general, the shift to imports had actually come much earlier. In the Caribbean and Central America, the Alliance for Progress had laid down the terms of a trade-based development policy under President Lyndon Johnson that proved equally palatable to later administrations. Rather than the Kennedy-era experiments with public infrastructure aid to the region, the Agency for International Development promoted private industries that would export cheap goods to the United States. The expectation was that sweatshops would mature into core industries with solid wages and benefits, and give America's unstable neighbors a middle-class bulwark against communism. Instead, the free-trade zones were locked in a race for the bottom, desperate to keep wages low and unions at bay so that the foreign investment would not shift to some other Third World source with even more desperate potential employees. In 1983, the Caribbean Basin Initiative gave clothing manufacturers an additional incentive to head for Haiti and Honduras by allowing the president to exempt many of their goods from U.S. import tariffs. By the mid-1980s, almost half of all apparel sold in the United States came from abroad.[16]

Wal-Mart's founder Sam Walton was not entirely comfortable with where the logic of low prices had taken the company. On the same Central American trip that sparked the Walton International Scholarship Program in 1984, he visited some of the sweatshops that supplied goods to Wal-Mart. What he saw evidently made an impression. Upon his return to Bentonville, Walton was contacted by Arkansas governor Bill Clinton, with whom the Republican retailer was on polite if not chummy terms. Would Walton consider contracting for textiles from an Arkansas firm that was failing in the face of competition from low-wage countries?[17]

Walton would. The resulting praise from the governor and the media made the next step an easier sell. In 1985, the company founder wrote to 3,000 of Wal-Mart's American suppliers, noting what they must already have known: more than a million and a half American jobs had been lost to imports in the first Reagan administration. In order to defend American free enterprise, the supplying companies needed to tighten their belts so that Wal-Mart could buy from them at competitive prices; in exchange, Wal-Mart would try to work with them to make their products salable through the giant company. There were savings in using U.S. suppliers, after all: shipping costs were lower, and cultural and linguistic barriers did not come into play. The "Buy American" campaign burnished the retailer's image among its core constituency while forcing domestic suppliers to try to meet Third World costs. "One of our big objectives," a Wal-Mart board member told reporter Bob Ortega, "was to put the heat on American manufacturers to lower their prices."[18]

But a series of media exposés after Walton's death in 1992 made it clear the program had become more style than substance. *Dateline NBC* confronted Walton's successor, CEO David Glass, with video evidence that the Kathie Lee Gifford signature clothing line was being manufactured under horrific conditions by children in Bangladesh. The *New York Daily News* revealed undocumented immigrants right in New York City sewing Kathie Lee fashions without pay. American trade unionists flew a fifteen-year-old girl from Honduras to testify to Congress about the sweatshop where she sewed the Wal-Mart products seventy hours a week for less than twenty-two dollars.[19]

Despite the immediate negative press, Wal-Mart learned from the incident that its shoppers and employees were evidently more loyal to the company than to the principle of "Buy American." Bentonville coordinated a full-fledged damage control campaign, rousing its own employees and those of its suppliers to attack the *Dateline* story. The resulting flood of phone calls to NBC jammed the network's switchboard.[20] The same Wal-Mart shoppers who approved of the company's "Buy American" efforts were nonetheless willing to buy Chinese if those were the cheapest products on offer.[21]

But it was Mexico, not China, that originally caused Wal-Mart to rethink its global vision from the standpoint of stores rather than factories. Wal-Mart's expansion into Mexico—its first attempt at retailing outside the United States—played a crucial symbolic role in the national debate over the North American Free Trade Agreement (NAFTA). It could only provide the imaginative framework for the NAFTA argument because it predated the treaty. In fact, the cross-border expansion grew out of an earlier era of economic and cultural integration around the Texas-Mexico border. For a brief but decisive moment in U.S. politics, the key to imagining free trade was Wal-Mart in Mexico.

In 1965, Mexico had begun experimenting with export-oriented maquiladoras along its northern border, where some areas enjoyed duty-free status to entice manufacturers.[22] Such efforts, however, did not attract much attention initially, nor were they meant to: Mexican policy from the 1940s to the 1980s remained committed to developing native industry for domestic consumption behind protective tariff walls, just as the United States and Britain had done in the nineteenth century.

Between 1940 and 1980, this strategy produced annual growth rates of over 6 percent and a steady rise in real wages. But the "Mexican Miracle" came at a price, one increasingly met through high-interest loans from American banks. In 1982, the Mexican finance minister was forced to go to Washington, hat in hand: the country could not honor its foreign payment schedule. In return for emergency loans, Mexico submitted to free-market restructuring, cutting social services, privatizing hundreds of state-owned enterprises, and joining the Uruguay Round of the General Agreement on Tariffs and Trade. The buying power of the Mexican minimum wage dropped by almost 70 percent between 1982 and 1991. Industrial wages fell by almost half; per capita basic food consumption dropped 30 percent.[23]

In early 1991, following announcements of negotiations for NAFTA, American investment in Mexico jumped to two and a half times its previous rate.[24] In this context, then, Wal-Mart's decision to enter Mexico's retail market represented part of a larger shift underway to realign the post–Cold War global geography from NATO and the Warsaw Pact into competing free-trade areas.[25] President George H. W. Bush negotiated the agreement with the help of the business-heavy Advisory Committee for Trade Policy and Negotiations.[26] A business coalition of more than 500 corporations—"a virtual lobbying Who's Who"—helped the administration secure Congressional approval for fast-tracking the treaty, or requiring an up-or-down vote without the possibility of amendments.[27] The constitutional division of labor that had often stymied free traders—commercial regulation to Congress, but foreign policy to the executive branch—could thus be short-circuited: It was to be the trade agreement hammered out by President Bush, or no trade agreement at all.

But the old Cold Warrior was not the visionary who could see it through to ratification. That job fell to Arkansan Bill Clinton, whose wife resigned from Wal-Mart's board to help her husband's presidential campaign in 1992.[28] Despite his party's resolution against NAFTA in 1991 and his own ambivalence toward it during the campaign, the new president threw his support to the treaty in 1993.[29] The key for business under the new administration was now to see the trade agreement through a scheduled vote in the House in mid-November. If they lost, and a new round of negotiations opened up, it might be years before they could muster the political will to pass another version, what with the recession and climbing unemployment.

The Business Roundtable swung into action. It organized 2,300 corporations into USA-NAFTA and assigned state captaincies to Roundtable members. The captains—all but four of whom had participated in the treaty negotiations through seats on the Bush-era advisory boards—mobilized unprecedented business unity in campaigning for public opinion through every conceivable media outlet, from op-eds to talking heads.[30] "You may also want to consider involving employees in a company-wide letter-writing campaign," suggested the Illinois NAFTA Coalition in a July 1993 memo to its members. Procter & Gamble, a major Wal-Mart vendor, promoted the treaty's potential to double the company's export market in a quarterly report to its 170,000 stockholders.[31] Wal-Mart made early appearances as a symbol for this export potential. "Here's a country with 86 million people, trying to grow and needing access to the kind of products we have here," said a USA-NAFTA council member. "I've been told by the leadership of Wal-Mart that they can't get enough American-made product into their stores they are now building in Mexico."[32]

Yet the fish weren't biting. Public support for NAFTA had been dropping steadily since the original fast-track vote. The lingering recession that had begun in 1990 and an unemployment rate holding at 7 percent raised middle-class fears about job loss. In the autumn of 1993, the proportion of Americans favoring NAFTA fell to less than half, according to the Gallup polls.[33]

It was at this juncture that Wal-Mart took the media limelight. The maquiladoras along the border, built for a generation by U.S. manufacturers in search of cheap labor, were not a camera-ready advertisement for economic integration. If this was what a free-trade zone looked like, American voters could hardly be blamed for opposing it. But U.S. retailers along the border provided another vision of life under NAFTA. It was precisely Wal-Mart's experience in South Texas that retail analysts cited in the early 1990s as a sign of good things to come in the company's Mexico expansion.[34]

Wal-Mart's 1991 joint venture with Mexican retail giant Grupo CIFRA S.A. was about more than retail homesteading on the other side of the Rio Grande. Rather, it coincided with three other acquisitions that together found new markets for the company at home and abroad. In the early 1990s Wal-Mart took its first big step toward incorporating food operations into the now-ubiquitous supercenters with the acquisition of the Texas grocery distributor McLane Company, as well as the purchase of a twenty-store Bentonville grocery chain and Western Merchandisers, a distributor of books, music, and videos.[35] Wal-Mart assured its internal audience that the four-part acquisition did not mean a wholesale remaking of the company's core: "Common corporate culture," explained *Wal-Mart World,* "is the framework that all four companies share with Wal-Mart." That shared culture included the "downhome values" that kept Western Merchandisers "humble"; the "honesty, integrity, and Christian principles" of McLane; and the Mexican enthusiasm for free trade.[36] In deference to potential national feeling, Mexico's first taste of Wal-Mart came under CIFRA's Aurrerá brand.[37] It was not until the fall of 1993 that a Wal-Mart Supercenter opened with that name in the working-class Mexico City neighborhood of Ixtapalapa.[38]

By that time, the debate over free trade had heated to a fever pitch. Congressional opponents of NAFTA argued that the experiment on the border had produced not a new, stable middle class of Mexicans but that hybrid haunting globalization, the peasant with the laser. On both sides of the border, asserted Democratic whip Dick Gephardt, he had seen Mexicans who were working in space-age automated factories, then going home to hovels without running water.[39] It was hard to imagine many customers for a Maytag dishwasher in the shanty towns.

By far the most robust line of defense against NAFTA came from labor, galvanized by the ten-to-one wage differential between the United States and Mexico. The AFL-CIO began organizing against the fast-track status back in 1990, even before business coalesced around supporting it. The unions gained high-profile help from an unexpected quarter when Ross Perot, a third-party presidential candidate in 1992, made his opposition to NAFTA a cornerstone of his campaign.[40] A year after the election, as debate over NAFTA heated up in the House of Representatives, the Texas billionaire's warning of the "giant sucking sound" from the south was reinvigorated. Thus by the fall of 1993, when the new Wal-Mart opened in Mexico City, the two major camps had staked out their positions: Was Mexico a vast reservoir of low-wage workers, willing to sell themselves to American companies for pennies on the dollar? Or was it an enormous untapped market, full of the same shop-happy rubes who roamed discount aisles in Arkansas and Texas?

Wal-Mart discovered which notes to hit for free trade's domestic

American audience. Late in the summer of 1993, the company had sent representatives to Washington for the International Mass Retailers Association lobbying trip. The trip had been intended to reiterate the industry's support in terms long familiar to the hosts. "NAFTA is a real key opportunity to bolster U.S. manufacturing," explained Bobby Martin, executive vice president and Wal-Mart's man on the NAFTA excursion.[41] The Clinton administration, of course, was receptive to this line of argument. The White House arranged meetings for the delegation with Secretary of the Treasury Lloyd Bentsen and U.S. trade representative Mickey Kantor that a participant described as "something of a pep rally."[42]

But in meetings with congressional representatives, the discount delegation awoke to the very real danger of NAFTA's failure.[43] Congressmen told the merchants that their constituent mail ran nine-to-one against ratification. NAFTA, the retailers learned, was "in deep trouble." The message from Capitol Hill was clear: If the retailers wanted to see NAFTA passed, it was up to them to persuade the Americans in their stores. "We'll have to fight every step of the way," warned Democratic senator Bill Bradley, the upper house's quarterback for NAFTA. "You will have to let everyone you employ know why this is important and get them involved in the process too." But these efforts alone would not be enough. In contrast to all other trade agreements since World War II, the NAFTA fight was being carried out in public, with significant grassroots involvement—mostly against its passage. Convincing employees had always been part of business's contribution. Now it would need to mobilize its customers, too.[44]

Back in Bentonville, the company wasted no time. CEO David Glass wrote to all of Wal-Mart's suppliers—the manufacturers of its products—encouraging them to "write or visit your member of Congress" and "become involved" in the fight to secure NAFTA's passage. Glass offered his assistance and asked to be updated on their activities.[45] Now the pro-NAFTA forces were back in the game. In mid-September, President Clinton himself reopened the offensive with a fiery speech that convened most of the state governors and three former presidents to demonstrate the bipartisan support for free trade. With the Cold War won, Americans faced a changing geography of "blocs." Asia and Europe would consolidate, so Americans needed to act fast to secure their leadership of the Western hemisphere. NAFTA had the potential to put Americans in the driver's seat of "a free trade zone stretching from the Arctic to the tropics, the largest in the world."[46]

A week later the International Mass Retail Association was back in Washington. Wal-Mart's corporate counsel Ralph Carter, under the title "director of Wal-Mart trade policy," spoke for the entire retail group in its testimony before the Trade Subcommittee of the House Ways and Means Committee on September 21, 1993.[47] NAFTA, he assured the congressional panel, was "right for America and especially right for American workers."[48]

In making his industry's case, the Wal-Mart trade policy director dismissed NAFTA's naysayers as nervous protectionists. The very mass consumption that had fueled the American century could not continue without moving into new territory, he explained to his congressional audience. In support, he pointed to Wal-Mart's experiences on the Texas-Mexico border, where eager consumers from the south pointed the way to a vast new market.[49]

Even better proof of his testimony was the Mexico City Wal-Mart Supercenter, which opened in early October to rave reviews. It did not take long for Bentonville and its pro-NAFTA allies to recognize a PR gold mine when they saw one. "Servando Infante, 39, a bank employee, said he doesn't know much about the NAFTA debate," reported a typical account. "But if the agreement means there will be more stores like Wal-Mart in Mexico, he's all for it."[50]

The opening day of the world's largest Wal-Mart was appropriate to the historical moment. Mariachi musicians and scantily clad spokesmodels were just the beginning, reported an Associated Press account that was widely carried in the United States. "Someone in a penguin costume does the cha-cha across the slippery tile floor of the 244,000-square-foot Wal-Mart Supercenter while amused customers watch. 'This place is enormous. You can get anything you want,' shopper Julieta Rodriguez said, 'Free trade has arrived.'"[51] These same high notes were to be reiterated constantly in the commentary flowing out of Ixtapalapa: the manic enthusiasm of newly globalized Mexican shoppers and their humble consumer naiveté. Their attitude toward this little slice of *Norte americana* bordered on religious devotion, the reports implied. One reporter followed a woman on her "pilgrimage" to "this country's newest shrine: Wal-Mart."[52] "It rises like a gleaming mirage," rhapsodized another account, where many came to gaze upon "such exotic made-in-the-U.S. wonders as Rollerblades, microwave popcorn and upholstered cat perches." The moral of the story, it turned out, was that the marveling Mexicans bought for the sheer joy of consuming. "'You Americans sell, we Mexicans buy,'" the article quoted a female shopper. "'It is good for both of us, no?'"[53]

This vision of free trade—Americans selling, people in poorer countries gratefully buying—beat out its shantytown rivals in the fall of 1993 to secure congressional ratification of NAFTA. Some of the most active companies in promoting NAFTA were precisely the manufacturing and financial giants whose interest in Mexico was suspect to many Americans: the more Westinghouse and American Express spoke of their abstract, high-minded allegiance to free trade, the less convincing they sounded.[54] But the Rollerblades in the Wal-Mart shopping cart were something else again. Images of Wal-Mart's Mexican customers flooded the press. And the audience that mattered most got a firsthand look.

The National Retail Federation selected fifty lawmakers to target with the full force of its lobbying muscle, pushing members to pressure their employees to write and fax Congress in support of the treaty.[55] And prominent among the undecided was Northwest Arkansas's own representative, a Bentonville native. This obstructionism from Republican Tim Hutchinson—alumnus of the evangelical Bob Jones University, ordained Southern Baptist pastor, and former history instructor at the evangelical, Walton-supported John Brown University—was a thorn in the side of his fellow Arkansans, both in Wal-Mart headquarters and in the White House. Hutchinson's chief concern was job loss. Many businesses, after all, had recently relocated to Arkansas for precisely the same attractions that Mexico now might be offering—low wages and a nonunion workforce straight off the farm.[56] In the first week in November, with the vote looming on the 18th, administration officials pleaded with the International Mass Retailers Association and Wal-Mart to "work on" the reluctant Hutchinson.[57]

The solution was a field trip to Ixtapalapa, to the world's largest Wal-Mart, where Hutchinson experienced an epiphany. There in the furthest outpost of the Bentonville retail empire, a store manager pointed out to Hutchinson a customer carrying a Skil saw, produced in a factory in Walnut Ridge, Arkansas. Over half of the products, in fact, came from the United States, and every day they were perused by over 35,000 Mexican shoppers. Hutchinson returned to Washington with his mind made up. "One of the real lasting impressions was the appetite for American products that exists in Mexico," he told fellow Arkansans.[58] And if the United States wasn't interested in feeding that appetite, he pointed out, surely Asia or Europe would be.[59]

With little more than a week to go before the vote, lobbying moved into overdrive. Hutchinson's conversion was interpreted as a triumph for Wal-Mart, and half a dozen hold-outs flipped.[60] Democrat John Pratt, representing part of South Carolina's textile region, reported that his trip to Mexico with the U.S. State Department had included a stop at the world's largest Wal-Mart. There he saw shelves stocked with South Carolina's own Springmaid sheets and Fruit of the Loom socks and tee-shirts, he explained to a constituent audience of union and environmental leaders firmly opposed to the treaty. Pratt pledged his support to NAFTA.[61] This line of reasoning also worked for New Jersey's representative Robert Franks, who visited the Mexico City Wal-Mart and watched excited middle-class consumers loading up their carts with children's toys, disposable baby wipes, soap—all made in the U.S.A. Three weeks later, he was off the fence, on the administration's side.[62]

Some of these last-minute congressional attitude adjustments were helped along by another key deployment of the Ixtapalapa Wal-Mart, this one by Vice President Al Gore. The White House had been looking for a splashy event to galvanize public opinion right before the House vote, and hit upon the idea of a televised debate between the urbane veep and the jug-eared Ross Perot, NAFTA's most high-profile opponent. Polls suggested that the twangy Texan annoyed many people so much that public support for NAFTA actually rose when poll responders discovered Perot opposed it. The strategy was to remind constituents what the anti-NAFTA forces looked like, and counter that vision with expert testimony.[63]

Perot fell for the bait. On November 9th, he went mano a mano with Gore on *Larry King Live,* and as one observer put it, "the vice president undressed Ross Perot."[64] "Did you see the Wal-Mart that opened in Mexico City on the news?" Gore asked his opponent. "It's the largest one in the world, if I understand it. They have seventy-two cash registers ringing constantly with people in that country—in Mexico—taking American products out of that store." If the United States would seize the day, that success could be replicated by countless other businesses.[65] The volume of constituent calls, which had been running heavily against the treaty, suddenly shifted.

Here, then, was the image that sold NAFTA: Mexico was not a backward reservoir of resentful toilers, but rather an incipient consumer behemoth. It had a lot in common with, say, Arkansas—who would have thought poor rural people could make such good shoppers? Outside the Mexican Wal-Mart store, a pair of bewildered reporters conceded, the city looked suspiciously like the Third World. But inside was "a First-World oasis of consumer goods."[66]

For some, Mexico's inner Wal-Mart even became the symbol for America's changed relationship not just to its southern neighbor, but to a world realigned by the end of the Cold War. "Failure to ratify the North American Free Trade Agreement could—I say could, not necessarily would—trigger a global economic collapse," warned David Nyhan, a liberal columnist for the *Boston Globe*. Nyhan reminded his readers that win or lose, the NAFTA vote would be followed immediately by a presidential trip to Seattle to talk trade with representatives from the rising economic powerhouses in Asia. Meanwhile, the clock was running down for official U.S. action to sign onto the Uruguay Round of the General Agreement on Tariffs and Trade, the big daddy of all economic integration treaties. Not just NAFTA, but free trade itself was up for a vote. "Do we go forward, into the future, and the interconnected world, stitched together by threads of trade into a tapestry of economic security? Or do we retreat, fall back into the sinkhole of protectionism, hiding behind tariff regulations, clinging to our dwindling oasis while the camel caravans of free trade divert to other routes?" America had a rendezvous with destiny, and the accompanying photo showed where: in the world's biggest Wal-Mart, in Ixtapalapa.[67]

The treaty passed the House on the night of November 17, 1993, in a vote that split more by geography than by party. The Sun Belt stood proudly and optimistically for a free-trade future against the anxious naysayers of Detroit. Clinton's mirror image, Georgia congressman Newt Gingrich, rallied his fellow Republicans and proclaimed, "This is a vote for history, larger than politics, larger than reelection, larger than personal ego."[68] The momentum of corporate support mobilized behind NAFTA and behind the symbol of the Mexico City Wal-Mart carried over into the successful campaign to ratify the Uruguay Round of the General Agreement on Tariffs and Trade less than a year after NAFTA went into effect. Ten thousand corporations organized into GATT-NOW, on the model of USA-NAFTA. Not one major business or industry association was left behind.[69]

As for Wal-Mart, NAFTA's new geography provided the proving ground for its international expansion. Two weeks after NAFTA took effect on January 1, 1994, Wal-Mart announced its acquisition of 122 Woolco stores across Canada, and went to work "Walmartizing" them. In 1997, Wal-Mart signaled confidence in its Mexico operations by buying up the controlling interest in the Mexican company CIFRA and adding its CEO Jerónimo Arango to the board of directors. The board also added a highly placed voice for free trade in its appointment of Paula Stern, the veteran chairwoman of the Reagan-era International Trade Commission and member of the Advisory Committee on Trade Policy and Negotiations under Clinton and later George W. Bush.[70] Tours of duty abroad became an exciting new field for stateside employees like Texans Erlinda and Chris Garza, who took their expertise to Monterrey after years spent managing stores in Texas and Arkansas.[71] The company was pleasantly surprised to find that in fact its culture traveled well and even gained from its association with "Latin passion," as *Fortune* put it. "I have never seen a Wal-Mart so rowdy," the head of the international division observed approvingly of a new store opening in Monterrey.[72] Once Mexico and Canada showed staying power, Wal-Mart took a much bolder approach to overseas ventures. The strategy of buying into established chains was replicated with Asda in the United Kingdom, Interspar in Germany, Seiyu in Japan, and Bompreco in Brazil.[73] By 2006, if Wal-Mart's international arm had established itself as an independent chain, it could have ended the year as the world's fourth largest retailer.[74] The same year, Wal-Mart's CEO Lee Scott joined Bill Gates and James Wolfensohn, former president of the World Bank, on a panel convened by the United Kingdom's Chancellor of the Exchequer to counsel that country on the best path to globalization.[75]

Through the 1990s, Wal-Mart's global vision shifted focus as it struggled to square its flag-waving patriotism and Christian entrepreneurial spirit with the demands of corporate globalism. It hearkened back to missionary internationalism, the free-trade faith that had seen American consumer goods as an opening wedge for Christian conversion and free-market democracy around the world. Jack Shewmaker recommended that all Wal-Mart executives make at least one trip abroad every year. "The world is getting smaller, and our stores are starting to look more and more alike," he explained. "The world is hungry for knowledge, information, freedom and our products. Everywhere I go I encounter people who want what we already have."[76] Despite language differences, the company explained in 1994, "Wal-Mart's concepts translate well."[77]

Epilogue: A Perfect Storm

Long before the first stirrings of Hurricane Katrina, even before the bulldozers began their ruckus on the banks of the Mississippi, the Wal-Mart on New Orleans's Tchoupitoulas Street was making headlines. The proposed site of the future Supercenter lay beneath the old St. Thomas housing project, once home to almost two thousand of the city's poor. Its sturdy, low-rise duplexes dated from the New Deal commitment to shelter one-third of a nation, artifacts of the era before massive towers warehoused the urban poor. Reserved for white tenants for a generation, St. Thomas finally bowed to Great Society desegregation in the mid-1960s. By 1980, all of its tenants were black, even as a wave of white bargain-hunters snapped up the nearby shotgun shacks and bungalows of New Orleans's quaint vernacular architecture. A decade later, St. Thomas was home to all the classic trappings of postindustrial poverty: its fifty acres housed mostly single mothers with annual incomes below $5,000, plagued by poor health, lousy schools, and alarming rates of violent crime. In 1996, the city officially gave up on St. Thomas and turned to a doomsday solution: a $25 million federal grant to raze most of the buildings. In their place, the plan promised, would rise new units evenly divided among low- and middle-class tenants, as well as resident-owned commercial sites.[1]

But once the bricks were down, the bare lot became a tantalizing tabula rasa. New plans cut the proposed low-income units back to fewer than two hundred, and instead added 780 luxury condominiums. In place of the expected small commercial sites for local businesses, a $28 million bond would allow the Wal-Mart Supercenter to rise tax-free on

the public land. The discount store's future customers would then contribute $20 million in sales taxes to the site's reconstruction, helping to
underwrite the condos as well as the public housing units. Fewer than
10 percent of the 800 families displaced from the St. Thomas project
would be allowed into the new development. "In reality," argued a critic,
"it's a way to get a lot of money for high-income housing." Renamed
"River Garden," the site would lure desirable residents with the pastel
pedestrianism of the New Urbanist design movement. And while the
big box store wasn't quite the period piece the architects had envisioned,
Wal-Mart did agree to landscape the parking lot.[2]

For the Arkansas-based company, its first stake in central New Orleans represented a form of urban homesteading. "The company started
in rural areas [because] people in those areas did not have access to
goods that other people did," explained a spokeswoman, and now that
rural Americans could buy brand-name goods in their Wal-Marts, the
company was extending that service to another population left behind
in national consumption. Besides, argued the River Garden developer,
the country had voted for Wal-Mart in the most democratic forum: the
marketplace. "Americans have decided they want discount shopping in
volume, and that's the real world," he explained succinctly.[3]

In 2001 former residents of St. Thomas and their white neighbors
packed a tense five-hour meeting of the New Orleans City Planning
Commission, arguing on opposite sides. The mostly white forces against
Wal-Mart saw their challenge to a subsidized big-box store as a stand for
the common good. The data was in: Wal-Mart didn't add jobs, it canni-
balized existing ones. It drove locally owned businesses under, homogenized communities, and degraded the landscape—and all with help
from the public purse. With the government contracting out its public
housing to for-profit developers, the tenants became loss leaders in a
slick real-estate deal. Did residents of this famously walkable city really
want to hike across acres of hot asphalt as Red Lobsters and Home De-
pots followed in the big blue wake of Wal-Mart? Was nothing sacred,
demanded preservationists?[4]

But many of the store's backers understood the sacred somewhat dif-
ferently, as several of the prominent African-American ministers in their
ranks attested. Earlier in the year, they had taken part in a conference to
train local congregations in the entrepreneurial arts of federal grant-
writing, construction partnerships, and tax credits. The two-day event

at historically black Xavier University positioned New Orleans churches to take advantage of President George W. Bush's planned White House Office of Faith-Based and Community Initiatives.[5] "We realized long ago we could not preach on Sunday without teaching throughout the week—trying to give people a living, sustaining gospel that's really going to change their circumstances and affect their lives," explained one of the participating pastors. "It's a natural thing for the church to be involved in empowering people." Following a national trend among black and white congregations alike, churches in the city had transformed themselves into business hubs. Church-owned enterprises in New Orleans included a self-storage company, an apartment complex, and a print shop. Business education classes joined Sunday schools as part of their outreach. The proposed Wal-Mart on Tchoupitoulas fit this entrepreneurial vision through its roundabout public-private redevelopment scheme. The arrangement to funnel the sales tax revenue from the stores built there offered some hope that these monies might eventually be used to bring some subsidized units back to St. Thomas. "Some of us are still stuck in 1965," explained the pastor of a New York African Methodist Episcopal church to the gathered New Orleanians. "We've reached the promised land, but too many of us don't know how to use the gifts."[6]

As the Tchoupitoulas fight ground toward the November City Council vote, the developers' public relations firm lent its organizational infrastructure to a pro–Wal-Mart rally of St. Thomas evictees. The ministers' references to the relevant history became more explicit. "The preservationists seek the resegregation of St. Thomas," said the Rev. Marie Galatas, a veteran civil rights activist. "The time has passed," asserted the Rev. Charles Southall, "when preservationists can tell predominantly African-American neighborhoods what can be built and what cannot be built."[7] Localism had not been a handmaiden of justice in the segregated South.

Wal-Mart won the vote, and after months of lawsuits, appeals, petitions, and inquiries, the faux-brick store went up. Even in a city almost synonymous with corruption, revelations of the sleazy deals behind River Garden raised eyebrows. Many of the "concerned citizens" who spoke up for the project turned out to be on the payroll. A mayoral ally received $350,000 in consulting fees from the developer; the Rev. Galatas accepted one tenth that sum. Slowly the fight eased out of the public spotlight.[8] Soon enough, there were bigger problems on Tchoupitoulas Street.

It's an unusually ill wind that blows no one good, and in the sodden aftermath of Hurricane Katrina, some observers found redemptive stories in two quarters: the market and the church. *The Economist* labeled Wal-Mart Stores, Inc., among the few "odd winners," noting that its efficient response and generosity had momentarily silenced the rising chorus of critics.[9] Vigilant for the upside of disaster, the *Wall Street Journal* was pleased to spotlight "the remarkable response of the business community" as an example of "what went right" for the Gulf Coast. And in its celebration of private-sector initiative, the journal wasn't shy about naming names: "The Federal Emergency Management Agency [FEMA] could learn some things from Wal-Mart Stores, Inc.," it elaborated, detailing the vast coordination efforts that kept essential goods flowing into the region's Wal-Marts even as the bumbling representatives of the public sector wept and whined on camera.[10]

During the dismal, disorganized official response to the broken levees, with the gutting of nonmilitary functions of government terrifyingly clear, it wasn't only the professional spokesmen of free-market supremacy who drew such a distinctly twenty-first-century conclusion. The *New York Times* recommended the country outsource disaster relief and let Wal-Mart take over emergency management in place of government, period—"WEMA" could replace FEMA.[11] The elected head of a New Orleans suburb declared that if "the American government would have responded like Wal-Mart has responded, we wouldn't be in this crisis."[12] Conservative activists had urged for a generation that Republicans shrink the state until it was small enough to be "drowned in a bathtub." Bathtub or no, it had certainly drowned.

Alongside the iconic corporation, the other entity that emerged from Katrina with its reputation enhanced was the church.[13] Hurricane Katrina trained a spotlight on the White House's determination to prove churches more effective than government. In relocating evacuees to Tulsa, Oklahoma, for example, FEMA bypassed the city's well-organized secular disaster relief network in favor of Catholic Charities, headquartered two hours away in Oklahoma City, and even sent one group of

New Orleanians to a remote Southern Baptist youth camp.[14] In Mississippi, the state agency charged with promoting President Bush's funding sources for religious charities found that the hurricane raised its profile among the state's churches. "At first," explained the director of the Mississippi Faith-Based Coalition, the churches were "more or less reluctant to connect with us," fearful that Big Brother would regulate them in exchange for the public monies distributed via state block grants. But they discovered that the program was less a Big Brother than a generous uncle, uninterested in oversight. Attendance quickly doubled at the monthly workshops on attracting government funds.[15] The state of Minnesota, somewhat off Katrina's path, nonetheless learned from the coast's example. Noting that the disaster proved how churches could help where government was useless, the Republican governor promptly opened a state office for channeling federal money to religious service groups.[16] By 2007, over 100 cities and 33 states had followed suit.[17]

The broken levees showed just how much separated the original Wal-Mart Country from its new frontiers. For all the transnational, multiracial, cross-class Christian enthusiasm for free enterprise, its devotees still stood in very different relationships to one another. The response to the epic calamity unfolded with such grisly ineptitude and callousness because many of New Orleans's citizens were already experiencing the face of neoliberalism that was more visible in Guatemala City than in Bentonville. In the United States, few disasters incited cries to replace the state with a store and a church, but that argument was familiar elsewhere. In places more thoroughly advanced down the neoliberal road, belonging to a church or working for a transnational corporation often structured life more concretely than did citizenship itself.[18]

For those who did not experience neoliberalism's worst effects, the devastated city served as an historical wormhole, a brief opening in time and space that placed the Sun Belt back into its original context. For hundreds of years, the American South and West in many ways resembled the other plantation and extraction societies of the colonized New World more than they did the northern Atlantic industrial zone—indeed, they spent much of their history under other flags. Forcibly incorporated into the industrial economy via the Civil War, they continued to function for another two generations very much like an internal banana republic, ruled by an enfranchised white settler class and a system of racial terrorism, sending raw materials and crops north to the factories and the cities. But they could claim a crucial privilege: Alone among similar American-owned or American-dominated agricultural zones in the Western hemisphere, the white settlers of the former Confederacy and frontier had representation in Washington. When in the twentieth century the federal government redistributed wealth from the industrial states into private hands in the Sun Belt, even poor whites in the South and West stood to gain. The postwar service sector that eclipsed the old industrial economy was built on a New Deal infrastructure. At the same time, as Nancy MacLean argues, the Sun Belt's free-market philosophy—cheap labor, low state investment in the public welfare, and open international markets for its commodities—survived intact from the South's nineteenth-century planters. Trent Lott, Mississippi's Republican senator, put it simply during the Reagan era: the party's goals "'from tax policy to foreign policy, from individual rights to neighborhood security' were 'all things [Confederate President] Jefferson Davis and his people believed in.'"[19] It was an overstatement, but one that might have sounded plausible on Tchoupitoulas Street that August.

The replacement of manufacturing with consumer services that turned New Orleans into a low-wage theme park and Wal-Mart into the world's largest private-sector employer is a tale familiar around the world. From New Orleans to Santiago to Vladivostok, economic restructuring eliminated public provisions to seduce footloose transnational capital. In the vacuum that was left by the eradication of the safety net, churches and other faith-based organizations became the provider of last resort. Their family values rendered care a private privilege awarded in defense of marriage, not a mutual social duty of citizens to one another. The irony was that both the corporations and the churches were already public-private partnerships by definition, built with public subsidy and dependent on state nurturance.[20]

The story of Wal-Mart and its world, however, also suggests that confining collective human endeavor to the market, the church, and the family is not an inevitable outcome of American history. Christian free enterprise did not grow from themes so commonsensical, so fundamentally appealing to a controlling public majority as to amount to our manifest destiny. To the contrary, it was an unstable compound, the product in part of impressive agglomerations of power and money.[21] But it was also the progeny of pragmatic responses to real needs, of idealistic hope in redemption, and of the elevation of service from its devalued position in the broader culture. The ideological work required to attach these human impulses to the market or contain them within a narrow definition of the sacred was breathtaking.

Surveying the free-market transitions imposed in places like post-Katrina New Orleans and post-invasion Iraq, Naomi Klein rightly draws attention to what she terms "disaster capitalism," or "the orchestrated raids on the public sphere in the wake of catastrophic events."[22] Quoting the free market's most influential recent spokesman, she offers us Milton Friedman's instructions for social change: "Only a crisis—actual or perceived—," wrote the Nobel Prize–winning economist in 1962, "produces real change. When that crisis occurs, the actions that are taken depend on the ideas that are lying around. That, I believe, is our basic function: to develop alternatives to existing policies, to keep them alive and available until the politically impossible becomes politically inevitable."[23]

Ideas cannot be kept alive for the next crisis without living hosts. The University of Chicago and the American Enterprise Institute could not by themselves sustain Milton Friedman's free-market utopia. Rather, the popular faith in Christian free enterprise attracted passionate support among many ordinary people. It was nurtured not only on the high planes of elite academe or in the hot-houses of well-funded think tanks, but also in the cultural apparatus of the Sun Belt service economy: discount stores, back offices, Christian business courses, missionary manuals, Wednesday night Bible study. It was not a simple matter of elite manipulation; it did not make political dupes of Kansans or Arkansans.

Rather, for many in the nation's old agricultural periphery, the gospel of free enterprise answered some of their most pressing needs. It compensated for the loss of the yeoman dream of self-sufficiency; it sanctified mass consumption; it raised degraded service labor to the status of a calling; it offered a new basis for family stability and masculine authority even as the logic of the market undermined both; for some whites it eased the dismantling of official white supremacy. The generation that moved from the farm to the store, and their children who filled marketing classes and offices, crafted an ideology of Christian free enterprise from their experience of a particular historical moment, a particular geography, and a particular religious ecology.

But the faithful also answered the needs of free enterprise itself. Markets, after all, render merely irrational many of the concerns we put at the center of our existence, concerns like art, justice, love, friendship, democracy, even worship itself. Within the closed system of economic logic, individuals have no principles, only preferences: a taste for freedom cannot be distinguished from a taste for french fries. Selling a child makes economic sense; caring for one does not. Markets in the real world, then, can run on self-interest only because other areas of life resist it. Christianity offered a sanctuary from which to renew human virtue, a higher authority when market logic became unbearable. This faith attracted enough adherents to keep the free market holy, and wholly available to the powerful. Wal-Mart and its world explain one way this process unfolded over decades of wrenching economic transformation, but others are possible.

For future generations, New Orleans' trial by flood in 2005 may stand with the fundamentalist violence of 2001 and the financial collapse of 2008 as key moments of reckoning for the new millennium. The defeat and defection of the Wal-Mart voters in the election of 2008 and the successful mobilization of quite different American traditions have roots in these three calamities. Our responses to them—war, "WEMA," and Wall Street welfare—may actually mark the end of the free-market crusade. The invisible hand and the hand of God are not easily mistaken for each other when the former proves so fallible.

Historians can only traffic in the past, but the headlines today begin to suggest 1933 rather than 1973. If an enduring social vision is to prevail, however, we will need to shed our industrial illusions. We will need to learn from Christian free enterprise that there is no bright line dividing hard issues from soft, economic concerns from cultural distractions, the bread from the roses. We will need, at last, to follow new leaders—Betty Dukes the Wal-Mart checker, Wanda Blue the hog processor, Donna Steele the home health aide, Armando Robles the sit-down striker, Linda Lloyd the living-wage activist. We will need a servant heart.[24]

Abbreviations in Notes

AA	*Austin American;* continued by *Austin American-Statesman*
AA-UO	Records of the Office of Academic Affairs, University of the Ozarks, Clarksville, Arkansas
ADG	*Arkansas Democrat-Gazette*
AG	*Arkansas Gazette*
BCDD	*Benton County* [Arkansas] *Daily Democrat;* continued by *Daily Record*
BCG-UO	Records of the Division of Business, Communications, and Government, University of the Ozarks, Clarksville, Arkansas
BHR	*Business History Review*
BW	*Business Week*
CIA	Chemical Industry Archives, Environmental Working Group, Washington, DC, www.chemicalindustryarchives.org
CSM	*Christian Science Monitor*
CT	*Christianity Today*
CW	*Chemical Week*
DNR	*Daily News Record*
DR	*Daily Record* [Benton County, Arkansas]
DSN	*Discount Store News*
FPCB	Records of the First Presbyterian Church, Bentonville, Arkansas; Special Collections, University of Arkansas Libraries, Fayetteville, Arkansas
JB Jr.	Correspondence, John Brown, Jr., University Archives, John Brown University, Siloam Springs, Arkansas

JBU	University Archives, John Brown University, Siloam Springs, Arkansas
JEE	*Journal of Economic Education*
JHE	*Journal of Higher Education*
JTR	Collected Papers of Senator Joseph T. Robinson, Special Collections, University of Arkansas Libraries, Fayetteville, Arkansas
MCMA	Minutes of the Chemical Manufacturers Association, Chemical Industry Archives, Environmental Working Group, Washington, DC, www.chemicalindustryarchives.org
ME	*Mountain Eagle* [University of the Ozarks, Clarksville, Arkansas]
NB	*Nation's Business*
NB-ES	*News Brief* [Enterprise Square, USA, Oklahoma Christian University, Oklahoma City, Oklahoma]
NOTP	*New Orleans Times-Picayune*
NW	*Newsweek*
NWAT	*Northwest Arkansas Times*
NYT	*New York Times*
OACH	Oklahoma Archives of Contemporary History, Oklahoma Christian University, Oklahoma City, Oklahoma
PBL-UO	Records of Phi Beta Lambda business honors society, University of the Ozarks, Clarksville, Arkansas
RCIU	Retail Clerks International Union Records, 1899–1979, Wisconsin Historical Society, Madison, Wisconsin; includes Retail Clerks International Protective Association records and Retail Clerks International Association records
SCLC	Records of the Springfield [Missouri] Central Labor Council, Ozarks Labor Union Archives, Missouri State University, Springfield, Missouri
SIFE	Students in Free Enterprise, Inc., Springfield, Missouri
SL	*SIFE Lines* [Students in Free Enterprise, Springfield, Missouri]
TA	*Threefold Advocate* [John Brown University, Siloam Springs, Arkansas]
TLEF	*Texas Law Enforcement Foundation Bulletin*
UFCW 322	Records of the United Food and Commercial Workers Local 322, Springfield, Missouri; Ozarks Labor Union Archives, Missouri State University, Springfield, Missouri; includes Retail Clerks International Association Local 322
UFCWRL	United Food and Commercial Workers Union Retired Leaders Oral History Project Interviews, 1980–1981, Wisconsin Historical Society, Madison, Wisconsin

USNWR	*U.S. News & World Report*
VSD	*Vital Speeches of the Day*
WMAR	*Wal-Mart Stores, Inc., Annual Report*
WMW	*Wal-Mart World*
WP	*Washington Post*
WSJ	*Wall Street Journal*

Notes

Prologue

1. Ryan Sager, "Revenge of the Wal-Mart Voters," *Real Clear Politics*, June 27, 2006, www.realclearpolitics.com/articles./2006/06/revenge_of_the_walmart_voters. html, accessed September 19, 2008; "Can Obama Win Back Wal-Mart Moms?" time.com/time/politics/article/0,8599,1839930,00.html#, accessed November 30, 2008; "The Wal-Mart Frontier," mymag.com/news/olitics/powergrip/50277, accessed November 30, 2008; "Mike Huckabee and the 'Wal-Mart Voter,'" June 30, 2006, http://mikehuckabeepresident2008.blogspot.com/2006/06/mike-huckabee-and-wal-mart-voter.html, accessed September 19, 2008.
2. Ralph Reed, quoted in Dan McGraw, "The Christian Capitalists," *USNWR* 118 (March 13, 1995): 55.
3. Sager, "Revenge of the Wal-Mart Voters," Bill McInturff quoted in Jane Sasseen with Dean Foust, "The Wal-Mart Sisterhood: Why Lower-Middle-Class White Women Could Be the Key to the Democratic Nomination—and Victory in the Fall," *BW,* April 28, 2008, 89.
4. Key among the earlier contributions to this literature, listed here with their original publication dates, are Dan T. Carter, *The Politics of Rage: George Wallace, the Origins of the New Conservatism, and the Transformation of American Politics* (New York: Simon & Schuster, 1995); James C. Cobb, *The Selling of the South: The Southern Crusade for Industrial Development, 1936–1980* (Baton Rouge, LA: Louisiana State University Press, 1982); Steve Fraser and Gary Gerstle, eds., *The Rise and Fall of the New Deal Order, 1930–1980* (Princeton: Princeton University Press, 1989); Thomas Byrne Edsall with Mary D. Edsall, *Chain Reaction:*

The Impact of Race, Rights, and Taxes on American Politics (New York: Norton, 1991); Bruce J. Schulman, *From Cotton Belt to Sun Belt: Federal Policy, Economic Development, and the Transformation of the South, 1938–1980* (New York: Oxford University Press, 1991); Thomas Sugrue, *The Origins of the Urban Crisis: Race and Inequality in Postwar Detroit* (Princeton: Princeton University Press, 1996). More recently, see Kevin M. Kruse, *White Flight: Atlanta and the Making of Modern Conservatism* (Princeton: Princeton University Press, 2007); Matthew D. Lassiter, *The Silent Majority: Suburban Politics in the Sunbelt South* (Princeton: Princeton University Press, 2007); and Robert O. Self, *American Babylon: Race and the Struggle for Postwar Oakland* (Princeton: Princeton University Press, 2005); and see below at note 8.

5. Ira Katznelson, *When Affirmative Action Was White: An Untold History of Racial Inequality in Twentieth Century America* (New York: W.W. Norton, 2005); see also Manning Marable, *How Capitalism Underdeveloped Black America: Problems in Race, Political Economy, and Society* (Boston: South End Press, 1983).

6. Kevin P. Phillips, *The Emerging Republican Majority* (New Rochelle, NY: Arlington House, 1969). On the failure of Phillips's "Southern strategy" and its replacement with "suburban populism," see Lassiter, *The Silent Majority*, 251–75.

7. Thomas Byrne Edsall, "The Changing Shape of Power: A Realignment in Public Policy," in *The Rise and Fall of the New Deal Order*, ed. Steve Fraser and Gary Gerstle (Princeton: Princeton University Press, 1989), 269–93; Mike Davis, *Prisoners of the American Dream: Politics and Economy in the History of the U.S. Working Class* (New York: Verso, 1999), 171–76.

8. The term comes from the path-breaking work of Lisa McGirr, *Suburban Warriors: The Origins of the New Christian Right* (Princeton: Princeton University Press, 2001); see also Donald T. Critchlow, *Phyllis Schlafly and Grassroots Conservatism: A Woman's Crusade* (Princeton: Princeton University Press, 2006); Michelle Nickerson, "Moral Mothers and Goldwater Girls," in David Farber and Jeff Roche, eds., *The Conservative Sixties* (New York: Peter Lang, 2003); Catherine Rymph, *Republican Women: Feminism and Conservatism from Suffrage to the Rise of the New Right* (Chapel Hill, NC: University of North Carolina Press, 2006).

9. Richard Viguerie, *The New Right: We're Ready to Lead* (Falls Church, VA: Viguerie Company, 1981); Bruce Schulman and Julian Zelizer, *Rightward Bound: Making America Conservative in the 1970s* (Cambridge, MA: Harvard University Press, 2008).

10. Godfrey Hodgson, *The World Turned Right Side Up: A History of the Conservative Ascendancy in America* (Boston: Houghton Mifflin, 1996), 180–83.

11. Linda Kintz, *Between Jesus and the Market: The Emotions That Matter in Right-Wing America* (Durham, NC: Duke University Press, 1997); McGirr,

Suburban Warriors: The Origins of the New American Right; Marjorie J. Spruill, "Gender and America's Right Turn," in Schulman and Zelizer, *Rightward Bound,* 71–89; Kristin Luker, *Abortion and the Politics of Motherhood,* California Series on Social Choice and Political Economy (Berkeley: University of California Press, 1984).

12. Mark Blyth, *Great Transformations: Economic Ideas and Institutional Change in the Twentieth Century* (Cambridge: Cambridge University Press, 2002), 126–201; David Harvey, *A Brief History of Neoliberalism* (Oxford: Oxford University Press, 2005). Military appropriations contracted under the Clinton administration, but the other parameters remained in place.

13. Thomas Frank, *What's the Matter with Kansas? How Conservatives Won the Heart of America* (New York: Metropolitan Books, 2004).

1. Our Fathers' America

1. Sarah Schafer, "A Welcome to Wal-Mart," *NW International* (Atlantic Edition), December 20, 2004, 36; Bruce Upbin, "Wall-to-Wall Wal-Mart," *Forbes* 173 (April 12, 2004): 78; Jerry Useem, "One Nation Under Wal-Mart," *Fortune* 147 (March 3, 2003): 66.

2. Mark Gimein, "Sam Walton Made Us a Promise," *Fortune* 145, no. 6 (March 18, 2002): 121–22, 128.

3. Interview with Ron Loveless, September 25, 2004. Interviews with Wal-Mart executives and other public figures appear in the text and endnotes with their actual names.

4. David B. Danbom, *Born in the Country: A History of Rural America* (Baltimore: Johns Hopkins University Press, 1995), 244–48; Jack Temple Kirby, *Rural Worlds Lost: The American South, 1920–1960* (Baton Rouge: Louisiana State University Press, 1987), 95–98.

5. Joel A. Carpenter, *Revive Us Again: The Reawakening of American Fundamentalism* (New York: Oxford University Press, 1997), 126–40; Razelle Frankl, "Transformation of Televangelism: Repackaging Christian Family Values," in *Media, Culture, and the Religious Right,* ed. Linda Kintz and Julia Lesage (Minneapolis: University of Minnesota Press, 1998), 163–89; Sara Diamond, *Spiritual Warfare: The Politics of the Christian Right* (Boston: South End Press, 1989), 57–60.

6. Kirby, *Rural Worlds Lost,* 119.

7. Useem, "One Nation Under Wal-Mart," 78.

8. "Utopia, Missouri," *Economist* 333, no. 7895 (December 24, 1994): 25–28; Aaron K. Ketchell, *Holy Hills of the Ozarks: Religion and Tourism in Branson, Missouri*

(Baltimore: Johns Hopkins University Press, 2007), 77; Hanna Rosin, "A 'Tubby' Ache for Jerry Falwell," *WP*, February 11, 1999, C1.

9. Customer survey respondent quoted in Ketchell, *Holy Hills*, 90.

10. Elizabeth L. Bland, "Country Music's New Mecca," *Time* 138, no. 8 (August 26, 1991): 64; "Utopia, Missouri"; Amy Feldman and Thomas Jaffe, "Image Trouble," *Forbes* 151, no. 11 (May 24, 1993): 18–19; Lisa Gubernick, "A Curb on the Ego," *Forbes* 150 (September 14, 1992): 418–20.

11. Margaret Mannix, "Nashville's Comeback Try," *USNWR* 117, no. 1 (July 4, 1994): 64–68.

12. Ketchell, *Holy Hills*, xxv.

13. Milton D. Rafferty, *The Ozarks, Land and Life* (Fayetteville: University of Arkansas Press, 2001), 209, 213–15.

14. "Utopia, Missouri"; Branson resident Gary Evans quoted in Bland, "Country Music's New Mecca."

15. "Utopia, Missouri."

16. Rogers Historical Museum, *Cultural Diversity in Benton County*, pamphlet (Rogers, AR: Rogers Historical Museum, 2001).

17. Brooks Blevins, "'In the Land of a Million Smiles': Twentieth-Century America Discovers the Arkansas Ozarks," *Arkansas Historical Quarterly* 61, no. 1 (Spring 2002): 1–35; Ketchell, *Holy Hills*, 194–201.

18. Thomas Hart Benton, "America's Yesterday," *Travel*, July, 1934; quoted in Blevins, "'Million Smiles,'" 27–28.

19. Anthony Harkins, *Hillbilly: A Cultural History of an American Icon* (New York: Oxford University Press, 2004), 186–88, 193–94, 198.

20. Kirby, *Rural Worlds Lost*, 40; Carl O. Sauer, "The Economic Problem of the Ozark Highland," *Scientific Monthly* 11, no. 3 (September 1920): 215–27.

21. Rafferty, *Ozarks*, 158–59.

22. On the use of this strategy in the South, see James C. Cobb, *The Selling of the South: The Southern Crusade for Industrial Development, 1936–1990* (Urbana: University of Illinois Press, 1993), 112.

23. Interview with Willis Shaw, September 9, 2004.

24. Interview with "June Whitehead," May 11, 2005. Oral history interviews with longtime hourly employees of Wal-Mart in Northwest Arkansas, conducted by the author in 2005, appear in the text and endnotes here with pseudonyms out of respect for their privacy. Original audiotapes of the interviews are held at the Shiloh Museum of Ozarks History, Springdale, Arkansas, along with a key to the pseudonyms used here.

25. Interview with "Alice Martin" and "Sherry Martin," May 2, 2005.

26. Interview with "June Whitehead."

27. Mike Davis, *City of Quartz: Excavating the Future in Los Angeles* (New York: Vintage Books, 1992), 31; Carl O. Sauer, *The Geography of the Ozark Highland of Missouri*, The Geographic Society of Chicago Bulletins (Chicago: University of Chicago Press, 1920), 186.

28. Martin J. Sklar, *The Corporate Reconstruction of American Capitalism, 1890–1916: The Market, the Law, and Politics* (Cambridge: Cambridge University Press, 1988), 49–53.

29. John G. Cawelti, *Apostles of the Self-Made Man: Changing Concepts of Success in America* (Chicago: University of Chicago Press, 1965); Judy Hilkey, *Character Is Capital: Success Manuals and Manhood in Gilded Age America* (Chapel Hill: University of North Carolina Press, 1997); Scott A. Sandage, *Born Losers: A History of Failure in America* (Cambridge, MA: Harvard University Press, 2005).

30. Nell Irvin Painter, *Standing at Armageddon: The United States, 1877–1919* (New York: W.W. Norton, 1987), 41–42; Neal Moore, "Ozarks Labor History," *Springfield [Missouri] Labor Record* 45, no. 3 (February 4, 1982): 1; Brooks Blevins, *Hill Folks: A History of Arkansas Ozarkers and Their Image* (Chapel Hill: University of North Carolina Press, 2002), 206; Elizabeth Sanders, *Roots of Reform: Farmers, Workers, and the American State, 1877–1917*, American Politics and Political Economy (Chicago: University of Chicago Press, 1999), 121.

31. From the "Cleburne Demands," a platform of the Farmers Alliance—the central precursor to the People's Party—composed in 1886 in Cleburne, Texas; quoted in Lawrence Goodwyn, *Democratic Promise: The Populist Moment in America* (New York: Oxford University Press, 1976), 79–80. On Arkansans' role, see Jeannie M. Whayne, et al., *Arkansas: A Narrative History* (Fayetteville: The University of Arkansas Press, 2002), 262–67.

32. "People's Platform of 1896," in *National Party Platforms, vol. I, 1840–1956*, comp. Donald Bruce Johnson (Urbana: University of Illinois Press, 1978), 104.

33. Sanders, *Roots of Reform*, 268–69; Ellis Wayne Hawley, *The New Deal and the Problem of Monopoly: A Study in Economic Ambivalence* (New York: Fordham University Press, 1995), 4–9; Sklar, *Corporate Reconstruction*, 179–332.

34. These are central arguments of Charles Postel, *The Populist Vision* (New York: Oxford University Press, 2007).

35. Ibid., 277–79; Sanders, *Roots of Reform*, 389–400.

36. Painter, *Standing at Armageddon*, 135–40.

37. Sklar, *Corporate Reconstruction*, 117–54.

38. Thomas Dionysius Clark, *Pills, Petticoats, and Plows: The Southern Country Store* (Indianapolis: Bobbs-Merrill, 1944), 78–79, 313–35; Goodwyn, *Democratic Promise*, 26–31; C. Vann Woodward, *Origins of the New South, 1877–1913*, A History of the South (Baton Rouge: Louisiana State University Press, 1999), 180–88.

39. Jonathan J. Bean, *Beyond the Broker State: Federal Policies Toward Small Business, 1936–1961,* Business, Society, and the State (Chapel Hill: University of North Carolina Press, 1996), 21–25; Alfred D. Chandler, *The Visible Hand: The Managerial Revolution in American Business* (Cambridge, MA: Belknap Press of Harvard University Press, 1977), 209–39; William Leach, *Land of Desire: Merchants, Power, and the Rise of a New American Culture* (New York: Pantheon Books, 1993), 29–32; Susan Strasser, *Satisfaction Guaranteed: The Making of the American Mass Market* (New York: Pantheon, 1989), 219–21.

40. Carl G. Ryant, "The South and the Movement Against Chain Stores," *Journal of Southern History* 39, no. 2 (May 1973): 211–12.

41. Charlie C. McCall, "Live and Let Live: An Address on the Foreign Chain Store Menace; by Charlie C. McCall, Attorney General of Alabama; as Broadcast over Radio Station KWKH, Shreveport, Louisiana," transcript of radio program segment, folder "KWKH Anti-Chain Store Broadcasts, 1929–1930," Archives and Special Collection, Louisiana State University Libraries, Shreveport, Louisiana, 5.

42. T. Eugene Beattie, "Public Relations and the Chains," *Journal of Marketing* 7, no. 3 (January 1943): 247–48; Godfrey M. Lebhar, *Chain Stores in America: 1859–1950* (New York: Chain Store Publishing Corporation, 1952), 156, 166; Nancy MacLean, *Behind the Mask of Chivalry: The Making of the Second Ku Klux Klan* (New York: Oxford University Press, 1994), 77–78; Boyce F. Martin, "The Independent, et al., Versus the Chains," *Harvard Business Review* 9, no. 1 (October 1930): 47.

43. Theodore N. Beckman and Herman Nolen, *The Chain Store Problem: A Critical Analysis* (New York: McGraw-Hill, 1938), 242; Harry W. Schacter, "War on the Chain Store," *The Nation* 130, no. 3383 (May 7, 1930): 544.

44. Ryant, "The South and the Movement Against Chain Stores."

45. Sandra Stringer Vance and Roy Vernon Scott, *Wal-Mart: A History of Sam Walton's Retail Phenomenon,* Twayne's Evolution of Modern Business Series (New York: Twayne Publishers, 1994), 26–27.

46. Hawley, *The New Deal and the Problem of Monopoly,* 262–63; Lebhar, *Chain Stores in America,* 240–76; Ryant, "The South and the Movement Against Chain Stores," 215–18; Richard S. Tedlow, *New and Improved: The Story of Mass Marketing in America* (New York: Basic Books, 1990), 214–26.

47. Bean, *Beyond the Broker State,* 26.

48. Schacter, "War on the Chain Store," 544. The immediate reference is to the modernist-Fundamentalist controversy within Protestantism; see George M. Marsden, *Fundamentalism and American Culture: The Shaping of Twentieth-Century Evangelicalism, 1870–1925* (New York: Oxford University Press, 1980), 171–75.

49. Edward G. Ernst and Emil M. Hartl, "Chains Versus Independents: IV. The Fighting Independents," *The Nation* 131, no. 3413 (December 3, 1930): 608.

50. Edward G. Ernst and Emil M. Hartl, "Chains Versus Independents: III. Chain Management and Labor," *The Nation* 131, no. 3412 (November 26, 1930): 576.
51. MacLean, *Mask of Chivalry*, 78.
52. Alan Brinkley, *Voices of Protest: Huey Long, Father Coughlin, and the Great Depression* (New York: Vintage Books, 1983), 146–48, 269.
53. "Chain Stores' Spy Sent among Foes," *NYT*, June 26, 1935, 39.
54. Mrs. Ken Calloway, "A National Problem; an Address on the Foreign Chain Systems; M M M Literature; by Mrs. Ken Calloway, Wife of the Corner Grocer, Taylorville, Illinois; as Broadcast Over Radio Station KWKH, Shreveport, Louisiana," transcript of radio program segment, folder "KWKH Anti-Chain Store Broadcasts, 1929–1930," Archives and Special Collection, Louisiana State University Libraries, Shreveport, Louisiana, 2.
55. "Inquiry Ordered on Retail 'Lobby,'" *NYT*, April 25, 1935, 38.
56. Ibid.; "Mercantile Group Upheld at Inquiry," *NYT*, October 11, 1935, 11.
57. Serial Set Vol. No. 9996, Session Vol. No. B, 74th Congress, 2nd Session, H.Rpt. 2373, "Report by the special committee of that part of House Resolution 203 relating to the organization and lobbying activities of the American Retail Federation," April 7, 1936, p. 7.
58. "Mercantile Group Upheld at Inquiry."
59. The classic elaboration of this thesis appears in Woodward, *Origins of the New South, 1877–1913*, 291–320.
60. Sanders, *Roots of Reform*, 244–61; William Graves, "Discounting Northern Capital: Financing the World's Largest Retailer from the Periphery," in *Wal-Mart World: The World's Biggest Corporation in the Global Economy*, ed. Stanley D. Brunn (New York: Routledge, 2006), 47–54.
61. Joe Bonner, letter, MS R563 18, JTR, Series 9, Subseries 2, 1936.
62. Representative Wright Patman (D-Texas, First Congressional District) speaking in the 75th Congress, 3d session, A707, and in a letter to the *Dallas News*, February 25, 1938; both quoted in Nancy Beck Young, *Wright Patman: Populism, Liberalism, & the American Dream* (Dallas: Southern Methodist University Press, 2000), 89.
63. MacLean, *Mask of Chivalry*, 77–78.
64. Forrest Loman Oilar, *Be Thou Prepared* (Boston: Meador, 1937), 147.
65. "Broadens Inquiry Into Retail 'Lobby,'" *NYT*, June 5, 1935, 16; *Hearings Before the Special Committee on Investigation, American Retail Federation, 74th Congress, 1st Session* (1935), 30–31.
66. George A. McArthur, letter, MS R563 18, JTR, Series 9, Subseries 2, July 24, 1935. Capitalization in original.
67. Cory Lewis Sparks, "Locally Owned and Operated: Opposition to Chain Stores,

1925–1940" (Ph.D. diss., Louisiana State University, 2000), 278–82; "Unliked Taxes: Help the Farmer Sell His Surplus Crop," *Time,* January 31, 1938, 54–56.

68. Jennifer Bair and Sam Bernstein, "Labor and the Wal-Mart Effect," in *Wal-Mart World,* ed. Brunn, 106–9.

69. Bob Ortega, *In Sam We Trust: The Untold Story of Sam Walton and How Wal-Mart Is Devouring America* (New York: Times Business, 1998), 284–303; Wal-Mart Watch, *Shameless: How Wal-Mart Bullies Its Way into Communities across America: A Wal-Mart Watch Special Report* (Washington, DC: Wal-Mart Watch, 2005).

2. The Birth of Wal-Mart

1. Charles Postel, *The Populist Vision* (New York: Oxford University Press, 2007); Elizabeth Sanders, *Roots of Reform: Farmers, Workers, and the American State, 1877–1917,* American Politics and Political Economy (Chicago: University of Chicago Press, 1999), 314–24.

2. On the Waltons' early financing arrangements, see Bob Ortega, *In Sam We Trust: The Untold Story of Sam Walton and How Wal-Mart Is Devouring America* (New York: Times Business, 1998), 52–53, 68–71. Godfrey M. Lebhar, *Chain Stores in America: 1859–1950* (New York: Chain Store Publishing Corporation, 1952), 154.

3. Sandra Stringer Vance and Roy Vernon Scott, *Wal-Mart: A History of Sam Walton's Retail Phenomenon,* Twayne's Evolution of Modern Business Series (New York: Twayne Publishers, 1994), 2.

4. Ibid., 4–6.

5. Ernest Hugh Shideler, "The Chain Store: A Study of the Ecological Organization of a Modern City" (Ph.D. diss., University of Chicago, 1927), VI: 16–19.

6. Ibid., VI: 7–8; Sandra S. Vance and Roy V. Scott, "Butler Brothers and the Rise and Decline of the Ben Franklin Stores: A Study in Franchise Retailing," in *Essays in Economic and Business History: Selected Papers from the Economic and Business Historical Society,* vol. 11 (East Lansing: Graduate School of Business Administration, Michigan State University, 1993), 258–71.

7. Susan Strasser, *Satisfaction Guaranteed: The Making of the American Mass Market* (New York: Pantheon, 1989), 235, 246.

8. See, for example, Terry Webster Shroyer, "An Analysis of the Control Policies Used in a Voluntary Variety Store Chain through the Study of Twenty-Five Ben Franklin Stores in Eastern Colorado" (Master's thesis, University of Colorado, 1957).

9. Vance and Scott, *Wal-Mart,* 9–14.

10. Ortega, *In Sam We Trust,* 49–56.

11. Vance and Scott, *Wal-Mart*, 23–33.

12. Vance H. Trimble, *Sam Walton: The Inside Story of America's Richest Man* (New York: Dutton, 1990), 78; Vance and Scott, *Wal-Mart*, 14, 52–3; Sam Walton and John Huey, *Sam Walton, Made in America: My Story* (New York: Doubleday, 1992), 35–36, 41, 110–12.

13. James Kindall, "Searching for Uncle Sam," *Star* [weekly insert of *Kansas City Star*], December 16, 1984, 24; direct quotation from Steve Trollinger.

14. Uncited clipping displayed at Wal-Mart Visitors' Center, Bentonville, Arkansas, 2005.

15. "People's Platform of 1896," in *National Party Platforms, Volume I, 1840–1956,* comp. Donald Bruce Johnson (Urbana: University of Illinois Press, 1978), 104–6.

16. Ira Katznelson, *When Affirmative Action Was White: An Untold History of Racial Inequality in Twentieth-Century America* (New York: W.W. Norton, 2005).

17. On federal promotion of agriculture in the early twentieth century, see Postel, *Populist Vision*, 278–79; Sanders, *Roots of Reform*, 391–94; on federal service to commerce in the 1920s, see William Leach, *Land of Desire: Merchants, Power, and the Rise of a New American Culture* (New York: Pantheon Books, 1993), 349–78.

18. Quoted in Lebhar, *Chain Stores in America: 1859–1950*, 196.

19. The presidential election of 1948 foreshadowed the Nixon-era defection of conservative whites from the Democratic to the Republican parties. In protest against the Democrats' adoption of a strong civil rights plank that year, white supremacist delegates from Mississippi and Alabama walked out of the convention. Segregationists quickly formed the States' Rights Democratic Party (the "Dixiecrats") and nominated Governor Strom Thurmond of South Carolina on a ticket that won four Deep South states. Jesse H. Jones was among those prominent Southern Democrats who never returned to the Democratic Party.

20. Joe R. Feagin, *Free Enterprise City: Houston in Political-Economic Perspective* (New Brunswick, NJ: Rutgers University Press, 1988), 121; Bascom N. Timmons, *Jesse H. Jones: The Man and the Statesman* (New York: Henry Holt, 1956), 389.

21. Feagin, *Free Enterprise City*, 51.

22. Ibid., 54, 60, 138.

23. Ibid., 51.

24. Arthur M. Schlesinger, Jr., *The Coming of the New Deal* (Boston: Houghton Mifflin, 1959), 429–32.

25. "Business-and-Government," *Fortune*, May 1940, 42; see also Schlesinger, *The Coming of the New Deal*, 425, 430; James S. Olson, *Saving Capitalism: The Reconstruction Finance Corporation and the New Deal, 1933–1940* (Princeton: Princeton University Press, 1988), 226–27. The Corporation's subsidiaries included the Commodity Credit Corporation, the Electric Home and Farm

Authority, the RFC Mortgage Company, the Federal National Mortgage Associa-
tion, and the Export-Import Bank. Its loans financed New Deal programs like the
Agricultural Adjustment Act, the Tennessee Valley Authority, and the Works
Progress Administration.

26. Torbjorn Sirevag, *The Eclipse of the New Deal* (New York: Garland, 1985), 79;
Timmons, *Jesse H. Jones,* 279–82.

27. Bethany E. Moreton, "The Soul of the Service Economy: Wal-Mart and the
Making of Christian Free Enterprise" (Ph.D. diss., Yale University, 2006), 47–49.

28. Jesse H. Jones to the American Bankers Association, Chicago, September 5, 1933,
quoted in Timmons, *Jesse H. Jones,* 200.

29. Jesse H. Jones interview, *NYT,* July 2, 1939; quoted in Olson, *Saving Capitalism,*
226.

30. Jeannie Whayne, "Darker Forces on the Horizon: Natural Disasters and Great
Depression," in *Arkansas: A Narrative History,* Jeannie M. Whayne, et al. (Fayette-
ville, AR: University of Arkansas Press, 2002), 303–35; *Report of Semi-Annual
Coordination Meeting of the Federal Departments and Agencies in Arkansas: United
States District Court Room, Federal Building, Little Rock, Arkansas, December 21,
1935* (Little Rock, AR: The Council, 1935), 72.

31. Ralph C. Kennedy Jr. and Thomas R. Rothrock, *John Brown of Arkansas* (Siloam
Springs, AR: John Brown University Press, 1966), 27, 39–42, 70; Rick Ostrander,
*Head, Heart, and Hands: John Brown University and Modern Evangelical Higher
Education* (Fayetteville: University of Arkansas Press, 2003), 17, 42–43, 94–95;
"Distinguished Visitors at Siloam Springs Fete," *South West American,* May 13,
1938.

32. Andrew Moreau and Randy Tardy, "Financier Stephens Dies at 84," *ADG,*
December 3, 1991, 10A.

33. John L. Fletcher, "Stephens Story: From Belt Buckles to Gas Companies," *AG,*
September 21, 1958.

34. Spencer Klaw, "They Don't Come Like Witt Stephens Any More," *Fortune,* May
1959, 158.

35. W. D. McClurkin, "Refunding Arkansas School Bonds," *Peabody Journal of
Education* 18, no. 3 (November 1940): 149.

36. Ernest Dumas, "Government 'Partner' of Brothers," *AG,* June 28, 1977, 1A, 5A.

37. Ibid.; Lance Kidd, "A Conversation with J. B. Hunt," *Arkansas Trucking Report* 4,
no. 6 (November/December 1999): 23.

38. Dumas, "'Partner,'" 1A, 5A; Kidd, "J. B. Hunt," 23; William Graves, "Discounting
Northern Capital: Financing the World's Largest Retailer from the Periphery," in
Wal-Mart World: The World's Biggest Corporation in the Global Economy, ed.
Stanley D. Brunn (New York: Routledge, 2006), 50. With the Stephens offer in

hand, Walton secured a hearing with a native Arkansan in New York's White, Weld & Co. investment bank; White, Weld wound up leading the IPO, with Stephens underwriting one third. Ortega, *In Sam We Trust*, 69–70.

39. Graves, "Discounting Northern Capital," 52–53. Graves finds that of the $257 billion in capital that Wal-Mart has brought in, roughly 40 percent comes from the Walton family and other Wal-Mart insiders, 25 percent from individual investors, and 35 percent from institutional investors, including major ones from California, the Northeast, and Europe.

40. Mary Anne Messick, *History of Baxter County [Arkansas] 1873–1973* (Mountain Home, AR: Mountain Home Chamber of Commerce, 1973), 320, quoted in Milton D. Rafferty, *The Ozarks, Land and Life* (Fayetteville: University of Arkansas Press, 2001), 213–14.

41. Rafferty, *Ozarks*, 73–74, 217–220.

42. Jeanne C. Biggar, *The Graying of the Sunbelt: A Look at the Impact of U.S. Elderly Migration*, Population Trends and Public Policy (Washington, DC: Population Reference Bureau, Inc., 1984), 1, 5–6, 15; James N. Gregory, *American Exodus: The Dust Bowl Migration and Okie Culture in California* (New York: Oxford University Press, 1989), 214–18.

3. Wal-Mart Country

1. Tonya McKiever, "Center Greeter Knows His Stuff," *DR*, June 6, 1997, 8A.

2. Interview with "Bea Scott," May 4, 2005.

3. Sam Walton and John Huey, *Sam Walton, Made in America: My Story* (New York: Doubleday, 1992), 41–42.

4. [Interview with the Waltons], *WMW*, October 1987, 2.

5. Interview with Ron Loveless, September 25, 2004.

6. Walton and Huey, *Sam Walton*, 42.

7. Walton quoted in Mary Jane Clemmer, "Walton Steals Show at Annual Meeting," *Benton County Daily Democrat*, June 8, 1984, 1.

8. Thomas O. Z. Graff and Dub Ashton, "Spatial Diffusion of Wal-Mart: Contagious and Reverse Hierarchical Elements," *Professional Geographer* 46, no. 1 (1994): 19–29, esp. 22–25.

9. See, for example, "The Other Manhattan: Manhattan, Ks.," *WMW*, February 1980, 16; "Vinita, 'Gateway to Grand Lake,'" *WMW*, March 1980, 16; "Nevada, Mo.: Site of Bushwhacker Days," *WMW*, April 1980, 16; "Fulton, Missouri—a Town Rich in History, Culture," *WMW*, May 1979, 16.

10. See, for example, "Nevada, Mo.," 16; "Fulton, Ky.: The Border-Straddlin' Town," *WMW*, May 1980, 16; "Five Managers Set to Open New Stores," *WMW*, December 1978, 6.

11. James C. Cobb, *The Selling of the South: The Southern Crusade for Industrial Development, 1936–1980* (Baton Rouge: Louisiana State University Press, 1982), 101–2; Nancy MacLean, "Southern Dominance in Borrowed Language: The Regional Origins of American Neoliberalism," in *New Landscapes of Inequality*, Jane L. Collins, Micaela di Leonardo, and Brett Williams (Sante Fe: School for Advanced Research Press, 2008), 21–37; Bruce J. Schulman, *From Cotton Belt to Sunbelt: Federal Policy, Economic Development, and the Transformation of the South, 1938–1980* (Durham: Duke University Press, 1994), 112–24, 163–64.

12. The Jones protegé was William L. Clayton, a native of Mississippi; Frederick J. Dobney, "Introduction," in *Selected Papers of Will Clayton*, ed. Frederick J. Dobney (Baltimore: Johns Hopkins University Press, 1971), 1–9; David Eakins, "Business Planners and America's Postwar Expansion," in *Corporations and the Cold War*, ed. David Horowitz (New York: Bertrand Russell Peace Foundation, 1969), 143–71.

13. Mark Ellis, Richard Barff, and Ann Markusen, "Defense Spending and Interregional Migration," *Economic Geography* 69, no. 2 (April 1993): 182–203; Joe R. Feagin, *Free Enterprise City: Houston in Political-Economic Perspective* (New Brunswick, NJ: Rutgers University Press, 1988); Ann Markusen, et al., *The Rise of the Gunbelt: The Military Remapping of Industrial America* (New York: Oxford University Press, 1991); Schulman, *From Cotton Belt to Sunbelt*, 135–73.

14. Barney Warf, "The Pentagon and the Service Sector," *Economic Geography* 69, no. 2 (April 1993): 125.

15. Lisa McGirr, *Suburban Warriors: The Origins of the New American Right* (Princeton: Princeton University Press, 2001); Thomas Allan Scott, *Cobb County, Georgia, and the Origins of the Suburban South: A Twentieth-Century History* (Marietta, GA: Cobb Landmarks and Historical Society, 2003); Philip Scranton, *The Second Wave: Southern Industrialization from the 1940s to the 1970s* (Athens: The University of Georgia Press, 2001); Jeff Sharlet, "Soldiers of Christ I: Inside America's Most Powerful Megachurch," *Harper's*, May 2005, 41–54.

16. On Arkansas, see Jeannie Whayne, "Dramatic Departures: Political, Demographic, and Economic Realignment," in *Arkansas: A Narrative History*, Jeannie M. Whayne, et al. (Fayetteville: University of Arkansas Press, 2002), 372–73; on the national realignment, see Kevin M. Kruse, *White Flight: Atlanta and the Making of Modern Conservatism* (Princeton: Princeton University Press, 2006); Matthew D. Lassiter, *The Silent Majority: Suburban Politics in the Sunbelt South* (Princeton: Princeton University Press, 2006); McGirr, *Suburban Warriors*.

17. Bethany E. Moreton, "The Soul of the Service Economy: Wal-Mart and the Making of Christian Free Enterprise" (Ph.D. diss., Yale University, 2006), 47–49.

18. Nelson Lichtenstein, "From Corporatism to Collective Bargaining: Organized Labor and the Eclipse of Social Democracy in the Postwar Era," in *The Rise and*

Fall of the New Deal Order, 1930–1980, ed. Steve Fraser, Gary Gerstle (Princeton: Princeton University Press, 1989), 120.

19. "Peace on Earth," *WMW,* December 1972, 8.

20. "Glowing Letters and Thank-You Notes," *WMW,* May [copy II] 1975, 4.

21. Stephen Koepp, with B. Russell Leavitt, "Make That Sale, Mr. Sam," *Time,* May 18, 1987, 54.

22. "Store Happenings," *WMW,* October 1975, 14.

23. "#717's 'Board of Directors,'" *WMW,* May 1990, 15.

24. James N. Gregory, "The Southern Diaspora and the Urban Dispossessed: Demonstrating the Census Public Use Microdata Samples," *Journal of American History* 82, no. 1 (June 1995): 111–12.

25. "['Dear Wal-Mart . . .']," *WMW,* October 1989, 9.

26. Emily Nelson, "Wal-Mart Customers Feel Free to Spend the Night in the Lot," *WSJ,* August 9, 1999, A1.

27. See, for example, "Western Days," *WMW,* September 1971, 7; "We See That . . . ," *WMW,* July 1972, 10–12; "We See That . . . ," *WMW,* April 1973, 4–5; "Store Happenings," *WMW,* May 1977, 13; "Store Happenings," *WMW,* March–April 1977, 23; Walton and Huey, *Made in America,* 112.

28. "#2 in a Hot Spot!" *WMW,* July 1971, III-5; "We See That . . . ," *WMW,* June 1974, 7.

29. "Western Days," 7.

30. "Claremore, Oklahoma—Will Rogers' Home, Heartland of State's Lovely 'Green Country,'" *WMW,* November 1978, 16.

31. "A Little Dramatization Goes a Long Way," *WMW,* June 1971, II-5.

32. "We See That . . . ," *WMW,* December 1971, 14.

33. "We See That . . . ," *WMW,* September 1973, 5; Roberta Parker, "Bill Sanders, V.I.P," *WMW,* August 1974, 5.

34. Dan Goetz, "Jasper Welcomes 'Goober' Home," *WMW,* April 1983, 5.

35. "Store Hosts Singer," *WMW,* February 1980, 6.

36. Grace Elizabeth Hale, "Commentary and Response: James N. Gregory: 'Southernizing the American Working Class': A Note on Region, Race, and Vision," *Labor History* 39, no. 2 (1998): 155–57.

37. Walton and Huey, *Sam Walton,* 137.

38. Interview with Bill Schwyhart, September 8, 2004.

39. Bob Ortega, *In Sam We Trust: The Untold Story of Sam Walton and How Wal-Mart Is Devouring America* (New York: Times Business, 1998), 16–19.

40. Austin Teutsch, *The Sam Walton Story* (New York: Berkley Books, 1991), 28.

41. Jacalyn Carfagno, "Walton Biography Thin on Drama," *USA Today,* November 21, 1990, 11B; Mindy Fetterman, "USA's Richest Person," *USA Today,* October 10, 1989, 1A.

42. Robert F. Hartley, *Marketing Mistakes,* 6th ed. (New York: John Wiley & Sons,

1995), 264. The Horatio Alger stories themselves actually depicted their young heroes' successes as the product of luck—perhaps a more apt template for the Sun Belt; see John G. Cawelti, *Apostles of the Self-Made Man: Changing Concepts of Success in America* (Chicago: University of Chicago Press, 1965), 109–12.

43. Robert Slater, *The Wal-Mart Decade: How a Generation of Leaders Turned Sam Walton's Legacy Into the World's #1 Company* (New York: Portfolio, 2003), 24.

44. Teutsch, *Sam Walton,* 13.

45. Jim M. Rountree, "Know Your Company," *WMW,* May 1976, 3.

46. Robert Slater, *The Wal-Mart Triumph* (New York: Portfolio, 2003), 78.

47. Ellen Neuborne, "Growth King Running Into Roadblocks," *USA Today,* April 27, 1993, 1B, 2B; "Sam Walton Made Us a Promise," *Fortune* 145, no. 6 (March 18, 2002): 120–24, 128.

48. Dan McGraw and John Simons, "The Birdman of Arkansas," *USNWR,* July 18, 1994, 42.

49. Personal communication with J. B. Hunt, September 8, 2004. Mr. Hunt died in 2006.

50. Roland Marchand, *Creating the Corporate Soul: The Rise of Public Relations and Corporate Imagery in American Big Business* (Berkeley: University of California Press, 1998), 85, 140–41.

51. Interview with Ron Loveless, September 25, 2004.

52. Sandra Stringer Vance and Roy Vernon Scott, *Wal-Mart: A History of Sam Walton's Retail Phenomenon,* Twayne's Evolution of Modern Business Series (New York: Twayne Publishers, 1994), 78.

53. Alan R. Raucher, "Dime Store Chains: The Making of Organization Men, 1880–1940," *BHR* 65, no. 1 (Spring 1991): 130–63; direct quotations from p. 153; p. 154 n. 47.

54. Daniel Scroop, "Local and National Identities in the Politics of Consumption: The Anti-Chain Store Movement Reconsidered," *History Compass* 6, no. 3 (2008): 953.

55. Raucher, "Dimestore Chains," 157–8; Lizabeth Cohen, *Making a New Deal: Industrial Workers in Chicago, 1919–1939* (New York: Cambridge University Press, 1990), 356–57.

4. The Family in the Store

1. Impact Fund et al., "Federal Judge Orders Wal-Mart Stores, Inc., the Nation's Largest Private Employer, to Stand Trial for Company-Wide Sex Discrimination," press release (San Francisco, June 22, 2004); www.impactfund.org/New/pages/press1/prs/062204.htm; accessed November 29, 2008.

2. Marc Bendick, Jr., *The Representation of Women in Store Management at*

Wal-Mart Stores, Inc., plaintiff's expert report, *Dukes v. Wal-Mart Stores, Inc.* (Washington, DC, 2003), VIII.53–54. See also Richard Drogin, *Statistical Analysis of Gender Patterns in Wal-Mart Workforce,* plaintiff's expert report, *Dukes v. Wal-Mart Stores, Inc.* (Berkeley, CA, 2003), 46; posted at www.walmartclass.com. An analysis of *Dukes v. Wal-Mart* is provided by Liza Featherstone, *Selling Women Short: The Landmark Battle for Workers' Rights at Wal-Mart* (New York: Basic Books, 2004).

3. Impact Fund et al., "Federal Judge."

4. Saskia Sassen, *Globalization and Its Discontents: Essays on the New Mobility of People and Money* (New York: New Press, 1998), 91. For a review of the historiography on the "labour aristocracy," see Eric Hobsbawm, *Workers: Worlds of Labour* (New York: Pantheon, 1984), 214–51; I use the term here much more loosely.

5. Stephanie McCurry, *Masters of Small Worlds: Yeoman Households, Gender Relations, and the Political Culture of the Antebellum South Carolina Low Country* (New York: Oxford University Press, 1995).

6. Elements of the companionate ideal of marriage were certainly widespread by the twentieth century, but the economic basis of family life was a more prominent feature of rural and working-class family ideology; see John D'Emilio and Estelle B. Freedman, *Intimate Matters: A History of Sexuality in America* (New York: Harper & Row, 1988), 265–74; Lillian B. Rubin, *Worlds of Pain: Life in the Working Class Family* (New York: Basic Books, 1976), 114–28; Susan Cahn, *Sexual Reckonings: Southern Girls in a Troubling Age* (Cambridge, MA: Harvard University Press, 2007), 147–49; Alfred P. Fengler, "The Effects of Age and Education on Marital Ideology," *Journal of Marriage and the Family* 35, no. 2 (May 1973): 264–71; Mary Neth, "Gender and the Family Labor System: Defining Work in the Rural Midwest," *Journal of Social History* 27, no. 3 (Spring 1994): 563–77; on the Ozarks specifically, see Janet Allured, "Ozark Women and the Companionate Family in the Arkansas Hills, 1870–1910," *Arkansas Historical Quarterly* 47 (Autumn 1988): 230–57.

7. In Wal-Mart's home tri-county area (later the Metropolitan Statistical Area of Fayetteville-Springdale-Rogers), the proportion of the population classified as "rural-farm" in the U.S. Census did not drop below half until 1950; in the United States as a whole, as early as 1920 only one-third of the population was thus classified. I am indebted to Tore Olsson for compiling these statistics.

8. Montaville Flowers, *America Chained: A Discussion of "What's Wrong with the Chain Store?"* (Pasadena: Montaville Flowers Publicists, Ltd., 1931), 280–81.

9. "Mr. Pro," "Shall We Curb the Chain Stores? Mr. Pro Attacks the Chains," *Readers' Digest* 33 (December 1938): 29; reprinted in Daniel Bloomfield, "Chain Stores and Legislation," in *Reference Shelf,* vol. 12, no. 7 (New York: H.W. Wilson Company, 1939), 29.

10. Nancy MacLean, *Behind the Mask of Chivalry: The Making of the Second Ku Klux Klan* (New York: Oxford University Press, 1994), 77.

11. J. M. Egan, letter, January 29, 1936, MS R563 18, series 9, subseries 2, JTR; Alan R. Raucher, "Dime Store Chains: The Making of Organization Men, 1880–1940," *BHR* 65, no. 1 (Spring 1991): 150–51.

12. Flowers, *America Chained,* 280–81.

13. Robert F. Chisholm, *The Darlings: The Mystique of the Supermarket* (New York: Chain Store Age Books, 1970), 125; Terry Webster Shroyer, "An Analysis of the Control Policies Used in a Voluntary Variety Chain through the Study of Twenty-Five Ben Franklin Stores in Eastern Colorado" (Master's thesis, University of Colorado, 1957), 83–84.

14. Ellis Wayne Hawley, *The New Deal and the Problem of Monopoly: A Study in Economic Ambivalence* (New York: Fordham University Press, 1995), 248.

15. Nancy F. Cott, *Public Vows: A History of Marriage and the Nation* (Cambridge, MA: Harvard University Press, 2000), 168–69.

16. Bob Ortega, *In Sam We Trust: The Untold Story of Sam Walton and How Wal-Mart Is Devouring America* (New York: Times Business, 1998), 69–71.

17. On the struggle to maintain an industrial labor force segmented by sex at midcentury, see Ruth Milkman, *Gender at Work: The Dynamics of Job Segregation by Sex During World War II,* The Working Class in American History (Urbana: University of Illinois Press, 1987); Nancy F. Gabin, *Feminism in the Labor Movement: Women and the United Auto Workers, 1935–1975* (Ithaca: Cornell University Press, 1990), 111–42. On the struggle for workplace equity since World War II more broadly, see Nancy MacLean, *Freedom Is Not Enough: The Opening of the American Workplace* (Cambridge, MA: Harvard University Press, with the Russell Sage Foundation, New York, 2006).

18. On the assumptions built into American social welfare provisions and their consequences, see Alice Kessler-Harris, *In Pursuit of Equity: Women, Men, and the Quest for Economic Citizenship in 20th-Century America* (Oxford: Oxford University Press, 2001).

19. David B. Danbom, *Born in the Country: A History of Rural America* (Baltimore: Johns Hopkins University Press, 1995), 234–40.

20. Steve Striffler, *Chicken: The Dangerous Transformation of America's Favorite Food* (New Haven: Yale University Press, 2005).

21. Farmer quoted in Margaret Bolsterli, "'Pretty Soon We Won't Even Be Us, Will We?' Prosperity, Urbanization and Cultural Change in Northwest Arkansas 1960–1997," unpublished paper in author's possession (C. 2000), 28.

22. On the midcentury rural shift from farming to trucking, see Shane Hamilton, *Trucking Century: The Road to America's Wal-Mart Economy* (Princeton: Princeton University Press, 2008), 100–34; on the long trend in off-farm

employment in the Ozarks, see Milton D. Rafferty, *The Ozarks: Land and Life* (Fayetteville: University of Arkansas Press, 2001), 80–81, 158–89, 173; on the pattern of women's off-farm work nationally in the twentieth century, see Danborn, *Born in the Country,* 250–51.

23. June Percival, "Store Happenings," *WMW,* September 1975, 11.

24. "We See That . . . ," *WMW,* January 1974, 10.

25. E.g., "Service Pins Awarded at Store Nos. 13 and 6," *WMW,* January 1974, 5.

26. Sam Walton and John Huey, *Sam Walton, Made in America: My Story* (New York: Doubleday, 1992), 170–71; Ortega, *In Sam We Trust,* 211.

27. Sandy Cinchon, "Grandma's Influence," *WMW,* June 1989, 28.

28. "Gainesville [Texas] Trio: Wal-Mart Boosters," *WMW,* February 1980, 14.

29. "Happiness Is . . . ," *WMW,* April 1972, 7.

30. "We See That . . . ," *WMW,* July 1973, 7, 10; "We See That . . . ," *WMW,* September 1973, 7.

31. "We See That . . . ," *WMW,* May 1974, 7.

32. "Gendarme of the TWX," *WMW,* April 1973, 2.

33. E.g., "We See That . . . ," *WMW,* December 1973, 5; "We See That . . . ," *WMW,* March 1974, 5.

34. "Store Happenings," *WMW,* May 1976, 13.

35. "Wal-Mart Blankets the Area," *WMW,* August 1971, 4.

36. Donna Love, "An Exercise in Customer Service," *WMW,* April 1983, 6; see also "We See That . . . ," *WMW,* March 1973, 7; "We See That . . . ," *WMW,* July 1973, 6; "We See That . . . ," *WMW,* August 1973, 4–5, 7.

37. "Memorial Day Sales Soar," *WMW,* July 1971, III-6; "We See That . . . ," *WMW,* December 1972, 7; "We See That . . . ," *WMW,* April 1973, 4.

38. "We See That . . . ," *WMW,* May 1975, 10.

39. Ibid., 8.

40. "We See That . . . ," *WMW,* February 1974, 9.

41. "New Briefs," *WMW,* August 1978, 13.

42. E.g., "We See That . . . ," *WMW,* December 1973, 6.

43. "Store Happenings," *WMW,* December 1975, 12.

44. "You're Gonna Love This One," *WMW,* October 1971, 15. For descriptions of turn-of-the-century office culture involving inversions of work hierarchies, and for similar conclusions about their uses in this earlier example of a feminized workplace, see Angel Kwolek-Folland, *Engendering Business: Men and Women in the Corporate Office, 1870–1930* (Baltimore: Johns Hopkins University Press, 1994), 161–62.

45. "We See That . . . ," *WMW,* September 1973, 7.

46. "Store Happenings," *WMW,* June 1977, 15.

47. "We See That . . . ," *WMW*, January 1975, 12.

48. E.g., "We See That . . . ," *WMW*, February 1975, 11; "'Walton's Winners,'" *WMW*, August 1974, 4; Interview with "Tammy Ellis" (2005).

49. "Store Happenings," *WMW*, August–September 1977, 15.

50. "Mrs. Bradford: A 105-Year Legend," *WMW*, September 1979, 7.

51. "Our Wal-Mart Family Tree," *WMW*, June/July 1992, 12–13.

52. Interview with "Alice Martin" and "Sherry Martin" (2005).

53. Sandra S. Vance and Roy V. Scott, "Sam Walton and Wal-Mart Stores, Inc.: A Study in Modern Southern Entrepreneurship," *Journal of Southern History* 58, no. 2 (May 1992): 244; [Interview with the Waltons], *WMW*, October 1987, 4; Ortega, *In Sam We Trust*, 60–61, 64–65.

54. Kristy Ely, "In the Beginning . . . A Visit with Those Who Were Part of Our Early Heritage," *WMW*, October 1989, 19.

55. Ortega, *In Sam We Trust*, 74; Ely, "In the Beginning," 19.

56. "We See That . . . ," *WMW*, October 1971, 11.

57. Todd Mason with Marc Frons, "Sam Walton of Wal-Mart: Just Your Basic Homespun Millionaire," *BW*, October 14, 1985, 147; "Year-End Meetings Focus on Company's Goals," *WMW*, March 1978, 16.

58. "1979: The Year Our People Made the Difference!" *WMW*, March 1980, 1.

59. "AIM Manuals Provide Training for Assistant Managers," *WMW*, March 1978, 10.

60. Jean Ann Bailey, "Associate's Wife Describes Wal-Mart as Caring 'Family,'" *WMW*, March 1979, 12.

61. Jay L. Johnson, "People Really Do Make the Difference," *Discount Merchandiser*, May 1989, 56.

62. Sam Walton, "11 Down, 3 to Go in '71," *WMW*, November 1971, 4.

63. "Associates Express Opinions on Wal-Mart Tranfers," *WMW*, November 1977, 4.

64. Ortega, *In Sam We Trust*, 93, 100, 105–8.

65. Jack Pate, "Knights of the Road," *DR*, June 6, 1997, 10A.

66. "A Truck Ride with Dad," *WMW*, July 1981, 21.

67. On sexual harassment as a deliberate and effective campaign of pressure against women's collective presence at work, rather than an individual affront, see Vicki Schultz, "Reconceptualizing Sexual Harassment," *Yale Law Journal* 107, no. 5 (March 1998): 1683–805; on the active participation of organized male workers in opposing women's equality on the job, see Marion Crain, "Sex Discrimination as Collective Harm," in *The Sex of Class: Women Transforming American Labor*, ed. Dorothy Sue Cobble (Ithaca: Cornell University Press, 2007), 103–9.

68. E.g., "We See That . . . ," *WMW*, December 1973, 5; "We See That . . . ," *WMW*, March 1974, 11; "We See That . . . ," *WMW*, May 1974, 10; "Store Happenings," *WMW*, December 1975, 12.

69. Ortega, *In Sam We Trust,* 360; Interview with "Angie Turner" (2005).

70. Ortega, *In Sam We Trust,* 359–60.

71. The incident, from a Wal-Mart logistics meeting in 1995, can be seen at www.youtube.com/watch?v=f2gpyodguk, accessed November 30, 2008.

72. Depositions of Melissa Howard and Deborah Gunter, respectively, quoted in Featherstone, *Selling Women Short,* 80–81, 46.

73. E.g., Edna Bonacich and Jake B. Wilson, "Global Production and Distribution: Wal-Mart's Global Logistics Empire (with Special Reference to the China/Southern California Connection)," in *Wal-Mart World: The World's Biggest Corporation in the Global Economy,* ed. Stanley D. Brunn (New York: Routledge, 2006), 227–42; Charles Fishman, *The Wal-Mart Effect: How the World's Most Powerful Company Really Works—and How It's Transforming the American Economy* (New York: Penguin, 2006); ATKearney, "Meeting the Retail RFID Mandate: A Discussion of the Issues Facing CPG Companies," (2003), www.atkearney.com/shared_res/pdf/Retail_RFID_S.pdf.

74. James Hoopes, "Growth Through Knowledge: Wal-Mart, High Technology, and the Ever Less Visible Hand of the Manager," in *Wal-Mart: The Face of Twenty-First Century Capitalism,* ed. Nelson Lichtenstein (New York: New Press, 2006), 83–104; on supply chains, see Bonacich and Wilson, "Global Production and Distribution."

5. Service Work and the Service Ethos

1. The proportion of married white women with children who participated in the paid labor force went from under 10 percent in 1940 to two-thirds by 1990; over the same period, nonwhite married women with children participated in the labor force at rates as much as twice as high. "Table Ba425-469: Female labor force participation rate, by race, marital status, and presence of children: 1880–1990 [Census estimates]," *Historical Statistics of the United States,* ed. Susan B. Carter et al. (Cambridge: Cambridge University Press, 2006).

2. K. Norman, "We See That . . . ," *WMW,* February 1974, 11.

3. "Seven Bright New Wal-Marts," *WMW,* July 1971, II-7; "We See That . . . ," *WMW,* November 1972, 14.

4. "We See That . . . ," *WMW,* December 1971, 14; Pat Plank, "Easter Festivities a Huge Success," *WMW,* June 1971, 6.

5. Pat Plank, "We See That . . . ," *WMW,* May 1972, 18.

6. "We See That," *WMW,* November 1972, 14.

7. Peggy L. Biggs, "[Dear Mr. Walton . . .]," *WMW,* February 1980, 12.

8. Interview with "Angie Turner" (May 26, 2005).

9. "Store Happenings," *WMW,* March–April 1976, 18.

10. "Store Happenings," *WMW*, May 1976, 13.

11. Interview with "Bea Scott," May 4, 2005.

12. "A Helping Hand," *WMW*, August 1974, 2.

13. Laura Gerke, "Belleville Associates Raise Money for Co-Worker," *WMW*, July 1978, 13.

14. "A Unique Get Well Message from Store no. 29," *WMW*, August 1974, 4.

15. "Region 2," *WMW*, April 1980, 9.

16. Nancy Brown, "We Get Letters," *WMW*, June 1979, 14.

17. "A Gesture Much Appreciated," *WMW*, November 1971, 11.

18. Interview with "Gina Dozier," April 29, 2005.

19. Interview with "Alice Martin" and "Sherry Martin," May 2, 2005.

20. Interview with Jim von Gremp, September 8, 2004.

21. Margaret A. Gilliam, *Wal-Mart Stores, Inc.,* Equity Research: Retail Trade (Boston: First Boston, 1988), 5.

22. Interview with "Alice Martin" and "Sherry Martin," May 2, 2005.

23. Interview with "Bea Scott," May 4, 2005. Selling discounted stock to employees as a tactic to keep a workplace "union-free" can be traced back at least to the 1920s; see Richard Gillespie, *Manufacturing Knowledge: A History of the Hawthorne Experiments,* Studies in Economic History and Policy: The United States in the Twentieth Century (Cambridge: Cambridge University Press, 1991), 18–19.

24. Interview with "Bea Scott," May 4, 2005.

25. Interview with "Pauline Crawford," May 3, 2005.

26. Interview with "Alice Martin" and "Sherry Martin," May 2, 2005.

27. Louis Uchitelle, "'Good' Jobs in Hard Times," *NYT,* October 3, 1993. Over the five years ending in 2007, Wal-Mart stock lost 23 percent of its value. Johanna Bennett, "No Business Like Show-Me Business," *Barron's Online,* October 22, 2007.

28. Charles Fishman, *The Wal-Mart Effect: How the World's Most Powerful Company Really Works—and How It's Transforming the American Economy* (New York: Penguin, 2006), 46–47.

29. They spent $3,620 per covered Wal-Mart employee for all benefits versus $4,834 per covered worker in the retail industry, on average, for health plan costs alone. The numbers err on the side of caution toward Wal-Mart since the calculation relies on the number of employees enrolled in Wal-Mart's health plan as the figure for benefits-eligible workers; in reality, only 62 percent of those eligible to be enrolled in Wal-Mart's health plan actually take the coverage. Human Rights Watch, *Discounting Rights: Wal-Mart's Violation of US Workers' Right to Freedom of Association* (2007), 43–44. http://hrw.org/reports/2007/us0507.

30. Interview with "June Whitehead," May 11, 2005.

31. Interview with "Alice Martin" and "Sherry Martin," May 2, 2005.

32. Interview with Jim von Gremp, September 8, 2004.

33. Interview with Ron Loveless, September 25, 2004.

34. Interview with "Bea Scott," May 4, 2005.

35. "Associate Writes Poem for Company," *WMW,* January 1980, 6.

36. Kate Bronfenbrenner and Robert Hickey, "Changing to Organize: A National Assessment of Union Strategies," in *Rebuilding Labor: Organizing and Organizers in the New Union Movement,* ed. Ruth Milkman and Kim Voss (Ithaca: Cornell University Press, 2004), 17–61; Peter T. Kilborn, "Why Labor Wants the Tired and Poor," *NYT,* October 29, 1995.

37. Greta Foff Paules, *Dishing It Out: Power and Resistance Among Waitresses in a New Jersey Restaurant,* Women in the Political Economy (Philadelphia: Temple University Press, 1991), 13–19; Karla Erickson and Jennifer L. Pierce, "Farewell to the Organization Man: The Feminization of Loyalty in High-End and Low-End Service Jobs," *Ethnography* 6, no. 3 (2005): 283–313. On the importance of the customer, see also Susan Porter Benson, *Counter Cultures: Saleswomen, Managers, and Customers in American Department Stores, 1890–1940,* The Working Class in American History (Urbana: University of Illinois Press, 1986), 128–31, 230–31, 263–64; Arlie Russell Hochschild, *The Managed Heart: Commercialization of Human Feeling* (Berkeley: University of California Press, 1983), 104–14; Pierrette Hondagneu-Sotelo, "Blow-Ups and Other Unhappy Endings," in Barbara Ehrenreich and Arlie Russell Hochschild, ed., *Global Woman: Nannies, Maids, and Sex Workers in the New Economy* (New York: Metropolitan Books, 2003), 55–69.

38. Interview with "Gail Hammond" and "Edna Guthry," May 2, 2005.

39. Interview with "Alice Martin" and "Sherry Martin," May 2, 2005.

40. Interview with "Tammy Ellis," May 13, 2005.

41. Interview with "June Whitehead," May 11, 2005.

42. Interview with "Eleanor Cook," May 5, 2005.

43. Interview with "Kathleen Hollins," May 26, 2005.

44. Interview with "Alice Martin" and "Sherry Martin," May 2, 2005.

45. See, in addition to works cited at note 37, Jennifer Johnson, *Getting By on the Minimum: The Lives of Working-Class Women* (New York: Routledge, 2002), 105–118.

46. Interview with "Gail Hammond" and "Edna Guthry," May 2, 2005.

47. Interview with "Kathleen Hollins," May 26, 2005.

48. Interview with "Alice Martin" and "Sherry Martin," May 2, 2005.

49. Patricia Armstrong, "Professions, Unions, or What?: Learning from Nurses," in *Women Challenging Unions: Feminism, Democracy, and Militancy,* ed. Linda Briskin and Patricia McDermott (Toronto: University of Toronto Press, 1993), 304–21; Dorothy Sue Cobble, "Introduction," in *The Sex of Class: Women*

Transforming American Labor, ed. Dorothy Sue Cobble (Ithaca: Cornell University Press, 2007), 7–8.

50. Sam Walton and John Huey, *Sam Walton, Made in America: My Story* (New York: Doubleday, 1992), 126–27.

51. Jay L. Johnson, "People Really Do Make the Difference," *Discount Merchandiser,* May 1989, 56.

52. Walton and Huey, *Made in America,* 126–31; John Tate paraphrased in Bob Ortega, *In Sam We Trust: The Untold Story of Sam Walton and How Wal-Mart Is Devouring America* (New York: Times Business, 1998), 86–90. Ortega found that of 2,300 hourly employees, only 128 took part in the first year of profit-sharing. The industry's high turnover meant then, as it would continue to mean, that very few actually qualified. Ortega, *In Sam We Trust,* 90. On the history of profit-sharing as a defensive mechanism to defuse labor agitation, see Daniel Nelson, *Managers and Workers: Origins of the New Factory System in the United States 1880–1920* (Madison: University of Wisconsin Press, 1975), 105–6.

53. "We Get Letters," *WMW,* January 1979, 14.

54. "We Can't Forget Those Glowing Letters" *WMW,* January 1975, 10.

55. Lisa Troyer, Charles W. Mueller, and Pavel I. Osinsky, "Who's the Boss? A Role-Theoretic Analysis of Customer Work," *Work and Occupations* 27, no. 3 (August 2000): 406–27; Erickson and Pierce, "Farewell to the Organization Man," 294–95; Benson, *Counter Cultures,* 263–65.

56. "We Can't Forget Those Glowing Letters," *WMW,* February 1976, 15.

57. Kessler-Harris, *Out to Work,* 135–41.

58. Mary Brubaker, "A Day in the Life of the Associate Hiring Process," *WMW,* April 1992, 30–31.

59. On the tensions between customers on the one hand and clerks or advertisers on the other, see Benson, *Counter Cultures,* 258–62; Roland Marchand, *Advertising the American Dream: Making Way for Modernity, 1920–1940* (Berkeley: University of California Press, 1985), 66–80.

60. Paules, *Dishing It Out,* 8–9, 132–36.

61. "Store Happenings," *WMW,* May 1977, 13.

62. A Wal-Mart Shopper, "From Wal-Mart Shoppers . . . [Letters]," *WMW,* June 1976, 16.

63. Interview with "Ann Tuttle," May 26, 2005.

64. Ruth Schwartz Cowan, *More Work for Mother: The Ironies of Household Technology from the Open Hearth to the Microwave* (New York: Basic Books, 1983), 83–85; Susan Strasser, *Satisfaction Guaranteed: The Making of the American Mass Market* (New York: Pantheon, 1989), 248–49.

65. "We See That . . . ," *WMW,* September 1974, 7.

66. "Around Wal-Mart," *WMW,* September 1992, 12.

67. "Store #35 Stages Retirement Party," *WMW,* July 1977, 5.

68. Nona Y. Glazer, *Women's Paid and Unpaid Labor: The Work Transfer in Health Care and Retailing* (Philadelphia: Temple University Press, 1993), 6.

69. A Ben Franklin customer, "From Wal-Mart Shoppers . . . [Letters]," *WMW,* June 1976, 16.

70. A Wal-Mart shopper, ibid.

71. Katherine Lamb, Ida Mae Shaw, and Mary O'Dell, "We Can't Forget Those Glowing Letters," *WMW,* May 1972, 14.

72. Eloise Wright, "Readers' Opinion," *WMW,* October 1974, 16.

73. Jim Rountree, "Communications: Customer Service Is Our Way—the Wal-Mart Way!" *WMW,* March 1974, 3.

74. Kristy Ely, "In the Beginning . . . A Visit with Those Who Were Part of Our Early Heritage," *WMW,* October 1989, 18.

75. Sam M. Walton, "A Message from Our President," *WMW,* August 1973, 2.

76. Lisa Belkin, "When Mom and Dad Share It All," *NYT Magazine,* June 15, 2008, 46–47; for a detailed breakdown of the division of household labor in the mid-1980s, see John P. Robinson and Geoffrey Godbey, *Time for Life: The Surprising Ways Americans Use Their Time* (University Park: Pennsylvania State University Press, 1997), 100.

77. This argument is drawn from Paules, *Dishing It Out,* chapters 4 and 5.

78. Nelson Lichtenstein, *State of the Union: A Century of American Labor* (Princeton: Princeton University Press, 2002), 118–22.

79. Ortega, *In Sam We Trust,* 7, 77.

80. Phil Moss, "What It's Like to Work for Wal-Mart," *Business Week Careers,* February 1987, 25.

81. Stephens Inc., "Stephens Incorporated Underwriting Follow-up: Wal-Mart Stores, Inc," *WMW,* September 1971, 8–11; Interview with "Alice Martin" and "Sherry Martin," May 2, 2005; manager quoted in Michael Bergdahl, *What I Learned from Sam Walton: How to Compete and Thrive in a Wal-Mart World* (Hoboken, NJ: John Wiley & Sons), 64–65.

82. Sam's Management Team, "To Whom It May Concern," February 13, 1993, and inserts 2, 3, Wal-Mart company files, Food and Allied Service Trades, AFL-CIO, Washington, DC; I am grateful to Jeffrey Fiedler for sharing these files with me.

83. Ortega, *In Sam We Trust,* 74; Bergdahl, *What I Learned from Sam Walton,* 62; Fishman, *The Wal-Mart Effect,* 29–30; Interview with "Gina Dozier."

84. Interview with "Alice Martin" and "Sherry Martin," May 2, 2005.

85. Interview with "Mark Higgins," May 25, 2005.

86. Interview with "Ann Tuttle," May 26, 2005.

87. Interview with "Angie Turner," May 26, 2005.

88. "Plaintiff's Pretrial Brief—Commission Sales Issues," (revised November 19, 1984), *EEOC v. Sears,* Civil Action No. 79-C-4373, U.S. District Court for the Northern District of Illinois, Eastern Division, p. 32; "Plaintiff's Pretrial Brief—Commission Sales Issues" (revised November 19, 1984), *EEOC v. Sears,* p. 34; "Trial Brief of Sears, Roebuck, and Co. (September/October 1984), *EEOC v. Sears,* pp. 10–13, all quoted in Ruth Milkman, "Women's History and the Sears Case," *Feminist Studies* 12, no. 2 (Summer 1986): 382, 384.

6. Revival in the Aisles

1. "Store Happenings," *WMW,* January 1978, 13.
2. "Toward a Hidden God," *Time,* April 8, 1966; Sydney E. Ahlstrom, *A Religious History of the American People* (New Haven: Yale University Press, 2004), 1082 n. 3.
3. Max Weber, *The Protestant Ethic and the Spirit of Capitalism,* trans. Talcott Parsons, with a foreword by R. H. Tawney (New York: Charles Scribner's Sons, 1958).
4. T. J. Jackson Lears, "From Salvation to Self-Realization: Advertising and the Therapeutic Roots of American Culture, 1880–1930," in *The Culture of Consumption,* ed. Richard W. Fox and T. J. Jackson Lears (New York, Pantheon, 1983), 1–38; Warren Susman, "Culture Heroes: Ford, Barton, Ruth," in *Culture as History: The Transformation of American Society in the Twentieth Century* (New York: Pantheon, 1984), 122–49.
5. Joel A. Carpenter, *Revive Us Again: The Reawakening of American Fundamentalism* (New York: Oxford University Press, 1997), 135–40, 148–50, 161–76.
6. Axel R. Schäfer, "The Cold War State and the Resurgence of Evangelicalism: A Study in the Public Funding of Religion Since 1945," *Radical History Review* 99 (Fall 2007): 19–50; Diana B. Henriques and Andrew Lehren, "Religion for Captive Audiences, with Taxpayers Footing the Bill," *NYT,* December 10, 2006.
7. On Southern consumption in this area, see Jack Temple Kirby, *Rural Worlds Lost: The American South, 1920–1960* (Baton Rouge: Louisiana State University Press, 1987), 115; Ted Ownby, *American Dreams in Mississippi: Consumers, Poverty, & Culture, 1830–1998* (Chapel Hill: University of North Carolina Press, 1999), 98–109; William Leach, *Land of Desire: Merchants, Power, and the Rise of a New American Culture* (New York: Pantheon, 1993), 9; see also Ira G. Zepp, *The New Religious Image of Urban America: The Shopping Mall as Ceremonial Center* (Niwot: University Press of Colorado, 1997), 12–15, 56–59; Alan R. Raucher, "Dime Store Chains: The Making of Organization Men, 1880–1940," *BHR* 65, no. 1 (Spring 1991): 130.
8. The contrast is to Leach, *Land of Desire,* 112–50.
9. Jeff Sellers, "Deliver Us from Wal-Mart?" *CT,* May 2005, 4.

10. Margaret A. Jacobs, "Workers' Religious Beliefs May Get New Attention," *WSJ*, August 22, 1995, B1.

11. Lizabeth Cohen, *A Consumer's Republic: The Politics of Mass Consumption in Postwar America* (New York: Vintage Books, 2003), 271–72, 489 n34.

12. David P. Thompson, "Session Records," February 1, 1954, mss. collection 950, vol. 5, FPCB (1989); David P. Thompson, "Session Records," April 11, 1955, mss. collection 950, vol. 5, FPCB; Virginia Williams, "Bentonville: Pioneers of Presbyterian Union," 950, FPCB (1989), 19; David P. Thompson, "Session Records," 950 (1955).

13. Gordon Garlington III, pastor of Bentonville First Presbyterian Church, quoted in Patricia May, "Walton, Wal-Mart Leave Their Mark on Northwest Arkansas," *DR Special Commemorative Edition,* April 5, 1992, 3.

14. Dan McGraw, "The Christian Capitalists," *USNWR* 118 (March 13, 1995): 52–56.

15. "Fundamentalism Sells," *WSJ*, February 6, 1995, A1, A4.

16. Sellers, "Deliver Us from Wal-Mart?" 40.

17. "Fundamentalism Sells."

18. Rob Moll, "Hurt by Success: Christian Bookstores Hit Hard by Competition from Wal-Mart," *CT* 48, no. 11 (November 2004): 21.

19. "Wal-Mart Check-Out Girls Do Check Out," *WMW*, July 1971, III-2; "We See That . . . ," *WMW*, August 1973, 5; "We Can't Forget These Glowing Letters," *WMW*, January 1975, 5; "Store Happenings," *WMW*, May 1977, 12; "Store Happenings," *WMW*, May 1976, 15.

20. Merrilyn Buchfink, "We Can't Forget These Glowing Letters," *WMW*, September 1974, 5.

21. Geri Kimbrell, "We Get Letters . . . ," *WMW*, October 1975, 4.

22. Neil Strauss, "Wal-Mart's CD Standards Are Changing Pop Music," *NYT*, November 12, 1996.

23. Sellers, "Deliver Us from Wal-Mart?" 40.

24. Linda Hicks, "Shocked: Death Announced at Morning Services," *DR Special Commemorative Edition,* April 5, 1992, 6.

25. "What's Happening in WMDC Number One," *WMW*, June 1976, 10.

26. "Associate's Book Published, Plans to Continue Writing," *WMW*, March 1979, 5.

27. "It Really Happened!" *WMW*, April 1972, 13.

28. "Working Women Balancing Priorities," *WMW* 19, no. 3 (May 1989): 16–21.

29. Interview with "Eleanor Cook," May 5, 2005.

30. Interview with "Ann Tuttle," May 26, 2005.

31. "Honesty Prevails," *WMW*, September 1973, 4.

32. "Honesty Prevails," *WMW*, April 1975, 16.

33. Jerry B. Smith, "Honesty Prevails," *WMW*, January 1975, 16.

34. "We See That . . . ," *WMW*, October 1972, 9.

35. "We See That . . . ," *WMW,* September 1973, 6.

36. "We See That . . . ," *WMW,* August 1973, 7.

37. "We See That . . . ," *WMW,* March 1974, 11; "We See That . . . ," *WMW,* April 1974, 11.

38. Aaron K. Ketchell, *Holy Hills of the Ozarks: Religion and Tourism in Branson, Missouri* (Baltimore: Johns Hopkins University Press, 2007); more generally, see R. Laurence Moore, *Selling God: American Religion in the Marketplace of Culture* (New York: Oxford University Press, 1994).

39. Stanley Burgess, "Perspectives on the Sacred: Religion in the Ozarks," *Ozarks-Watch: The Magazine of the Ozarks* 2, no. 2 (Fall 1988).

40. Gary Farley, "The Wal-Martization of Rural America and Other Things," *OzarksWatch: The Magazine of the Ozarks* 2, no. 2 (Fall 1988).

41. Ralph Burrage, "Patterns of Evangelism in First Baptist Church, Springdale, Arkansas, 1970–1994," *Baptist History and Heritage* 30, no. 1 (January 1995): 32–40.

42. www.fbcs.net/pastor/, accessed July 7, 2008; Greg Warner, "Ronnie Floyd Nomination Sparks Talk of Weak SBC Support, Fire-Truck Baptistry," *Associated Baptist Press,* May 11, 2006, www.apbnews.com/1021.article, accessed July 7, 2008.

43. Erin Curry, "Ronnie Floyd, on Fox News, Discusses Pulpits and Politics," *Baptist Press,* August 2, 2004, www.bpnews.net/bpnews.asp?ID=18792, accessed July 7, 2008.

44. www.fbcs.net/pastor/, accessed July 7, 2008.

45. Dean M. Kelley, *Why Conservative Churches Are Growing: A Study in Sociology of Religion with a New Preface for the ROSE Edition,* Reprints of Scholarly Excellence, no. 11 (Macon, GA: Mercer University Press, 1986); Roger Finke and Rodney Stark, *The Churching of America, 1776–2005: Winners and Losers in Our Religious Economy* (New Brunswick, NJ: Rutgers University Press, 2005), 244–53.

46. "Poplar Bluff: Missouri's Gateway to Recreation," *WMW,* November 1979, 16.

47. Interview with Jack Gray, July 15, 2004.

48. RCIA Local 322, "Executive Board Minutes," manuscript log, UFCW 322 (1970), 86.

49. Interview with Jack Gray, July 15, 2004.

50. Karen Nussbaum, "Working Women's Insurgent Consciousness," in *The Sex of Class: Women Transforming American Labor,* ed. Dorothy Sue Cobble (Ithaca: Cornell University Press, 2007), 171.

51. On these trends nationally, see Carpenter, *Revive Us Again;* Robert Wuthnow, *The Restructuring of American Religion: Society and Faith Since World War II* (Princeton: Princeton University Press, 1988).

52. Gary Harrell, unpublished manuscript in author's possession, 62.

53. A specific inspiration for worship style at the Fellowship Bible Church of Northwest Arkansas was B. Joseph Pine II and James H. Gilmore, *The Experience Economy: Work Is Theater & Every Business a Stage* (Cambridge, MA: Harvard Business School Press, 1999). On lay leadership, see Harrell, 70–72. I am indebted to the Rev. Harrell and to the Rev. Dr. Robert Cupp for guidance on this history.

54. Wuthnow, *The Restructuring of American Religion,* 92–93; Carpenter, *Revive Us Again,* 162–76; Kelley, *Why Conservative Churches Are Growing.*

55. Interview with Dr. H. D. McCarty, May 20, 2003; Mickey Anders, "Apologetics [sermon, First Christian Church, Pikeville, Kentucky], May 1, 2005, www.pikevillefirstchristianchurch.org/Sermons/Sermon20050501.html; Michael D. Bates, October 15, 2003, "Batesline," www.batesline.com/archives/000260.html; www.venturesforchrist.com/about_us.html; all accessed September 21, 2006.

56. Interview with Dr. H. D. McCarty, May 20, 2003.

57. John Marquette, "The Shepherds of Pinewood," *Horizon,* Spring 2003, 12.

58. Lorrie Wolfenkoehler, "It's a Beautiful Day in the Neighborhood," *Horizon,* Spring 2003, 17.

59. Ahlstrom, *A Religious History of the American People,* 951.

60. Shana Aborn, "Do You Take God to Work with You?" *Women's Faith & Spirit,* Spring 2003.

61. David W. Miller, *God at Work: The History and Promise of the Faith at Work Movement* (Oxford: Oxford University Press, 2007), 67.

62. Robert K. Gilmore, "The Church as Entertainment," *OzarksWatch: The Magazine of the Ozarks* 2, no. 2 (Fall 1988).

7. Servants unto Servants

1. Transcript of address by Paul Faulkner to Wal-Mart Managers Meeting, February 20, 1987, Flagler Productions, Inc., Lenexa, KS. Flagler reference number 00243A.

2. www.acu.edu/centennial/profiles/paul_faulkner.html, accessed September 20, 2008.

3. Lizabeth Cohen, *A Consumer's Republic: The Politics of Mass Consumption in Postwar America* (New York: Vintage Books, 2003), 18–19; Meg Jacobs, *Pocketbook Politics: Economic Citizenship in Twentieth-Century America* (Princeton: Princeton University Press, 2005). Both Jacobs and Cohen demonstrate consumerist politics as a project specifically of organized labor, politically active progressives and radicals, and Northern and African-American women. The Wal-Mart shoppers of the 1970s and 1980s represent a different set of actors in the story of American mass consumption.

4. Ann Braude, "Women's History Is American Religious History," in *Retelling U.S.*

Religious History, ed. Thomas A. Tweed (Berkeley: University of California Press, 1997), 87–107.

5. "Work, Ambition: Sam Walton," *Wal-Mart Stores Inc. 20th Anniversary [Special Supplement to BCDD],* October 24, 1982, 27.

6. Bill Saporito, "And the Winner Is Still . . . Wal-Mart," *Fortune,* May 2, 1994, 64.

7. Union organizer quoted in Mark Gimein, "Sam Walton Made Us a Promise," *Fortune* 145, no. 6 (March 18, 2002), 130.

8. Interview with "Eleanor Cook," May 5, 2005.

9. Interview with "Ann Tuttle," May 26, 2005.

10. Michael Bergdahl, *What I Learned from Sam Walton: How to Compete and Thrive in a Wal-Mart World* (Hoboken, NJ: John Wiley & Sons), 64.

11. Sam M. Walton, "Message from Sam Walton : Teamwork, Involvement Key to Manager's Success," *WMW,* June 1979, 2.

12. A. Jane Dunnett and Stephen J. Arnold, "Falling Prices, Happy Faces: Organizational Culture at Wal-Mart," in *Wal-Mart World: The World's Biggest Corporation in the Global Economy,* ed. Stanley D. Brunn (New York: Routledge, 2006), 89.

13. Linda Kintz, *Between Jesus and the Market: The Emotions that Matter in Right-Wing America* (Durham, NC: Duke University Press, 1997), 29. Emphasis added. Kintz is quoting Christian advice authors Beverly LaHaye and Elisabeth Elliott.

14. Interview with "Eleanor Cook," May 5, 2005.

15. "The 'Peggy' Curtain," *WMW,* June 1977, 7.

16. "Store Happenings," *WMW,* May 1976, 13; "What's Happening in WMDC Number One," *WMW,* June 1976, 10.

17. "'Welcome!' Begins Training Program," *Wal-Mart Stores Inc. 20th Anniversary [Special Supplement to BCDD],* October 24, 1982, 28–29.

18. Jean Wilkins, "Opportunities for Personal Growth—Unlimited!" *WMW,* April 1983, 9.

19. Interview with "June Whitehead," May 11, 2005.

20. Interview with "Alice Martin" and "Sherry Martin," May 2, 2005.

21. Interview with "Bea Scott," May 4, 2005.

22. Interview with "Ann Tuttle," May 26, 2005.

23. T. J. Jackson Lears, "From Salvation to Self-Realization: Advertising and the Therapeutic Roots of American Culture, 1880–1930," in *The Culture of Consumption,* ed. Richard W. Fox and T. J. Jackson Lears (New York: Pantheon, 1983), 36–37; Warren Susman, "Culture Heroes: Ford, Barton, Ruth," in *Culture as History: The Transformation of American Society in the Twentieth Century* (New York: Pantheon, 1984), 122–49.

24. Saporito, "And the Winner Is Still . . . Wal-Mart," 68.

25. Sam M. Walton, "Message to Associates: Our Focus for '92," *WMW,* February 1992, 5. The company actively promoted this association in training materials

today; see Dunnett and Arnold, "Falling Prices, Happy Faces," 83; Barbara Ehrenreich, Nickel and Dimed: On (Not) Getting By in America (New York: Metropolitan Books, 2001), 157.

26. "Promise," 122.

27. Don M. Frick, *Robert K. Greenleaf: A Life of Servant Leadership* (San Francisco: Berrett-Koehler Publishers, 2004), 293.

28. Frederick Winslow Taylor, *The Principles of Scientific Management* (New York: W.W. Norton, 1967), 47.

29. Daniel Nelson, *Managers and Workers: Origins of the New Factory System in the United States, 1880–1920* (Madison: University of Wisconsin Press, 1975), 65.

30. Herbert A. Simon, quoted in Stephen P. Waring, *Taylorism Transformed: Scientific Management Theory Since 1945* (Chapel Hill: University of North Carolina Press, 1991), 66.

31. Nelson, *Managers and Workers,* 150.

32. Waring, *Taylorism Transformed;* Ronald G. Greenwood, Alfred A. Bolton, and Regina A. Greenwood, "Hawthorne Half a Century Later: Relay Assembly Participants Remember," *Journal of Management* 9 (Fall 1983): 217–31.

33. The following very general sketch of management theory draws heavily on Mauro Guillén, *Models of Management: Work, Authority, and Organization in a Comparative Perspective* (Chicago: University of Chicago Press, 1994), 30–90; and Waring, *Taylorism Transformed.* I am indebted to Rakesh Khurana for suggesting these guides.

34. William H. Whyte Jr., *The Organization Man* (New York: Simon and Schuster, 1956), 37.

35. Rosabeth Moss Kanter, *Men and Women of the Corporation* (New York: Basic Books, 1977), 23–25.

36. Daniel Bell, *The Coming of Post-Industrial Society: A Venture in Social Forecasting; Special Anniversary Edition with a New Foreword by the Author* (New York: Basic Books, 1999), 17.

37. W. Jack Duncan, *Great Ideas in Management: Lessons from the Founders and Foundations of Managerial Practice* (San Francisco: Jossey-Bass, 1989), 187–89; Waring, *Taylorism Transformed,* 133–42.

38. Douglas McGregor, *The Human Side of Enterprise* (New York: McGraw-Hill, 1960).

39. Robert R. Blake and Jane Srygley Mouton, *The Managerial Grid* (Houston: Gulf Publishing Company, 1964), 18.

40. Guillén, *Models of Management,* 76.

41. "Communications Seminars Teach Variety of Skills: The Arts of Listening, Speech and Writing," *WMW,* November 1977, 8–9.

42. Robert Wuthnow, *Sharing the Journey: Support Groups and America's New Quest*

for Community (New York: Free Press, 1994), 4–7, 40–44; David W. Miller, *God at Work: The History and Promise of the Faith at Work Movement* (Oxford: Oxford University Press, 2007), 31–34; Matthew J. Raphael, *Bill W. and Mr. Wilson: The Legend and Life of A.A.'s Cofounder* (Amherst: University of Massachusetts Press, 2000), 71–72; see also Kurt W. Back, *Beyond Words: The Story of Sensitivity Training and the Encounter Movement* (New York: Russell Sage Foundation, 1972), esp. 47–76.

43. Frick, *Robert K. Greenleaf,* 277–79; Martin Luther King, Jr., "The Drum Major Instinct," www.stanford.edu/group/King/publications/sermons/680204.000_Drum_Major_Instinct.html.

44. "Bennett Sims Teaches Managers the Gospel of Servant Leadership," *Atlanta Journal-Constitution,* May 4, 1987, C1.

45. James F. Hind, "The Perfect Executive," *WSJ,* December 18, 1989, A10.

46. Barrie Richardson, "[Book Review]," *Business Horizons* 22, no. 3 (June 1979): 91–92.

47. Frick, *Robert K. Greenleaf,* 257–60; Ken Blanchard and Phil Hodges, *Lead Like Jesus: Lessons from the Greatest Leadership Role Model of All Times* (Nashville: W Publishing Group, 2005).

48. James Dobson, *Dare to Discipline* (Wheaton, IL: Tyndale House Publishers, 1976), 49–50.

49. Dan Gilgoff, *The Jesus Machine: How James Dobson, Focus on the Family, and Evangelical America Are Winning the Culture Wars* (New York: St. Martin's Press, 2007), xii.

50. Michael Lienesch, *Redeeming America: Piety and Politics in the New Christian Right* (Chapel Hill: University of North Carolina Press, 1993), 61–63.

51. Ron Burks and Vicki Burks, *Damaged Disciples: Casualties of Authoritarian Churches and the Shepherding Movement* (Grand Rapids: Zondervan, 1992); S. David Moore, *The Shepherding Movement: Controversy and Charismatic Ecclesiology* (London: T&T Clark International, 2003); Sara Diamond, *Spiritual Warfare: The Politics of the Christian Right* (Boston: South End Press, 1989), 111–19.

52. www.vft.ag.org/theologicalbasis.cfm, accessed November 20, 2005.

53. Gustav Niebuhr, "Southern Baptists Declare Wife Should 'Submit' to Her Husband," *NYT,* June 10, 1998, A24.

54. Elizabeth Brusco, *The Reformation of Machismo: Evangelical Conversion and Gender in Colombia* (Austin: University of Texas Press, 1995), 3. See also John Burdick, *Looking for God in Brazil: The Progressive Catholic Church in Urban Brazil's Religious Arena* (Berkeley: University of California Press, 1993), 86–113; Cecília Loreto Mariz and Maria das Dores Campos Machado, "Pentecostalism and Women in Brazil," in *Power, Politics, and Pentecostalism in Latin America,* ed.

Edward L. Cleary and Hannah W. Stewart-Gambinno (Boulder, CO: Westview, 1997), 41–54; Anna L. Peterson, "'The Only Way I Can Walk': Women, Christianity, and Everyday Life in El Salvador," in *Christianity, Social Change, and Globalization in the Americas,* ed. Anna L. Peterson, Manuel A. Vásquez, and Philip J. Williams (New Brunswick, NJ: Rutgers University Press, 2001), 25–44. In the U.S. context, see Brenda Brasher, *Godly Women: Fundamentalism and Female Power* (New Brunswick, NJ: Rutgers University Press, 1998); Nancy Tatom Ammerman, *Bible Believers: Fundamentalists in the Modern World* (New Brunswick, NJ: Rutgers University Press, 1987), 134–46; R. Marie Griffith, *God's Daughters: Evangelical Women and the Power of Submission* (Berkeley: University of California Press, 1997).

55. Laura and James Majors, and RuthAnn and Mike Harvey, quoted in Elizabeth Kadetsky, "Women of the Christian Right," *Glamour,* February 1995; reprinted in Melvin I. Urofsky and Martha May, eds., *The New Christian Right: Political and Social Issues* (New York: Garland Publishing, 1996), 286–91.

56. Michael S. Kimmel, "Patriarchy's Second Coming as Masculine Renewal," in *Standing on the Promises: The Promise Keepers and the Revival of Manhood,* Dane S. Claussen (Cleveland, OH: Pilgrim Press, 1999), 115.

57. McCartney interviewed October 7, 1997; quoted in Clella Iles Jaffe, "Promise Keepers Welcomed Home by Wives," in *Standing on the Promises*, 136.

58. www.promisekeepers.org/paffnews252#212.

59. I do not mean to suggest that the conflict between paid and unpaid employment was a new one; see, for example, Dorothy Sue Cobble, *The Other Women's Movement: Workplace Justice and Social Rights in Modern America* (Princeton: Princeton University Press, 2004), 121–44. However, the responses to the "double day" by labor union women in urban, industrial settings of the mid-twentieth century that Cobble analyzes are distinct from those of Christian service workers in Wal-Mart Country of the 1970s and 1980s.

60. W. Bradford Wilcox, *Soft Patriarchs, New Men: How Christianity Shapes Fathers and Husbands* (Chicago: University of Chicago Press, 2004), 114, 127–28; John P. Robinson and Geoffrey Godbey, *Time for Life: The Surprising Ways Americans Use Their Time* (University Park: Pennsylvania State University Press, 1997), 100.

61. The ratio of annual average annual earnings of women and men employed full time in 2007 was 77.8. Institute for Women's Policy Research, "The Gender Wage Gap: 2007," http://www.iwpr.org; accessed November 26, 2008.

62. For a review of the literature on the "motherhood penalty," see Shelley J. Correll, Stephen Benard, and In Paik, "Getting a Job: Is There a Motherhood Penalty?" *American Journal of Sociology* 112, no. 5 (March 2007): 1297–1338; on hours spent in parenting, see Lisa Belkin, "When Mom and Dad Share It All," *NYT Magazine,* June 15, 2008, 44–51, 74, 78.

63. Kintz, *Between Jesus and the Market*, 39–40.

64. Connaught "Connie" Marshner, quoted in William C. Martin, *With God on Our Side: The Rise of the Religious Right in America* (New York: Broadway Books, 1996), 182.

65. Aihwa Ong, *Buddha is Hiding: Refugees, Citizenship, the New America* (Berkeley: University of California Press, 2003), 212–13; David Martin, *Pentecostalism: The World Their Parish* (Oxford: Blackwell Publishing, 2002), 99–100.

66. Arlie Hochschild, *The Second Shift: Working Parents and the Revolution at Home* (New York: Viking Press, 1989).

67. This argument is made by Wilcox, *Soft Patriarchs, New Men*, 132–38. For a review of the data showing persistent inequalities in the household division of labor between the sexes in the period 1965 to 1995 and for a confirmation of the failure of an egalitarian gender ideology to increase men's contribution to housework, see Susan M. Bianchi, Melissa A. Milkie, Liana C. Sayer, and John P. Robinson, "Is Anyone Doing the Housework? Trends in the Gender Division of Household Labor," *Social Forces* 79, no. 1 (September 2000), 191–228. Bianchi et al. find that an overall decline in the total number of hours that women spend on housework, and some increase in the number that men spend (particularly on the more discretionary chores like yard work or repairs), has narrowed the gap between them since 1965. Most of this narrowing was accomplished by 1985, however. Subsequently, women have continued to perform roughly twice as much unpaid domestic labor as men in coupled households, and more of it in the "core" tasks of daily cooking and cleaning. The presence of children increases this gap significantly.

68. Wilcox, *Soft Patriarchs, New Men,* 154, 171–72.

69. Jaffe, "Promise Keepers Welcomed Home by Wives," 137.

70. The quoted term comes from Hochschild, *The Second Shift,* p. 12.

71. Bob Mumford, "Fatherpower," *New Wine Magazine,* April 1978, 4–10. An audio version was circulated on cassettes beginning in 1977; Burks and Burks, *Damaged Disciples,* 122.

72. David Waterman, "The Care and Feeding of Growing Christians," *Eternity,* September 1979, 16.

73. Joel A. Carpenter, *Revive Us Again: The Reawakening of American Fundamentalism* (New York: Oxford University Press, 1997), 306 n.17.

74. Bob Mumford, www.lifechangers.org/html2/about_bob.php, accessed August 24, 2006.

75. For example, Kent Marts, "Friends Remember Folksy Mr. Sam as Very Uncommon Common Man," *DR Special Commemorative Edition,* April 5, 1992, 1, 6; Angel Hernandez, "Front Range Wal-Mart Workers Mourn Death of Boss and Friend," *Rocky Mountain News,* April 6, 1992.

76. Arthur Markowitz, "Mr. Sam: Wal-Mart's Patriarch," *DSN* 28, No. 23 (December 18, 1989): 88.

77. Ellen Neuborne, "Book Promotions Hit Small Towns," *USA Today,* June 16, 1992, 5B; Meg Cox, "Walton Memoir Puts Marketers on Rural Route," *WSJ,* June 11, 1992, B1.

78. The theological reference here is to a variety of clear biblical prohibitions of usury, e.g., Exodus 22:25–27; Leviticus 25:35–37; Ezekiel 18:7–9, 13, 17.

79. Don Soderquist, *The Wal-Mart Way: The Inside Story of the Success of the World's Largest Company* (Nashville: Thomas Nelson Publishers, 2005), 1–2.

80. Alice G. Sargent and Ronald J. Stupak, "Managing in the 90's: The Androgynous Manager," *Training and Development Journal* 43, no. 12 (December 1989): 30–31.

81. Michael J. Chrasta, "The Religious Roots of the Promise Keepers," in *The Promise Keepers: Essays on Masculinity and Christianity,* ed. Dane S. Claussen (Jefferson, NC: McFarland & Company, 2000), 26.

82. Audio of Bishop Boone's testimony at the September 2006 "Values Voter Summit" is available at http://thinkprogress.org/2006/09/26/anti-gay-summit/.

83. Kimmel, "Patriarchy's Second Coming," 113–14.

84. Although Colorado's Amendment 2 passed in 1992 with 54 percent of the vote, it never went into effect because of legal challenges and was ultimately declared unconstitutional by the United States Supreme Court in 1996.

85. Bill McCartney quoted in Kimmel, "Patriarchy's Second Coming," 119; see also Lauren Berlant, "The Theory of Infantile Citizenship," in *The Queen of America Goes to Washington City: Essays on Sex and Citizenship (Series Q)* (Durham, NC: Duke University Press, 1997), 25–54; Kintz, *Between Jesus and the Market,* 265–71.

86. Jasmyne Cannick, "Gays Lose Advocate with Death of Mrs. King," *Pacific News Service,* February 3, 2006, at http://news.pacificnews.org/news/view, accessed November 29, 2006.

87. George N. Lundskow, *Awakening to an Uncertain Future: A Case Study of the Promise Keepers,* American University Studies Series VII: Theology and Religion (New York: Peter Lang, 2002), 67.

88. Wilcox, *Soft Patriarchs, New Men,* 46, 79.

89. Matthew D. Lassiter, "Inventing Family Values," in *Rightward Bound: Making America Conservative in the 1970s,* ed. Bruce J. Schulman and Julian E. Zelizer (Cambridge, MA: Harvard University Press, 2008), 13–28; Martin, *With God on Our Side,* 168–90.

90. Susan Friend Harding, *The Book of Jerry Falwell: Fundamentalist Language and Politics* (Princeton: Princeton University Press, 2000), 196.

91. On the changing economic valuation of children, see Viviana A. Zelizer, *Pricing*

the Priceless Child: The Changing Social Value of Children (New York: Basic Books, 1985); on the homosexual imagined as insatiable consumer, see Ann Pellegrini, "Consuming Lifestyle: Commodity Capitalism and Transformations in Gay Identity," in *Queer Globalizations: Citizenship and the Afterlife of Colonialism,* ed. Arnaldo Cruz-Malavé and Martin F. Manalansan IV (New York: New York University Press, 2002), 134–45.

92. "A Tombstone for Baby Joshua," *WMW,* April 1990, 15.

93. Kristin Luker, *Abortion and the Politics of Motherhood,* California Series on Social Choice and Political Economy (Berkeley: University of California Press, 1984), quoted phrase from p. 193.

94. Julie Ingersoll, *Evangelical Christian Women: War Stories in the Gender Battles* (New York: New York University Press, 2003), 52–53.

95. David Harrington Watt, "The Private Hopes of American Fundamentalists and Evangelicals, 1925–1975," *Religion and American Culture* 1, no. 2 (Summer 1991): 164–65.

96. Martin, *With God on Our Side,* 341.

97. Roy Beck, "Washington's Profamily Activists: How They Made 'Family Values' This Year's Hottest Political Issue," *CT* 36 (November 9, 1992): 21–23; Martin, *With God on Our Side,* 303.

98. John P. Bartowski, *The Promise Keepers: Servants, Soldiers, and Godly Men* (New Brunswick, NJ: Rutgers University Press, 2004), 6.

99. Wilcox, *Soft Patriarchs, New Men,* 96.

100. For a summary of the scholarship on nineteenth-century interpretations of masturbation and prostitution, see John D'Emilio and Estelle B. Freedman, *Intimate Matters: A History of Sexuality in America* (New York: Harper & Row, 1988), 66–73, 130–38; on bureaucrats as perverts, see David K. Johnson, *The Lavender Scare: The Cold War Persecution of Gays and Lesbians in the Federal Government* (Chicago: University of Chicago Press, 2004), 92–98; on temperance, see Paul E. Johnson, *A Shopkeeper's Millennium: Society and Revivals in Rochester, New York, 1815–1837* (New York: Hill & Wang, 1978), 121–28.

101. Janet Rugg, "People to People," *WMW,* May 1992, 4.

102. In 1980, for the first time, the U.S. Census found more than half of all married women in the labor force. "Table Ba579-582: Labor force participation rate for married women, by age and presence of children: 1948–1999," *Historical Statistics of the United States,* Millennial Edition On Line, ed. Susan B. Carter, Scott Sigmund Gartner, Michael R. Haines, Alan L. Olmstead, Richard Sutch, and Gavin Wright (Cambridge: Cambridge University Press, 2006).

103. Haynes Bonner Johnson, *Sleepwalking Through History: America in the Reagan Years* (New York: Anchor Books, 1992), 113–15; George Gilder, *Men and Marriage*

(Gretna, LA: Pelican, 1993; orig. pub. *Sexual Suicide,* 1973), 39, quoted in Kintz, *Between Jesus and the Market,* 169.

104. Kintz, *Between Jesus and the Market,* 157.

8. Making Christian Businessmen

1. Mark Blyth, *Great Transformations: Economic Ideas and Institutional Change in the Twentieth Century* (Cambridge: Cambridge University Press, 2002), 167–69; Barry Bluestone and Bennett Harrison, *The Deindustrialization of America: Plant Closings, Community Abandonment, and the Dismantling of Basic Industry* (New York: Basic Books, 1982), 95; Bluestone and Harrison, *The Great U-Turn: Corporate Restructuring and the Polarizing of America* (New York: Basic Books, 1988), 3–5; Mike Davis, *Prisoners of the American Dream: Politics and Economy in the History of the U.S. Working Class* (New York: Verso, 1999), 208–9; Ralph Landau, Timothy Taylor, and Gavin Wright, "Introduction," in *The Mosaic of Economic Growth,* ed. Ralph Landau, Timothy Taylor, and Gavin Wright (Stanford, CA: Stanford University Press, 1996), 9, n2.

2. In much of the world, "neoliberalism" is a familiar name for the twentieth-century movement of economists to link their belief in market supremacy and noninterventionist government to Enlightenment theories of private property as the foundation of personal liberty—classical liberalism, selectively interpreted. American political terminology makes this a confusing title, however, since neoliberal economic theories are associated with conservatives (including conservative Democrats). However, no suitable alternative is widely recognized, and there are signs that "neoliberalism" is gaining currency in the United States; I use it here for lack of a better term. This summary of neoliberalism draws heavily on James Ferguson, "Introduction," *Global Shadows: Africa in the Neoliberal World Order* (Durham, NC: Duke University Press, 2006), 1–23; Nancy Folbre, *The Invisible Heart: Economics and Family Values* (New York: New Press, 2001); David Harvey, *A Brief History of Neoliberalism* (Oxford: Oxford University Press, 2005); and Robert Kuttner, *Everything for Sale: The Virtues and Limits of Markets* (New York: Alfred A. Knopf, 1997).

3. Elizabeth A. Fones-Wolf, *Selling Free Enterprise: The Business Assault on Labor and Liberalism, 1945–60,* History of Communication (Urbana: University of Illinois Press, 1994); Naomi Klein, *The Shock Doctrine: The Rise of Disaster Capitalism* (New York: Metropolitan Books, 2007); Kim Phillips-Fein, "Top-Down Revolution: Businessmen, Intellectuals, and Politicians Against the New Deal, 1945–1964," *Enterprise & Society* (2006): 686–94; Fred Turner, *From Counterculture to Cyberculture: Stewart Brand, the Whole Earth Network, and the Rise of Digital Utopianism* (Chicago: University of Chicago Press, 2007).

4. Interview with Jim von Gremp, September 8, 2004.

5. Ferold Arend, "Store Talk: Definition of 'Tactful,'" *WMW*, February 1972, 16.

6. "Words to Manage By," *WMW*, January 1978, 14.

7. Arend, "Store Talk: Definition of 'Tactful,'" 16; Terry Webster Shroyer, "An Analysis of the Control Policies Used in a Voluntary Variety Store Chain Through the Study of Twenty-Five Ben Franklin Stores in Eastern Colorado," unpublished master's thesis (Boulder, CO: University of Colorado, 1957), i.

8. "What Is Your Score?" *WMW*, August 1973, 3.

9. Bob Ortega, *In Sam We Trust: The Untold Story of Sam Walton and How Wal-Mart Is Devouring America* (New York: Times Business, 1998), 60.

10. Don Soderquist, *The Wal-Mart Way: The Inside Story of the Success of the World's Largest Company* (Nashville: Thomas Nelson Publishers, 2005), 120.

11. Jim Rountree, "A Meaningful Year," *WMW*, January 1975, 3.

12. "An Important First for Wal-Mart!" *WMW*, July 1973, 4; Betty McAllister, "OTS," *WMW*, September 1974, 15.

13. Sam M. Walton, "Message from Sam Walton," *WMW*, April 1975, 2.

14. Tim Caldwell, "Wal-Mart Begins New Concept in Advanced Training Seminar," *WMW*, July 1978, 10.

15. "Headquarters Personnel Participate in Communications Seminar," *WMW*, November 1975, 1–2.

16. Bette Hendrix, "Counting Our Blessings," *WMW*, January 1976, 3.

17. "Headquarters Personnel Participate in Communications Seminar."

18. Betty McAllister, "Editorial: 'Happy 1976,'" *WMW*, January 1976, 2.

19. Interview with Jim von Gremp, September 8, 2004.

20. Betty Baker, "The Word Processing Center—How It Works," *WMW*, February 1977, 11–12.

21. Glenn Habern, "Computers and Technology at Wal-Mart Today," *WMW*, April 1983, 15.

22. Sandra Stringer Vance and Roy Vernon Scott, *Wal-Mart: A History of Sam Walton's Retail Phenomenon*, Twayne's Evolution of Modern Business Series (New York: Twayne Publishers, 1994), 94.

23. Randall Balmer, *Mine Eyes Have Seen the Glory: A Journey Into the Evangelical Subculture in America*, 4th ed. (Oxford: Oxford University Press, 2006), 62–65; Joel A. Carpenter, *Revive Us Again: The Reawakening of American Fundamentalism* (New York: Oxford University Press, 1997), 23–24, 128–131.

24. For a first-hand account of this communications revolution and its context, see Richard A. Viguerie and David Franke, *America's Right Turn: How Conservatives Used New and Alternative Media to Take Power* (Chicago: Bonus Books, 2004).

25. William Martin, "The Christian Right and American Foreign Policy," *Foreign Policy* 114 (Spring 1999): 71.

26. Robert Wuthnow, *The Restructuring of American Religion: Society and Faith Since World War II* (Princeton, NJ: Princeton University Press, 1988), 184.

27. Aaron K. Ketchell, *Holy Hills of the Ozarks: Religion and Tourism in Branson, Missouri* (Baltimore: Johns Hopkins University Press, 2007), 87–88.

28. E. William George, letter to John Brown, Jr., JB Jr., folder: letters by JB Jr. 1957–1968, October 20, 1967.

29. Ortega, *In Sam We Trust,* 99–100.

30. Vance and Scott, *Wal-Mart,* 95; Ortega, *In Sam We Trust,* 131–133.

31. Vance H. Trimble, *Sam Walton: The Inside Story of America's Richest Man* (New York: Dutton, 1990), 277.

32. John Huey, "Wal-Mart: Will It Take Over the World?" *Fortune,* January 30, 1989, 55; Soderquist, *The Wal-Mart Way: The Inside Story of the Success of the World's Largest Company.*

33. http://larryholder.blogspot.com/2008/02/my-early-days-with-wal-mart-data.html; accessed July 15, 2008.

34. Turner, *From Counterculture to Cyberculture;* the quoted phrase, reports Turner, appeared in Stewart Brand's opening statement to every edition of the *Whole Earth Catalog* (1969–1971); Ibid., 82.

35. Between 1959 and 1997, actual skilled high-tech jobs like systems analysts and code-writers grew only from 3.4 percent of all U.S. jobs to 6.6 percent; even at a paradigmatic high-tech corporation like Intel, three-quarters of the jobs are for routine clerical, sales, production, or maintenance work. Anthony P. Carnevale and Stephen J. Rose, "Inequality and the New High-Skilled Service Economy," in *Unconventional Wisdom: Alternative Perspectives on the New Economy,* Jeff Madrick (New York: Century Foundation Press, 2000), 147.

36. "We Get Letters . . . ," *WMW,* December 1975, 6.

37. Ferold Arend quoted in Ortega, *In Sam We Trust,* 90–91.

38. Sam Walton and John Huey, *Sam Walton, Made in America: My Story* (New York: Doubleday, 1992), 169.

39. Interview with Jim von Gremp, September 8, 2004.

40. Joseph Guilianno, "Automation's Time Is Now," *Chain Store Age Executive with Shopping Center Age* 51 (September 1975): 49.

41. "Recruiting: A Necessity for a Growing Company," *WMW,* November 1979, 1, 3.

42. "Management Trainee Program Has High Success, Low Turnover," *WMW,* January 1978, 11; "Recruiting: A Necessity," 1, 3.

43. "Management Trainee Program Has High Success."

44. Michael Bergdahl, *What I Learned from Sam Walton: How to Compete and Thrive in a Wal-Mart World* (Hoboken, NJ: John Wiley & Sons), 153.

45. Ibid., 154.

46. Ibid., 151.

47. Thomas D. Snyder, ed., *120 Years of American Education: A Statistical Portrait* (National Center for Education Statistics, 1993), 65–66, http://nces.ed.gov/pubs93/93442.pdf. U.S. Census Bureau, *Population Profile of the United States: 2000 (Internet Release)* (2001), fig. 8-2, http://www.census.gov/population/pop-profile/2000/profile2000.pdf.

48. Howard Brick, "Optimism of the Mind: Imagining Postindustrial Society in the 1960s and 1970s," *American Quarterly* 44, no. 3 (September 1992): 348–80.

49. Daniel Bell, *The Coming of Post-Industrial Society: A Venture in Social Forecasting; Special Anniversary Edition with a New Foreword by the Author* (New York: Basic Books, 1999), 269.

50. Bergdahl, *What I Learned from Sam Walton,* 151.

51. College of the Ozarks, *Bulletin* (Clarksville, AR, 1969–70), 15.

52. Vernon McDaniel, "Milestone at Ozarks: Arkansas's Oldest College Marks Its 125th Year This Week; New Era Dawns," *AG,* October 25, 1959, 2E.

53. See Michael Mumper and Pamela Vander Ark, "Evaluating the Stafford Student Loan Program: Current Problems and Prospects for Reform," *JHE* 62, no. 1 (January–February 1991): 62–78; Deborah A. Verstegen, "Education Fiscal Policy in the Reagan Administration," *Educational Evaluation and Policy Analysis* 12, no. 4 (Winter 1990): 360–63, 369; Dru Shockley, "New Legislation Tightens Student Federal Aid," *TA* 53, no. 3 (November 6, 1986): 4.

54. "1982 'Interesting Year' in History of College," *ME,* May 14, 1982, 2.

55. Terry Wade, "C of O Students—Distinct," *ME,* February 12, 1971, 4.

56. Robert L. George, "Annual Report of the Combined Departments of Business Education and Economics," BCG-UO (1948); Robert L. George, "Annual Report of the Departments of Business and Economics," BCG-UO (1949).

57. Robert L. George, "Annual Report of the Departments of Business and Economics, The College of the Ozarks," BCG-UO (1950); Robert L. George, "Annual Report of the Department of Business, The College of the Ozarks," BCG-UO (1951).

58. Mrs. J. K. Harrison, "Annual Report of the Department of Business, The College of the Ozarks," BCG-UO (1959), 6–7; D. W. Blackburn, "Annual Report of the Department of Business, The College of the Ozarks," BCG-UO (1957), 3.

59. Blackburn, "Annual Report of the Department of Business, The College of the Ozarks," 5.

60. Harrison, "Annual Report of the Department of Business, The College of the Ozarks," 2, 6–7; more generally, see W. J. Cash, *The Mind of the South* (New York: Vintage Books, 1969), 322.

61. Mrs. J. K. Harrison, "Annual Report of the Department of Business, The College of the Ozarks," BCG-UO (1960), 5, 7.

62. "Union National Bank," report, scrapbook, PBL-UO (1972).

63. "Arkansas Highway Department," report, scrapbook, PBL-UO (1972).

64. "Arkansas Gazette," report, scrapbook, PBL-UO (1972).

65. "Arkansas Best Corporation," report, scrapbook, PBL-UO (1972).

66. Herman Houston, "Western Arkansas Telephone Company," report, scrapbook, PBL-UO (1972), 1–2.

67. "Arkansas Best Corporation."

68. PBL grew out of the high-school vocational organization Future Business Leaders of America, on the model of the Future Farmers of America, which had offered agribusiness a direct link to the public schools since 1928.

69. "Annual Activities Report 1976," PBL-UO (1976), 24.

70. "Annual Activities Report 1978," PBL-UO (1978), 25; "Annual Activities Report 1979," PBL-UO (1979), 36–37.

71. "Annual Activities Report 1983," PBL-UO (1983), 6, Appendix F; "Business Report," PBL-UO (1985), 13.

72. "Annual Activities Report 1975," PBL-UO (1975), 40.

73. "Annual Activities Report 1981," PBL-UO (1981), 32.

74. Bruce J. Schulman, *The Seventies: The Great Shift in American Culture, Society, and Politics* (New York: Free Press, 2001), 131–40; quotation from p. 138.

75. "Annual Activities Report 1974," PBL-UO (1974), 21–22.

76. "Annual Activities Report 1978," 25; "Annual Activities Report 1979," 36–37.

77. "Division of Business Enterprise," unpublished rept., BCG-UO (1988).

78. "Annual Activities Report 1979," 33.

79. "'Project Awareness,'" PBL-UO (1979), 1.

80. "Business Report," PBL-UO (1984), 10; Schulman, *The Seventies,* 135.

81. On the long tradition of individual success through positive thinking, see John G. Cawelti, *Apostles of the Self-Made Man: Changing Concepts of Success in America* (Chicago: University of Chicago Press, 1965), 201–36 ; Alfred Anthony Griswold, "New Thought: A Cult of Success," *American Journal of Sociology* 40, no. 3 (November 1934): 475–93; T. J. Jackson Lears, "From Salvation to Self-Realization: Advertising and the Therapeutic Roots of American Culture, 1880–1930," in *The Culture of Consumption,* ed. Richard W. Fox and T. J. Jackson Lears (New York: Pantheon, 1983), 1–38.

82. "Most Outstanding Project—Event 4," PBL-UO (1980), 4–5.

83. "Annual Activities Report 1981," 29; Johnson County Chamber of Commerce, "Board of Directors Minutes," scrapbook, PBL-UO (1977); "Annual Activities Report 1975," 29–30.

84. "Annual Activities Report 1975"; "Annual Activities Report 1982," PBL-UO (1982); "C of O to Implement Recruiting Program," *ME,* November 18, 1983, 1.

85. "Annual Activities Report 1978," 31; "Annual Activities Report 1975," 21–22.

86. "Helen Walton . . . Leadership and Dedication," *ME,* November 4, 1983, 3.

87. McDaniel, "Milestone at Ozarks," 2E; Thomas H. Campbell, *Good News on the Frontier: A History of the Cumberland Presbyterian Church* (Memphis: Frontier Press, 1965). Wade, "C of O Students—Distinct," 4.

88. Robert J. Smith, "Walton Says Project Isn't Legacy but Love," *ADG* [*Northwest Arkansas Edition*], May 24, 2005.

89. Steve Shaner, "Walton Heads Campaign," *ME*, October 31, 1985, 3.

9. Evangelizing for Free Enterprise

1. Donald M. Kendall, "The Generation Gap: Economic Illiteracy," *VSD* 37 (February 1, 1971): 245–46.

2. William L. Bird, Jr., '*Better Living': Advertising, Media, and the New Vocabulary of Business Leadership, 1935–1955* (Evanston, Ill.: Northwestern University Press, 1999); Elizabeth A. Fones-Wolf, *Selling Free Enterprise: The Business Assault on Labor and Liberalism, 1945–60,* History of Communication (Urbana: University of Illinois Press, 1994); Kim Phillips-Fein, "Top-Down Revolution: Businessmen, Intellectuals, and Politicians Against the New Deal, 1945–1964," *Enterprise & Society 7,* no. 4 (December 2006): 686–94.

3. Dan Harrison, "A Broader Role for Business?" *Chain Store Age Executive with Shopping Center Age* 53 (February 1977): 11.

4. Henry C. Wallach, "Generation Gap," *NW* 76 (October 12, 1970): 98; Ronald Reagan, "Free Enterprise Economics," *VSD* 39 (January 15, 1973): 196–201.

5. Bird, '*Better Living,*' 163–81, 183–84; Fones-Wolf, *Selling Free Enterprise,* 189–217; Roland Marchand, *Creating the Corporate Soul: The Rise of Public Relations and Corporate Imagery in American Big Business* (Berkeley: University of California Press, 1998), 212–13, 295–301.

6. Paul Davenport, "Former Arizona Governor Dead at 88," *AP State & Local Wire,* August 26, 1998; Joseph Stocker, "Compulsory Free Enterprise: Brainwashing the Classrooms," *Nation,* December 17, 1973, 653; quotation from Arizona legislator Jim Skelly.

7. Stocker, "Brainwashing the Classrooms," 654; the quoted materials are by Weldon P. Shofstall.

8. Sheila Harty, *Hucksters in the Classroom: A Review of Industry Propaganda in Schools* (Washington, DC: Center for the Study of Responsive Law, 1979), 78. See also John P. Manzer, "What to Do (and Not to Do) When Johnny Can't Define Profit," *WSJ,* September 15, 1983, 30.

9. Harty, *Hucksters in the Classroom,* 85–88.

10. Burton Yale Pines, *Back to Basics* (New York: William Morrow and Company, 1982), chapters 1 and 2.

11. "How a Company Changes Youngsters' Lives," *NB,* September 1972, 17.

12. Priscilla Schwab, "Introducing Johnny and Mary to the World of Business," *NB*, January 1978, 57.

13. "Spreading Economic Education Across the Country," *NB*, January 1978, 63–64.

14. Vernon Louviere, "Panorama of the Nation's Business: A Company's Salesman for Our Economic System," *NB*, February 1976, 82; direct quotation from W. Richard Bryan of Goodyear Tire and Rubber Co.

15. Vernon Louviere, "Speaking up for the Free Enterprise System," *NB*, October 1976, 80.

16. Irving Kristol, "On 'Economic Education,'" *WSJ*, February 18, 1976, 20.

17. Though my intellectual debt to Michael Denning is too pervasive to tease out in every instance, I originally encountered this particular point, expressed in essentially these terms, in a 2002 lecture of his.

18. Jean Seligmann et al., "The Golden Passport," *NW*, May 14, 1979, 110; "Courses That Lead to Jobs Are Taking Over on Campus," *USNWR*, December 15, 1975, 50ff; Thomas D. Snyder, Alexandra G. Tan, and Charlene M. Hoffman, *Digest of Education Statistics 2003* (Washington, DC: National Center for Education Statistics; U.S. Department of Education Institute of Education Sciences, 2004), 316 table 252; Thomas L. Wheelen, "Top Managements' Perspective of Business Education—a Preliminary Summary Report," *Academy of Management Proceedings* (1972): 289.

19. "Courses That Lead to Jobs," 50.

20. Jennifer Washburn, *University, Inc.: The Corporate Corruption of Higher Education* (New York: Basic Books, 2005), 57. See also the papers of the Working Group on Globalization and Culture, *Breaking Down the Ivory Tower: The University in the Creation of Another World*, 2005, www.yale.edu/laborculture/work_culture.html.

21. Merrill Sheils et al., "Bonus for Businessmen," *NW*, June 7, 1976, 84; Carl M. Larson, "Management Assistance for the Small Businessman: A Joint Program of SBA and the University," *Journal of Small Business Management* 12 (1974): 6; "On the Way: A New Round of Help for Small Business," *USNWR*, August 30, 1976, 38; "Spotlight on Small Business," *NB*, May 1973, 12. A parallel project, the Small Business Incubators, began in the same years but focused on the commercialization of technologies developed at major research universities.

22. SBA press release (May 1976); quoted on the Web site of the Association of Small Business Development Centers, www.asbdc-us.org; accessed October 11, 2006.

23. House of Representatives, *Hearing Before the Subcommittee on SBA and SBIC Authority and General Small Business Problems of the Committee on Small Business.* 96th Cong., 1st sess., 1979, 9–12. Quotations from Congressman Neal Smith and from William H. Mauk, SBA deputy administrator, respectively.

24. www.asbdc-us.org (accessed October 11, 2006); Sheils, "Bonus for Businessmen."

25. The metaphor is from the political economist Susan Strange, elaborated in her *Casino Capitalism* (London: Basil Blackwell, 1986).

26. Roberta Graham, "Free Advice Pays Off for Small Business," *NB*, February 1979, 50.

27. Sheils, "Bonus for Businessmen."

28. Larson, "Management Assistance," 8–9.

29. Ronald Alsop, "Capitalism 101: Programs to Teach Free Enterprise Sprout on College Campuses," *WSJ*, May 10, 1978, 1.

30. Snyder, Tan, and Hoffman, *Digest of Education Statistics 2003*, 316 table 252.

31. James J. Kilpatrick, "Why Students Are Hostile to Free Enterprise," *NB* 63, no. 7 (July 1975): 11–12; "Enterprise Square Teaches Economics," *Saturday Oklahoman & Times* [*Oklahoma City, OK*], March 7, 1992, 10.

32. Schwab, "Introducing Johnny and Mary," 58–59.

33. "Foundations of a Better Society?" *Industry Week*, April 20, 1981, 49.

34. Henry E. Metzner and Edwin C. Sims, "Student Attitudes Toward the Free Enterprise System," *JEE* 10, no. 1 (Autumn 1978): 46–50.

35. James "Jack" Gray, "Organizing Report to James Suffridge, President of RCIA," January 12, 1966, M8–580, Reel 41, RCIU.

36. RCIA Local 322, "Executive Board Minutes," manuscript log, December 12, 1968, UFCW 322, 57.

37. Springfield Central Labor Council, "Minutes," January 13, 1969, box 6, folder "1969," Records of the Springfield [Missouri] Central Labor Council, Ozarks Labor Union Archives, Missouri State University, Springfield, Missouri.

38. "Business Report," March 11, 1985, PBL-UO, 9; "Epsilon Psi Chapter 1611 Annual Activities Report," April 4, 1977, PBL-UO, 33.

39. "PBL Spin-Off Markets Toy," *Bulletin of the College of the Ozarks*, March 1977.

40. "Annual Activities Report 1975," PBL-UO, 21–22. The Labor-HEW Appropriations Act of 1970 made $1.5 million in federal funds available to encourage cooperative education in colleges and universities. A contemporaneous review of the program's potential noted the "important implications for fund-raising" created by bringing university personnel in touch with area businesses. James R. Davis, "Cooperative Education: Prospects and Pitfalls," *JHE* 42, no. 2 (February 1971): 136, 142.

41. Patricia May, "Walton Name Signifies Giving," *ADG*, March 2, 1991.

42. "PBL to Sponsor Business Symposium," *ME*, October 21, 1983, 1.

43. "Annual Activities Report 1978," PBL-UO (1978), 24.

44. "Epsilon Psi Chapter 1611 Annual Activities Report," April 4, 1977, PBL-UO, 15.

45. Randy Hilton, "Memo to All Business Division Faculty," April 8, 1985, AA-UO.

46. Randy Hilton, letter to Fritz Ehren, April 25, 1985, file "Entrepreneur Proposal," AA-UO.

47. Randy Hilton et al., "Minutes: Division of Business Administration First Strategic Planning Session," April 18, 1985, AA-UO, 2.

48. Ibid., 2–4.

49. Randy Hilton et al., "Division of Business Administration major entrepreneurship," April 18, 1985, file "Entrepreneur Proposal," AA-UO.

50. John A. Hornaday, "Research About Living Entrepreneurs," in *Encyclopedia of Entrepreneurship,* ed. Calvin A. Kent, Donald L. Sexton, and Karl A. Vesper (Englewood Cliffs, NJ: Prentice-Hall, 1982), 30; Jerome A. Katz, *2004 Survey of Endowed Positions in Entrepreneurship and Related Fields in the United States* (Kansas City, MO: Ewing Marion Kauffman Foundation, 2004), 6 fig. 1, fig. 2.

51. Hilton, "Division of Business Administration major entrepreneurship"; interview with Professor Robert Hilton, February 17, 2003.

52. "Center for Entrepreneurship," http://webs.wichita.edu, accessed June 22, 2006.

53. Karl H. Vesper, *Entrepreneurship Education: A Bicentennial Compendium* (Milwaukee: Society for Entrepreneurship Research and Application, 1976); unpaginated.

54. Karl H. Vesper, *Entrepreneurship Education 1985* (Wellesley, MA: Center for Entrepreneurial Studies, Babson College, 1985), 220, 207.

55. Calvin A. Kent, "The Treatment of Entrepreneurship in Principles of Economics Textbooks," *JEE* 20, no. 2 (Spring 1989): 611.

56. Quoted in Vesper, *Entrepreneurship Education: A Bicentennial Compendium.*

57. John A. Walsh and Jerry F. White, "Converging on the Characteristics of Entrepreneurs," in *Frontiers of Entrepreneurship Research 1981: Proceedings of the 1981 Conference on Entrepreneurship at Babson College,* ed. Karl H. Vesper (Wellesley, MA: Babson College, 1981), 511.

58. Vesper, *Entrepreneurship Education: A Bicentennial Compendium.*

59. Vesper, *Entrepreneurship Education 1985,* 304.

60. Gifford Pinchot, *Intrapreneuring: Why You Don't Have to Leave the Corporation to Become an Entrepreneur* (New York: Harper & Row, 1985).

61. Donald M. Dible, *Up Your OWN Organization! A Handbook for the Employed, the Unemployed, and the Self-Employed on How to Start and Finance a New Business* (Santa Clara, CA: Entrepreneur Press, 1971). Subsequent editions dropped the reference to unemployment, and eventually replaced it with "entrepreneur."

62. Stephen H. Norwood, *Strikebreaking and Intimidation: Mercenaries and Masculinity in Twentieth-Century America* (Chapel Hill: University of North Carolina Press, 2002), 15, 26.

63. http://webs.wichita.edu/?=markl&p=pizzahut; accessed December 1, 2008.

64. Vesper, *Entrepreneurship Education 1985,* xii, quotation on p. xiii.

65. James S. Fairweather, "Academic Research and Instruction: The Industrial Connection," *JHE* 60, no. 4 (July 1989): 393–94.

66. Clay Chandler, "New Business Incubators Are Started as Money Makers," *WP,* August 29, 1988, F25; Karl Vesper, "Research on Education in Entrepreneurship," in *Encyclopedia of Entrepreneurship,* ed. Calvin A. Kent, Donald L. Sexton, and Karl A. Vesper (Englewood Cliffs, NJ: Prentice-Hall, 1982), 326; Wayne S. Brown, "Commentary on Entrepreneurship Education," in *Encyclopedia of Entrepreneurship,* 347.

67. "Foundations of a Better Society?"; William F. May, "Corporate Support of Higher Education," *Proceedings of the Academy of Political Science* 30, no. 1 (May 1970): 147–50.

68. Roger M. Blough, "Agenda for the 1970s," *Proceedings of the Academy of Political Science* 30, no. 1 (May 1970): 176.

69. W. O. Beeman, *Oklahoma Christian College: Dream to Reality: The Story of the First Twenty Years, 1950–1970* (Delight, AR: Gospel Light Publishing Company, 1970), 117–19. "Oklahoma City: Center of Education," *Esquire,* December 1966, 174–75. The labor cost savings that OCU realized from this experiment in automation came in part through government subsidy of the infrastructure: a $279,850 federal grant from the U.S. Department of Health, Education, and Welfare; Housing and Urban Development loans totaling $1.49 million; and subsequent state financing of $1 million. Beeman, *Oklahoma Christian College,* 123–25.

70. Carl P. Zeithaml and George H. Rice, Jr., "Entrepreneurship/Small Business Education in American Universities," *Journal of Small Business Management* 25, no. 1 (January 1987): 46–48.

71. Ibid.

72. Pines, *Back to Basics,* 60.

73. Zeithaml and Rice, Jr., "Entrepreneurship/Small Business Education in American Universities," 50.

74. Emily Sachs, "JBU: A Dream Come True," *Morning News* [Springdale, AR], August 16, 1999, A3.

75. John E. Brown, "Editorial: Jesse H. Jones, Our Next President," *Christian Fellowship* XX, no. 39, 40 (May 17, 1938): 1–2.

76. Rick Ostrander, *Head, Heart, and Hands: John Brown University and Modern Evangelical Higher Education* (Fayetteville: University of Arkansas Press, 2003), 140–45, 156–62, 176–78; Sound Generation co-founder John Coates quoted on 161.

77. May, "Walton Name Signifies Giving."

78. Kathy Buller, [untitled, ca. 1988], file "Trustees, Board of—Committees," folder "Trustees," JBU; John Brown University, "Promise Keepers, Soderquist Host Ethics Conference for CEOs," press release, May 18, 2005, www.jbu.edu/news/press_releases/release.asp?id=2157, accessed December 1, 2008.

79. Buller, [untitled]; John Brown University, "Promise Keepers, Soderquist Host Ethics Conference for CEOs."

80. Don Soderquist, *The Wal-Mart Way: The Inside Story of the Success of the World's Largest Company* (Nashville, TN: Thomas Nelson Publishers, 2005).

81. John R. Duke, Jr., "American Studies: Improving a College, Improving a Nation," unpublished paper in author's possession (Harding University, 1997), 18–20.

82. Ibid.; Appendix A, "List of Speakers," pp. 20, 22, 24.

83. Harding University, "The Dream Continues," promotional pamphlet, file "Publicity—Harding," HU (1992).

84. Duke, Jr., "American Studies," 22–23.

85. Gazette Press Services, "Harding Program Called Big Factory of Radical Right Propaganda in U.S," *AG*, September 20, 1964, 1A–2A.

86. *Newsweek*, December 4, 1961, 20; quoted in Donald P. Garner, "George S. Benson: Conservative, Anti-Communist, Pro-Americanism Speaker" (Ph.D. diss., Wayne State University, 1963), 5 n2.

87. *NYT*, May 9, 1961; quoted in Garner, "George S. Benson," 23 n.

88. This is a principal argument of both Royce Money, "Church-State Relations in the Churches of Christ since 1945: A Study in Religion and Politics" (Ph.D. diss., Baylor University, 1975) and Richard T. Hughes, *Reviving the Ancient Faith: The Story of Churches of Christ in America* (Grand Rapids, MI: William B. Eerdsman Publishing Co., 1996).

89. This account of George Benson and Harding College (University) draws heavily on L. Edward Hicks, *"Sometimes in the Wrong, but Never in Doubt": George S. Benson and the Education of the New Religious Right* (Knoxville: University of Tennessee Press, 1994), 4; George Benson, interviewed in 1985, quoted on p. 3.

90. Garner, "George S. Benson," 61.

91. Hughes, *Reviving the Ancient Faith*, 155–56.

92. Ibid., 157–59.

93. Garner, "George S. Benson," 75, quoted material from p. 23; Hicks, *"Sometimes in the Wrong,"* 65.

94. Gazette Press Services, "Big Factory," 1A–2A.

95. Hicks, *"Sometimes in the Wrong . . .,"* 51–65.

96. Lori Lyn Bogle, *The Pentagon's Battle for the American Mind: The Early Cold War* (College Station: Texas A&M University Press, 2004), 151–52.

97. Bogle, *Pentagon's Battle*, 146.

98. Arthur J. Weitzman, "Should Courses on Communism Be Offered in Colleges and Universities?" *JHE* 33, no. 3 (March 1962): 167.

99. Duke, Jr., "American Studies," 5–10.

100. National Education Program, "Important New Tool Available," *The National Program Letter/American Citizenship Letter*, January 1983, 7.

101. Duke, Jr., "American Studies," Appendix A, "List of Speakers," p. 17.

102. Don P. Diffine, "IV. Proof That Free Enterprise Delivers the Goods," *The Entrepreneur,* January 1999, 10; Don P. Diffine, "How Does Wal-Mart Do It?" *The Entrepreneur,* August 1991, 21.

103. Bob Reely, "Center's First Year a Good One," *Forum* [publication of Harding University Center for Management Excellence] 1, no. 2 (April 1983); Bethany E. Moreton, "Make Payroll, Not War: Business Culture as Youth Culture, 1970–1981," in Bruce Schulman and Julian Zelizer, eds., *Rightward Bound: Making America Conservative in the 1970s* (Cambridge, MA: Harvard University Press, 2008).

104. Enterprise Square USA, press release, March 5, 1992, folder "Auxiliary Enterprises—Enterprise Square," OACH.

105. "Gallup Study Triggers Search for Effective Economics Education Method," *NB-ES* 1, no. 1 (Winter 1980): 2; Jan Eskridge, "Selling Free Enterprise in a Theme Park Atmosphere," *Oklahoma Business* 9, no. 7 (July 1979): 20.

106. Jim Etter, "Mr. Fixit Keeps the Razzledazzle in Enterprise Square," *Oklahoma Today* 34, no. 1 (Winter 1983–84): 12.

107. "The Enterprising Mind Behind Enterprise Square," *NB-ES* 2, no. 1 (Winter 1982): 2, 3, 4.

108. Charles Gaylor, "Enterprise Square Time Capsule Ceremony Closes Jubilee," undated clipping, folder "Auxiliary Enterprises—Enterprise Square," OACH; "An Enterprising Teaching Tool," *Oklahoma City Times,* October 14, 1980, 30.

109. "An Enterprise Square Who's Who," *NB-ES* 2, no. 1 (Winter 1982): 4.

110. "Award-Winning Scriptwriters Drafting Scenarios for Animation Segments," *NB-ES* 1, no. 1 (Winter 1980): 3; Eskridge, "Selling Free Enterprise," 20.

111. "Ground Broken for Enterprise Square, U.S.A., Construction Underway for 1982 Grand Opening!" *NB-ES* 1, no. 2 (Fall 1980): 1; quotations from Covey Bean, "Enterprise Square Ground-Breaking Ceremonies Held," undated clipping, folder "Auxiliary Enterprises-Enterprise Square," OACH.

112. Randy Ellis, "Enterprise Square Gets Rave Reviews," *Sunday Oklahoman,* November 21, 1982.

113. Jim Etter, "Mr. Fixit," 12.

114. Enterprise Square USA, "A Fast Tour of Enterprise Square, U.S.A." [undated promotional brochure], OACH, 1.

115. Ibid.

116. Eskridge, "Selling Free Enterprise," 21.

117. "David North Gets Down to Business Games," *News Brief* 2, no. 1 (Winter 1982): 2; Enterprise Square USA, "Economics Computer Games" [undated promotional material], OACH.

118. Enterprise Square USA, "Tour Notes" [exhibit guide], OACH (1982), 1.

119. Etter, "Mr. Fixit," 12.

120. Enterprise Square USA, "America's Most Entertaining Educational Attraction" [undated promotional brochure], folder "Auxiliary Enterprises—Enterprise Square," OACH.

121. "Soviet Students Visit ESUSA While in States," *Report from Enterprise Square, USA* 2 (Summer 1990): 3.

122. "Rowland to Retire from Position at OC," *Edmond [OK] Evening Sun,* September 13, 1990, B2.

123. "Where Do You See ESUSA? Everywhere," *Report from Enterprise Square, USA* 1 (Summer 1989): 3.

124. Oklahoma Christian College, "Want a Business Education? Take a Look at Oklahoma Christian College" [undated recruiting pamphlet], folder "Colleges, Business, 195?–1999," OACH.

10. Students in Free Enterprise

1. The 1909 Mondell Act doubled the homestead allotment from 160 to 320 acres, making farming on arid lands seem just plausible enough to lure thousands of newcomers to bankruptcy.

2. Gil Henshaw, *Lea, New Mexico's Last Frontier* (Hobbs, NM: *Hobbs Daily News-Sun,* 1976), 109, 193–218; Gailanne Dill, "Lea County: Diversifying as It Grows," *New Mexico Business Journal,* September 1977.

3. SIFE, "1989 Expo Winners," *SL* 5, no. 1 (Summer 1989): 20.

4. Carol Hymowitz, "Independent Program Puts College Students on Leadership Path," *WSJ,* January 14, 2003.

5. Stephanie Armour, "While Hiring at Most Firms Chills, Wal-Mart's Heats Up," *USAToday.com,* August 25, 2002.

6. www.sife.org, accessed April 25, 2006.

7. Ryan Olson, "Students Bullish About Building Businesses," *Enterprise Record* [Chico, CA], April 3, 2005.

8. SIFE, *SL* 5, no. 1 (Summer 1989).

9. Ibid.; direct quotation from Suzanne Alford.

10. Karl H. Vesper, *Entrepreneurship Education 1985* (Wellesley, MA: Center for Entrepreneurial Studies, Babson College, 1985), xii.

11. I take this term from Amanda Ciafone and Mandi Jackson, with thanks.

12. James Gilbert, *A Cycle of Outrage: America's Reaction to the Juvenile Delinquent in the 1950s* (New York: Oxford University Press, 1986), 29, 63–66; Austin L. Porterfield, *Youth in Trouble: Studies in Delinquency and Despair,* Publications in the Social Sciences (Fort Worth: The Leo Potishman Foundation, 1946), 38.

13. "Brief History . . . Big Progress," *TLEF* 1, no. 1 (February 1957); "Millionth

Crimemobile Visitor Feted in Mineral Wells," *TLEF* 1, no. 6 (July 1957): 1; "Crimemobile Supervisor Bill Squier . . . [photo caption]," *TLEF* 1, no. 8 (September 1957): 3.

14. Robert T. Davis, "Biographical Information on Robert T. (Sonny) Davis," unpublished paper in author's possession (2005); the author is very grateful to Mr. Davis for supplying this and other relevant documents.

15. Waggoner Carr, "Attorney General's Youth Conference 1964 Summary Report," Mss. 2225, A24008 V88 1964 Sum.c.1, Texas State Library, Austin, Texas, 2.

16. Ernestine Wheelock, "Travis County Youth Council: Teenagers Grow 'Taller' in New Self-Help Project," undated clipping, *AA,* folder "Texas Youth Conference (4th: 1966: Austin Tex.)," -Q-HQ 796 T459 1966 TXC, Center for American History, University of Texas, Austin, Texas; Don Adams, "Beginning Here Today: Nationwide Interest Shown in Texas Youth Conference," *AA,* August 18, 1966.

17. John Masher, "Youth Program Urged for Texas," *Dallas News,* April 2, 1960. Despite the acclaim, however, the Texas approach was not unique; see William Graebner, *The Engineering of Consent: Democracy and Authority in Twentieth-Century America* (Madison: University of Wisconsin Press, 1987), 142–43, 168–80.

18. Jane Srygley Mouton and Robert R. Blake, *Synergogy: A New Strategy for Education, Training, and Development* (San Francisco: Jossey-Bass Publishers, 1984), 5; for the authors' place among the human relations theorists of the postwar years, see Kurt W. Back, *Beyond Words: The Story of Sensitivity Training and the Encounter Movement,* 2nd ed. (New Brunswick, NJ: Transaction, 1987), 164; Stephen P. Waring, *Taylorism Transformed: Scientific Management Theory Since 1945* (Chapel Hill: University of North Carolina Press, 1991), 109–15.

19. Davis, "Biographical Information on Robert T. (Sonny) Davis"; Mauro F. Guillén, *Models of Management: Work, Authority, and Organization in a Comparative Perspective* (Chicago: University of Chicago Press, 1994), 64–65.

20. Paul Rothaus and Robert T. Davis, *The Art of Leadership, A manual for group leaders developed by the National Leadership Institute under a grant from the Humble Oil Education Foundation* (Austin, TX: National Leadership Institute, 1968), [unpaginated].

21. Patricia Evridge Hill, *Dallas: The Making of a Modern City* (Austin, TX: University of Texas Press, 1996), 129–61.

22. Darwin Payne, *Big D: Triumphs and Troubles of an American Supercity in the 20th Century,* rev. ed. (Dallas: Three Forks Press, 2000), 328.

23. Michael V. Hazel, *Dallas: A History of the "Big D",* Fred Rider Cotton Popular History Series, no. 11 (Austin, TX: Texas State Historical Association, 1997), 53; Payne, *Big D,* 354–56.

24. Harold F. Boss, *How Green the Grazing: 75 Years at Southwestern Life, 1903–1978* (Dallas: Taylor Publishing Company, 1978), 272–75, 282–83; Payne, *Big D,* 13–16.

25. Joe Simnacher, "Margaret Mary 'Margie' Gurley Seay: Taught Bible Classes to Many at HP Church," *Dallas Morning News,* February 24, 2006.

26. D. W. Nauss, "Retiring Bill Seay Remains on Deck," *Dallas Times-Herald,* October 4, 1984, 1; Rosalie McGinnis, "Love for Dallas Changed Career," *Houston Post,* undated clipping, vertical file "William H. Seay," Center for American History, University of Texas, Austin, Texas; "Noted Texan Seay, 77, Dies," *AA,* April 14, 1997.

27. Boss, *How Green the Grazing,* 283–84.

28. Student response quoted in "We Say: Fantastic! Students Say: Fantastic!" *Southwestern Life News,* May/June 1975, 31; Denny Griswold, [untitled], *Public Relations News,* XXVII, no. 5 (February, 1971), 4.

29. Davis, "Biographical Information on Robert T. (Sonny) Davis."

30. Boss, *How Green the Grazing,* 285.

31. Ibid.

32. Jim Rountree, "Communications: How Others See Us," *WMW,* November 1978, 3.

33. Lizabeth Cohen, *A Consumer's Republic: The Politics of Mass Consumption in Postwar America* (New York: Vintage Books, 2003), 346, 357–63.

34. Ralph Nader, Mark Green, and Joel Seligman, *Taming the Giant Corporation: How the Largest Corporations Control Our Lives* (New York: W.W. Norton, 1976).

35. John R. Duke, Jr., "American Studies: Improving a College, Improving a Nation," unpublished paper in author's possession (Harding University, 1997), Appendix A, "List of Speakers," p. 15.

36. Thomas Byrne Edsall, *The New Politics of Inequality* (New York: W.W. Norton, 1984), 113.

37. Morton Mintz, "GM, Ford Units Criticized on WWII Role," *WP,* February 27, 1974, A4; Associated Press, "High Court Rebuffs Author," *NYT,* April 17, 1984, C16.

38. Edsall, *The New Politics of Inequality,* 113.

39. Louis E. Davis, "Changing Values in the Workplace," in George A. Steiner, *Business and Its Environment* (Los Angeles: University of California, 1977), 262.

40. Bennett Harrison and Barry Bluestone, *The Great U-Turn: Corporate Restructuring and the Polarizing of America* (New York: Basic Books, 1988), 5–8; and see above, Chapter 8, n. 1.

41. SIFE, *Students in Free Enterprise 1980–81 National Competition,* Program, Austin, Texas, 1981.

42. Ibid.

43. Edsall, *The New Politics of Inequality,* 121–25, 128.

44. Kim Moody, *An Injury to All: The Decline of American Unionism* (New York: Verso, 1988), 128–30; Marc Linder, *Wars of Attrition: Vietnam, the Business*

Roundtable, and the Decline of Construction Unions 2nd rev. ed. (Iowa City: Fănpìhuà Press, 2000); David C. Korten, *When Corporations Rule the World* (West Hartford, CT: Kumarian Press and Berrett Kohler, 1995), 143–44.

45. This account of the Business Roundtable's defeat of labor reform is based on Sar A. Levitan and Martha R. Cooper, *Business Lobbies: The Public Good and the Bottom Line* (Baltimore: Johns Hopkins University Press, 1984), 121–35.

46. Sam Walton, "Message from Sam Walton," *WMW*, February 1978, 2; see also Jim Rountree, "Communications: Let's Stand Up and Be Counted," *WMW*, April 1978, 3.

47. "How to Write a Letter to Your Congressman," *WMW*, July 1978, 7.

48. Levitan and Cooper, *Business Lobbies*, 120–36, 52, 54.

49. Burton Yale Pines, *Back to Basics: The Traditionalist Movement that Is Sweeping America* (New York: William Morrow, 1982), 61.

50. Mayme Lucille Hamlett, *To Noonday Bright: The Story of Southwest Baptist University 1878–1984* (Bolivar, MO: Southwest Baptist University, 1984), 1–4, 316–17; www.sbuniv.edu/library/uarchive/timeln1.htm, accessed April 7, 2006.

51. Interview with Dr. James Sells, March 17, 2005.

52. Hamlett, *To Noonday Bright*, 344–45.

53. Interview with Dr. James Sells, March 17, 2005.

54. Ibid.

55. Ibid.

56. "Gene Taylor National Free Enterprise Center Dedication Ceremony," University Archives, Hutchens Library of Southwest Baptist University, Bolivar, Missouri (1982).

57. Students in Free Enterprise, *National Conference Program* (Bolivar, MO, 1984); Alvin Rohrs, "Open-Space Zoning and the Taking Clause: A Two-Part Test," *Missouri Law Review* 46 (1981): 868–74.

58. John Kerr, "Pass It On," *Inc.*, December 1995, 100–102; at www.inc.com/magazine/19951201/2515.html, accessed December 10, 2008.

59. Ibid.; interview with Dr. James Sells, March 17, 2005.

60. Kerr, "Pass It On."

61. Pines, *Back to Basics*, 62. Justin Dart was a close friend of Reagan's dating from the latter's years as the governor of California. He became heavily involved in the Business Roundtable during the 1970s, and in association with the National Federation of Independent Business, the National Association of Manufacturers, and the U.S. Chamber of Commerce, Dart established the Center for the Study of Private Enterprise at the University of Southern California.

62. SIFE, *National Conference Program*.

63. Ibid.

64. Frances Frank Marcus, "New Orleans Hotel Business Depressed Since Fair," *NYT,* June 25, 1985; Allen R. Myerson, "A Big Casino Wager That Hasn't Paid Off," *NYT,* June 2, 1996.

65. SIFE, *National Conference Program.*

66. Christopher Elliott, "For Passengers, a Weary Feeling of Bankruptcy Fatigue," *NYT,* September 15, 2005; Melvin A. Brenner, "It's Time to Rethink Deregulation," *NYT,* December 3, 1992. Pan Am collapsed in 1991.

67. SIFE, *National Conference Program.*

68. "New Staff Members Lead SIFE Recruiting Efforts," *SL* (Summer–Fall 1985), 3; "SIFE Incentive Encourages Creativity," *SL* (Summer–Fall 1985), 3; "SIFE Video Tape Available for Loan," *SL* (Summer–Fall 1985), 6; "Recruitment: 1985 Drive Begins in Early Summer," *SL* (Summer–Fall 1985), back cover.

69. Interview with Dr. James Sells; SIFE, "Leaders of the Ozark . . .," *SL* (Summer–Fall 1985), 3.

70. Bob Ortega, *In Sam We Trust: The Untold Story of Sam Walton and How Wal-Mart Is Devouring America* (New York: Times Business, 1998), 94.

71. Ortega, *In Sam We Trust,* 94, 101.

72. J. Mark Holmes, "SIFE Board Meeting," memo to SIFE corporate sponsors, University Archives, Hutchens Library of Southwest Baptist University, Bolivar, Missouri.

73. SIFE, "Chairman's Club Formed," *SL* 1, no. 2 (Winter 1985): 3.

74. SIFE, "Wal-Mart Fellowships Announced," *SL* 2, no. 2 (Winter 1987): 11.

75. SIFE, "Tenth Anniversary International Exposition," program (Memphis, TN, 1986).

76. Kerr, "Pass It On."

77. "Wal-Mart is #1 with SIFE," *SL,* Spring 1991, 6–7.

78. Lubbock Christian University Students in Free Enterprise, "Free Enterprise: America's Rx for Success," in SIFE, *1988/89 Training Manual* (Springfield, MO: SIFE, 1988).

79. Debbie Howell, "SIFE Nears 25th Anniversary of Preparing Business Execs," *DSN* 38, no. 12 (June 21, 1999): 19.

11. "Students Changing the World"

1. SIFE, *All About Economic Freedom,* videotape recording (1989).

2. SIFE, "SIFE Has Record Year—Again!" *A Year in Review* (1991): 1.

3. For the Friedmans' own recollections of this project, see Milton Friedman and Rose D. Friedman, *Two Lucky People: Memoirs* (Chicago: University of Chicago Press, 1998), 471–515; quotation from p. 471.

4. Mary Sennholz, "Leonard Read, the Founder and Builder," *Freeman* 46, no. 5 (May 1996), 348–54.

5. Ibid.

6. Richard Cockett, *Thinking the Unthinkable: Think-Tanks and the Economic Counter-Revolution, 1931–1983* (London: Fontana Press, 1995), 109.

7. Elizabeth A. Fones-Wolf, *Selling Free Enterprise: The Business Assault on Labor and Liberalism, 1945–60,* History of Communication (Urbana: University of Illinois Press, 1994), 195–96.

8. Leonard E. Read, "I, Pencil," reprinted in *Freeman* 46, no. 5 (May 1996), 274–278.

9. SIFE, "1990 Fifteenth Anniversary International Exposition Recap," *SL* 6, no. 1 (Summer 1990): 19.

10. William Walstead and Michael Watts, "Teaching Economics in the Schools: A Review of Survey Findings," *JEE* 13, no. 2 (Spring 1985): 135–46.

11. Debra Phillips, "Higher Learning: For Students in SIFE, Learning Is Anything but Business as Usual," *Entrepreneur,* March 1998, 44.

12. SIFE, "1986 Fall Workshops Prepare Students for SIFE Success," *SL* 2, no. 2 (Winter 1987): 7.

13. SIFE, *Students in Free Enterprise,* videotape recording (1990).

14. SIFE, *Salute to Students in Free Enterprise,* videotape recording (c. 1991).

15. SIFE, "SIFE Q&A," *SL* 2, no. 1 (Summer 1986): 2.

16. SIFE, "Leadership Training Key to SIFE Performance," *SL* 1, no. 2 (Winter 1985): 3.

17. SIFE, "Training Motivates Students for SIFE Success," *SL* 1, no. 2 (Winter 1985): 5.

18. SIFE, "1986 Fall Workshops," *SL* 2, no. 2 (Winter 1987): 4.

19. SIFE, "John Bates Retires," *SL* 3, no. 1 (Summer 1987): 9.

20. Donald P. Diffine, "Launching and Sustaining a SIFE Program," in SIFE, *1988/89 Training Manual* (Springfield, MO: SIFE, 1988), 43.

21. SIFE, "Recruitment Successful for 85–86 Academic Year," *SL* 1, no. 2 (Winter 1985): 2.

22. SIFE, "SIFE Q&A," 2.

23. Ibid.

24. SIFE, *Salute to Students in Free Enterprise.*

25. From the American Citizenship Center program 1968–69, quoted in W. O. Beeman, *Oklahoma Christian College: Dream to Reality: The Story of the First Twenty Years, 1950–1970* (Delight, AR: Gospel Light Publishing Company, 1970), 148–149.

26. SIFE, "Coors Becomes SIFE Lines Sponsor," *SL* 1, no. 3 (Spring 1986): 2.

27. SIFE, "New Contributors Info," *SL* 1, no. 3 (Spring 1986). The contributors list for the spring of 1986 put the Adolph Coors Company in the $5,000 to $10,000

range and the Adolph Coors Foundation in the $1,000 to $5,000 range. Although these were significant donations to SIFE of the 1980s, it is important to put them in perspective. The Adolph Coors Foundation gave an initial $250,000 to the Paul Weyrich project that became the Heritage Foundation. In other words, Coors was a major funder of SIFE, but SIFE was not a major recipient of Coors funding.

28. SIFE, "Halliday/Acers Boost SIFE in Southwest Region," *SL* 1, no. 2 (Winter 1985): 3.

29. SIFE, "SIFE Receives Six-Figure Gift from Congressman Rudd," *SL* 3, no. 1 (Summer 1987): 2.

30. SIFE, "Standard Oil New Sponsor," *SL* 1, no. 3 (Spring 1986): 2.

31. http://www.sife.org/united_states/support/recognition/plaster_building.asp, accessed June 11, 2006.

32. SIFE, "SIFE Q&A," 2.

33. SIFE, "Comments from SIFE President Alvin Rohrs," *SL* 2, no. 1 (Summer 1986): 7.

34. Rick Alm, "One of KC's Top Conventions Says Farewell," *Kansas City Star,* May 20, 2006.

35. SIFE, "Interviews Set for Exposition," *SL* 1, no. 3 (Spring 1986): 5.

36. SIFE, "A Letter of Thanks from a SIFE Student," *SL* 1, no. 3 (Spring 1986): 6.

37. SIFE, "Near Misses . . . SIFE Students Do Succeed," *SL* 2, no. 1 (Summer 1986): 3.

38. SIFE, "Comments from SIFE President Alvin Rohrs," 7.

39. SIFE, "SIFE Connection Leads to Student Becoming an Entrepreneur," *SL* 2, no. 2 (Winter 1987): 4.

40. SIFE, "SIFE Pays Off in Dividends," *SL* 3, no. 1 (Summer 1987): 3.

41. SIFE, *All About Economic Freedom.*

42. Ronald Reagan, "Remarks at the Los Angeles, California, County Board of Supervisors' Town Meeting," March 3, 1982; "Grace Commission Chairman Addresses Ozarks Banquet," *SL,* Summer–Fall 1985, 6. The Grace Commission's findings included recommendations that the federal government outsource more work to private contractors, reduce welfare and Social Security benefits, and make Defense Department bidding more competitive. Separate reviews by the Congressional Budget Office and the General Accounting Office deemed its conclusions exaggerations, and its recommendations for closing unnecessary military facilities politically unfeasible. "Ads by Grace Back Cuts in U.S. Budget," *NYT,* December 11, 1984, A-28. Andrew Schneider, "A Town Left to Die" and "The History of W.R. Grace & Company," both in the *Seattle Post-Intelligencer,* November 18, 1999; Andrew Schneider, "W.R. Grace Indicted on Asbestos Deaths," *Seattle Post-Intelligencer,* February 8, 2005.

43. "Students Fight Government Waste," *SL,* Summer–Fall 1985, 7.

44. SIFE, "Business Roundtable Donates 'Halt the Deficit' Materials," *SL* 1, no. 2 (Winter 1985): 2.

45. Anahad O'Conner, "James Keogh, 89, Who Was *Time* Editor and Wordsmith for Nixon, Dies," *NYT,* May 14, 2006.

46. Robert Kaiser, "Big Business Moving to Get Off the Bandwagon of Reaganomics," *WP,* March 29, 1982, A8; quoted in Sar A. Levitan and Martha R. Cooper, *Business Lobbies: The Public Good and the Bottom Line* (Baltimore: Johns Hopkins University Press, 1984), 59–60. Sidney Blumenthal, "Whose Side Is Business on, Anyway?" *NYT Magazine,* October 25, 1981, 29. Howell Raines, "President Terms Views of Business a Disappointment," *NYT,* March 19, 1982, A1; Howell Raines, "Executives Bid Reagan Cut Deficit," *NYT,* March 13, 1982, section 2, p. 31.

47. David W. Schumann, Jan M. Hathcote, and Susan West, "Corporate Advertising in America: A Review of Published Studies on Use, Measurement, and Effectiveness," *Journal of Advertising* 20, no. 3 (1991): 52; Edwin McDowell, "Why the Digest, Finally, Wants to Make Money," *NYT,* February 9, 1986. "Business Roundtable; Americans Send Postcards Urging Action on the Federal Deficit," *Business Wire,* April 24, 1985.

48. For an overview of these changes, see Leslie Wayne, "The New Face of Business Leadership," *NYT,* May 22, 1983.

49. SIFE, "Grant Made Available by the Business Roundtable," *SL* 1, no. 3 (Spring 1986): 3.

50. SIFE, *Students in Free Enterprise.*

51. SIFE, "Student Project: Lubbock Christian College," *SL* 1, no. 3 (Spring 1986): 6.

52. SIFE, "Tenth Anniversary Exposition Recap," *SL* 2, no. 1 (Summer 1986): 6.

53. SIFE, "Near Misses . . . Outstanding Outreach Programs," *SL* 3, no. 1 (Summer 1987): 15.

54. SIFE, "The Business Roundtable Halt the Deficit Winners," *SL* 5, no. 1 (Summer 1989): 27.

55. SIFE, "The Business Roundtable Halt the Deficit Awards $1,000 Each," *SL* 4, no. 1 (Summer 1988): 22.

56. SIFE, "Near Misses . . . Outstanding Outreach Programs," 15.

57. SIFE, *1988/89 Training Manual,* 27.

58. "Everybody's Business," *WMW,* January 1992, 28–29. From his experience organizing small groups around the country with Campus Crusade for Christ, Burkett founded Christian Financial Concepts in 1976 to offer advice on "Biblical principles of handling money." In addition to several bestsellers on Christian money management, Burkett hosted four radio programs carried on over one thousand stations. http://www.crown.org/larry/biography.asp.

59. Clay Chandler, "Opportunity Has Passed for Deficit Deal, Many Experts Fear; Calls for a Balanced Budget Fade in Election Debate as Interest Rates Rise," *WP,* March 20, 1996, D1.

60. Arnold H. Lubasch, "200 Million Agent Orange Settlement Is Upheld by U.S.

Appeals Court," *NYT,* April 22, 1987, B3. The decision did not consider the connection between Agent Orange and the veterans' injuries proved, and it pointed out the complicating factor of the government's potential culpability in ordering Agent Orange be used.

61. An investigation by a House committee concluded in 1984 that "During 1981, 1982, and 1983, top-level officials of the Environmental Protection Agency violated their public trust by disregarding the public health and environment, manipulating the Superfund program for political purposes, engaging in unethical conduct, and participating in other abuses." Quoted in Haynes Bonner Johnson, *Sleepwalking Through History: America in the Reagan Years* (New York: Anchor Books, 1992), 171. As Johnson points out, the chemical industry was particularly conspicuous in the EPA's misconduct during the early Reagan years. For relevant examples, see "EPA Official Resigns; Role of Dow Chemical Cited," *CSM,* May 2, 1983, 2; Philip Shabecoff, "Acting E.P.A. Chief Is Said to Be Ready to Quit Post Today," *NYT,* March 25, 1983, A1; Robert Jr. Kilborn, "US Chemical Industry Decides to Clean Up Its Deteriorating Image," *CSM,* December 8, 1983, 8.

62. Stuart Diamond, "Insurance Against Pollution Is Cut," *NYT,* March 11, 1985, A1.

63. "The Dow Chemical Company Liability Crisis Awards $500 Each," *SL* 4, no. 1 (Summer 1988): 22; Chemical Manufacturers Association, "Exhibit B: CMA Grassroots System Progress Report," appended to "Agenda—Meeting of CMA Board of Directors," October 21, 1985, MCMA, doc. no. CMA 074512-CMA 074513, CIA.

64. Daniel B. Moskowitz, "The Chemical Industry Fights for Tort Reform," *CW,* March 19, 1986, 76; Daniel B. Moskowitz, "State Tort Reform: A Faster Track," *CW,* March 18, 1987, 16.

65. "Chemical Manufacturers Association State Affairs Committee Annual Report to the CMA Board of Directors," September 15, 1986, MCMA, doc. no. CMA 075891, CIA.

66. "Chemical Manufacturers Association State Affairs Committee," November 13, 1986, MCMA doc. no. 084390, CIA.

67. "Chalk Up Some Victories for Tort Reform," *CW,* July 1, 1987, 40.

68. SIFE, *1988/89 Training Manual,* 21.

69. "The Dow Chemical Company Liability Crisis Awards $500 Each," 22.

70. Lubbock Christian University SIFE, "Free Enterprise: America's Rx for Success," in SIFE, *1988/89 Training Manual* [appendix], p. 5.

71. Lubbock Christian University SIFE, "Free Enterprise: America's Rx for Success," in SIFE, *1988/89 Training Manual.*

72. SIFE of Southern Illinois University, [untitled report], SIFE, *1988/89 Training Manual* [appendix], 2.

73. SIFE, "Student Project: State Fair Community College," *SL* 1, no. 3 (Spring 1986):

7; Al Slavin, "Budd Co. Buys Missouri Aluminum Company," *Crain's Detroit Business*, June 5, 2000, 50.

74. Joel Kotkin, "Made in USA," *Inc.*, March 1985, 48.

75. SIFE, Salute to Students in Free Enterprise; SIFE, *1988/89 Training Manual*, 29; Don P. Diffine, "Launching and Sustaining a SIFE Program," 44.

76. SIFE, *1988/89 Training Manual*, 22, 24; for additional examples of this widespread practice, see also SIFE, "Tenth Anniversary Exposition Recap," 5; SIFE, "Near Misses: Outstanding Outreach Programs," 15.

77. SIFE, "Near Misses . . . Outstanding Outreach Programs," 15.

78. Professor John Bates, Kent State University, quoted in SIFE, "John Bates Retires," *SL* 3, no. 1 (Summer 1987), 9.

79. SIFE, "You'll be Missed, Professor Dykes," *SL* 2, no. 1 (Summer 1986): [back cover].

80. Ronald Alsop, "Capitalism 101: Programs to Teach Free Enterprise Sprout on College Campuses," *WSJ*, May 10, 1978, 1.

81. Michael L. King, "Corporations Back Campus Missionaries for Free Enterprise," *WSJ*, June 21, 1979, 1.

82. SIFE, "1986 Fall Workshops Prepare Students for SIFE Success," 8; SIFE, "John Bates Retires," 9.

83. SIFE, "Meet SIFE Faculty Advisors," *SL* 2, no. 2 (Winter 1987): 5.

84. Peggy D. Keck, "Analysis of the Areas of Money Management Dealt with in the Holy Bible" (Ph.D. diss., University of Oklahoma, 1968).

85. SIFE, "Finalist Awards—Holiday Inns, Inc. $1,500 Each," *SL* 3, no. 1 (Summer 1987): 16.

86. Harding University Students in Free Enterprise, "Stars and Stripes Forever."

87. "Students in Free Enterprise of Southern Illinois University" in SIFE, *1988/89 Training Manual*.

88. SIFE, "National Federation of Independent Business," *SL* 2, no. 1 (Summer 1986): 11.

89. Interview with Alvin Rohrs, *Nation's Business Today*, May 5, 1989.

90. Ibid.

91. SIFE, "SIFE Opens Operations Center in Springfield," *SL* 2, no. 2 (Winter 1987): 4.

92. R. Heath Larry, 1978, quoted in Thomas Byrne Edsall, *The New Politics of Inequality* (New York: W.W. Norton & Co., 1984), 108; Levitan and Cooper, *Business Lobbies*, 51.

93. Executive Vice President W. Dean Cannon, Jr., in *Savings and Loan News*, September, 1978, p. 66; quoted in Edsall, *The New Politics of Inequality*, 115.

94. Levitan and Cooper, *Business Lobbies*, 51.

95. Burton Yale Pines, *Back to Basics* (New York: William Morrow and Company, 1982), 246–47.

96. Kara Isham, "Jackie Clifford Shewmaker Store of Knowledge," *ADG*, August 29, 2004.

97. Bob Ortega, *In Sam We Trust: The Untold Story of Sam Walton and How Wal-Mart Is Devouring America* (New York: Times Business, 1998), 129–31.

98. Isham, "Jackie Clifford Shewmaker Store of Knowledge."

99. "Pacific Dunlop Limited and GNB, Inc," *PR Newswire*, October 5, 1987.

100. Cynthia Grenier, "Conquering of the Capital," *Washington Times*, April 29, 1995, B2.

101. Mrs. Gaines joined GOPAC in 1985, and chaired it from 1993 to 1997. On her career, see *Bush's $800,000 Pledge Break* (Washington, DC: Common Cause, 2003). Paul Farhi, "Kenneth Tomlinson Quits Public Broadcasting Board," *WP*, November 4, 2005, C1. Tom O'Meilia, "GOP Activist Gets Public Media Post," *Palm Beach [FL] Post*, September 28, 2005, 13A; Ken Auletta, "Big Bird Flies Right: How Republicans Learned to Love PBS," *New Yorker*, June 7, 2004, 42–48.

102. Gay Hart Gaines, "Rep. Gingrich's Generosity," *WP*, May 14, 1994, A22.

103. Gay Hart Gaines, "GOPAC as a Target of Opportunity," *WP*, July 14, 1995, A21.

104. Gay Hart Gaines, "GOPAC Trains Leaders in Conservative Ideals," *NYT*, September 7, 1994, A22.

105. From a 1990 GOPAC memo to Republican candidates entitled "Language: A Key Mechanism of Control"; quoted in David Corn, "Gingrich-izing Public Broadcasting," September 27, 2005, http://www.thenation.com/blogs/capitalgames.

106. The Public Affairs Council was founded in 1954 as the Effective Citizens' Organization (ECO), with backing from General Electric and Standard Oil, among many other corporate powerhouses. Its mission was to foster greater corporate involvement in politics.

107. SIFE, "New Contributors Info," 8; Lou Dubose, Jan Reid, and Carl M. Cannon, *Boy Genius: Karl Rove, the Brains Behind the Remarkable Political Triumph of George W. Bush* (New York: PublicAffairs, 2003), 19–20, 21–22.

108. SIFE, "Seven New SIFE Board Members Elected," *SL*, Spring 1991, 13; http://www.mosportshalloffame.com/inducteebio, accessed June 1, 2006.

109. Lubbock Christian University SIFE, "Free Enterprise: America's Rx for Success."

110. Harding University SIFE, "Stars and Stripes Forever."

111. Diffine, "Launching and Sustaining a SIFE Program."

112. SIFE, *Annual Report* (Springfield, MO, 1989), 4.

113. Jaan Van Valkenburgh, "'Hero,' Other Students Go to Bat for Business at Meet," *Commercial Appeal [Memphis, TN]*, April 18, 1996, 9B.

114. SIFE, "SIFE Alumni Enjoy High Achievements," *SL*, Spring 1991, 14.

115. John Kerr, "Pass It On," *Inc.*, December 1995.

116. "Students in Free Enterprise Opens Doors in Business," *Chain Drug Review*, October 14, 2002, 90.

117. Ronald Reagan, "Address to Members of the British Parliament," June 8, 1982.

118. SIFE, "1988 International Exposition Recap," *SL* 4, no. 1 (Summer 1988): 20.

119. SIFE, *1988/89 Training Manual*, 24.

120. SIFE, *1988/89 Training Manual*, 21. Pan American is now known as the University of Texas–Pan American.

121. http://www.atlasusa.org/directory/institute_profile.php?refer=directory&org_id=77; accessed June 13, 2006.

122. Joseph L. McCarthy, "Monterrey Miracle," *Chief Executive*, July 1, 1993.

123. Cárdenas quoted in translation in Sarah Babb, *Managing Mexico: Economists from Nationalism to Neoliberalism* (Princeton: Princeton University Press, 2001), 70.

124. McCarthy, "Monterrey Miracle."

125. J. Rolando Espinosa Ramirez, "Desarrollo Histórico de la Intervención Estatal en la Economía Mexicana," in *La Falacia de la Economía Mixta Mexicana*, ed. J. Rolando Espinosa Ramirez, Ludwig von Mises, and Óscar H. Ver Ferrer (Mexico: Centro de estudios en economía y educación, A.C., 1989), 31.

126. SIFE, "Finalist Awards—Holiday Corporation $1,500 Each," *SL* 2, no. 1 (Summer 1986): 8.

127. This was Soon Young Choi, owner of the Shindongah business group and chairman of Korea Life Insurance. On his career, see Soo-Jeong Lee, "South Korean Tycoon Alleges Bribes Were Given to Kazakstan's President," *AP Newswires*, November 5, 2001; Lee Sung-yul, "Shindongah Group Chairman Sentenced to 5-Year Jail Term," *Korea Herald*, July 28, 1999; "Court Rules Korea Life is Free to Try to Revitalize Itself," *AsiaPulse News*, August 31, 1999; Kwak Young-sup, "U.S. Investment Fund Panacom Competing to Acquire Korea Life," *Korea Herald*, May 28, 1999; John Burton, "Korea Life Auction Aborted After Axa and MetLife Quit," *Financial Times*, May 20, 1999, 33; "Former Shindongah Head Gets Longer Jail Term for Capital Flight," *Asia Africa Intelligence Wire*, January 5, 2005.

128. SIFE, *Salute to Students in Free Enterprise*.

129. SIFE, "SIFE Goes Global," *A Year in Review* (1991): 5.

130. Stanley N. Gaines, "Chairman's Letter," SIFE, *Annual Report* (Springfield, MO, 1990).

12. On a Mission

1. Paul Harvey, "Latin Youth Is a Sam Walton Success," updated clipping, vertical file "John Brown University," Special Collections, University of Arkansas Libraries, Fayetteville, AR.

2. John Williamson, "What Washington Means by Policy Reform," in Williamson, ed., *Latin American Economic Adjustment: How Much Has Happened?* (Washing-

ton, DC: Institute for International Economics, 1990), 7–20; Ronald Reagan on magic quoted in Walter Lafeber, *Inevitable Revolutions: The United States in Central America*, 2nd ed. (New York: W.W. Norton, 1993), 285.

3. Peter H. Smith, *Talons of the Eagle: Dynamics of U.S.-Latin American Relations* (New York: Oxford University Press, 1996), 236–42.

4. Sara Diamond, *Spiritual Warfare: The Politics of the Christian Right* (Boston: South End Press, 1989), 164–72; Virginia Garrard-Burnett, *Protestantism in Guatemala: Living in the New Jerusalem* (Austin: University of Texas Press, 1998), 120, 140, 157; Greg Grandin, *Empire's Workshop: Latin America, the United States, and the Rise of the New Imperialism* (New York: Metropolitan Books, 2006), 124–29, 150–56; David Stoll, *Is Latin America Turning Protestant? The Politics of Evangelical Growth* (Berkeley: University of California Press, 1990), 180–93; Manuel A. Vásquez and Marie Friedman Marquardt, *Globalizing the Sacred: Religion Across the Americas* (New Brunswick, NJ: Rutgers University Press, 2003), 197–223; Office of Public Diplomacy quoted in Grandin, 124.

5. Grandin, *Empire's Workshop*, 71.

6. Brenda J. McClain, "Waltons Donate $3.6 Million for Central American Scholarships," Press release, May 20, 1985, vertical file "Sam Walton," Special Collections, University of Arkansas Libraries, Fayetteville, Arkansas, 2.

7. "Waltons Give $3.6 Million," *AG*, May 21, 1985, 1A.

8. *The Report of the President's National Bipartisan Commission on Central America;* Foreword by Henry A. Kissinger (New York: MacMillan Publishing, 1984), 119.

9. *The Report of the President's National Bipartisan Commission on Central America,* 113; see also the account in William M. LeoGrande, *Our Own Backyard: The United States in Central America, 1977–1992* (Chapel Hill: University of North Carolina Press, 1998), 246–50.

10. *The Report of the President's National Bipartisan Commission on Central America,* 64.

11. From 1950 to 1979, land devoted to growing two major export crops alone— sugar and cotton—grew almost tenfold, which in turn swelled the population of landless peasants by 300 percent. By 1978, the ratio of land under export cultivation to land under subsistence production was ninety to one; child malnutrition soared, growing 51 percent in Nicaragua and 46 percent in El Salvador in the decade following 1965. Christian Smith, *Resisting Reagan: The U.S. Central America Peace Movement* (Chicago: University of Chicago Press, 1996), 9–10, table 1.1.

12. *The Report of the President's National Bipartisan Commission on Central America,* 86–87; LeoGrande, *Our Own Backyard: The United States in Central America, 1977–1992,* 67. On the changes in educational funding that encouraged private-sector involvement, see Michael Mumper and Pamela Vander Ark, "Evaluating

the Stafford Student Loan Program: Current Problems and Prospects for Reform," *JHE* 62, no. 1 (January–February 1991): 65–66; Deborah A. Verstegen, "Education Fiscal Policy in the Reagan Administration," *Educational Evaluation and Policy Analysis* (1990): 360–63, 369; Dru Shockley, "New Legislation Tightens Student Federal Aid," *TA* 53, no. 3 (November 6, 1986): 4.

13. "Waltons Give $3.6 Million," 1A.

14. Interview with Professor Rickey J. Casey, August 5, 2002.

15. Larry Rohter, "Gabriel Lewis Galindo, 68, Veteran Panamanian Diplomat," *NYT*, January 1, 1997, 47; *America Weekly Report,* December 21, 1979, 86; "Gabriel Lewis Galindo," *The [Glasgow] Herald,* December 26, 1996, 20; Linda Feldman, "Noriega Opposition-in-Exile Becomes Lobbying Force in US," *CSM,* March 7, 1988, 3.

16. The Walton family later became major donors to the University of Arkansas.

17. "Helen Walton . . . Leadership and Dedication," *ME,* November 4, 1983, 3. On the connection between Stephens and Lewis Galindo, see Frederick Kempe, *Divorcing the Dictator: America's Bungled Affair with Noriega* (New York: G.P. Putnam's Sons, 1990), 219, 227.

18. "New Program Established," *ME,* September 19, 1985, 1.

19. Kirkpatrick quoted in LeoGrande, *Our Own Backyard: The United States in Central America, 1977–1992,* 581.

20. "Waltons Give $3.6 Million," 6A.

21. Marcia Hernandez, "Foreign Students Adjusting to Culture Change," *TA,* November 8, 1985, 7.

22. "Waltons Give $3.6 Million," 1A.

23. Interview with Professor Rickey J. Casey, August 5, 2002. The Moravian church was the institutional vehicle for indigenous Miskitu opposition to the Sandinistas, an armed resistance that Susan Hawley argues was deeply grounded in Moravian Protestantism; Susan Hawley, "Protestantism and Indigenous Mobilisation: The Moravian Church among the Miskitu Indians of Nicaragua," *Journal of Latin American Studies* 29, no. 1, (February 1997), 11–29.

24. Cindy Parrish, "Brown, Rudd Travel South of the Border," *TA,* April 8, 1987, 1.

25. Tim Peter, "Sanford to Recruit Walton Students," *TA,* April 26, 1991, 7; Amy L. Sherman, *The Soul of Development: Biblical Christianity and Economic Transformation in Guatemala* (New York: Oxford University Press, 1997), 141.

26. Raquel Ventura, "Rev. Munos [sic] Speaks," *ME,* March 23, 1988, unpaginated.

27. David Tucker, David R. Sanford, and Rickey J. Casey, *Walton Central America Scholarship Program Director's Manual* (1992), 10.

28. Interview with "Doug Ross," November 22, 2003. In this chapter, in order to ensure the privacy of the students, staff, and alumni of the program, I have provided pseudonyms to any interview informant who does not appear in the

printed public record or in the previous chapters. If I do not provide pseudonyms in the text, as in the case of shorter direct quotations, I cite the interviews by date only.

29. Interview with WISP alumnus, October 5, 2003.

30. Interview with WISP alumnus, October 14, 2003.

31. Interview with WISP alumnus, October 3, 2003.

32. Interview with "Federico López Bolaños," September 9, 2003.

33. Lindy Baines, "South Africa Situation Has No Clear, Easy Solutions," *Bison* [University of the Ozarks], November 8, 1985, 3. Rhodesia became Zimbabwe in 1980, but the student author used the country's colonial name.

34. Randy Doyle, "Putting Your Money Where Your Heart Is," *TA,* March 13, 1986.

35. Jane Gore and Linda Ford, "Apathy Is Escape While Living in Nuclear Age," *Bison,* February 25, 1983, 8.

36. See Smith, *Resisting Reagan.*

37. "With 1,888 Miles and 77 Days and Nine Pairs of Running Shoes Behind Him, Dennis Godby Ran Out of Little Rock Saturday, Headed for Washington, D.C.," *ADG,* February 17, 1985; Smith, *Resisting Reagan,* 64.

38. "With 1,888 Miles."

39. Jeff Smolla, "Central America Is Hot Topic," *ME,* March 7, 1985, 4.

40. John E. Brown III, "One Small Step in Central America," typescript "Commentary," folder "Walton Scholarship Program," JBU, pp. 2–3.

41. Shawn Goodpasture, "Central American Students to Receive Aid," *Bison,* April 5, 1985, 16.

42. See William I. Robinson, "Globalization, the World System, and 'Democracy Promotion' in U.S. Foreign Policy," *Theory and Society* 25 (October 1996): 615–65.

43. Hernandez, "Foreign Students Adjusting to Culture Change," 7.

44. Isaac Cascante, "Special Feature: Central Americans Graduations," *ME,* November 18, 1988, 3.

45. John T. Anderson, "John Brown Provides Tutors to Develop Skills in English and in Community Service," *Morning News* [Springdale, AR], December 14, 1995; Jennie Lindgren, "Responding to a Need," *Northwest Arkansas Times,* November 30, 1994.

46. Interview with Professor Rickey J. Casey, August 5, 2002.

47. Harding University SIFE, "Stars and Stripes Forever," in SIFE, *1988/89 Training Manual* (Springfield, MO: SIFE, 1988).

48. Interview with WISP alumna, October 11, 2003.

49. Interview with WISP alumna, October 1, 2003.

50. Sheila Underwood, "Central Americans Add to Harding's Melting Pot," *Bison,* November 8, 1985, 12. Church of Christ worship excludes musical instruments, so all sacred singing is unaccompanied.

51. Isaac Cascante, "Walton Scholars," *ME*, October 21, 1988, 1.

52. Interview with WISP alumnus, October 14, 2003.

53. Interview with "Carlos Estrada Román," October 10, 2003.

54. Lina Arzu, quoted in Underwood, "Central Americans," 12.

55. Cindy Parrish, "Studies That Go Places," *TA*, February 26, 1988, 5.

56. Interview with "Jeff Simmons," September 24, 2003; "Minutes of the Board Committee on Academic Affairs," AA, 1985.

57. "Hopes Are High for New Instructor," *ME*, September 19, 1985, 3.

58. Elizabeth Morales, "Panamanians vs Americans," *ME*, December 15, 1987, 4.

59. Joey Lessin, "Students Respond to Conflict in Panama," *TA*, February 2, 1990, 1–2.

60. "Students Arrive," *Johnson County* [Arkansas] *Graphic*, August 1986, 1.

61. Cindy Dawson, "Economic Impact of Foreign Students" [Unsourced clipping circa 1995 in file "International Studies," folder "International Students," JBU] (n.d.).

62. Charmayne Ring, "Odette Chooses JBU for Atmosphere," *TA*, October 14, 1988, 4.

63. Students of Latin American and other "Third World" Christianities rightly emphasize their independence from First World leadership. See Edward L. Cleary, "Introduction: Pentecostals, Prominence, and Politics," in *Power, Politics, and Pentecostals in Latin America*, ed. Edward L. Cleary and Hannah W. Stewart-Gambino (Boulder, CO: Westview Press, 1997), 1–24; Douglas Petersen, "The Formation of Popular National Autonomous Pentecostal Churches in Central America," in *Conference Papers on the Theme "To the Ends of the Earth"* (Gaithersburg, MD: Society for Pentecostal Studies, 1994), 13; Susan Hoeber Rudolph and James Piscatori, eds., *Transnational Religion and Fading States* (Boulder, CO: Westview Press, 1997); Everett Wilson, "Guatemalan Pentecostals: Something of Their Own," in *Power, Politics, and Pentecostals in Latin America*, 139–62.

64. Jeffrey Swanson, *Echoes of the Call: Identity and Ideology among American Missionaries in Ecuador* (New York: Oxford University Press, 1995), 83–90; interview with "Doug Ross," November 22, 2003.

65. Interview with "Doug Ross," November 22, 2003.

66. Ibid.

67. Joel A. Carpenter, *Revive Us Again: The Reawakening of American Fundamentalism* (New York: Oxford University Press, 1997), 170–86; Axel R. Schäfer, "The Cold War State and the Resurgence of Evangelicalism: A Study of the Public Funding of Religion Since 1945," *Radical History Review* 99 (Fall 2007), 35–40; Wayne Warner, "Flying *Ambassadors* of Goodwill: The Story of Two Converted World War II Planes," *Assemblies of God Heritage* (Winter 1986), 3–4, 13–14.

68. Samuel Escobar, *The New Global Mission: The Gospel from Everywhere to Everyone* (Downers Grove, IL: InterVarsity Press, 2003), 25.

69. Stoll, *Is Latin America Turning Protestant?* 90–94. The Lausanne Covenant, which formally codified the movement's key principles at the 1974 meeting, stated, "The gospel does not presuppose the superiority of any culture to another . . . Missions have all too frequently exported with the gospel an alien culture . . . Christ's evangelists must humbly seek to empty themselves of all but their personal authenticity in order to become the servants of others." Lausanne Committee on World Evangelization, *Lausanne Covenant*, signed July 25, 1974; http://www.lausanne.org/lausanne-1974/lausanne-covenant.html; accessed December 12, 2008.

70. J. Herbert Kane, *Winds of Change in the Christian Mission* (Chicago: Moody Press, 1973), 14.

71. Ibid., 101.

72. Ibid., 24.

73. Ibid., 33.

74. On racial reconciliation among evangelical men, see L. Dean Allen, "Promise Keepers and Racism: Frame Resonance as an Indicator of Organizational Vitality," *Sociology of Religion* 61:1 (2000), 55–72; John P. Bartkowski, *The Promise Keepers: Servants, Soldiers, and Godly Men* (New Brunswick, NJ: Rutgers University Press, 2004), 61–64.

75. Rich Mullikin, "Walton Scholar Program Gaining in Name, Popularity," *BCDD*, May 24, 1992.

76. Robert S. McCord, "Sam Walton on Politics, Management, Merchandising and Iraq," *Arkansas Inc. [Supplement to AG]*, October 15, 1990, 8–9.

77. Sharon Stanbrough, "Graduate Covers Costa Rican Political Leaders," *TA*, October 16, 1987, 8.

78. Robert Tillet, quoted in Mike Rodman, "Christian Colleges Spread Democracy," *ADG*, November 8, 1993, 5B.

79. Virginia Garrard-Burnett, *Protestantism in Guatemala*, 128.

80. Manuel Francisco Ayau Cordón, *Mis Memorias y Mis Comentarios Sobre la Fundacion de la Universidad Francisco Marroquin y Sus Antecedentes* (Ciudad de Guatemala: Editorial UFM-IDEA, 1988); Rigoberto Juarez-Paz, *El Nacimiento de una Universidad* (Ciudad de Guatemala: Ediciones Papiro, 1995); *Guatemala: Never Again! REMHI/Recovery of Historical Memory Project: The Official Report of the Human Rights Office, Archdiocese of Guatemala* (New York: Orbis Books, 1999), 209, 214.

81. John E. Brown III, "One Small Step in Central America," folder "Walton Scholarship Program," JBU, pp. 2–3.

82. Tucker, Sanford, and Casey, *Walton Central America Scholarship Program Director's Manual*, 38.

83. Interview with "Doug Ross," November 22, 2005.

84. Personal communication from WISP alumnus, October 14, 2003; interview with WISP alumnus, October 14, 2003.

85. Interview with "Roberto Guzman Ayala," September 9, 2003.

86. Interview with WISP alumna, October 11, 2003.

87. Interview with WISP alumnus, October 5, 2003.

88. Interview with "Federico López Bolaños," September 9, 2003.

89. Interview with WISP alumnus, October 14, 2003.

90. Interview with WISP alumna, October 4, 2003.

91. Patti Fasig, "Sam Walton's Wisdom Means More Than His Wealth," *TA,* September 25, 1986, 2.

92. John E. Brown III, "Walton Visit with International Students—Success," *TA,* October 9, 1986, 3.

93. Interview with WISP alumna, October 4, 2003.

94. Rickey J. Casey, *Walton Central American Scholarship Program Annual Report* (Clarksville, AR: University of the Ozarks, 1993), 25; Rickey J. Casey, *Walton Central American Scholarship Program Annual Report* (Clarksville, AR: University of the Ozarks, 1994), 1; Rickey J. Casey, *Walton Central American Scholarship Program Annual Report* (Clarksville, AR: University of the Ozarks, 1995), 16.

95. Interview with "Federico López Bolaños," September 9, 2003.

96. Interview with "Isabel Rueda Navas," October 4, 2003.

97. Interview with "Federico López Bolaños," September 9, 2003. Knowledge as a form of property has received unprecedented legal status through the 1995 implementation of Trade Related Intellectual Property Rights, or TRIPS, in the Uruguay round of the General Agreement on Tariffs and Trade.

98. Interview with "Olga Nuñez," September 20, 2003.

99. Quoted in interview with "Doug Ross," November 22, 2005.

100. Interview with "Jeff Simmons," September 24, 2003.

101. Interview with WISP alumna, October 1, 2003.

102. "Uribe Deja su Puesto en Wal-Mart Centroamérica," *El Financiero,* December 17, 2006.

103. *Guatemala: Never Again!* 290; Leigh Binford, *The El Mozote Massacre* (Tucson: University of Arizona Press, 1996), 146–67.

104. Second interview with "Carlos Estrada Román," October 12, 2003.

13. Selling Free Trade

1. Byron McCauley, "Patriotism Energizes Annual Meeting This Year," *AG,* June 8, 1991, 1C, 8C; Kimberly J. Slavan and with Mary Brubaker and Steve Weeks,

"Shareholders' 1991 Meeting," *WMW*, June/July 1991, 10–15; Mary Jo Schneider, "The Wal-Mart Annual Meeting: From Small-Town America to a Global Corporate Culture," *Human Organization* 57, no. 3 (Fall 1998): 293–295.

2. Schneider, "The Wal-Mart Annual Meeting," 294, 296.

3. Taft quoted in Matthew Frye Jacobsen, *Barbarian Virtues: The United States Encounters Foreign Peoples at Home and Abroad, 1876–1917* (New York: Hill & Wang, 2000), 22–23.

4. This is a central argument of Christina Klein, *Cold War Orientalism: Asia in the Middlebrow Imagination, 1945–1961* (Berkeley: University of California Press, 2003). For Latin America, the formal diplomatic apparatus to this postwar integration was the Rio Pact of 1948 and the corresponding Bogotá Economic Charter of the Organization of American States, formulated the same year; the de facto mechanism of enforcement, however, was the United States' overwhelming economic influence in the region. Walter LaFeber, *Inevitable Revolutions: The United States in Central America*, 2nd ed. (New York: W.W. Norton, 1993), 94–99.

5. Marcelo Bucheli, "United Fruit Company in Latin America," in Steve Striffler and Mark Moberg, *Banana Wars: Power, Production, and History in the Americas* (Durham, NC: Duke University Press, 2003), 89–90; Piero Gleijeses, *Shattered Hope: The Guatemalan Revolution and the United States, 1944–1954* (Princeton, NJ: Princeton University Press, 1999).

6. At the Asian-African Conference in Bandung, Indonesia, in 1955 and the Afro-Asian People's Solidarity Conference in Cairo two years later, leaders of dozens of former colonies protested the pressure to ally their countries with either of the superpowers. Melani McAlister, *Epic Encounters: Culture, Media, and U.S. Interests in the Middle East since 1945*, updated ed. (Berkeley: University of California Press, 2005), 90.

7. Klein, *Cold War Orientalism*, 50–56. As Melani McAlister makes clear, however, these religious linkages were not always the ones Washington would have favored; see McAlister, *Epic Encounters: Culture, Media, and U.S. Interests in the Middle East since 1945*, 84–124.

8. R. Andrew Chesnut, *Born Again in Brazil: The Pentecostal Boom and the Pathogens of Poverty* (New Brunswick, NJ: Rutgers University Press, 1997), 47, 65–66; Jean Comaroff and John L. Comaroff, "Millennial Capitalism: First Thoughts on a Second Coming," *Public Culture* 12, no. 2 (2000): 314; Mark R. Mullins, "The Empire Strikes Back: Korean Pentecostal Mission to Japan," in *Charismatic Christianity as a Global Culture*, ed. Karla Poewe (Columbia, SC: University of South Carolina Press, 1994), 92; Jeff Sharlet, "Soldiers of Christ I: Inside America's Most Powerful Megachurch," *Harper's*, May 2005, 41–54.

9. David Chilton, *Productive Christians in an Age of Guilt-Manipulators: A Biblical Response to Ronald J. Sider* (Tyler, TX: Institute for Christian Economics, 1981),

126; quoted in Michael Lienesch, *Redeeming America: Piety and Politics in the New Christian Right* (Chapel Hill, NC: University of North Carolina Press, 1993), 109.

10. Greg Grandin, *Empire's Workshop: Latin America, the United States, and the Rise of the New Imperialism* (New York: Metropolitan Books, 2006), 147–50; Linda Kintz, *Between Jesus and the Market: The Emotions That Matter in Right-Wing America* (Durham, NC: Duke University Press, 1997), 193–7.

11. Regent University, *Graduate Catalog 1994–96* (Virginia Beach, VA: Regent University, 1994), p. 61; quoted in Linda Kintz, *Between Jesus and the Market*, 232.

12. Misha Petrovic and Gary G. Hamilton, "Making Global Markets: Wal-Mart and Its Suppliers," in *Wal-Mart: The Face of Twenty-First Century Capitalism*, ed. Nelson Lichtenstein (New York: New Press, 2006), 128.

13. Sam M. Walton, "Message from Sam Walton," *WMW*, May 1976, 2.

14. Phyllis Overstreet, "Bring It Home to the U.S.A.: Wal-Mart's Import Program—Sharpening Our Merchandise Strategy," *WMW*, June 1989, 18.

15. Hedrick Smith, "Who Calls the Shots in the Global Economy?" (2004), http://www.pbs.org/wgbh/pages/frontline/shows/walmart/secrets/shots.html, accessed May 20, 2006.

16. Greg Grandin, *Empire's Workshop*, 48–49; Harold Molineu, *U.S. Policy Toward Latin America: From Regionalism to Globalism*, 2nd ed. (Boulder, CO: Westview Press, 1990), 123–125; Bob Ortega, *In Sam We Trust: The Untold Story of Sam Walton and How Wal-Mart Is Devouring America* (New York: Times Business, 1998), 204.

17. This account is drawn directly from Ortega, *In Sam We Trust*, 202–3.

18. Ibid., 202–7; board member quoted anonymously on p. 207.

19. Dana Frank, *Buy American: The Untold Story of Economic Nationalism* (Boston: Beacon Press, 1999), 200–207. Ortega, *In Sam We Trust*, 223–25, 332–35.

20. Ibid., 243–44.

21. By 2003, Wal-Mart accounted for 10 percent of American imports from China; Anthony Bianco and Wendy Zellner, "Is Wal-Mart Too Powerful?" *BW*, October 6, 2003, 103; Matthew Benjamin, "China Conundrum," *USNWR* 135, no. 8 (September 15, 2003), 37–38.

22. William P. Avery, "Domestic Interests in NAFTA Bargaining," *Political Science Quarterly* 113, no. 2 (1998): 287; Altha J. Cravey, *Women and Work in Mexico's Maquiladoras* (Lanham, MD: Rowman & Littlefield, 1998), 10–16.

23. Having nurtured domestic industry and increased the middle class during the "Mexican Miracle" decades of the 1950s and 1960s, the continued state subsidy to domestic private industry kept prices high and made Mexican products less competitive in export markets. These costs were compounded by a fixed exchange rate that overvalued the peso to hold down inflation, making up the

difference between the currency's real value and its exchange rate through mounting public debt. The reckoning was delayed by two economic developments of the 1970s: first, the high-interest lending spree of U.S. banks, fueled by their burgeoning deposits of "petrodollars" from the Middle East; and, second, the discovery of oil in the Mexican state of Tabasco in 1974, just as oil prices began hitting historic highs. By the time the petroleum boom came to an end in 1982, the country's interest payments amounted to half of its exports, and thirteen American banks had $16 billion invested in Mexico, almost half of their total combined capital. Rather than allow the borrowers to default on their North American private-sector loans, the Reagan administration produced a high-interest public loan and engineered a bailout through the International Monetary Fund (IMF) that required radical restructuring of the Mexican economy along free-market lines. The question of continuing down this road was raised by the 1988 Mexican national elections pitting the Harvard-trained pro–free trader Carlos Salinas de Gortari against the son of former president Lázaro Cárdenas del Río, the man still revered by many for nationalizing the country's oil wealth in 1938. The race looked uncharacteristically close, and with the future of free trade on the line, it was suddenly announced in the midst of the vote count that the computer system had crashed. When it was restored, Salinas was proclaimed the winner by the government of his own party, already in power. Following this disputed win, Salinas pushed through legislation expanding on the structural adjustments, including expanded incentives for foreign investment and the repeal of the 1982 bank nationalization.

Sarah Babb, *Managing Mexico: Economists from Nationalism to Neoliberalism* (Princeton: Princeton University Press, 2001), 106–7, 113–116; Kim Moody, "The Corporate Redesign of Latin America," *Latin American Perspectives* 22, no. 1: Labor and the Free Market in the Americas (Winter 1995): 100–1; John Ross, *The Annexation of Mexico: From the Aztecs to the I.M.F.* (Monroe, ME: Common Courage Press, 1998), 170–74; Ian Vásquez, "The Brady Plan and Market-Based Solutions to the Debt Crises," *Cato Journal* 16, no. 2 (Fall 1996): 233–34; K. Larry Stone, "CRS Report for Congress: NAFTA Decisions and U.S.-Mexico Relations," *North American Free Trade Agreement: Issues and Implications* (Washington, DC: Congressional Research Service, 1993), 2–3.

24. Moody, "The Corporate Redesign of Latin America," 106.
25. Canada and the United States negotiated a precursor agreement in 1988, to considerably less fanfare in the United States.
26. Avery, "Domestic Interests in NAFTA Bargaining," 285.
27. Ibid., 284. The fast-tracking lobbying umbrella group, the Coalition for Trade Expansion, included the Business Roundtable, the National Association of

Manufactures, the U.S. Chamber of Commerce, the Emergency Committee for American Trade, and the National Foreign Trade Council.

28. Ortega, *In Sam We Trust*, 214.

29. Clinton's support came with the price tag of supplemental agreements intended to address labor and environmental concerns, but their minor scope and weak enforcement mechanisms did little to win approval among those opposed to NAFTA's ratification. Avery, "Domestic Interests in NAFTA Bargaining," 299–304.

30. Michael C. Drieling, "The Class Embeddedness of Corporate Political Action: Leadership in Defense of the NAFTA," *Social Problems* 47, no. 1 (February 2000): 21–48; David C. Korten, *When Corporations Rule the World* (West Hartford, CT, and San Francisco: Kumarian Press and Berrett Koehler Publishers, 1995), 145. Sarah Anderson, John Cavanagh, and Sandra Gross, *NAFTA's Corporate Cadre: An Analysis of the USA-NAFTA State Captains* (Washington, DC: Institute for Policy Studies, 1993), 3.

31. Stefan Fatsis, "Companies Supporting NAFTA Turn up the Heat," *Las Vegas Review-Journal*, September 28, 1993.

32. Joanna Ramey, "Coalition Forms to Push NAFTA Over Hurdles," *HFD-The Weekly Home Furnishings Newspaper*, October 26, 1992.

33. Drieling, "Corporate Political Action," 24.

34. Jonathan J. Ginns, *Wal-Mart Ventures Into Mexico*, Case 9-793-071 (Boston, MA: Harvard Business School Publishing Division, 1992), 1; Ellen Neuborne, "Wal-Mart: Mexico Offers Rich Retail Market," *USA Today*, July 12, 1991, 3B; Rosalind Smith, "U.S. Retailers Looking South for New Growth; Mexico's Young Consumers Are Target," *Press-Enterprise* [*Riverside, CA*], November 7, 1993.

35. Ortega, *In Sam We Trust*, 148–50; Sandra Stringer Vance and Roy Vernon Scott, *Wal-Mart: A History of Sam Walton's Retail Phenomenon*, Twayne's Evolution of Modern Business Series (New York: Twayne Publishers, 1994), 124–35. Today Wal-Mart Supercenters outnumber Wal-Mart Stores by almost two to one.

36. "New Horizons," *WMW*, January 1992, 8–11.

37. Jill Lettich, "Execs Eye Impact of Free Trade with Mexico," *DSN*, December 7, 1992.

38. Janet Duncan, "Mexican Retailer Takes Aim at Wal-Mart," *Reuters News*, September 23, 1993.

39. Richard A. Gephardt, "North American Free Trade Agreement: I Will Vote Against This NAFTA [September 21, 1993]," speech, *VSD* 60, no. 1 (October 16, 1993): 22–29.

40. Avery, "Domestic Interests in NAFTA Bargaining," 288.

41. Joyce Barrett, "Retailers Told to Teach Customers, Workers the Benefits of NAFTA," *DNR*, August 4, 1993.

42. Calvin Woodward, "NAFTA Talks Mean Business," *Hamilton Spectator*, August 4, 1993.

43. "IMRA Mobilizes Support for Floundering NAFTA," *DSN*, August 16, 1993.

44. Joyce Barrett, "Congress Tells Top Retailers: You Sell NAFTA," *Women's Wear Daily*, August 4, 1993.

45. Fatsis, "Companies Supporting NAFTA Turn up the Heat"; "Wal-Mart Seeks Aid on NAFTA," *DNR* 23, no. 165 (August 27, 1993): 4.

46. William J. Clinton, "Remarks at the Signing Ceremony for the North American Free Trade Agreement Supplemental Agreements [September 14, 1993]," *Weekly Compilation of Presidential Documents* 29, no. 7 (September 20, 1993): 1754–59.

47. "U.S. House of Representatives—Part 2, Tuesday, September 21, 1993," *Federal News Service Daybook*, September 21, 1993.

48. "Wal-Mart Makes Statement Supporting Trade Agreement," *Journal Record*, September 23, 1993.

49. Ken Rankin, "Retailers Urge OK on NAFTA," *DSN*, October 4, 1993.

50. Tracey Eaton, "A Shopper's Heaven: Mexicans Make Wal-Mart Country's Newest Shrine," *Dallas Morning News*, October 24, 1993, 1H.

51. Associated Press, "Free Trade Going on in Mexico: Changes Already Exist, Despite Treaty Debate," *Rocky Mountain News*, October 2, 1993.

52. Eaton, "Shopper's Heaven."

53. Carol Byrne, "How Mexico Sees NAFTA; A Melon Baller Becomes Symbol of Trade Relations," *Star-Tribune* [*Minneapolis-St. Paul*], November 14, 1993.

54. See Jésus Velasco, "Reading Mexico, Understanding the United States: American Transnational Intellectuals in the 1920s and 1990s," *Journal of American History* 86, no. 2 (1999).

55. Anne D'Innocenzio, "Businesses Hike Tempo on NAFTA Push," *DNR*, November 9, 1993, 8.

56. John Haman, "Predicting the NAFTA-Math," *Arkansas Business* 10, no. 46 (November 15, 1993): 18; Cravey, *Women and Work in Mexico's Maquiladoras*, 49–51.

57. D'Innocenzio, "Businesses Hike Tempo on NAFTA Push."

58. Haman, "Predicting the NAFTA-Math."

59. "White House: We Have 6 More Pro-NAFTA Votes in House; Claims Arkansas Congressman Among Those Who Have Joined Group," *DNR*, November 10, 1993, 5.

60. Ibid.

61. Susan McKenzie, "Mexico Trip May Sway Spratt," *Herald* [*Rock Hill, SC*], November 13, 1993, 1A. "The New Deal: NAFTA—Textile and Apparel Industries," *DSN*, December 6, 1993.

62. "Republican Congressman from NJ Supports NAFTA," *AP Political Service,* November 11, 1993.

63. George J. Church, "It's Just That Close," *Time* 142, no. 20 (November 15, 1993): 38.

64. Former congressman and pro-NAFTA congressional coordinator Bill Frenzel (R-Minnesota), quoted in Kenneth J. Cooper, "House Approves U.S.-Mexico-Canada Trade Pact on 234 to 200 Vote, Giving Clinton Big Victory," *WP,* November 18, 1993, A1.

65. "Wal-Mart in Mexico City Draws Thousands to Buy U.S. Products," *St. Louis Post-Dispatch,* November 11, 1993.

66. Del Jones and Ellen Neuborne, "Goods Go South; Made in USA Means Sales in Mexico," *USA Today,* November 16, 1993, 1B.

67. David Nyhan, "The Big Roll Call: NAFTA, or Else," *Boston Globe,* November 14, 1993.

68. Cooper, "House Approves U.S.-Mexico-Canada Trade Pact."

69. Drieling, "Corporate Political Action," 24 n.5.

70. WMAR 1997, 4. Recent biographical data on Paula Stern from www.leadingauthorities.com/13007/Paula_Stern,_PhD.htm, accessed May 22, 2006.

71. WMAR 1997, 15.

72. Bill Saporito, "And the Winner Is Still . . . Wal-Mart," *Fortune,* May 2, 1994, 70.

73. Petrovic and Hamilton, "Making Global Markets," 128–29.

74. Michael Exstein, Credit Suisse Group; paraphrased in Geraldo Samor, Cecilie Rohwedder, and Ann Zimmerman, "Innocents Abroad? Wal-Mart's Global Sales Rise as It Learns from Mistakes," *WSJ,* May 16, 2006, B1.

75. Larry Elliott, "Brown's Globalisation Panel of 'Wise Men' Attacked from All Sides," *Guardian,* March 22, 2006.

76. "Shewmaker: Retailers Need Global Outlook to Compete," *DSN* 37, no. 11 (June 8, 1998): 42.

77. WMAR 1994, 9.

Epilogue

1. Lisa Selin Davis, "New Orleans Faces Off with Wal-Mart," *Preservation Online,* March 19, 2004; Constance L. Hays, "For Wal-Mart, New Orleans Is Hardly the Big Easy," *NYT,* April 27, 2003.

2. Land-use attorney William Borah quoted in Davis, "New Orleans Faces Off with Wal-Mart"; Hays, "For Wal-Mart, New Orleans is Hardly the Big Easy"; Bruce Nolan, "Church Conference Gets Down to Business; Leaders Preach Economic Health," *NOTP,* January 6, 2001.

3. Daphne Moore and Maurice Pres Kabacoff quoted in Hays, "For Wal-Mart, New Orleans Is Hardly the Big Easy."

4. Bruce Eggler, "Wal-Mart Conflict Creates Odd Allies; Crowds Pack Public Hearing," *NOTP*, October 24, 2001; "House Divided; Historic Preservationists Struggle to Redefine Their Mission in Hopes of Bridging Longtime Schisms of Race," *NOTP*, December 9, 2001.

5. Though the Office of Faith-Based and Community Initiatives (OFBCI) was established, its funding never reached a fraction of the $8 billion per year George W. Bush had promised while campaigning in 2000. David Kuo, deputy director of the OFBCI in 2002 and 2003, relates how the White House used seminars like the one at Xavier in the run-up to the 2004 election to appeal to nonwhite Christian leaders and activists in all the key battleground states. David Kuo, *Tempting Faith: An Inside Story of Political Seduction* (New York: Free Press, 2006), 212.

6. The Rev. Gregg Thomas and the Rev. Floyd Flake quoted in "Down to Business."

7. "Cries of Racism Enter Debate Over Wal-Mart; Black Groups Blast Web Site as Attempt at 'Political Extortion,'" *NOTP*, November 13, 2001; Bruce Eggler and Lyn Jensen, "Post-Katrina Frustration Fuels Many Candidates," *NOTP*, April 12, 2006.

8. "Wal-Mart: The Hits Just Keep on Coming" (2002), http://www.urbanconservancy.org/issues/walmart; Frank Donze, "Oliver Thomas Enters Prison Today; He Says He's Trying to Forgive Himself," *NOTP*, January 3, 2008.

9. "When Government Fails," *Economist* 376, no. 8443 (September 8, 2005).

10. "Private FEMA," *WSJ*, September 8, 2005; Ann Zimmerman and Valerie Bauerlein, "At Wal-Mart, Emergency Plan Has Big Payoff," *WSJ*, September 12, 2005; George Melloan, "What Are the Lessons of Katrina?" *WSJ*, September 13, 2005.

11. John Tierney, "From FEMA to WEMA," *NYT*, September 20, 2005.

12. Aaron F. Broussard, president of Jefferson Parish, speaking on the television show *Meet the Press*, September 4, 2005; quoted in Michael Barbaro and Justin Gillis, "Wal-Mart at the Forefront of Hurricane Relief," *WP*, September 6, 2005, D1. According to Barbaro's report, Wal-Mart contributed $20 million in cash relief, as well as about 100 truckloads of merchandise and food for 100,000 emergency meals.

13. Robert Wuthnow, *Saving America? Faith-Based Services and the Future of Civil Society* (Princeton, NJ: Princeton University Press, 2004), 14.

14. David Kirp, "Faith-Based Disaster," *San Francisco Chronicle*, September 19, 2005, B5.

15. Jacqueline Johnson quoted in "More Faith-Based Initiatives After Katrina," Hurricanes Archives Section (MSNBC.com, 2005), www. msnbc.msn.com/id/9852785; direct quote from Jacqueline Johnson.

16. "More Faith-Based Initiatives After Katrina."

17. Diana B. Henriques and Andrew Lehren, "Religion for Captive Audiences, with Taxpayers Footing the Bill," *NYT*, December 10, 2006.

18. James Ferguson, "Governing Extraction: New Spatializations of Order and Disorder in Neoliberal Africa," in James Ferguson, *Global Shadows: Africa in the Neoliberal World Order* (Durham, NC: Duke University Press, 2006), 194–210; Susanne Hoeber Rudolph, "Introduction: Religion, States, and Transnational Civil Society," in Susanne Hoeber Rudolph and James Piscatori, ed., *Transnational Religion and Fading States* (Boulder, CO: Westview Press, 1997), 1–24.

19. Nancy MacLean, "Southern Dominance in Borrowed Language: The Regional Origins of American Neoliberalism," in Jane L. Collins, Micaela di Leonardo, and Brett Williams, eds., *New Landscapes of Inequality: Neoliberalism and the Erosion of Democracy in America* (Santa Fe, NM: School for Advanced Research Press, 2008), 21–25; Trent Lott quoted on p. 22.

20. Lisa Duggan, *The Twilight of Equality? Neoliberalism, Cultural Politics, and the Attack on Democracy* (Boston: Beacon Press, 2004); Janet R. Jakobsen and Ann Pellegrini, *Love the Sin: Sexual Regulation and the Limits of Religious Tolerance* (New York: New York University Press, 2003), 133–148; Philip Mattera and Anna Purinton, *Shopping for Subsidies: How Wal-Mart Uses Taxpayer Money to Finance Its Never-Ending Growth* (Washington, DC: Good Jobs First, 2004); Axel R. Schäfer, "The Cold War State and the Resurgence of Evangelicalism: A Study of the Public Funding of Religion Since 1945," *Radical History Review* 99 (Fall 2007): 19–50.

21. See, for example, Elizabeth Fones-Wolf, *Selling Free Enterprise: The Business Assault on Labor and Liberalism, 1945–1960* (Urbana: University of Illinois Press, 1995); Kim Phillips-Fein, *Invisible Hands: The Making of the Conservative Movement from the New Deal to Reagan* (New York: W.W. Norton, 2009); James K. Galbraith, *The Predator State: How Conservatives Abandoned the Free Market and Why Liberals Should, Too* (New York: Free Press, 2008).

22. Naomi Klein, *The Shock Doctrine: The Rise of Disaster Capitalism* (New York: Metropolitan Books, 2007), 6.

23. Milton Friedman, quoted in Klein, *Shock Doctrine*, 6.

24. Liza Featherstone, "Down and Out in Discount America," *The Nation*, January 8, 2005, 11–15; Steven Greenhouse, "Workers at Pork Plant in North Carolina Vote to Unionize After a 15-Year Fight," *NYT*, December 13, 2008, A10; George Packer, "The Hardest Vote," *New Yorker*, October 13, 2008; Michael Luo and Karen Ann Cullotta, "Even Workers Surprised by the Success of Factory Sit-In," *NYT*, December 13, 2008, A9; Carolyn Crist, "Group Seeks Higher Wage," *Red and Black* [University of Georgia], February 29, 2008; www.econjustice.org.

Acknowledgments

It takes a village to write a book, and I only wish the virtual village I have depended on for this one could be gathered into a single small town, maybe in the Ozarks. My first thanks are to the people who sheltered, fed, and taught me while I was on the road, and whose friendship was the greatest gift of this process: Leslie Abadie; Danielle Amico; Margaret Bolsterli; John, Thea, and Thomas Boyne; David Chappell; the Rev. Lowell and Kathy Grisham; Kate Howe; Louis Hyman; Michael Jo; Karon Reese; Beth Schweiger; Katherine Sloan; Olivia Sordo; Steve Striffler; Harley and Eli Ungar; and J. T. Way. If I build it, will y'all come?

During those years on Route 66 and the Pan-American Highway, many people shared with me their insights on the Retail Clerks International Association, Students in Free Enterprise, Wal-Mart Stores, Inc., and the Walton International Scholarship Program. Without their help, there would be no story to tell. Respect for privacy is an Ozarks tradition, and though virtually no one who contributed to this project put any conditions on the use of the material, I have generally kept proper names out of the text except where they also appear in published sources. I must therefore thank them here collectively, anonymously, but very sincerely. After meals, prayers, and many illuminating conversations with these veterans, I hope my respect and gratitude are evident. If they would not all agree with everything in these pages, I trust they will not feel their perspectives have been misrepresented.

The expertise and patience of professional archivists was equally crucial to this research. My thanks to my historical colleagues at the Baker

Library Historical Collections, Harvard Business School; the Benton-ville Public Library; the Biblioteca Ludwig von Mises, Universidad Francisco Marroquín; the Brackett Library Archives and Special Collections, Harding University; the Center for American History, University of Texas; the Chicago Historical Society; the Horn Library Archives and Special Collections, Babson College; the Hutchens Library, Southwestern Baptist University; the John Brown University Library and Archives; the Mullins Library Special Collections, University of Arkansas; the Noel Memorial Library Archives and Special Collections, Louisiana State University–Shreveport; the Oklahoma Archive of Contemporary History of the Beam Library, Oklahoma Christian University; the Ozarkiana Collection and the Ozarks Labor Union Archives of Meyer Library, Missouri State University; the Robson Library, University of the Ozarks; the Springfield-Greene County Library; the Rogers Historical Museum; the Shiloh Museum of Ozarks History; the Sterling Memorial Library, Yale University; the Texas State Archives; Widener Library, Harvard University; and the Wisconsin Historical Society. I am especially grateful for the expert help of Gay Bland, Andrea Cantrell, J. J. Compton, Marie Demeroukas, Nancy Godleski, Laura Linard, Allyn Lord, Carolyn Reno, R. C. Rybnikar, Alison Scott, Geoffrey Stark, and Susan Young, a treasured friend as well as a respected colleague. Bob Ortega inexplicably allowed me to interrupt his family vacation to go through his private archives in the garage. Thank you also to everyone at the respective headquarters of Students in Free Enterprise and the Food and Allied Services Trades for the kind permission to rummage through files and clog up the offices and for the hospitality of those I was inconveniencing. Equal Rights Advocates in San Francisco generously provided documents from *Dukes* v. *Wal-Mart*. Thank you as well for research guidance to Scott Henson, Cathy Mitchell, Danalynn Recer, and to Mary Lyn Villanueva of Flagler Productions.

Through their high standards and even higher ideals, my extraordinary mentors Nancy Cott, Michael Denning, Glenda Gilmore, and Jim Scott modeled the joy of committed labor and opened whole worlds to me. Learning from them and from Jean Christophe Agnew, Jennifer Baszile, Jon Butler, Hazel Carby, David Emmons, Peter Frost, Paul Gilroy, Robert Johnston, Gil Joseph, Regina Kunzel, Ken Lockridge, Lynn Murchison, Steve Pitti, and Bill Wagner was an object lesson in how service work compels its best practitioners to give far beyond the call of duty. Thank you; on my best days in this line of work, I hope I can live up to y'all.

Especially because the research trail took me so far from my real home, I was deeply dependent on the generous communities that took me in as a regular hanger-on. For their sustained offerings of good ideas and good fellowship, I thank the Tepoztlán Institute for the Transnational History of the Americas; the Program in Agrarian Studies; the Market Cultures Colloquium; the Marxist Reading Group; the American Academy of Arts and Sciences; the Charles Warren Center; the Boston University Institute of Political History; the Harvard Workshop on the Political Economy of Modern Capitalism (and its associated poker crew); the Working Group on Globalization and Culture; and my stalwart writing group, originally convened through the generosity of the Schlesinger Library at Radcliffe. For the joy of these intellectual barn-raisings and the hard work that kept them functioning, thank you especially to Sven Beckert, Kristina Boylan, Laura Briggs, Victoria Cain, Amanda Ciafone, Rebecca Davis, Christine Desan, Rossen Djagalov, Eileen Ford, Taylor Fravel, Daniel Gilbert, Victor Macías Gonzalez, Reiko Hillyer, the Rev. Jennifer Hughes, Sara Amelia Espinosa Islas, Mandi Jackson, Kay Mansfield, Serena Mayeri, Gladys McCormick, Ajay Mehrotra, Christina Moon, Anthony Mora, Claire Nee Nelson, Jocelyn Olcott, Julia Ott, Naomi Paik, Arthur Patton-Hock, Rebecca Rix, Laura Scales, Bruce Schulman, Julieta Sierra, Ageeth Sluis, Olga Sooudi, Patricia Meyer Spacks, Ann Stiles, Laura Trice, Pamela Voekel, Ben Waterhouse, Kirsten Weld, Elliott Young, and Julian Zelizer.

For an inquiry into the service economy, two other groups of teachers were equally indispensable: the Graduate Employees and Students Organization/Federation of Hospital and University Employees in New Haven, and the Economic Justice Coalition in Athens. Thank you to Alison Bruey, Kathleen Cambor, Amy Chazkel, Victoria Langland, Elaine Lewinnek, Linda Lloyd, Ray McNair, Ted Mellilo, Humberto Mendoza, Michael Mullins, Matthew Pulver, Shana Redmond, Anita Seth, Kristie Starr, and Stephen Vella for connecting the theory to the practice.

Most recently, the extraordinary students at the seminar tables and Living Wage meetings at the University of Georgia animated this book and its author whenever either one was flagging. I am especially grateful for all I learned from Jenny Aszman, Matthew Boynton, Katie Carson, Leslie Dunsmore, Bobbie Fair, Daleah Goodwin, Brad Hill, Maggie

Kilgo, Liz Kinnamon, Perry McCall, Keri Leigh Merritt, Tore Olsson, Alex Palmour, Manisa Prema, Meredith Rainey, Rachel Salmons, Blake Scott, Sherri Sheu, Allison Stouffer, Audrey Turner, Hannah Waits, Taryn Weil, and Billye Young. Can we call this my thank-you note?

Greater love hath no scholar than to critique a colleague's entire manuscript. Although the book's shortcomings are mine alone, any virtues are the product of many people's intellectual generosity: In addition to others already mentioned, thank you to Joyce Seltzer, Kate Brick, and the three anonymous reviewers for Harvard University Press for putting the flabby drafts through boot camp at double speed; and to Margot Canaday, Janet Jakobsen, Allan Kulikoff, and my Fairy Godmentor, Nancy MacLean. For segments of the argument, other valued interlocutors included many mentioned elsewhere and Darren Dochuk, Lisa Duggan, Leon Fink, Dana Frank, Gerald Friedman, Tom Geoghagen, Sarah Hammond, Anya Jabour, Sandra Koelle, Sarosh Kuruvilla, Jana Lipman, Laura Lovett, Rob MacDougal, Noam Maggor, William Mass, Manuela Meyer, Melani McAlister, Eugene McCarraher, Bruce Nelson, Jodie Pavilack, Kim Phillips-Fein, Ann Pellegrini, Susie Porter, Josie Saldaña, Andrew Sandoval-Strausz, Alexandra Stern, Kathryn Stockton, Lisa Szefel, Dorian Warren, and Angela Zito. Long Di, Kathi Nehls, Tore Olsson, Brad Reese, and the incomparable Sherri Sheu provided indispensable aid in the final stages of research. Sheila Barnett, Jeannette Estruth, and Brenda Luke all went way beyond the call of duty to accommodate the pace of revisions; thank you, and forgive me.

For their contributions at other points, I'm grateful to many more colleagues, any one of whom would be an ornament to an ideal scholarly village: Tonio Andrade, Rick Casey, Rohan D'Souza, John Eglin, Walter Friedman, Willard Gatewood, Greg Grandin, Doug Guthrie, Cindy Hahamovitch, Randy Hilton, Robert Hilton, Kristen Hoganson, Jeanette Keith, Rakesh Kurana, Stephen L. McIntyre, Scott Nelson, Rick Ostrander, John Ozment, Patrick Rael, Mary Jo Schneider, Chris Tilly, George Trumbell, Joe Walenciak, and Jeannie Whayne. My first three semesters of teaching coincided with my last three semesters of writing, and I appreciate the support of my University of Georgia colleagues who bore with me through this unlovely combination, especially that of Derrick Aldridge, Stephen Berry, Melissa Blair, Brooke Campbell, Jim Cobb, Victoria Davion, Brian Drake, Shane Hamilton, Kelly Happe, Cecilia Herles, Doris Kadish, Michael Kwass, Ari Levine, Tricia Lootens,

Laura Mason, Stephen Mihm, Molly Moreland Meyers, Blaise Parker, Patricia Richards, Reinaldo Román, Claudio Saunt, Paul Sutter, Susan Thomas, and Montgomery Wolf. A particular thanks to Susan Mattern and Amy Ross, and for the support of my department heads Chris Cuomo and Robert Pratt at every stage.

Despite my shameless couch-surfing, creating the archives for this project over several years was an expensive process. I appreciate the chance to acknowledge the generous support I received from the following sources: for preliminary research, thank you to the Center for Religion in American Life Summer Research Grant; the Chace Family Fellowship; the Coca-Cola World Fund at Yale Summer Travel Grant; a Foreign Language and Area Studies summer language grant from the U.S. Department of Education; a John Perry Miller Summer Research Grant from the Yale Graduate School of Arts and Sciences; a summer research grant from the Program in Agrarian Studies; the Yale Center for International and Area Studies Research Grant; and a Yale Department of History Alumni Fund grant. I appreciated the major backing subsequently provided by the Myrna Bernath Fellowship in the History of International Relations from the Society for Historians of American Foreign Relations; an Alfred D. Chandler Traveling Fellowship from the Baker Library of the Harvard Business School; the Louisville Institute Fellowship for Research on American Religion; a Mellon Summer Research Grant in Women's and Gender History from the Schlesinger Library at Radcliffe; the Charlotte F. Newcombe Fellowship of the Woodrow Wilson Foundation; the Social Science Research Council Program on the Corporation as a Social Institution; the Social Science Research Council Program on Philanthropy and the Non-Profit Sector; and the Visiting Scholar Program of the American Academy of Arts and Sciences. At the University of Georgia, thank you to the Office of the Dean, the Institute for Women's Studies, the Department of History, and the Office of the Vice President for Research for a first book subvention grant and a research grant for access to a late-breaking source. Thank you to my sponsors and other fellows, who provided significant moral support and intellectual sustenance along with the more tangible aid.

But the support whose price was above rubies came from my beloved family, from whom this book has demanded so much. Any insight it can claim about labors of love and responsibilities of justice are wholly theirs. Thank you to my mother and father, a constant inspiration; my brother Elliott, a lifelong teacher; and my extended family, a gift—Gail, Penelope, Michael, Swen, Ulrike, John, Haley, and Jennifer. Finally, the debt I cannot repay belongs to Pamela Voekel, who faithfully leads by serving every day of her life, and whose brilliance is only matched by her generous spirit. This book is dedicated to her, for her mind and heart are on every page.

Index